CURRICULUM:
QUEST FOR RELEVANCE

CURRICULUM:

Quest for Relevance

Second Edition

Edited by WILLIAM VAN TIL, *Indiana State University*

Houghton Mifflin Company   Boston
Atlanta   Dallas   Geneva, Ill.   Hopewell, N.J.   Palo Alto   London

Library of Congress Catalog Card Number: 73-14023
ISBN: 0-395-17787-1   •

For a Person and a Group—
Bee, my wife, and the members of the
Association for Supervision and Curriculum
Development, my curriculum organization.
They believe in the importance of people.

CONTENTS

The Critics of the Critics

PART TWO: CURRICULAR ALTERNATIVES 107

Free, Alternative, and Open Schools

Cautions and Reminders

PART THREE: CURRICULUM TODAY 227

Approaches to Curriculum

PREFACE

Although my publishers and I call this book a revision, it comes close to being a new book. Twenty-nine new readings have been added. Only nineteen of the readings in the original 1971 edition have been retained. The revised book now includes four parts, rather than three, and one of these, *Curricular Alternatives*, is completely new.

Curriculum: Quest for Relevance is, I believe, a curriculum book with a difference: its contents focus on today and tomorrow, rather than on yesterday. Its four parts focus on current criticisms of the curriculum, curricular alternatives, curriculum today, and curriculum for the future. Part One reports the trenchant views of today's compassionate critics, the critics of compulsory education, and the critics of the critics. Part Two presents views on free, alternative, and open schools, with some cautions and reminders. Part Three discusses current approaches to the curriculum, racism and ethnic education, and changing the curriculum; many of these articles first appeared in a special curriculum issue of *Phi Delta Kappan* which I edited. Part Four is tomorrow-oriented, and offers some of the most promising educational futurist thinking yet available in article and pamphlet form.

My role as editor included developing the above organization from among the possible alternatives, selecting the contributors from current curriculum literature, and writing the introductions and the selection headnotes.

Curriculum: Quest for Relevance is designed for use in a variety of curriculum courses, such as curriculum development, curriculum theory and practice, elementary curriculum and secondary curriculum. Because of its present-future orientation, some educators may use it as the basic text for a course; others may find it a useful supplement to books more oriented toward the past. *Curriculum: Quest for Relevance* should be especially helpful in orientation programs for new teachers and in-service programs for experienced teachers.

My thanks go, above all, to those whose writings appear in this volume and to their publishers.

In the first edition I thanked students in my doctoral seminars on curriculum at Indiana State University whose advice and recommendations helped in the development of this book of readings: Theodore Kowalski, John S. Burd, Martha K. Hedley, O. Pierre Lee, Vera Channels, James C. Campbell, Sister Joanne Golding, Betty Jean Searcy, Rita Schrenker, Ronald M. Leathers, Edwin A. Gray, and David N. Kelsey. In this second edition I again wish to thank students in my doctoral seminars in curriculum during 1972 and 1973 for their advice and recommendations, including Raymond A. Cusic, R. Joseph Dixon, Raymond H. Ernest, Gary L. Gueldner, Eugene L. Jones, Bruce F. Mills, Patroba E. Ondiek, John P. Schmeling, and Larry D. Vandeventer.

I also wish to thank those who reviewed this revised edition as a whole. They are Elsie J. Alberty, Professor, College of Education, Ohio State University, Columbus, Ohio; Virgil A. Clift, Professor of Education, New York University, New York City; and Jessie J. DuBois, Reading Specialist, Indiana State University, Terre Haute, Indiana.

My thanks to my research assistants at Indiana State University, Larry D. Vandeventer and R. Joseph Dixon, and to my secretaries Donna Fisher and Sandy Sievers.

Thanks to my editors and the staff at Houghton Mifflin Company.

Thanks to the Association for Supervision and Curriculum Development, the John Dewey Society, and the National Society of College Teachers of Education for entrusting their presidencies to me during the 1960s and teaching me much in the process.

And thanks for being granted Bee; as always, her editing and advice were of high importance to me.

WILLIAM VAN TIL
Lake Lure
Terre Haute, Indiana

PART ONE

CONTEMPORARY
CRITICISMS
OF
THE
CURRICULUM

*Today the major criticisms of the American
school curriculum stem from those
dissatisfied with "the way it is." They regard
the standard curriculum as sterile, lifeless,
coercive, indifferent to the actual lives of
children and youth, and blind to the
problems of the times. The failure of
American education is reported under such
titles as* The Way It Spozed To Be, How
Children Fail, Compulsory Mis-education,
Educating Contra Naturam, The
Underachieving School, The Vanishing
Adolescent, The High School Revolutionaries,
Growing Up Absurd, The Naked Children,
The Angel Inside Went Sour. *The smell of
death pervades some titles:* Our Children
Are Dying, Murder in the Classroom, Death
at an Early Age, School Is Dead, How to
Survive in Your Native Land.
   *Part One of this anthology is devoted to
the views of authors dissatisfied with the*

1

American school curriculum today and to the emerging criticism of these views by other authors.

The history of American education demonstrates that waves of criticism of the school curriculum accompany tides of dissatisfaction with the existing social order. For instance, historian R. Freeman Butts has cogently demonstrated that during the eighteenth and nineteenth centuries, as Americans rejected aristocracy in favor of an emerging democracy, the curriculum of American schools moved from elitist programs toward universal public education. In the late nineteenth and early twentieth centuries, as social problems again changed, the traditional curriculum was challenged by the progressive critics, as historian Lawrence A. Cremin has demonstrated in The Transformation of the School.

The same relationship has prevailed in recent decades. In the early 1950s the public school curriculum was repeatedly assailed as socialistic, communistic, atheistic, and unpatriotic by right wing individuals and reactionary forces. This assault took place while Senator Joseph McCarthy was charging subversion in governmental, intellectual, and even military circles—a period termed the "era of McCarthyism." Many educators remained silent but some responded at substantial risk to their own careers. Defenses of American education were difficult to mount in the climate of the times. (Should an honor roll of the defenders of education against the unwarranted criticism of the early 1950s ever be compiled, it should include such names as Harold Benjamin, Willard Goslin, Virgil Rogers, Richard Barnes Kennan, Ernest Melby, Robert A. Skaife, William H. Burton, and others.)

In the middle and later 1950s the major criticisms of the school curriculum came from supporters of academic education. Carefully distinguishing themselves from the right wing reactionaries, and reiterating that they were not "enemies of the schools," the spokesmen for academic programs assailed progressive education. They opposed the progressive educators' emphasis upon the importance of the individual learner, interdisciplinary education, problem-centered instruction, and curricular content related to the individual's life experiences. Ironically, the viewpoint of yesterday's academic critics is precisely the opposite of that expressed by today's critics of "the way it is." The educational views of historian Arthur E. Bestor and Admiral Hyman G. Rickover are antithetical to the opinions of John Holt, Herbert Kohl, Jonathan Kozol, George Dennison, James Herndon, and others among today's critics of the schools.

The academic critics reflected a dissatisfaction with the schools which grew out of attitudes widespread in the America of the mid 1950s. The cold war with the Soviet Union was at its most frigid. The amiable relations characterizing Soviet leader Brezhnev's June 1973 visit to the United States were inconceivable in the mid 1950s. American fears were mounting as to the ability of American science and technology to compete with the Russians. Calls for manpower trained in science and mathematics were sounded. With the launching of the Russian Sputnik in 1957, American social hysteria increased, and the schools proved to be a handy scapegoat. Life magazine called for the closing of the "carnival" in the schools; intellectual leaders who had not been in an elementary or secondary school since their own graduations loftily condemned the schools for lack of academic rigor. The appropriately-titled National Defense Education Act followed swiftly in 1958. Projects in the separate academic disciplines proliferated; heavy emphasis was placed on the fields singled out for favor in the National Defense Education Act: science, mathematics, modern languages, and guidance. The schools struggled to adapt to the new dispensation. Once again, dissatisfaction with the social order created and sanctioned criticisms of the curriculum of American schools.

In the early 1960s, a proposal fostered by Jerome S. Bruner's The Process of Education relating to the structure of the disciplines was the talk of educational circles. The "disciplines proposal" stressed that each of the scholarly disciplines has an innate structure or logic which can provide a means of teaching that subject on any level in a meaningful and rigorous way. The function of instruction, according to Bruner, was to introduce the student to the several modes of inquiry used in the disciplines. Concepts, relationships, and principles were stressed in curriculum development. By the 1960s, substantial government and foundation funds were invested in various projects conceived along these lines. The disciplines proposal supplied an ideology which unified and solidified the otherwise disparate and even competitive approaches of projects in the various subject fields.

By the late 1960s some grim realities facing society, and human problems facing children and youth, had taken precedence in the public mind over the cold war, competition with the Russians, scientific expertise, and the like. America was then engaged in a frustrating hot war in Vietnam and the nation was confronted by racial antagonism at home. People were worried about disadvantaged Americans who could find no place in the economy, and alienated young people who repudiated American society. Social priorities changed. In an era of black dissent, which affected all institutions in American society; of student dissent, which began in the colleges and spread into the high schools; of alienation and disillusion; of dissatisfaction with formal schooling; and of real and palpable survival-threatening problems, dissatisfaction permeated the social order. And with it came new criticisms and new demands upon the curriculum of American schools. Educators especially worried about the lives children led in our schools.

Part One of this book focuses on the pro and con of this criticism which persists in the 1970s. Excerpts follow from the writings of the *dissenting critics and of critics of the critics. The interrelationships among the ideas of the new critics and of the critics of the new critics will be discussed in the remainder of this introduction.*

Part One opens with a prologue by the editor, written in the early 1960s to express a conviction that the issues raised by progressive educators were not obsolete, though the attention of curriculum workers seemed to have turned elsewhere. The editor concluded:

The central questions posed and the relevant contributions toward workable answers for our times made by such interpreters of the progressive movement in education are not obsolete. They must and will persist. In time, they will be embodied in the form of new proposals for modern education, new syntheses which build upon predecessors, as is common in the world of ideas. The overanxious gravediggers, and those who currently give them comfort, will discover as this twentieth century rolls along that what they have mistaken for a corpse is indeed very much alive.

This contention was supported during the later 1960s by the emergence of a school of thought still so new that no satisfactory name has yet been coined for it. The young teachers who are its spokesmen have been called "the romantic critics," "the radical critics," and other names which similarly miss the mark. In this book they will be called "the compassionate critics," for their common characteristic seems to be a sympathetic concern for the welfare of children and youth. Many of them began as formal teachers, but soon recognized the inanity and inappropriateness of the traditional curriculum for the situations in which they found themselves, and began instead to focus upon children and youth.

The first of the compassionate critics to be heard (and the first from whom we present a selection) was John Holt in 1964. In How Children Fail, *Holt repeatedly illustrates from his own private-school teaching experiences how children's fears of failing contribute to actual failure. The notion of the curriculum as an essential body of knowledge seems to Holt to contribute to this self-fulfilling prophecy of expected failure and actual failure. He calls for schools in which each child would satisfy his curiosity, develop his abilities, and pursue his interests in his own way. Thus Holt aligns himself with a child-centered approach to education*

Meanwhile James Herndon (represented in this new edition by an excerpt from his latest book, How to Survive in Your Native Land) *began reporting, first in* Harper's *magazine and then in* The Way It Spozed To Be, *his experiences teaching in a ghetto school in an unnamed West Coast metropolis. In his account of his defeats, Herndon writes with sympathy and wry "black humor" of the lives of teachers and students in a 98% Negro urban school. For both, nothing is ever "the way it spozed to be." The curriculum is not merely ineffectual, it is positively harmful. He ends his book on a note of despair: "But frankly, I have almost no hope that there will be any significant change in the way we educate our children—for that, after all, would involve liberty, the last thing we may soon expect—and so I have thought mainly to describe one time for you, parents, kids, readers, the way it is."* Later he taught in a suburb and described further reactions in How to Survive in Your Native Land.

Herbert Kohl (*represented here by an excerpt from his first book*, 36 Children) *is a vital, sensitive, and amazingly ingenious teacher. Faced with 36 sixth grade black children in East Harlem, Kohl first tried to retain the standard curriculum. But the burden of irrelevance was too heavy; he could not communicate with his children. So, a bit at a time, he abandoned the formal curriculum in favor of another kind of education, which first took place in ten-minute "breaks." An analysis of words the children actually used developed into a study of language and myths, and the children began writing about their own lives.* Kohl's 36 Children *is an exciting story of success in creating a curriculum out of the teacher's imagination and the children's experiences. Yet it has bitter overtones, such as Kohl's description of his attempt to learn what had happened to his children years later: "I stopped searching; don't want to know the full extent of misery and tragedy of the children's present lives. Recently one of the kids told me: 'Mr. Kohl, one good year isn't enough. . . .'"*

In New York City, Herbert Kohl and his 36 children successfully created a curriculum and got away with it. In Boston, Jonathan Kozol, a substitute teacher with an assignment in a fourth grade class made up largely of black children, tried to develop a curriculum related to students' lives and to establish some genuine contacts with children— and was fired by school officials for deviation from the established fourth grade course of study. Of all of the compassionate critics, Kozel is the most politically sensitive, probably because of his extensive encounters with the school authorities. He deals not only with the inadequacies of the curriculum for black children but also with the broader school and societal situation which prompted the title of his book: Death at an Early Age: The Destruction of the Hearts and Minds of Negro Children in the Boston Public Schools. *Kozol is an earnest and angry young man, and after reading his description of his experiences, the reader will understand why. Kozol reappears in Part Two of this anthology to urge more emphasis on social problems and hard skills in free schools.*

George Dennison, *in* The Lives of Children, *tells of his experiences with 23 children and three full-time teachers at the First Street School, a "minischool" in New York City. Dennison is a man of patience, courage, and integrity. In the First Street School he held to his convictions about freedom and learning under adverse conditions,* including physical attacks. His ruthlessly realistic depiction of the obscenity and violence which marked the children's relationship to their environment is unsurpassed in the literature of the compassionate critics. The quoted excerpts can only partially convey the depth of the problems which characterize the lives of his children. Unlike most of the compassionate critics, Dennison recognizes his intellectual debt to precedent. Some of his fellow critics, overly impressed with the novelty of their approaches, misinterpret or deprecate their heritage from the child-centered wing of the progressive education movement. In general, the compassionate critics are long on wisdom about children and short on knowledge of the educational leaders who preceded their own generation. Dennison, however, draws from Dewey and Tolstoy, in addition to A. S. Neill and Paul Goodman.

Following Dennison, James Herndon is represented with an amusing quotation from How to Survive in Your Native Land in which he reports on his recent encounters with children and teachers in a middle class suburban junior high school. How to Survive in Your Native Land is even wilder and more free-wheeling than Herndon's first book, The Way It Spozed to Be.

Another kind of probing criticism of education comes from those who challenge the social and educational axiom of the desirability of compulsory education, terming it, in Paul Goodman's ringing phrase, "compulsory mis-education." They call for "free choice, with no processing whatever," and attempt to refute the assumptions upon which the American system of free universal public education is based. To them, compulsory education is a tool used by the Establishment to manipulate children into conformity with and acceptance of a sick society.

The first of the critics of compulsory education to be quoted is the historian Theodore Roszak. Roszak is a spokesman for the "counter-culture," a view of the world which is sharply critical of Establishment ways and strongly supportive of their repudiation by a variety of dissenting forces. Taking as his point of departure Leo Tolstoy's views on education, he inveighs against an educational system which seems to him contrary to the nature of man. Roszak came to the attention of contemporary curriculum workers particularly through his television address to the Association for Supervision and Curriculum Development in 1970, an expanded version of which is reproduced in this volume.

Though Paul Goodman had vigorously condemned compulsory education in many of his writings, it remained for Ivan Illich to bring a massive denunciation of required schooling before a wide reading public through Deschooling Society, excerpted here. Illich's experiences in Latin America had led him to the conclusion that schooling does harm to poor people. He asserted his belief in education disassociated from *the process of schooling. Society, not school, must educate, said Illich. His views are expanded upon in* Deschooling Society *and in articles.*

The views of the compassionate critics are being examined in the 1970s by some students of contemporary education. They charge the compassionate critics with overdependence on a child-centered school. To some observers, the critics of compulsory education have put their fingers on the tragic flaw in the educational process. To others, critics of compulsory education seem to be burning down the railroad station rather than rebuilding it while the trains keep running. Nor are the curriculum reformers who reconstructed separate subject disciplines exempt from today's counter criticism.

One critic of the views of the compassionate critics is an experienced controversialist, Sidney Hook, who recently retired as a professor of philosophy after a long career at New York University. Hook believes that the compassionate critics have grossly misinterpreted the progressive views of John Dewey, on whom Hook has been a long time specialist. Hook's article is particularly condemnatory of the result of this purported misinterpretation in higher education. As a social activist, he has recently been prominent in the University Center for Rational Alternatives, an organization defending academic freedom and liberty against what Hook conceives to be misguided student revolutionary excesses.

In moderate tones, John H. Fischer, a former school superintendent and now the president of Teachers College, Columbia University, comes to the defense of school systems against the opponents of compulsory education. He readily accepts criticisms of current weaknesses but does not find a way out in leaving schooling "to the uncertain enthusiasms of voluntary enterprise." His call is that "the public schools be reformed, preserved, and strengthened."

An epilogue to various criticisms and reforms comes from a much-discussed book, Charles E. Silberman's Crisis in the Classroom, a report of a study by the Carnegie Corporation. In the excerpts selected from his insightful and extremely provocative report, Silberman stresses the importance of purposes in education as he accounts for the failure of the recent movement to reform the curriculum through reconstructing separate subject disciplines. More than eight years after the editor of this anthology asked, "Is Progressive Education Obsolete?" and answered that it is not, Silberman underlined the importance of the questions raised by the leaders of the progressive movement.

What follows, then, is representative of the latest major criticism of the American school curriculum and the emerging response to that criticism. The critics vary in the degree of their penetration and analytic power; they range, as well, from moderate to revolutionary. They may be more powerful in their analysis of what is wrong than persuasive in *their proposals of what to do about it. But they are all vigorous, forceful, and sometimes eloquent. The contemporary critics are well worth reading in full; excerpts alone cannot do full justice to them and their ideas. They have much to say and they are in dead earnest. The same comments apply to the emerging critics of the critics. The scholars reported here who question the adequacy of the proposals of the compassionate critics, or who defend universal free public education, or who stress philosophical goals, cannot be dismissed as social reactionaries, for they are not. Each has been active in the struggle for better democratic education. But they have reached conclusions as to preferable roads that are somewhat different from the views of the compassionate critics and the advocates of deschooling and the reformers of separate subject matter fields.*

PROLOGUE: IS PROGRESSIVE EDUCATION OBSOLETE?

WILLIAM VAN TIL

In 1962, the editor of this anthology contended in a Saturday Review *article that the questions raised by such progressive educators as John Dewey, William Heard Kilpatrick, George Counts, and Boyd H. Bode were inescapable and that their contributions to workable answers must be taken into account by American education. Consequently, he held, progressive education is not obsolete.*

The article appeared during a period when curriculum leaders seemed absorbed with technology, organizational innovation, and the structure of the disciplines proposal. However, since publication, this article has been reprinted in more than a dozen anthologies on contemporary education. Apparently it struck a sensitive nerve. Keep the date in mind as you read.

Is progressive education outmoded? One's first impulse is to say "yes." Who today, among the voices being heard on education, is talking about the concerns which characterized many leaders of education during the first half of the twentieth century? Specifically, who today is talking about the ideas which occupied John Dewey, George Counts, Boyd H. Bode, and William Heard Kilpatrick, those symbols of the intellectual leadership of the "new education," symbols of the varied versions of the progressive movement in education? Practically nobody; at least nobody who is being heard widely.

Instead, American education in the early 1960s is engrossed with the application of technology to education, with competing new proposals for organization of the school program, and with stress on reconstruction of academic disciplines. The mass media foster the interest in technology, organization, and disciplines. If an educator tries to be heard on more fundamental aspects, he often encounters the silent treatment.

The Industrial Revolution has finally reached education. As a result, matters of technology have virtually become table talk in education today. In professional discussions and in the mass media reporting we hear constantly about educational television, language laboratories, courses on film, and programmed learning through teaching machines.

A second stress in today's education emphasizes organization of the school program. Proposals are varied and often conflicting. They include such organizational proposals as team teaching, the dual progress

William Van Til, "Is Progressive Education Obsolete?" *Saturday Review*, February 17, 1962, pp. 56–57, 82–84. Copyright 1962 Saturday Review, Inc.

plan, the non-graded school, and increasing the course requirements within the existing Carnegie unit structure.

Currently, a third stress is the new interest in the academic disciplines. In part, the emphasis is upon updating knowledge through efforts by specialists in the disciplines. The work of such groups as the Physical Science Study Committee and the varied mathematics programs at Yale, Maryland, and Illinois are watched intently. Science, mathematics, and foreign languages ride high as the favored fields of the national government, which has become a significant curriculum maker on the elementary and high school levels. The fields of English and physical education make frantic and failing attempts to latch onto the benefits of the National Defense Education Act; leadership in reconstruction of the curriculum in these fields has been assumed by the College Entrance Examination Board and by a football coach, respectively. There are indications that Commissioner McMurrin intends to attempt to do for the arts as well as for English what post-Sputnik apprehension did for the sciences. Rumors, alarms, and confusions surround the status of the social studies. The phrase "structures of the disciplines" is being bandied about, with none too clear a definition emerging as yet.

Technology, organization, and the disciplines seem a far cry from the philosophical, social, and psychological ideas that engaged the leaders of the progressive movement in education in the first half of the twentieth century. There appears to have been a change in "fashions in ideas," to use the chilling and accurate phrase Irwin Edman coined for a phenomenon of our times. Consequently, progressive education seems outmoded. Lawrence A. Cremin even consigned it to history in his "The Transformation of the School: Progressivism in American Education, 1876–1957." He began his preface as follows: "The death of the Progressive Education Association in 1955 and the passing of its journal, *Progressive Education*, two years later marked the end of an era in American pedagogy. Yet one would scarcely have known it from the pitifully small group of mourners at both funerals." Martin Mayer recapitulated the Cremin position in his widely read book, "The Schools."

One might readily conclude that progressive education is outmoded save for a stubborn fact. The fact is that the questions raised by the progressive movement in education are not obsolete. They will not die. They cannot be killed. They cannot be exorcised by any voodooism yet known to technology, organization, or the reconstruction of disciplines which remains aloof from these questions.

The basic questions which men like John Dewey, William Heard Kilpatrick, George Counts, and Boyd H. Bode raised are inescapable questions: What are the aims of education? Upon what foundations should the school program be built? Given such aims and foundations, what should the schools teach? To these probing and fundamental questions, matters of organization and technique, while important, are necessarily subordinate.

The progressive education movement of the first half of the twentieth century, symbolized by Dewey, Kilpatrick, Counts, and Bode, was essentially a quest for workable answers for our times to questions such as these. No one claims that the Holy Grail was found; no one claims that the questioners came up with final, definitive, eternal answers. The "new educators" did not completely agree among themselves on workable answers for our times. But at least the "new educators" asked the right questions.

One wing of the progressive movement sought the answers primarily in the potential of the individual learner. A pioneer in this respect was the man whose ninetieth birthday was celebrated on November 20, 1961—William Heard Kilpatrick. Many of today's schoolmen will remember Kilpatrick's classes in the Horace Mann Auditorium of Teachers College, Columbia University. Hundreds attended each session, yet the quiet man with the mane of white hair used committees and reports so skillfully that each student found opportunities to speak out and battle over ideas.

The heart of Kilpatrick's first major contribution to education, "The Project Method," was founded on his faith in the potential of the individual learner. In back of the recurrent Kilpatrickian phrases which valued "purposeful activity," "intrinsic motivation," "planning," in back of his opposition to "extrinsic subject matter" which disregarded individuals, in back of his opposition to meaningless rote learning, lay Kilpatrick's belief that clues to significant content can be found within the learner and can be developed fully in collaboration with a mature adult who fosters self-direction and independent thought. The later Kilpatrick increased his stress on the importance of social orientation and the urgency of meeting social problems. But the mark Kilpatrick lastingly left on the progressive movement still derives largely from his faith in the potentiality of the learner when that potentiality is cultivated by skillful and sensitive teachers. To many educators, probably to most, insight into the relationship between the individual and his education was the major contribution of the progressive education which Kilpatrick espoused, though he was concerned for philosophical and social, as well as psychological, foundations. And—mistake it not—the insight derived from Kilpatrick made a massive contribution to education in an era that had lost sight of the importance of the learner and his purposes and potential.

A second wing of the progressive movement set forth answers to the perennial questions of aims, foundations, and content largely in terms of the society which surrounded the schools. George Counts, a battler for socially oriented schools in a democracy, serves as a symbol of this emphasis. To George Counts, for instance, the times cried out for an education realistically geared to the new social order which was emerging. He threw his eloquent challenge to the Progressive Education Association assembled in convention in 1932. He amplified his ideas in the pamphlet "Dare the Schools Build A New Social Order?" and for years educators found themselves forced to face the issues Counts raised. Whether one condemned aspects of his viewpoint as indoctrination and a potential abuse of the method of intelligence, thus classifying it as a new liberal's version of authoritarianism, or whether one hailed it as a realistic recognition of the overpowering importance of social problems, as an indication that the social sciences had come of age, an educator who heard Counts had to take into account stress on society. The role of education with respect to social change and to reform was an imperative and recurrent theme with Counts and his fellow social reconstructionists. The pivotal place of social realities in education could not be forgotten after Counts was heard, even though indoctrination might be repudiated.

George Counts lived his faith. He helped turn back Communist infiltration of teachers' unions. He was a tower of strength in the Liberal Party; he was a candidate for public office and in the vanguard of social movements of his time. He is still active in his retirement.

To others equally immersed in the progressive movement, democratic values were central to all considerations. For instance, to Boyd H. Bode, the Lincoln-like man from Illinois who made his major contribution through Ohio State University, the crucial need was for the clarification of differences between the democratic way of life and the way of its authoritarian competitors. As he saw it, the road out of value confusion led through a remorseless and unremitting use of the method of intelligence in human affairs. To Bode, progressive education was at the crossroads and a child-centered view would never suffice. Nor was indoctrination the road to a better world. He conducted his classes in philosophy of education through the Socratic method and he fostered thought with every heckling, humorous, or trenchant exchange of ideas in the day-by-day learning experiences.

I venture for your consideration the bold hypothesis that each of these men touched on part of the whole, that each perceived and particularly stressed an aspect of education which we neglect at our peril, that each succeeded nobly, and, where he failed, failed gallantly in building the "new education." Each asked the right questions; each responded with relevant contributions toward workable answers for our times.

The thinker who came closest to the reconciliation of the individual, society, and philosophical foundations—was the extraordinary John Dewey, whose centennial was celebrated by the John Dewey Society three years ago through meetings in scores of universities across the nation. The word "extraordinary" is used advisedly. During his long lifetime, this incredible man lived a full life as a person, participated in social and civic action, conducted the most famous laboratory school in history, became the father figure of the progressive education movement (and, to shift the analogy, sometimes served as mother hen by reconciling conflicts and even smoothing ruffled feathers in the flock), became a towering figure in philosophy, and, in the process, managed to leave for posterity a legacy of 5,000 pages of articles and 18,000 pages in book form.

Yet even Dewey, prodigious though his endeavors were, never achieved extensive translation of his ideas into a new curriculum. Underbrush in philosophy needed to be cleared. After his Laboratory School experimentation, and after setting forth his pedagogical creed in such books as "The School and Society" and "Democracy and Education," Dewey gave himself to this Herculean labor as he built his philosophy of experimentalism. He constantly reacted to trends and tendencies in progressive education, as he did in his critique "Experience and Education." He made only occasional critical forays into program building. He would be the first to admit, were he alive, that much remained to be done to implement his ideas on what he preferred to term simply "education," rather than "progressive education."

So we turn back to the thinking of representative intellectual leaders of the progressive movement in education, not in any spirit of ancestor worship, but for the inescapable questions they raised and for the insights they contributed toward workable solutions for our times. Cremin says it well in his final paragraphs: "There remained a timelessness about many of the problems the progressives raised and the solutions they proposed. . . . And for all the talk about pedagogical breakthroughs and crash programs, the authentic progressive vision remained strangely pertinent to the problems of mid-century America. Perhaps it only awaited the reformulation and resuscitation that would ultimately derive from a larger research and reform in American life and thought." With these words Cremin partially redeems the strange inconsistency of pointing out brilliantly in early chapters that social currents created progressive education well before the official establishment of a Progressive Education Association, yet conveying the impression in his final chapter that the demise of an organization and a magazine meant the death of progressive education. The fact that ideas live beyond organizations apparently escaped the overanxious gravediggers who gleefully greeted Cremin's book as the definitive obituary for progressive education as a force in American ideas.

The questions raised and many of the tentative answers ventured by the early leaders of progressive education are not dead nor will they die. In time, the sponsors of new educational technology, the advocates of varied forms of educational organization, the proponents of study of the structure of separate disciplines, must face the inescapable questions and consider the possible solutions proposed.

The problem for sponsors and users of programmed learning through teaching machines does not lie in the capacity of the machine to produce positive reinforcement, whether it takes the form of a kind word, a pat on the head, or, indeed, a bottle of Coca-Cola. Given technical ingenuity, a reinforcing reward will be forthcoming. The harder problem for sponsors and users of the teaching machine is whether positive reinforcement will be used to bring nearer George Orwell's "1984" and Aldous Huxley's "Brave New World," or whether programmed learning, using positive reinforcement selectivity and with discrimination, will reduce the skill-drudgery of education and free teachers and students for more humane aspects of learning and human development, such as creativity, the use of reflective thought, and experiences in freedom. Consider, for instance, this quotation from "Walden Two," a Utopia envisioned by the pioneer of teaching machines, B. F. Skinner of Harvard, a Utopia which appears to some of us an authoritarian nightmore world of behavioristic conditioning. T. E. Frazier, spokesman for "Walden Two," says approvingly, "Now that we *know* how positive reinforcement works and why negative doesn't . . . we can be more deliberate, and hence more successful, in our cultural design. We can achieve a sort of control under which the controlled, even though they are following a code much more scrupulously than was ever the case under the old system, nevertheless *feel free*. They are doing what they want to do, not what they are forced to do. That's the source of the tremendous power of positive reinforcement—there's no restraint and no revolt. By a careful cultural design, we control not the final behavior, but the *inclination* to behave—the motives, the desires, the wishes.

"The curious thing is that in that case *the question of freedom never arises.*"

In the light of this quotation we can understand why Aldous Huxley recently reminded us in "Brave New World Revisited" that it may be later than we think. He wrote as his conclusion, "The older dictators fell because they never could supply their subjects with enough bread, enough circuses, enough miracles and mysteries. Nor did they possess a really effective system of mind-manipulation. . . . Under a scientific dictator, education will really work—with the result that most men and women will grow up to love their servitude and will never dream of revolution. There seems to be no good reason why a thoroughly scientific dictatorship should ever be overthrown."

The problem before the sponsors of educational television is not how wide a circle over six states, or indeed a nation, can be reached by a plane flying for Midwest Airborne Television. Nor is it bouncing beams off satellites for global television. Technology will solve those problems.

The real problem is whether the device will realize the gloomy prophecy of an old Vanderbilt University professor who once said at a meeting of the American Association of University Professors, "Gentlemen, the time is coming when one Harvard University professor will determine through his history course on television what history is taught in the United States—and even if it's Arthur Schlesinger, Jr., I say the hell with it!"—or whether imaginative educational TV will provide learners with a magic carpet to a wider world of experience made at once more expansive and more closely detailed.

The problem before the sponsors and users of team teaching is not precisely how many students to instruct at any given time in any given space. It is not whether a new magical number combination, proposed for better staff utilization, or some flexible magic of numbers out of Lexington, Massachusetts, will take the place of the former magic number—25 or 30 in each classroom. Experience and, we hope, genuine controlled experimentation, will supply the answer here. The real problem is whether team teaching actually will improve learning, whether it will evolve toward emphasis on the *interrelationships* of subject matter, whether it can provide sufficient personalized contacts with teachers and sufficient firsthand experiences by students to enable young people to deal with significant problems.

The problem before the sponsors and users of the dual progress plan is not the technical difficulty of introducing specialized science, mathematics, and arts teachers into elementary school organization through the demonstrations at Ossining and Long Beach in New York. The real problem for the sponsors and users of the dual progress plan is recognized by the originator of the plan as whether the dual progress plan will or will not better answer some of Dewey's persistent queries; George Stoddard poses the issue in his new book, "The Dual Progress Plan," which should be read along with the Association for Supervision and Curriculum Development pamphlet, "The Self-Contained Classroom," for differing organizational approaches to possibly compatible goals.

The problem before the liberal arts professors currently reconstructing and updating knowledge in such disciplines as physics, biology, and mathematics is not whether they can cram all of man's new knowledge into separate watertight compartments, which will then be siphoned off during the elementary and high school years. They can't. Even if they could, they would endlessly face true obsolescence, for knowledge swiftly dates and, like fish, won't keep. The real problem, of which some of the reconstructors of disciplines are aware and of which others appear quite unaware, is whether the scholars can identify concepts in their new knowledge which can be made meaningful to children and youth, appropriate to both the general and specialized education needed for living in today's society, crucial in the process of critical thinking and problem solving—or whether their reconstructed and amplified knowledge, however new, will prove to be inert subject matter in Alfred North Whitehead's sense.

The problem for those who are studying the structures of the disciplines may be first to make clear what they mean. Granted that they can and do, the question will face them as to whether their studies of structures of disciplines are to be achieved as culminations built upon the experience of learners, as Dewey recommended. Or will their studies of structures of disciplines be evasions of problems central to general education, formal orientations to content which bear little relationship to how young people live and learn?

One can derive little encouragement for the future of study of the structure of the disciplines from the views of Charles B. Keller, director of the John Hay Fellows Program, who believes "too many social studies teachers have emphasized the creation of good citizens rather than the content and discipline of their subjects." He says, "Attitudes cannot be taught in formal classroom situations. We weaken education —and schools—when we try to do so. What students should do in school is to study subjects and become acquainted with facts and ideas. Subjects as such have disciplines that will help to develop students' minds." Is this the conception of educational aims and psychology of learning which is to characterize the new advocacy of studying the structure of disciplines? Surely this was not the conception of Arthur W. Foshay when, in his presidential address to the Association for Supervision and Curriculum Development in 1961, he advised "that we educators take directly into account the nature of the organized bodies of knowledge, in addition to the nature of the growing child and the nature of our society, as we try to make curriculum decisions."

If their work is to have meaning, rather than to be innovation for unclear purposes, the sponsors and users of the new technology, organization, and approaches to disciplines must come to terms with the questions that engaged the intellectual leadership of the progressive movement in education. Questions of "why" and "what" have necessary precedence over questions of "how" and "when." The inescapable questions relate to the aims of education, the foundations of the program, and what the schools should teach as appropriate content based on such aims and foundations.

Is, then, the progressive movement in education obsolete? I think not. The questions raised by the "new education" are remorseless, inevitable, demanding. The answers provided by the intellectual leaders of the progressive movement were promising beginnings, useful leads, valid foreshadowings.

When considerations of "why" are dodged, we get prescriptions which simply cannot be appraised. One cannot truly evaluate the proposals made in widely read books which are characterized by indifference to aims and purposes in the early chapters and which then constantly smuggle in unanalyzed value assumptions through the remainder of the pages. Two knights entered in the educational jousting show this tendency: both the great and good James B. Conant and the provocative and prancing Martin Mayer.

Conant, for instance, does not set forth aims for education in "The American High School Today." Yet he steadily makes assumptions as to what knowledge is of most worth.

In "Slums and Suburbs," Conant says, "It is after visits to schools like these that I grow impatient with both critics and defenders of public education who ignore the realities of school situations to engage in fruitless debate about educational philosophy, purposes, and the like. These situations call for action, not hair-splitting arguments." Yet "Slums and Suburbs" is permeated with proposals for action which must be based on philosophic assumptions.

In "The Schools," Martin Mayer colorfully rejects all possible formulations of aims. He says, "It is well to rid oneself immediately of this business of 'the aims of education.' Discussions on this subject are among the dullest and most fruitless of human pursuits. Whatever the ideal general 'aims of education' may be, they certainly cannot be accomplished in schools." He then proceeds to lace through his book individualistic approbations and denunciations based on his acceptance of undefined aims.

One of the myths of our times is that the several tendencies which characterized what is broadly termed progressive education prevailed, were fully achieved, and are now being repudiated. This sedulously cultivated myth is incomprehensible. The reality is that progressive education has never been tried on any significant scale.

As the inescapable queries reassert themselves and the tentative proposals of the varied interpretations of progressive education are reconsidered, educators will find it necessary to utilize the insights of Dewey, Bode, Counts, and Kilpatrick. An education which takes into account the individual, his society, and his values—an education which builds upon the soundest possible scholarship derivative from psychological, social, and philosophical foundations—is imperative in developing a curriculum appropriate for twentieth-century man.

The central questions posed and the relevant contributions toward workable answers for our times made by such interpreters of the progressive movement in education are not obsolete. They must and will persist. In time, they will be embodied in the form of new proposals for modern education, new syntheses which build upon our predecessors, as is common in the world of ideas. The overanxious gravediggers, and those who currently give them comfort, will discover as this twentieth century moves along that what they have mistaken for a corpse is indeed very much alive.

THE COMPASSIONATE CRITICS

HOW CHILDREN FAIL

JOHN HOLT

John Holt, who has taught at both the high school and elementary levels, describes in his summary from How Children Fail *the deadly connection between fear of failing and actual failure by children. As early as 1964, Holt, an eloquent and compassionate critic, implored educators to focus on children rather than on the promulgation of the formal curriculum. His call was heard by kindred spirits and his influential first book went into several printings.*

John Holt now writes articles and reviews for major magazines and acts as a consultant to experimentally oriented schools. He has written several books; among his recent publications are What Do I Do Monday? *(New York: E. P. Dutton, 1970), and* Freedom and Beyond *(New York: E. P. Dutton, 1972).*

Nobody starts off stupid. You have only to watch babies and infants, and think seriously about what all of them learn and do, to see that, except for the most grossly retarded, they show a style of life, and a desire and ability to learn that in an older person we might well call genius. Hardly an adult in a thousand, or ten thousand, could in any three years of his life learn as much, grow as much in his understanding of the world around him, as every infant learns and grows in his first three years. But what happens, as we get older, to this extraordinary capacity for learning and intellectual growth?

What happens is that it is destroyed, and more than by any other one thing, by the process that we misname education—a process that goes on in most homes and schools. We adults destroy most of the intellectual and creative capacity of children by the things we do to them or make them do. We destroy this capacity above all by making them afraid, afraid of not doing what other people want, of not pleasing, of making mistakes, of failing, of being *wrong*. Thus we make them afraid to gamble, afraid to experiment, afraid to try the difficult and the unknown. Even when we do not create children's fears, when they come to us with fears ready-made and built-in, we use these fears as handles to manipulate them and get them to do what we want. Instead of trying to whittle down their fears, we build them up, often to monstrous size. For we like children who are a little afraid of us, docile, deferential children, though not, of course, if they are so obviously afraid that they threaten our image of ourselves as kind, lovable people whom there is no reason to fear. We find ideal the kind of "good" children who are just enough afraid of us to do everything we want, without making us feel that fear of us is what is making them do it.

We destroy the disinterested (I do *not* mean *un*interested) love of learning in children, which is so strong when they are small, by encouraging and compelling them to work for petty and contemptible rewards—gold stars, or papers marked 100 and tacked to the wall, or A's on report cards, or honor rolls, or dean's lists, or Phi Beta Kappa keys—in short, for the ignoble satisfaction of feeling that they are better than someone else. We encourage them to feel that the end and aim of all they do in school is nothing more than to get a good mark on a test, or to impress someone with what they seem to know. We kill, not only their curiosity, but their feeling that it is a good and admirable thing to be curious, so that by the age of ten most of them will not ask questions, and will show a good deal of scorn for the few who do.

In many ways, we break down children's convictions that things make sense, or their hope that things may prove to make sense. We do it, first of all, by breaking up life into arbitrary and disconnected hunks of subject matter, which we then try to "integrate" by such artificial and irrelevant devices as having children sing Swiss folk songs while they are studying the geography of Switzerland, or do arithmetic problems about rail-splitting while they are studying the boyhood of Lincoln. Furthermore, we continually confront them with what is senseless, ambiguous, and contradictory; worse, we do it without knowing that we are doing it, so that, hearing nonsense shoved at them as if it were sense, they come to feel that the source of their confusion lies not in the material but in their own stupidity. Still further, we cut children off from their own common sense and the world of reality by requiring them to play with and shove around words and symbols that have little or no meaning to them. Thus we turn the vast majority of our students into the kind of people for whom all symbols are meaningless; who cannot use symbols as a way of learning about and dealing with reality; who cannot understand written instructions; who, even if they read books, come out knowing no more than when they went in; who may have a few new words rattling around in their heads, but whose mental models of the world remain unchanged and, indeed, impervious to change. The minority, the able and successful students, we are very likely to turn into something different but just as dangerous: the kind of people who can manipulate words and symbols fluently while keeping themselves largely divorced from the reality for which they stand; the kind of people who like to speak in large generalities but grow silent or indignant if someone asks for an example of what they are talking about; the kind of people who, in their discussions of world affairs, coin and use such words as megadeaths and megacorpses, with scarcely a thought to the blood and suffering these words imply.

We encourage children to act stupidly, not only by scaring and confusing them, but by boring them, by filling up their days with dull, repetitive tasks that make little or no claim on their attention or demands on their intelligence. Our hearts leap for joy at the sight of a roomful of children all slogging away at some imposed task, and we are all the more pleased and satisfied if someone tells us that the children don't really like what they are doing. We tell ourselves that this drudgery, this endless busywork, is good preparation for life, and we fear that without it children would be hard to "control." But why must this busywork be so dull? Why not give tasks that are interesting and demanding? Because, in schools where every task must be completed and every answer must be right, if we give children more demanding tasks they will be fearful and will instantly insist that we show them how to do the job. When you have acres of paper to fill up with pencil marks, you have no time to waste on the luxury of thinking. By such means children are firmly established in the habit of using only a small part of their thinking capacity. They feel that school is a place where they must spend most of their time doing dull tasks in a dull way. Before long they are deeply settled in a rut of unintelligent behavior from which most of them could not escape even if they wanted to. . . .

Behind much of what we do in school lie some ideas, that could be expressed roughly as follows: (1) Of the vast body of human knowledge, there are certain bits and pieces that can be called essential, that everyone should know; (2) the extent to which a person can be considered educated, qualified to live intelligently in today's world and be a useful member of society, depends on the amount of this essential knowledge that he carries about with him; (3) it is the duty of schools, therefore, to get as much of this essential knowledge as possible into the minds of children. Thus we find ourselves trying to poke certain facts, recipes, and ideas down the gullets of every child in school, whether the morsel interests him or not, even if it frightens him or sickens him, and even if there are other things that he is much more interested in learning.

These ideas are absurd and harmful nonsense. We will not begin to have true education or real learning in our schools until we sweep this nonsense out of the way. Schools should be a place where children learn what they most want to know, instead of what we think they ought to know. The child who wants to know something remembers it and uses it once he has it; the child who learns something to please or appease someone else forgets it when the need for pleasing or the danger of not appeasing is past. This is why children quickly forget all but a small part of what they learn in school. It is of no use or interest to them; they do not want, or expect, or even intend to remember it. The only difference between bad and good students in this respect is that the bad students forget right away, while the good students are careful to wait until after the exam. If for no other reason, we could well afford to throw out most of what we teach in school because the children throw out almost all of it anyway.

The notion of a curriculum, an essential body of knowledge, would be absurd even if children remembered everything we "taught" them. We don't and can't agree on what knowledge is essential. The man who has trained himself in some special field of knowledge or competence thinks, naturally, that his specialty should be in the curriculum. The classical scholars want Greek and Latin taught; the historians shout for more history; the mathematicians urge more math and the scientists more science; the modern language experts want all children taught French, or Spanish, or Russian; and so on. Everyone wants to get his specialty into the act, knowing that as the demand for his special knowledge rises, so will the price that he can charge for it. Who wins this struggle and who loses depends not on the real needs of children or even of society, but on who is most skillful in public relations, who has the best educational lobbyists, who best can capitalize on events that have nothing to do with education, like the appearance of Sputnik in the night skies.

The idea of the curriculum would not be valid even if we could agree what ought to be in it. For knowledge itself changes. Much of what a child learns in school will be found, or thought, before many years, to be untrue. I studied physics at school from a fairly up-to-date text that proclaimed that the fundamental law of physics was the law of conservation of matter—matter is not created or destroyed. I had to scratch that out before I left school. In economics at college I was taught many things that were not true of our economy then, and many more that are not true now. Not for many years after I left college did I learn that the Greeks, far from being a detached and judicious people surrounded by chaste white temples, were hot-tempered, noisy, quarrelsome, and liked to cover their temples with gold leaf and bright paint; or that most of the citizens of Imperial Rome, far from living in houses in which the rooms surrounded an atrium, or central court, lived in multi-story tenements, one of which was perhaps the largest building in the ancient world. The child who really remembered everything he heard in school would live his life believing many things that were not so.

Moreover, we cannot possibly judge what knowledge will be most needed forty, or twenty, or even ten years from now. At school, I studied Latin and French. Few of the teachers who claimed then that Latin was essential would make as strong a case for it now; and the French might better have been Spanish, or better yet, Russian. Today the schools are busy teaching Russian; but perhaps they should be teaching Chinese, or Hindi, or who-knows-what? Besides physics, I studied chemistry, then perhaps the most popular of all science courses; but I would probably have done better to study biology, or ecology, if such a course had been offered (it wasn't). We always find out, too late, that we don't have the experts we need, that in the past we studied the wrong things; but this is bound to remain so. Since we can't know what knowledge will be most needed in the future, it is senseless to try to teach it in advance. Instead, we should try to turn out people who love learning so much and learn so well that they will be able to learn whatever needs to be learned.

How can we say, in any case, that one piece of knowledge is more important than another, or indeed, what we really say, that some knowledge is essential and the rest, as far as school is concerned, worthless? A child who wants to learn something that the school can't and doesn't want to teach him will be told not to waste his time. But how can we say that what he wants to know is less important than what we want him to know? We must ask how much of the sum of human knowledge anyone can know at the end of his schooling. Perhaps a millionth. Are we then to believe that one of these millionths is so much more important than another? Or that our social and national problems will be solved if we can just figure out a way to turn children out of schools knowing two millionths of the total, instead of one? Our problems don't arise from the fact that we lack experts enough to tell us what needs to be done, but out of the fact that we do not and will not do what we know needs to be done now.

Learning is not everything, and certainly one piece of learning is as good as another. One of my brightest and boldest fifth graders was deeply interested in snakes. He knew more about snakes than anyone I've ever known. The school did not offer herpetology; snakes were not in the curriculum; but as far as I was concerned, any time he spent learning about snakes was better spent than in ways I could think of to spend it; not least of all because, in the process of learning about snakes, he learned a great deal more about many other things than I was ever able to "teach" those unfortunates in my class who were not interested in anything at all. In another fifth-grade class, studying Romans in Britain, I saw a boy trying to read a science book behind the cover of his desk. He was spotted, and made to put the book away, and listen to the teacher; with a heavy sigh he did so. What was gained here? She traded a chance for an hour's real learning about science for, at best, an hour's temporary learning about history—much more probably no learning at all, just an hour's worth of daydreaming and resentful thoughts about school.

It is not subject matter that makes some learning more valuable than others, but the spirit in which the work is done. If a child is doing the kind of learning that most children do in school, when they learn at all—swallowing words, to spit back at the teacher on demand—he is wasting his time, or rather, we are wasting it for him. This learning will not be permanent, or relevant, or useful. But a child who is learning naturally, following his curiosity where it leads him, adding to his mental model of reality whatever he needs and can find a place for, and rejecting without fear or guilt what he does not need, is growing— in knowledge, in the love of learning, and in the ability to learn. He is on his way to becoming the kind of person we need in our society, and that our "best" schools and colleges are *not* turning out, the kind of person who, in Whitney Griswold's words, seeks and finds meaning, truth, and enjoyment in everything he does. All his life he will go on learning. Every experience will make his mental model of reality more complete and more true to life, and thus make him more able to deal realistically, imaginatively, and constructively with whatever new experience life throws his way.

We cannot have real learning in school if we think it is our duty and our right to tell children what they must learn. We cannot know, at any moment, what particular bit of knowledge or understanding a child needs most, will most strengthen and best fit his model of reality. Only he can do this. He may not do it very well, but he can do it a hundred times better than we can. The most we can do is try to help, by letting him know roughly what is available and where he can look for it. Choosing what he wants to learn and what he does not is something he must do for himself.

There is one more reason, and the most important one, why we must reject the idea of school and classroom as places where, most of the time, children are doing what some adult tells them to do. The reason is that there is no way to coerce children without making them afraid, or more afraid. We must not try to fool ourselves into thinking that this is not so. The would-be progressives, who until recently had great influence over most American public school education, did not recognize this—and still do not. They thought, or at least talked and wrote as if they thought, that there were good ways and bad ways to coerce children (the bad ones mean, harsh, cruel, the good ones gentle, persuasive, subtle, kindly), and that if they avoided the bad and stuck to the good they would do no harm. This was one of their greatest mistakes, and the main reason why the revolution they hoped to accomplish never took hold.

The idea of painless, non-threatening coercion is an illusion. Fear is the inseparable companion of coercion, and its inescapable consequence. If you think it your duty to make children do what you want, whether they will or not, then it follows inexorably that you must make them afraid of what will happen to them if they don't do what you want. You can do this in the old-fashioned way, openly and avowedly, with the threat of harsh words, infringement of liberty, or physical punishment. Or you can do it in the modern way, subtly, smoothly, quietly, by withholding the acceptance and approval which you and others have trained the children to depend on; or by making them feel that some retribution awaits them in the future, too vague to imagine but too implacable to escape. You can, as many skilled teachers do, learn to tap with a word, a gesture, a look, even a smile, the great reservoir of fear, shame, and guilt that today's children carry around inside them. Or you can simply let your own fears, about what will happen to you if the children don't do what you want, reach out and infect them. Thus the children will feel more and more that life is full of dangers from which only the goodwill of adults like you can protect them, and that this goodwill is perishable and must be earned anew each day.

The alternative—I can see no other—is to have schools and classrooms in which each child in his own way can satisfy his curiosity, develop his abilities and talents, pursue his interests, and from the adults and older children around him get a glimpse of the great variety and richness of life. In short, the school should be a great smörgåsbord of intellectual, artistic, creative, and athletic activities, from which each child could take whatever he wanted, and as much as he wanted, or as little. When Anna was in the sixth grade, the year after she was in my class, I mentioned this idea to her. After describing very sketchily how such a school might be run, and what the children might do, I said, "Tell me, what do you think of it? Do you think it would work? Do you think the kids would learn anything?" She said, with utmost conviction, "Oh, yes, it would be wonderful!" She was silent for a minute or two, perhaps remembering her own generally unhappy schooling. Then she said thoughtfully, "You know, kids really like to learn; we just don't like being pushed around."

No, they don't; and we should be grateful for that. So let's stop pushing them around, and give them a chance.

36 CHILDREN

HERBERT KOHL

If a "born teacher" exists it is Herbert Kohl, the author of 36 Children; *his account of learning to teach the hard way is a contemporary classic. The irrelevant curriculum accounted for his initial difficulties. Yet he rallied, won the children over, and developed a curriculum for sixth graders which combined creativity with academic accomplishment.*

After three years in the New York City schools, Kohl directed a teachers' and writers' group and worked with parent groups in Harlem for community participation in education. He wrote The Open Classroom *(New York: The New York Review, 1969), "a handbook for teachers who want to work in an open environment." Later he worked in Berkeley, California, on the development of alternative schools.*

The books arrived the next morning before class. There were twenty-five arithmetic books from one publisher and twelve from another, but in the entire school there was no complete set of sixth-grade arithmetic books. A few minutes spent checking the first day's arithmetic assignment showed me that it wouldn't have mattered if a full set had existed, since half the class had barely mastered multiplication, and only one child, Grace, who had turned in a perfect paper, was actually ready for sixth-grade arithmetic. It was as though, encouraged to believe that the children couldn't do arithmetic by judging from the school's poor results in teaching it, the administration decided not to waste money on arithmetic books, thereby creating a vicious circle that made it even more impossible for the children to learn.

From *36 Children* by Herbert Kohl, pp. 9–10, 16–17, 21–29. Copyright © 1967 by Herbert Kohl. Reprinted by arrangement with The New American Library, Inc., New York, New York.

The situation was almost as dismal in reading—the top class of the sixth grade had more than half its members reading on fourth-grade level and only five or six children actually able to read through a sixth-grade book. There were two full sets of sixth-grade readers available, however, and after the arithmetic situation I was grateful for anything. Yet accepting these readers put me as a teacher in an awkward position. The books were flat and uninteresting. They only presented what was pleasant in life, and even then limited the pleasant to what was publicly accepted as such. The people in the stories were all middle-class and their simplicity, goodness, and self-confidence were unreal. I couldn't believe in this foolish ideal and knew that anyone who had ever bothered to observe human life couldn't believe it. Yet I had to teach it, and through it make reading important and necessary. Remembering the children, their anxiety and hostility, the alternate indifference, suspicion, and curiosity they approached me with, knowing how essential it is to be honest with children, I felt betrayed by the books into hypocrisy. No hypocrite can win the respect of children, and without respect one cannot teach.

One of the readers was a companion to the social studies unit on the growth of the United States and was full of stories about family fun in a Model T Ford, the first wireless radio in town, and the joys of wealth and progress. The closest the book touched upon human emotion or the real life of real children was in a story in which children accepted a new invention before their parents did, even though the adults laughed at the children. Naturally, everything turned out happily.

The other reader was a miscellany of adventure stories (no human violence or antagonists allowed, just treasure hunts, animal battles, close escapes), healthy poems (no love except for mother, father, and nature), and a few harmless myths (no Oedipus, Electra, or Prometheus). I also managed to get twenty dictionaries in such bad condition that the probability of finding any word still intact was close to zero.

The social studies texts (I could choose from four or five) praised industrial America in terms that ranged from the enthusiastic to the exorbitant. Yet the growth of modern industrial society is fascinating, and it was certainly possible to supplement the text with some truth. I decided to work with what was given me and attempt to teach the sixth-grade curriculum as written in the New York City syllabus, ignoring as long as possible the contradictions inherent in such a task.

The class confronted me, surrounded by my motley library, at nine that second morning and groaned.

"Those phoney books?"

"We read them already, Mr. Kohl."

"It's a cheap, dirty, bean school."

My resolve weakened, and I responded out of despair.

"Let me put it straight to you. These are the only books here. I have no more choice than you do and I don't like it any better. Let's get through them and maybe by then I'll figure out how to get better ones."

The class understood and accepted the terms. As soon as the books were distributed the first oral reading lesson began. Some children volunteered eagerly, but most of the class tried not to be seen. The children who read called out the words, but the story was lost. I made the lesson as easy as possible by helping children who stumbled, encouraging irrelevant discussion, and not letting any child humiliate himself. It was bad enough that more than half the class had to be forced to use books they couldn't read.

The lesson ended, and a light-skinned boy raised his hand.

"Mr. Kohl, remember that ten minutes you gave us yesterday? Couldn't we talk again now? We're tired after all this reading."

I wasn't sure how to take Robert's request. My initial feeling was that he was taking advantage of me and trying to waste time. I felt, along with the official dogma, that no moment in school should be wasted—it must all be pre-planned and structured. Yet why shouldn't it be "wasted"? Hadn't most of the class wasted years in school, not merely moments? . . .

I tried for the next six weeks to use the books assigned and teach the official curriculum. It was hopeless. The class went through the readers perfunctorily, refused to hear about modern America, and were relieved to do arithmetic—mechanical, uncharged—as long as nothing new was introduced. For most of the day the atmosphere in the room was stifling. The children were bored and restless, and I felt burdened by the inappropriateness of what I tried to teach. It was so dull that I thought as little as the children and began to despair. Listening to myself on the growth of urban society, realizing that no one else was listening, that though words were pronounced the book was going unread, I found myself vaguely wondering about the children.

But there were moments. The ten-minute breaks between lessons grew until, in my eyes, the lessons were secondary. Everything important happening in the classroom happened between lessons.

First it was the piano, Leverne wanting to play, picking up a few tunes, teaching them to other children, to Charisse and Desiree, to Grace, Pamela, and Maurice. Then it was the six of them asking me to teach them to read music and their learning how in one afternoon.

There was Robert Jackson. I took time to look at his art, observe him working. He was good, accurate; he thought in terms of form and composition. Seeing I was interested, other children told me of Robert's reputation and the neighborhood legend about him—when he was four, his mother gave him a pencil as a pacifier, and he began to draw. They told of the money he made drawing, of his ability to draw "anything."

I watched the girls gossiping, talking about records, parties, boys. After a few days, talk of the summer was exhausted. The children began wandering about the room looking for things to do. They seemed relaxed and eager to work then, though bored and restless during lessons. Unwilling to lose this will and energy I brought checkers and chess to school as well as magazines and books. I developed the habit of taking five minutes in the morning to describe what I had brought in. I sketched the history of chess and told the class about the wise man who asked a king, as reward for a favor, for the number of grains of wheat that resulted from placing one on the first square of a checker-board and then progressively doubling the amount until the whole board was occupied. I commented that the king went broke, and that afternoon, to my surprise, three children told me I was right and showed me how far they'd gotten trying to figure out how much wheat the king owed the wise man.

The checkers provided quite a lesson for me. Only four of the boys in the class knew how to play. Two of them grabbed one set while another set was grabbed by Sam, a tall, respected boy who nevertheless could not play checkers. He sat down with one boy who could play and managed a game with the help of the fourth boy who could play. Within a few days all of the boys knew how to play. The boys also learned that the laws of physical dominance in the class didn't coincide with the laws of checker dominance, and learned to accept this. Over a period of a few weeks the rights of winners and losers were established and respected. During the first few days there were fights, the board was frequently knocked to the floor, and the game was called "cheap" and "phoney." But nothing very serious or extended could develop in a ten- or fifteen-minute period, and whenever things seemed a bit tight I quickly ended the break and the class returned to "work." After a week six or seven boys retained their interest in checkers while three began to explore chess. They grabbed the game, asked me to show them how to set up the men and make the moves, and then they took over. Within a week, two more boys had joined them in developing an idiosyncratic version of chess (when they forgot the moves they were too proud to ask me) which satisfied them very well.

Leverne stuck to the piano and Robert drew while several other boys kept searching the room for something to do. One of them, Ralph, showed me a copy of the *New York Enquirer* one day and asked me what I thought about it. I facetiously remarked that he could probably do better and stick closer to the truth. Two days later he asked me what I'd meant, and struggling to remember what I'd said, I came up with the idea that he report what went on in his neighborhood. He looked at me strangely and asked me if I meant it. I said, "Sure," and he sat down and wrote, though it took him nearly a month to show me what he was doing. The girls were more interested in magazines that I had brought in, and some of them asked me for books. . . .

September 25 was the day of the first Patterson-Liston fight. I had been reading Patterson's *Victory Over Myself* and brought it to school with me. I asked the class if they knew of the fight and they laughed. Sides had been drawn for days, bets made; several of the boys were going to see the televised fight at the RKO, and others defensively claimed relatives and friends who would be in attendance. I read from Patterson's book and talked of the family photograph he tried to remove his face from. We talked of self-hatred and confidence, of the fighters' personalities, of good and bad, winners and losers. Many of the kids wanted Patterson to win, but they were too cynical to believe that he would just because he was a good person. He had to win with his fists.

Some girls felt the whole thing was brutal though they reluctantly admitted that the fight fascinated them too. An argument broke out about the fighters' size and the money involved. I remembered seeing some facts about the fight in *The New York Times* that morning, found two charts, and put them on the board.

The class studied them intently, the first thing they had all looked at so closely all year. They checked off the characteristics and their implications: Patterson younger, maybe faster; Liston older but bigger, heavier, longer reach, stronger . . . Then one boy rebelled and said facts weren't everything, personality counted and Patterson had to be more confident. A girl countered by saying Liston was too confident and a big head who thought too much of himself.

After a while the discussion turned to the money and trouble arose —what were ancillary rights, how could you tell what 55 percent, 12½ percent, and 45 percent of the money earned was, could the fighters be sure they weren't being cheated? "Domestic" created problems as well as "promoter." The kids wanted to know who made the guarantee to the fighters, whether it was verbal or written, how much the government took. The questions were real and the curiosity genuine. I answered as many as I could without preaching or handing out dictionaries, without pausing for a lesson on percentage or saying, "Don't you wish you could read now?" The children knew what they couldn't do, and were grateful for the fact that one time in school a teacher answered their questions when they needed answering, and didn't make them feel foolish for asking in the first place.

It was eleven thirty when the discussion ended so I gave the class the rest of the morning off. Some of the children immediately set to copying the charts on the blackboard. Someone borrowed *Victory Over Myself* and a group of children sat looking at the photographs in the book. The morning passed effortlessly and well. At noon I noticed that the book had disappeared, and over the next three months it periodically reappeared in someone else's hands until Patterson must have ceased interesting the children and it appeared on my desk one day.

That afternoon I expected the children to come in as excited and

FACTS ON TITLE FIGHT

Place—Comiskey Park, Chicago, capacity 49,000.
Promoter—Championship Sports, Inc.
Time—10:30 P.M., Eastern daylight time.
Television—Closed circuit with Chicago and approximate 100-mile radius blacked out.
Radio—Nationwide by American Broadcasting Company (also foreign broadcasts to eight countries).
Closed circuit TV proceeds—$2,000,000 guaranteed. About $4,000,000 expected.
Radio proceeds (domestic and foreign—about $400,000.
Movie proceeds (Post-Fight showing)—about $550,000.
Estimated gate—$750,000.
Estimated attendance—35,000.
Fighters' shares—Patterson, 55 percent of ancillary rights (Closed circuit TV, radio, movies) and 45 percent of net gate; Liston, 12½ per cent of net in all revenue phases.
Prices of seats—$100, $50, $30, $20 and $10.
Scoring—Referee and two judges; 5-point maximum a round.
Return bout—If Liston wins, return bout within a year. Percentage, 30 percent for each fighter and 40 percent for promoter.

HOW RIVALS COMPARE

PATTERSON		LISTON
27 years	Age	28 years
189 lbs.	Weight	212 lbs.
6 feet	Height	6 ft. 1 in.
71 in.	Reach	84 in.
16½ in.	Neck	17½ in.
40 in.	Chest (Normal)	44 in.
42 in.	Chest (Expanded)	46½ in.
32½ in.	Waist	33 in.
14½ in.	Biceps	16½ in.
12¾ in.	Fist	14 in.
21½ in.	Thigh	25½ in.
6 in.	Wrist	8½ in.
15½ in.	Calf	12 in.
9½ in.	Ankle	12 in.

enthusiastic about what had occurred that morning as I was. But it was as if nothing had happened at all. The next day was worse. The children came in sleepy and irritable, wanting to hear nothing of the fight, of school, of anything. Money had been lost, people had argued. Things had happened on the streets the night before—the kids looked at me as if to say "You just can't understand." Charisse actually said:

"Mr. Kohl, we're tired. Let's do reading instead of talking."

One day Ralph cursed at Michael and unexpectedly things came together for me. Michael was reading and stumbled several times.

Ralph scornfully called out, "What's the matter, psyches, going to pieces again?" The class broke up and I jumped on that word "psyches."

"Ralph, what does *psyches* mean?"

An embarrassed silence.

"Do you know how to spell it?"

Alvin volunteered. "S-i-k-e-s."

"Where do you think the word came from? Why did everybody laugh when you said it, Ralph?"

"You know, Mr. Kohl, it means, like crazy or something."

"Why? How do words get to mean what they do?"

Samuel looked up at me and said: "Mr. Kohl, now you're asking questions like Alvin. There aren't any answers, you know that."

"But there are. Sometimes by asking Alvin's kind of questions you discover the most unexpected things. Look."

I wrote *Psyche*, then *Cupid*, on the blackboard.

"That's how *psyche* is spelled. It looks strange in English, but the word doesn't come from English. It's Greek. There's a letter in the Greek alphabet that comes out *psi* in English. This is the way *psyche* looks in Greek."

Some of the children spontaneously took out their notebooks and copied the Greek.

"The word *psyche* has a long history. *Psyche* means mind or soul for the Greeks, but it was also the name of a lovely woman who had the misfortune to fall in love with Cupid, the son of Venus, the jealous Greek goddess of love. . . ."

The children listened, enchanted by the myth, fascinated by the weaving of the meaning of *psyche* into the fabric of the story, and the character, Mind, playing tricks on itself, almost destroying its most valuable possessions through its perverse curiosity. Grace said in amazement:

"Mr. Kohl, they told the story and said things about the mind at the same time. What do you call that?"

"*Myth* is what the Greeks called it."

Sam was roused.

"Then what happened? What about the history of the word?"

"I don't know too much, but look at the words in English that come from *Cupid* and *Psyche*."

I cited *psychological, psychic, psychotic, psychodrama, psychosomatic, cupidity*—the children copied them unasked, demanded the meanings. They were obviously excited.

Leaping ahead, Alvin shouted: "You mean words change? People didn't always speak this way? Then how come the reader says there's a right way to talk and a wrong way?"

"There's a right way now, and that only means that's how most people would like to talk now, and how people write now."

Charles jumped out of his desk and spoke for the first time during the year.

"You mean one day the way we talk—you know, with words like *cool* and *dig* and *sound*—may be all right?"

"Uh huh. Language is alive, it's always changing, only sometimes it changes so slowly that we can't tell."

Neomia caught on.

"Mr. Kohl, is that why our reader sounds so old-fashioned?"

And Ralph.

"Mr. Kohl, when I called Michael *psyches*, was I creating something new?"

Someone spoke for the class.

"Mr. Kohl, can't we study the language we're talking about instead of spelling and grammar? They won't be any good when language changes anyway."

We could and did. That day we began what had to be called for my conservative plan book "vocabulary," and "an enrichment activity." Actually it was the study of language and myth, of the origins and history of words, of their changing uses and functions in human life. We began simply with the words *language* and *alphabet*, the former from the Latin for tongue and the latter from the first two letters of the Greek alphabet. Seeing the origin of *alphabet* and the relationship of *cupidity* to Cupid and *psychological* to Psyche had a particularly magical effect upon the children. They found it easy to master and acquire words that would have seemed senseless and tedious to memorize. Words like *psychic* and *psychosomatic* didn't seem arbitrary and impenetrable, capable of being learned only painfully by rote. Rather they existed in a context, through a striking tale that easily accrued associations and depth. After a week the children learned the new words, asked to be tested on them, and demanded more.

"Vocabulary" became a fixed point in each week's work as we went from Cupid and Psyche to Tantalus, the Sirens, and the Odyssey and the linguistic riches that it contains. We talked of Venus and Adonis and spent a week on first *Pan* and *panic*, *pan-American*, then *pandemonium*, and finally on *demonic* and *demons* and *devils*. We studied *logos*, *philos*, *anthropos*, *pathos*, and their derivatives. I spun the web of *mythos* about language and its origins. I went to German (*kindergarten*), Polynesian (*taboo*), or Arabic (*assassin*), showing what a motley open-ended fabric English (and for that matter any living language) is. The range of times and peoples that contributed to the growth of today's American English impressed me no less than it did the class. It drove me to research language and its origins; to reexplore myth and the dim origins of man's culture; and to invent ways of sharing my discoveries with the children.

The children took my words seriously and went a step farther. Not content to be fed solely words that grew from sources that I, the teacher, presented, they asked for words that fitted unnamed and partially articulated concepts they had, or situations they couldn't adequately describe.

"Mr. Kohl, what do you call it when a person repeats the same thing over and over again and can't stop?"

"What is it called when something is funny and serious at the same time?"

"What do you call a person who brags and thinks he's big but is really weak inside?"

"Mr. Kohl, is there a word that says that something has more than one meaning?"

The class became word-hungry and concept-hungry, concerned with discovering the "right" word to use at a given time to express a specific thought. I was struck by the difference of this notion of rightness and "the right way" to speak and write from the way children are supposed to be taught in school. They are supposed to acquire correct usage, right grammar and spelling, the right meaning of a word, and the right way to write a sentence. Achievement and I.Q. tests give incomplete sentences and the child is instructed to fill in the "right" word. Many teachers correct children's writing on the basis of a canon of formal rightness without bothering to ask what the children's words mean. I did the same thing myself.

I noticed that the children frequently said that they were bad at their friends, or their parents, or some teacher who angered them. They insisted upon describing a certain type of anger as "being bad at," and I kept telling them that it was wrong because "to be bad at" someone doesn't exist in English. And in a way I was "right"; it didn't exist, nor did the concept it was trying to express exist in English as I spoke and wrote it. But the children did mean "to be bad at," and meant something very specific by it. "To be bad" is a way of defying authority and expressing anger at the same time, as indicating one's own strength and independence. The use of "bad" here is ironical and often admiring. One child explained to me that down South a "bad nigger" was one who was strong enough and brave enough to be defiant of the white man's demands no matter how much everyone else gave in. Only later did I discover Bessie Smith in J. C. Johnson's "Black Mountain Blues," using "bad" in the same way as the kids:

> Back on Black Mountain a child would smack your face
> Back on Black Mountain a child would smack your face
> Babies cry for liquor and all the birds sing bass.
>
> Black Mountain people are bad as they can be
> Black Mountain people are bad as they can be
> They uses gun powder just to sweeten their tea

I think that before we talked about language and myth the children, if they thought about it at all, felt that most words were either arbitrary labels pinned on things and concepts the way names seem to be pinned onto babies, or indicators of connections amongst these labels. These "labels" probably represented the way the adult world capriciously decided to name things. I doubt whether the children ever thought of adults as having received language from yet other adults even more remote in time. My pupils must have found the language of their teachers strange and arbitrary indeed. The "right" language of school texts and middle-class teachers must have seemed threatening and totalitarian, especially since the only living words the children knew and used were the words they used on the streets, words teachers continually told them were "wrong" and "incorrect."

The idea that words were complex phenomena with long and compelling histories was never presented to the children. I doubt many teachers entertained it. The canons of the schools pretend that a small preselected segment of the language of the moment is an eternally correct and all-inclusive form. This form is embodied in basic word lists and controlled vocabulary readers, as if the mastering of language consists of learning a list of fifty or a hundred words by rote. The use of language in human life is continually avoided or ignored, as if it poses too great a threat to "correctness" and "rightness." No wonder then that the children showed so persistently and ingeniously how much they feared and avoided the language of the schools.

Later in the semester I taught the class a lesson on naming, a topic that seems deceptively simple yet minimally encompasses history, psychology, sociology, and anthropology. I put everybody's full name on the blackboard, including my own, and asked the class how people got names. The answer was, naturally, from their parents who made the choice—but not the full choice, it emerged, when Michael remembered that his parents' surnames came from their parents. Then how far back can you go? The children thought and Grace raised a delicate question. If the names go back through the generations how come her name wasn't African since her ancestors must have been? In answer I told the class about my own name—Kohl, changed from Cohen, changed from Okun, changed from something lost in the darkness of history; one change to identify the family as Jewish, one change to deny it. Then I returned to the question of slave names and the destruction of part of the children's African heritage that the withholding of African names implied.

Neomia said that she knew of someone who changed his name because he wanted to start a new life, and Sam told the class that his brother called himself John X because X meant unknown and his original African name was unknown. We talked of people who named their children after famous men and of others who gave exotic names. From there the discussion went on to the naming of animals—pets, wild animals, racehorses; things—boats, houses, dolls; and places. The class knew by that time in the school year that one doesn't talk of words in isolation from human lives and history, and by then I had begun to know what to teach.

The emphasis on language and words opened the children to the whole process of verbal communication. Things that they had been struggling to express, or worse, had felt only they in their isolation thought about, became social, shareable. Speaking of things, of inferiority and ambiguity, or irony and obsession, brought relief, and perhaps for the first time gave the children a sense that there were meaningful human creations that one could discover in a classroom.

Yet not all concepts have been verbalized, and the children frequently talked of having feelings and desires that no words I gave them expressed adequately. They had to create new words, or develop new forms of expression to communicate, and that can neither be taught nor done upon command. We could go to the frontier, however, and speak about the blues, about being bad or hip or cool—about how certain ways of living or historical times created the need for new words. We talked about the nuclear age, the smallness of the modern world, the jargon of democracy and communism, integration and segregation. The children looked in awe at *Finnegans Wake* and Joyce's monumental attempt to forge a new language; they listened to Bob Dylan, recorded the words of soul songs and classical blues, read poetry. We started out talking about words and ended up with life itself. The children opened up and began to display a fearless curiosity about the world.

I sense that I've jumped ahead too quickly, for the whole thing happened slowly, almost imperceptibly. There were days of despair throughout the whole year, and I never learned how to line the class up at three o'clock. There were days when Alvin was a brilliant inspiring pupil at ten and the most unbearable, uncontrollable nuisance at eleven thirty; when after a good lesson some children would turn angry and hostile, or lose interest in everything. There were small fights and hostilities, adjustments and readjustments in the children's relationships to each other and to me. I had to enlarge my vision as a human being, learn that if the complex and contradictory nature of life is allowed to come forth in the classroom there are times when it will do so with a vengeance.

I still stuck to the curriculum as much as possible. The social studies was impossible so I collected the books and returned them to the bookroom. It was too painful to see the children twist their faces into stupid indifference and hear their pained dull answers accompanied by nervous drumming on the desks.

"New York is a large modern country."

"The Hudson is an important ocean."

"The Industrial Revolution was a benefit to all."

Better drop it altogether, try anything so long as it didn't humiliate the children. These answers were not a function of the children's lack of experience, as the hopelessly respectable anti-poverty program believes; rather they were a direct response to the institutionalized hypocrisy that is characteristic of schools in the United States today.

I brought part of my library to school and temporarily substituted it for social studies. The children were curious about those Greeks and Latins who contributed so many words and concepts to our language. I brought in books on Greek and Roman architecture and art, as well as Robert Graves's version of the *Iliad*, a paperback translation of Apuleius' *Cupid and Psyche*, the *Larousse Encyclopedia of Mythology*, and anything else that seemed relevant or interesting. I showed the books to the children and let them disappear into their desks. It was made clear that the books were to be read, the pages to be turned. If someone reads a book so intensely that the book is bruised it is flattering to the book.

For three-quarters of an hour a day the Pantheon circulated along with Floyd Patterson and J. D. Salinger, Partridge's dictionary of word origins made its way through the class with Langston Hughes and the Bobbsey twins. Anything I could get my hands on was brought to class—a great deal remained unread, and some books I hadn't read myself shocked and surprised the class. They were sexy and popular. Later that year my supervisor told me I was running a very effective individualized reading program. That may have been it, but the truth seemed simpler and less structured. I overwhelmed the class with books, many of which I loved, and let them discover for themselves what they liked. There were no reports to be written, no requirements about numbers of pages to be read. Some children hardly read at all, others devoured whatever was in the room. The same is true of my friends.

Robert Jackson grabbed a book on Greek architecture, copied floor plans and perspective drawings, and finally, leaping out of the book, created a reasonably accurate scale model of the Parthenon. Alvin and Michael built a clay volcano, asked for and got a chemistry book which showed them how to simulate an eruption. Sam, Thomas, and Dennis fought their way through war books; through the Navy, the Seabees, the Marines, and the Paratroops. The girls started with the Bobbsey twins and worked through to romantic novels and, in the case of a few, Thurber and O. Henry. I learned that there were no books to fear, and having been divested of my fear of idleness, I also wasn't worried if some children went through periods of being unable to do anything at all. . . .

DEATH
AT
AN
EARLY
AGE

JONATHAN KOZOL

Jonathan Kozol, author of Death at an Early Age, *taught in Newton, Massachusetts, after being fired in Boston, and continued to write. Then he became active in developing "free schools."*

The poem which triggered the Jonathan Kozol dismissal in Boston was "Ballad of the Landlord" by Langston Hughes. The poem recounts a social protest by a black tenant against his inadequate housing, the conflict with his landlord which follows, and the resultant jailing of the black tenant. The simple yet eloquent ballad contains no profanity or obscenity whatsoever.

The attitudes of many teachers, I suppose, are derived over the course of years from the kinds of books they use. Many of the books we had at school were very bad for many reasons, and none of them that I recall was very good. I was promised a certain amount of new material during the year, but this material did not appear. The only new material that I had received by the middle of the winter was an expensive boxed edition of *The Bobbsey Twins*. The old books with which we were already saddled confirmed for me almost all of the criticism that I had ever heard about conventional texts, except that perhaps the ones we had outstripped the criticism a little. Of four biographical series that were available in our Fourth Grade classrooms, out of a total of 140 biographies of famous men and women, there was one that had to do with a Negro. That one was George Washington Carver. The geography book given to my pupils and kept within their desks or on their shelves, was about eighteen years old in substance, though it was somewhat newer than that by renewal of copyright. In this book, typical of many others in its title as it was also in approach and manner, a traditional American cross-country journey was traced. During this journey there wasn't one mention, hint, whisper or glimmer of a dark-skinned face. Reading it without any outside source of information, you would have had no reason to suspect either the past history or present existence of a Negro race. The chapter on the South described an idyllic and fantasied landscape in the heart of Dixie: pastoral home of hard-working white citizens, contented white children and untroubled white adults. Cotton production was studied, and a vicarious journey to a Mississippi plantation was undertaken, without ever a reference to, or picture of, a dark-skinned person.

37

The history book could not get by in the same manner. It had to speak of Negroes because it had to speak of slavery. It did this, however, in a manner that seemed reluctant and half-hearted. "Men treasure freedom above all else," the narrative told us at one point. But it balanced this out by telling us beforehand that "most Southern people treated their slaves kindly. 'Our slaves have good homes and plenty to eat. When they are sick, we take care of them . . .'" In the final event I think that the author came out on the side of emancipation, but he did this in a tone and style which were so lukewarm and insipid as to be without effect. The language used throughout was coy and awkward: "In the dictionary we find that one meaning of the word 'civil' is 'polite.' The Civil War was not a polite one. It was a war between the states of Our America . . ." A final verdict on the War Between the States was the following: "No one can truly say, 'The North was right' or 'The Southern cause was the better.' Remember, each side fought for the ideals it believed in. For in Our America all of us have the right to our beliefs."

The material about the Civil War was not the only disturbing section in this book, but it is the part that seems most relevant. It would always have been simple enough, if I had been obliged to use that section, just to skip over the offensive pages—or, better, not to skip them but rather to read them with the children and then to deal with them critically. Since that time, I have done this in many situations and I do it frequently today. Nonetheless, the fact remained: The book had been printed. The book had been stocked and ordered. The book stood within our bookshelves and it was looked into by dozens of children every day. I wondered for how many years it would continue to misrepresent reality in this manner and to how many future thousands of Negro children it would spread the sad word that their people in bondage did not have the imagination to be free?

There is a school in Boston named for William Lloyd Garrison. It was at this school that the class to which I have referred received twenty-five substitute teachers in the fall of 1964. I once had a chance to work for a few mornings with a group of Fourth, Fifth and Sixth Grade pupils from the Garrison School. I asked them if they would tell me, child by child, the most important facts about the man for whom their school was named. A long silence met my question and then I discovered, by asking some other questions, that not one of these children had the slightest idea either of who he was or what he had done. No principal, no teacher, it appeared, had ever told them. Some of them had been in that school for six or seven years. They had all studied geography. They had all studied history. They had all, I suppose, talked of current events. Their teachers presumably also had some idea of what was going on in the world and could find the affiliation between this, the present day, and the beliefs of the man whose name had been given to their school. The school happened to be one of the most totally segregated (96.8 per cent) in all of Boston. Yet none of these children knew who William Lloyd Garrison was. So long as a school that is 96.8 per cent Negro can stand in the name of William Lloyd Garrison and so long as teachers and principals are unable to tell the children in whose name their building stands, then I don't think it will be surprising that geography and history books will also resort to evasions about America and it will not be surprising either that Negro children, growing a little older, will look back with cynicism and surely without forgiveness upon the white teachers who have denied them even this much self-knowledge and who have disseminated among them these crippling ideas and desiccating lies. . . .

Perhaps a reader would like to know what it is like to go into a new classroom in the same way that I did and to see before you suddenly, and in terms you cannot avoid recognizing, the dreadful consequences of a year's wastage of real lives. [Editor's note: Kozol is now describing a different school.]

You walk into a narrow and old wood-smelling classroom and you see before you thirty-five curious, cautious and untrusting children, aged eight to thirteen, of whom about two-thirds are Negro. Three of the children are designated to you as special students. Thirty per cent of the class is reading at the Second Grade level in a year and in a month in which they should be reading at the height of Fourth Grade performance or at the beginning of the Fifth. Seven children out of the class are up to par. Ten substitutes or teacher changes. Or twelve changes. Or eight. Or eleven. Nobody seems to know how many teachers they have had. Seven of their lifetime records are missing: symptomatic and emblematic at once of the chaos that has been with them all year long. Many more lives than just seven have already been wasted but the seven missing records become an embittering symbol of the lives behind them which, equally, have been lost or mislaid. (You have to spend the first three nights staying up until dawn trying to reconstruct these records out of notes and scraps.) On the first math test you give, the class average comes out to 36. The children tell you with embarrassment that it has been like that since fall.

You check around the classroom. Of forty desks, five have tops with no hinges. You lift a desk-top to fetch a paper and you find that the top has fallen off. There are three windows. One cannot be opened. A sign on it written in the messy scribble of a hurried teacher or some custodial person warns you: DO NOT UNLOCK THIS WINDOW IT IS BROKEN. The general look of the room is as of a bleak-light photograph of a mental hospital. Above the one poor blackboard, gray rather than really black, and hard to write on, hangs from one tack, lopsided, a motto attributed to Benjamin Franklin: "*Well begun is half done.*" Everything, or almost everything like that, seems a mockery of itself.

Into this grim scenario, drawing on your own pleasures and memories, you do what you can to bring some kind of life. You bring in some cheerful and colorful paintings by Joan Miro and Paul Klee. While the paintings by Miro do not arouse much interest, the ones by Klee become an instantaneous success. One picture in particular, a watercolor titled "Bird Garden," catches the fascination of the entire class. You slip it out of the book and tack it up on the wall beside the doorway and it creates a traffic jam every time the children have to file in or file out. You discuss with your students some of the reasons why Klee may have painted the way he did and you talk about the things that can be accomplished in a painting which could not be accomplished in a photograph. None of this seems to be above the children's heads. Despite this, you are advised flatly by the Art Teacher that your naïveté has gotten the best of you and that the children cannot possibly appreciate this. Klee is too difficult. Children will not enjoy it. You are unable to escape the idea that the Art Teacher means herself instead.

For poetry, in place of the recommended memory gems, going back again into your own college days, you make up your mind to introduce a poem of William Butler Yeats. It is about a lake isle called Innisfree, about birds that have the funny name of "linnets" and about a "bee-loud glade." The children do not all go crazy about it but a number of them seem to like it as much as you do and you tell them how once, three years before, you were living in England and you helped a man in the country to make his home from wattles and clay. The children become intrigued. They pay good attention and many of them grow more curious about the poem than they appeared at first. Here again, however, you are advised by older teachers that you are making a mistake: Yeats is too difficult for children. They can't enjoy it, won't appreciate it, wouldn't like it. You are aiming way above their heads . . . Another idea comes to mind and you decide to try out an easy and rather well-known and not very complicated poem of Robert Frost. The poem is called "Stopping By Woods on a Snowy Evening." This time, your supervisor happens to drop in from the School Department. He looks over the mimeograph, agrees with you that it's a nice poem, then points out to you—tolerantly, but strictly—that you have made another mistake. "Stopping By Woods" is scheduled for Sixth Grade. It is not "a Fourth Grade poem," and it is not to be read or looked at during the Fourth Grade. Bewildered as you are by what appears to be a kind of idiocy, you still feel reproved and criticized and muted and set back and you feel that you have been caught in the commission of a serious mistake.

On a series of other occasions, the situation is repeated. The children are offered something new and something lively. They respond to it energetically and they are attentive and their attention does not waver. For the first time in a long while perhaps there is actually some real excitement and some growing and some thinking going on within that one small room. In each case, however, you are advised sooner or later that you are making a mistake. Your mistake, in fact, is to have impinged upon the standardized condescension on which the entire administration of the school is based. To hand Paul Klee's pictures to the children of this classroom, and particularly in a twenty-dollar volume, constitutes a threat to this school system. It is not different from sending a little girl from the Negro ghetto into an art class near Harvard Yard. Transcending the field of familiarity of the administration, you are endangering its authority and casting a blow at its self-confidence. The way the threat is handled is by a continual and standardized underrating of the children: They can't do it, couldn't do it, wouldn't like it, don't deserve it . . . In such a manner, many children are tragically and unjustifiably held back from a great many of the good things that they might come to like or admire and are pinned down instead to books the teacher knows and to easy tastes that she can handle. This includes, above all, of course, the kind of material that is contained in the Course of Study.

Try to imagine, for a child, how great the gap between the outside world and the world conveyed within this kind of school must seem: A little girl, maybe Negro, comes in from a street that is lined with carcasses. Old purple Hudsons and one-wheel-missing Cadillacs represent her horizon and mark the edges of her dreams. In the kitchen of her house roaches creep and large rats crawl. On the way to school a wino totters. Some teenage white boys slow down their car to insult her, and speed on. At school, she stands frozen for fifteen minutes in a yard of cracked cement that overlooks a hillside on which trash has been unloaded and at the bottom of which the New York, New Haven and Hartford Railroad rumbles past. In the basement, she sits upon broken or splintery seats in filthy toilets and she is yelled at in the halls. Upstairs, when something has been stolen, she is told that she is the one who stole it and is called a liar and forced abjectly to apologize before a teacher who has not the slightest idea in the world of who the culprit truly was. The same teacher, behind the child's back, ponders audibly with imagined compassion: "What can you do with this kind of material? How can you begin to teach this kind of child?"

Gradually going crazy, the child is sent after two years of misery to a pupil adjustment counselor who arranges for her to have some tests and considers the entire situation and discusses it with the teacher and finally files a long report. She is, some months later, put onto a waiting-list some place for once-a-week therapy but another year passes before she has gotten anywhere near to the front of a long line. By now she is fourteen, has lost whatever innocence she still had in the back seat of the old Cadillac and, within two additional years, she will be ready and eager for dropping out of school.

Once at school, when she was eight or nine, she drew a picture of a rich-looking lady in an evening gown with a handsome man bowing before her but she was told by an insensate and wild-eyed teacher that what she had done was junk and garbage and the picture was torn up and thrown away before her eyes. The rock and roll music that she hears on the Negro station is considered "primitive" by her teachers but she prefers its insistent rhythms to the dreary monotony of school. Once, in Fourth Grade, she got excited at school about some writing she had never heard about before. A handsome green book, brand new, was held up before her and then put into her hands. Out of this book her teacher read a poem. The poem was about a Negro—a woman who was a maid in the house of a white person—and she liked it. It remained in her memory. Somehow without meaning to, she found that she had done the impossible for her: she had memorized that poem. Perhaps, horribly, in the heart of her already she was aware that it was telling about her future: fifty dollars a week to scrub floors and bathe little white babies in the suburbs after an hour's street-car ride. The poem made her want to cry. The white lady, the lady for whom the maid was working, told the maid she loved her. But the maid in the poem wasn't going to tell any lies in return. She knew she didn't feel any love for the white lady and she told the lady so. The poem was shocking to her, but it seemed bitter, strong and true. Another poem in the same green book was about a little boy on a merry-go-round. She laughed with the class at the question he asked about a Jim Crow section on a merry-go-round, but she also was old enough to know that it was not a funny poem really and it made her, valuably, sad. She wanted to know how she could get hold of that poem, and maybe that whole book. The poems were moving to her . . .

This was a child in my class. Details are changed somewhat but it is essentially one child. The girl was one of the three unplaced special students in that Fourth Grade room. She was not an easy girl to teach and it was hard even to keep her at her seat on many mornings, but I do not remember that there was any difficulty at all in gaining and holding onto her attention on the day that I brought in that green book of Langston Hughes.

Of all of the poems of Langston Hughes that I read to my Fourth Graders, the one that the children like most was a poem that has the title "Ballad of the Landlord." . . . This poem may not satisfy the taste of every critic, and I am not making any claims to immortality for a poem just because I happen to like it a great deal. But the reason this poem did have so much value and meaning for me and, I believe, for many of my students, is that it not only seems moving in an obvious and immediate human way but that it *finds* its emotion in something ordinary. It is a poem which really does allow both heroism and pathos to poor people, sees strength in awkwardness and attributes to a poor person standing on the stoop of his slum house every bit as much significance as William Wordsworth saw in daffodils, waterfalls and clouds. At the request of the children later on I mimeographed that poem and, although nobody in the classroom was asked to do this, several of the children took it home and memorized it on their own. I did not assign it for memory, because I do not think that memorizing a poem has any special value. Some of the children just came in and asked if they could recite it. Before long, almost every child in the room had asked to have a turn.

All of the poems that you read to Negro children obviously are not going to be by or about Negro people. Nor would anyone expect that all poems which are read to a class of poor children ought to be grim or gloomy or heart-breaking or sad. But when, among the works of many different authors, you do have the will to read children a poem by a man so highly renowned as Langston Hughes, then I think it is important not to try to pick a poem that is innocuous, being like any other poet's kind of poem, but I think you ought to choose a poem that is genuinely representative and then try to make it real to the children in front of you in the way that I tried. I also think it ought to be taken seriously by a teacher when a group of young children come in to him one morning and announce that they have liked something so much that they have memorized it voluntarily. It surprised me and impressed me when that happened. It was all I needed to know to confirm for me the value of reading that poem and the value of reading many other poems to children which will build upon, and not attempt to break down, the most important observations and very deepest foundations of their lives. . . .

. . . I was standing in front of the class and they were listening to a record I had brought in. The record was a collection of French children's songs. We had been spending the month reading and talking about Paris and about France. As lunch-time drew near I decided to let the children listen to the music while they were having their meal. While the record was playing, a little signal on the wall began to buzz. I left the room and hurried to the Principal's office. A white man whom I had never seen before was sitting by the Principal's desk. This man, bristling and clearly hostile to me, as was the Principal, instantly attacked me for having read to my class and distributed at their wish the poem I have talked about that was entitled "Ballad of the Landlord." It turned out that he was the father of one of the white boys in the class. He was also a police officer. The mimeograph of the poem, in my handwriting, was waved before my eyes. The Principal demanded to know what right I had to allow such a poem—not in the official Course of Study—to be read and memorized by the children in my class. I said I had not asked anyone to memorize it but that I would defend the poem and its use against her or anyone on the basis that it was a good poem. The Principal became incensed with my answer and blurted out that she did not consider it a work of art. I remember that I knew right away I was not going to give in to her. I replied, in my own anger, that I had spent a good many years studying poetry and that I was not going to accept her judgment about a poem that meant that much to me and to my pupils. Although I did not say it in these words, it was really a way of telling her that I thought myself a better judge of poetry than she. I hope that I am.

The parent attacked me, as well, for having forced his son to read a book about the United Nations. I had brought a book to class, one out of sixty or more volumes, that told about the U.N. and its Human Rights Commission. The man, I believe, had mistaken "human rights" for "civil rights" and he was consequently in a patriotic rage. The Principal, in fairness, made the point that she did not think there was anything really wrong with the United Nations, although in the report that she later filed on the matter, she denied this for some reason and said, instead, "I then spoke and said that I felt there was no need for this material in the classroom." The Principal's report goes on to say that, after she dismissed me to my own room, she assured the parent that "there was not another teacher in the district who would have used this poem or any material like it. I assured him that his children would be very safe from such incidents."

As the Principal had instructed, I returned to my class, where the children had remained quiet and had not even opened up their lunch because I had not told them to and they were patiently waiting for me to come back. We had our lunch and listened to more music and did the rest of our lessons and at quarter to two, just before school ended, the Principal called me back again. She told me I was fired. This was about eight days before· the end of school. I asked her whether this was due to the talk we had had earlier but she said it was not. I asked her if it was due to an evaluation, a written report, which I had sent in on the compensatory program about a week before. This was a report that I had written, as all teachers had, in answer to a request from the School Department and in which I had said that the program seemed to me to be very poor. I was told, at the time I passed it in, that the Principal had been quite angry. But again she said it was not that. I asked her finally if my dismissal was at her request and she said, No, it came from higher up and she didn't know anything about it except that I should close up my records and leave school and not come back. She said that I should not say good-bye to the children in my class. I asked her if she really meant this and she repeated it to me as an order.

I returned to my class, taught for ten more minutes, then gave assignments for the following morning as if I would be there and saw the children file off. After all but one were gone, that one, a little girl, helped me to pile up the books and posters and pictures with which I had tried to fill the room. It took an hour to get everything out and when it was all in my car it filled up the back seat and space behind it and the floor, as well as the floor and half the seat in front. Outside my car, on the sidewalk, I said good-bye to this one child and told her that I would not be back again. I told her I had had a disagreement with the Principal and I asked her to say good-bye to the other children. I regretted very much now that I had not disobeyed the Principal's last order and I wished that I could have had one final chance to speak to all my pupils. The little girl, in any case, took what I had said with great solemnity and promised that she would relay my message to the other children. Then I left the school.

The next morning, an official who had charge of my case at the School Department contradicted the Principal by telling me that I was being fired at her wish. The woman to whom I spoke said the reason was the use of the poem by Langston Hughes, which was punishable because it was not in the Course of Study. She also said something to me at the time that had never been said to me before, and something that represented a much harder line on curriculum innovation than I had ever seen in print. No literature, she said, which is not in the Course of Study can *ever* be read by a Boston teacher without permission from someone higher up. When I asked her about this in more detail, she said further that no poem anyway by any Negro author can be considered permissible if it involves suffering. I thought this a very strong statement and I asked her several times again if that was really what she meant. She insisted that it was.

I asked if there would be many good poems left to read by such a standard. Wouldn't it rule out almost all great Negro literature? Her answer evaded the issue. No poetry that described suffering was felt to be suitable. The only Negro poetry that could be read in the Boston schools, she indicated, must fit a certain kind of standard or canon. The kind of poem she meant, she said by example, might be a poem that "accentuates the positive" or "describes nature" or "tells of something hopeful." Nothing was wanted of suffering, nothing that could be painful, nothing that might involve its reader in a moment of self-questioning or worry. If this is an extremely conservative or eccentric viewpoint, I think that it is nonetheless something which has to be taken seriously. For an opinion put forward in the privacy of her office by a School Department official who has the kind of authority that that woman had must be taken to represent a certain segment of educational opinion within the Boston school system and in some ways it seems more representative even than the carefully written and carefully prepared essays of such a lady as the Deputy Superintendent. For in those various writings Miss Sullivan unquestionably has had one ear tuned to the way they were going to come across in print and sound in public whereas, in the office of a central bureaucratic person such as the lady with whom I now was talking, you receive an absolutely innocent and unedited experience in what a school system really feels and believes.

The same official went on a few minutes later to tell me that, in addition to having made the mistake of reading the wrong poem, I also had made an error in bringing in books to school from the Cambridge Public Library. When I told her that there were no books for reading in our classroom, except for the sets of antiquated readers, and that the need of the children was for individual reading which they would be able to begin without delay, she told me that that was all very well but still this was the Boston school system and that meant that you must not use a book that the Cambridge Library supplied. She also advised me, in answer to my question, that any complaint from a parent means automatic dismissal of a teacher anyway and that this, in itself, was therefore sufficient grounds for my release. When I repeated this later to some Negro parents they were embittered and startled. For they told me of many instances in which they had complained that a teacher whipped their child black and blue or called him a nigger openly and yet the teacher had not been released. It seemed obvious to them, as it seems to me, and would to anyone, that a complaint from a white police officer carries more weight in the Boston school system than the complaint of the mother of a Negro child.

I asked this official finally whether I had been considered a good teacher and what rating I had been given. She answered that she was not allowed to tell me. An instant later, whimsically reversing herself, she opened her files and told me that my rating was good. The last thing she said was that deviation from a prescribed curriculum was a serious offense and that I would never be permitted to teach in Boston again. The words she used were these: "You're out. You cannot teach in the Boston schools again. If you want to teach why don't you try a private school someday?"

THE LIVES OF CHILDREN

GEORGE DENNISON

It is difficult to excerpt from The Lives of Children, *for many of George Dennison's best insights are contained in his detailed reporting of interrelationships among students and staff. But the account of José's problems reproduced here provides some insights into the way Dennison conceives of the curriculum and the learner. Dennison's book should be read as a whole, for the experiences and moods of both teachers and learners at the First Street School changed throughout the year as described in* The Lives of Children. *Dennison has taught in preschool, primary, and preparatory school, and has worked with severely disturbed children.*

There is no need to add to the criticism of our public schools. The critique is extensive and can hardly be improved on. The processes of learning and teaching, too, have been exhaustively studied. One thinks of the books of Paul Goodman, John Holt, Greene and Ryan, Nat Hentoff, James Herndon, Jonathan Kozol, Herbert Kohl; and of such researches as those of Bruner and Piaget; and of Joseph Featherstone's important *Report*. The question now is what to do. In the pages that follow, I would like to describe one unfamiliar approach to the problems which by now have become familiar. And since "the crisis of the schools" consists in reality of a great many crises in the lives of children, I shall try to make the children of the First Street School the real subject of this book. There were twenty-three black, white, and Puerto Rican in almost equal proportions, all from low-income families in New York's Lower East Side. About half were on welfare. About half, too, had come to us from the public schools with severe learning and behavior problems.

Four things about the First Street School were unusual: first, its small size and low teacher/pupil ratio; second, the fact that this luxurious intimacy, which is ordinarily very expensive, cost about the same per child as the $850 annual operating costs of the public schools; third, our reversal of conventional structure, for where the public school conceives of itself merely as a place of instruction, and puts severe restraints on the relationships between persons, we conceived of ourselves as an environment for growth, and accepted the relationships between the children and ourselves as being the very heart of the school; and fourth, the kind of freedom experienced by teachers and pupils alike.

Freedom is an abstract and terribly elusive word. I hope that a context of examples will make its meaning clear. The question is not really one of authority, though it is usually argued in that form. When adults give up authority, the freedom of children is not necessarily increased. Freedom is not motion in a vacuum, but motion in a continuum. If we want to know what freedom is, we must discover what the continuum is. "The principle," Dewey remarks, "is not what justifies an activity, for the principle is but another name for the continuity of the activity." We might say something similar of freedom: it is another name for the fullness and final shape of activities. We experience the activities, not the freedom. The mother of a child in a public school told me that he kept complaining, "They never let me *finish* anything!" We might say of the child that he lacked important freedoms, but his own expression is closer to the experience: activities important to him remained unfulfilled. Our concern for freedom is our concern for fulfillment—of activities we deem important and of persons we know are unique. To give freedom means to stand out of the way of the formative powers possessed by others.

Before telling more of the school, I must say that I was a partisan of libertarian values even before working there. I had read of the schools of A. S. Neill and Leo Tolstoy. I had worked in the past with severely disturbed children, and had come to respect the integrity of the organic processes of growth, which given the proper environment are the one source of change in individual lives. And so I was biased from the start and cannot claim the indifference of a neutral observer. Events at school did, however, time and again, confirm the beliefs I already held—which, I suppose, leaves me still a partisan, though convinced twice over. Yet if I can prove nothing at all in a scientific sense, there is still a power of persuasion in the events themselves, and I can certainly hope that our experience will arouse an experimental interest in other parents and teachers.

But there is something else that I would like to convey, too, and this is simply a sense of the lives of those who were involved—the jumble of persons and real events which did in fact constitute our school. The closer one comes to the facts of life, the less exemplary they seem, but the more human and the richer. Something of our time in history and our place in the world belongs to Vicente screaming in the hallway, and José opening the blade of a ten-inch knife—even more than to Vicente's subsequent learning to cooperate and José to read. So, too, with other apparently small details: the fantasy life and savagery of the older boys, the serenity and rationality of the younger ones, teachers' moments of doubt and defeat. Learning, in its essentials, is not a distinct and separate process. It is a function of growth. We took it quite seriously in this light, and found ourselves getting more and more involved in individual lives. It seems likely to me that the actual features of this involvement may prove useful to other people. At the same time, I would like to try to account for the fact that almost all of our children improved markedly, and some few spectacularly. We were obviously doing something right, and I would like to hazard a few guesses at what it might have been. All instruction was individual, and that was obviously a factor. The improvement I am speaking of, however, was not simply a matter of learning, but of radical changes in character. Where Vicente had been withdrawn and destructive, he became an eager participant in group activities and ceased destroying everything he touched. Both Eléna and Maxine had been thieves and were incredibly rebellious. After several months they could be trusted and had become imaginative and responsible contributors at school meetings. Such changes as these are not accomplished by instruction. They proceed from broad environmental causes. Here again, details which may seem irrelevant to the business of a school will give the reader an idea of what these causes may have been. A better way of saying this is that the business of a school is not, or should not be, mere instruction, but the life of the child.

This is especially important under such conditions as we experience today. Life in our country is chaotic and corrosive, and the time of childhood for many millions is difficult and harsh. It will not be an easy matter to bring our berserk technocracy under control, but we *can* control the environment of the schools. It is a relatively small environment and has always been structured by deliberation. If, as parents, we were to take as our concern not the instruction of our children, but the lives of our children, we would find that our schools could be used in a powerfully regenerative way. Against all that is shoddy and violent and treacherous and emotionally impoverished in American life, we might propose conventions which were rational and straightforward, rich both in feeling and thought, and which treated individuals with a respect we do little more at present than proclaim from our public rostrums. We might cease thinking of school as a place, and learn to believe that it is basically relationships: between children and adults, adults and adults, children and other children. The four walls and the principal's office would cease to loom so hugely as the essential ingredients.

It is worth mentioning here that, with two exceptions, the parents of the children at First Street were not libertarians. They thought that they believed in compulsion, and rewards and punishments, and formal discipline, and report cards, and homework, and elaborate school facilities. They looked rather askance at our noisy classrooms and informal relations. If they persisted in sending us their children, it was not because they agreed with our methods, but because they were desperate. As the months went by, however, and the children who had been truants now attended eagerly, and those who had been failing now began to learn, the parents drew their own conclusions. By the end of the first year there was a high morale among them, and great devotion to the school.

We had no administrators. We were small and didn't need them. The parents found that, after all, they approved of this. They themselves could judge the competence of the teachers, and so could their children—by the specific act of learning. The parents' past experience of administrators had been uniformly upsetting—and the proof, of course, was in the pudding: the children were happier and *were* learning. As for the children, they never missed them.

We did not give report cards. We knew each child, knew his capacities and his problems, and the vagaries of his growth. This knowledge could not be recorded on little cards. The parents found—again—that they approved of this. It diminished the blind anxieties of life, for grades had never meant much to them anyway except some dim sense of *problem*, or some dim reassurance that things were all right. When they wanted to know how their children were doing, they simply asked the teachers.

We didn't give tests, at least not of the competitive kind. It was important to be aware of what the children knew, but more important to be aware of *how* each child knew what he knew. We could learn nothing about Maxine by testing Eléna. And so there was no comparative testing at all. The children never missed those invidious comparisons, and the teachers were spared the absurdity of ranking dozens of personalities on one uniform scale.

Our housing was modest. The children came to school in play-torn clothes. Their families were poor. A torn dress, torn pants, frequent cleanings—there were expenses they could not afford. Yet how can children play without getting dirty? Our uncleanliness standard was just right. It looked awful and suited everyone.

We treated the children with consideration and justice. I don't mean that we never got angry and never yelled at them (nor they at us). I mean that we took seriously the pride of life that belongs to the young—even to the very young. We did not coerce them in violation of their proper independence. Parents and children both found that they approved very much of this.

Now I would like to describe the school, or more correctly, the children and teachers. I shall try to bring out in detail three important things:

1) That the proper concern of a primary school is not education in a narrow sense, and still less preparation for later life, but the present lives of the children—a point made repeatedly by John Dewey, and very poorly understood by many of his followers.

2) That when the conventional routines of a school are abolished (the military discipline, the schedules, the punishments and rewards,

the standardization), what arises is neither a vacuum nor chaos, but rather a new order, based first on relationships between adults and children, and children and their peers, but based ultimately on such truths of the human condition as these: that the mind does not function separately from the emotions, but thought partakes of feeling and feeling of thought; that there is no such thing as knowledge *per se*, knowledge in a vacuum, but rather all knowledge is possessed and must be expressed by individuals; that the human voices preserved in books belong to the real features of the world, and that children are so powerfully attracted to this world that the very motion of their curiosity comes through to us as a form of love; that an active moral life cannot be evolved except where people are free to express their feelings and act upon the insights of conscience.

3) That running a primary school—*provided it be small*—is an extremely simple thing. It goes without saying that the teachers must be competent (which does not necessarily mean passing courses in a teacher's college). Given this *sine qua non*, there is nothing mysterious. The present quagmire of public education is entirely the result of unworkable centralization and the lust for control that permeates every bureaucratic institution.

In saying this, I do not mean that the work in a free school is easy. On the contrary, teachers find it taxing. But they find it rewarding, too—quite unlike the endless round of frustrations experienced by those at work in the present system. . . .

Perhaps after these excerpts from the journal, something of our intimate, informal style may be apparent. What may not be so obvious is that there was any connection between this style and the advances in learning made by the children. And here we come to one of the really damaging myths of education, namely, that learning is the result of teaching; that the progress of the child bears a direct relation to methods of instruction and internal relationships of curriculum. Nothing could be farther from the truth. Naturally we want good teachers. Naturally we want a coherent curriculum (we need not impose it in standardized forms). But to cite these as the effective causes of learning is wrong. The causes are in the child. When we consider the power of mind of a healthy eight-year-old—the avidity of the senses, the finesse and energy of observation, the effortless concentration, the vivacious memory—we realize immediately that these powers possess true magnitude in the general scale of things. Beside them, the subject matter of primary education can hardly be regarded as a difficult task. Yet the routine assumption of school professionals is that somehow or other learning is difficult.

Why is it, then, that so many children fail? Let me put it bluntly: it is because our system of public education is a horrendous, life-destroying mess. The destruction is primary. The faculties themselves, the powers of mind, are nipped in the bud, or are held inoperative, which eventually comes to the same thing.

There is no such thing as learning except (as Dewey tells us) in the continuum of experience. But this continuum cannot survive in the classroom unless there is reality of encounter between the adults and the children. The teachers must be themselves, and not play roles. They must teach the children, and not teach "subjects." The child, after all, is avid to acquire what he takes to be the necessities of life, and the teacher must not answer him with mere professionalism and gimmickry. The continuum of experience and reality of encounter are destroyed in the public schools (and most private ones) by the very methods which form the institution itself—the top-down organization, the regimentation, the faceless encounters, the empty professionalism, and so on.

Eléna and Maxine suddenly began assimilating schoolwork at a fantastic rate. Their lessons were brief and few, yet in a year and a half both girls covered more than three years' work. Maxine, who had been behind in everything, was reading three years beyond her age level. But the truth is that there was nothing unusual in this, though certainly it seems to be rare. I mean that the girls found it *easy*. José gradually reversed his long-standing habit of total failure. He began to learn. His progress was slow, but his experience was much like that of the girls. I mean that he discovered—just barely glimpsed—the easiness of learning. And invariably, when he glimpsed it, a very particular laughter bubbled out of him, expressing release.

The experience of learning is an experience of wholeness. The child feels the unity of his own powers and the continuum of persons. His parents, his friends, his teachers, and the vague human shapes of his future form one world for him, and he feels the adequacy and reality of his powers within this world. Anything short of this wholeness is not true learning. Children who store up facts and parrot the answers (as John Holt has described in *How Children Fail*) invariably suffer a great deal of anxiety. If they are joined to the continuum of persons, it is not by the exercise of their powers, but by the suppression of their needs. Rebellious children are more loyal to their instincts, but they suffer the insecurity of conflict with the persons who form the continuum of life.

The really crucial things at First Street were these: that we eliminated—to the best of our ability—the obstacles which impede the natural growth of mind; that we based everything on reality of encounter between teacher and child; and that we did what we could (not enough, by far) to restore something of the continuum of experience within which every child must achieve his growth. It is not remarkable that under these circumstances the children came to life. They had been terribly bored, after all, by the experience of failure. For books *are* interesting; numbers are, and painting, and facts about the world.

Let me put this in more specific terms by saying a few words about José. At the same time, I would like to show that what are widely regarded as "learning problems" are very often simply problems of school administration.

José had failed in everything. After five years in the public schools, he could not read, could not do sums, and had no knowledge even of the most rudimentary history or geography. He was described to us as *having* "poor motivation," *lacking* "reading skills," and (again) *having* "a reading problem."

Now what are these *entities* he possessed and lacked? Is there any such thing as "a reading problem," or "motivation," or "reading skills"?

To say "reading problem" is to draw a little circle around José and specify its contents: syllables, spelling, grammar, etc.

Since we are talking about a real boy, we are talking about real books, too, and real teachers and real classrooms. And real boys, after all, do not read syllables but words; and words, even printed words, have the property of voice; and voices do not exist in a void, but in very clearly indicated social classes.

By what process did José and his schoolbook come together? Is this process part of his reading problem?

Who asks him to read the book? *Someone* asks him. In what sort of voice and for what purpose, and with what concern or lack of concern for the outcome?

And who wrote the book? For whom did they write it? Was it written for José? Can José actually partake of the life the book seems to offer?

And what of José's failure to read? We cannot stop at the fact that he draws a blank. How does he do it? What does he do? It is impossible, after all, for him to sit there *not listening*. He is sitting there doing something. Is he daydreaming? If so, of what? Aren't these particular daydreams part of José's reading problem? Did the teacher ask him what he was thinking of? Is his failure to ask part of José's reading problem?

Printed words are an extension of speech. To read is to move outward toward the world by means of speech. Reading is conversing. But what if this larger world is frightening and insulting? Should we, or should we not, include fear and insult in José's reading problem?

And is there a faculty in the mind devoted to the perception and recollection of *abc*? Or is there just one intelligence, modified by pleasure, pain, hope, etc. Obviously José has little skill in reading, but as I have just indicated, reading is no small matter of syllables and words. Then reading skills are no small matter either. They, too, include his typical relations with adults, with other children, and with himself; for he is fiercely divided within himself, and this conflict lies at the very heart of his reading problem.

José's reading problem is José. Or to put it another way, there is no such thing as a reading problem. José hates books, schools, and teachers, and among a hundred other insufficiencies—*all of a piece*—he cannot read. Is this a reading problem?

A reading problem, in short, is not a fact of life, but a fact of school administration. It does not describe José, but describes the action performed by the school, i.e., the action of ignoring everything about José except his response to printed letters.

Let us do the obvious thing for a change, and take a look at José. This little glimpse of his behavior is what a visitor might have seen during José's early months at the First Street School.

He is standing in the hallway talking to Vicente and Julio. I am sitting alone in the classroom, in one of the student's chairs. There is a piece of paper in front of me, and on it a sentence of five words. The words appear again below the sentence in three columns so that each word is repeated a number of times. Now since José came to us with a reading problem, let us see what relation we can find between these one dozen syllables and the extraordinary behavior he exhibits.

He had been talking animatedly in the hall. Now as he comes to join me, his face contracts spasmodically and the large gestures of his arms are reduced to almost nothing. There is no one near him, and he is absolutely free to refuse the lesson, yet he begins to squirm from side to side as if someone were leading him by the arm. He hitches up his pants, thrusts out his lower lip, and fixes his eyes on the floor. His forehead is lumpy and wrinkled like that of a man suffering physical pain. His eyes have glazed over. Suddenly he shakes himself, lifts his head, and squares his shoulders. But his eyes are still glassy. He yawns abruptly and throws himself into the chair beside me, sprawling on the tip of his spine. But now he turns to me and smiles his typical smile, an outrageous bluff, yet brave and attractive. "Okay, man—let's go." I point to the sentence and he rattles it off, for his memory is not bad and he recalls it clearly from the day before. When I ask him to read the same words in the columns below, however, he repeats the sentence angrily and jabs at the columns with his finger, for he had not read the sentence at all but had simply remembered it. He guffaws and blushes. Now he sits up alertly and crouches over the paper, scanning it for clues: smudges, random pencil marks, his own doodles from the day before. He throws me sagacious glances, trying to interpret the various expressions on my face. He is trying to reconstruct in his mind *the entire sequence* of yesterday's lesson, so that the written words will serve as clues to the spoken ones, and by repeating the spoken ones he will be able to seem to read. The intellectual energy—and the acumen—he puts into this enterprise would more than suffice for learning to read. It is worth mentioning here that whenever he comes upon the written word "I," he is thrown into confusion, though in conversation he experiences no such difficulty.

Now what are José's problems? One of them, certainly, is the fact that he cannot read. But this problem is obviously caused by other, more fundamental problems; indeed, his failure to read should not be described as a problem at all, but a symptom. We need only look at José to see what his problems are: shame, fear, resentment, rejection of others and of himself, anxiety, self-contempt, loneliness. None of these were caused by the difficulty of reading printed words—a fact all the more evident if I mention here that José, when he came to this country at the age of seven, had been able to read Spanish and had regularly read to his mother (who cannot read) the post cards they received from the literate father who had remained in Puerto Rico. For five years he had sat in the classrooms of the public schools literally growing stupider by the year. He had failed at everything (not just reading) and had been promoted from one grade to another in order to make room for the children who were more or less doomed to follow in his footsteps.

Obviously not all of José's problems originated in school. But given the intimacy and freedom of the environment at First Street, his school-induced behavior was easy to observe. He could not believe, for instance, that anything contained in books, or mentioned in classrooms, belonged by rights to himself, or even belonged to the world at large, as trees and lampposts belong quite simply to the world we all live in. He believed, on the contrary, that things dealt with in school belonged somehow to school, or were administered by some far-reaching bureaucratic arm. There had been no indication that he could share in them, but rather that he would be measured against them and be found wanting. Nor did he believe that he was entitled to personal consideration, but felt rather that if he wanted to speak, either to a classmate or to a teacher, or wanted to stand up and move his arms and legs, or even wanted to urinate, he must do it more or less in defiance of authority. During his first weeks at our school he was belligerent about the most innocuous things. Outside of school he had learned many games, as all children do, unaware that they are engaged in "the process of learning." Inside the school this ability deserted him. Nor had it ever occurred to him that one might deliberately go about the business of learning something, for he had never witnessed the whole forms of learning. What he had seen was reciting, copying, answering questions, taking tests—and these, alas, do not add up to learning. Nor could he see any connection between school and his life at home and in the streets. If he had heard our liberal educators confessing manfully, "We are not getting through to them," he would have winced with shame and anger at that little dichotomy "we/them," for he had been exposed to it in a hundred different forms.

One would not say that he had been schooled at all, but rather that for five years he had been indoctrinated in the contempt of persons, for contempt of persons had been the supreme fact demonstrated in the classrooms, and referred alike to teachers, parents, and children. For all practical purposes, José's inability to learn consisted precisely of his school-induced behavior. . . .

HOW TO SURVIVE IN YOUR NATIVE LAND

JAMES HERNDON

The "black humor" of James Herndon is even more on display in How to Survive in Your Native Land *than in his earlier book,* The Way It Spozed To Be (*New York: Simon and Schuster,* 1965, 1968). *Although he has moved from a ghetto school attended by blacks to a suburban junior high school attended by whites, Herndon still views the educational world as a spectacle at which he is not sure whether to laugh or cry. He ruefully portrays his suburban school as dedicated to teaching about ancient Egypt; he helps his students find relief from tedium through elaborate kite-flying projects.*

Toward the end, his book becomes a series of essays and squibs. One of the latter, reporting the dominant place of flax in the curriculum, is reproduced here. His account should strike a sympathetic note with any reader who has encountered in his own experiences some bit of content meaningless to him yet apparently an obsession of the school.

Smiley's Bar and Bait Shop School was the only school I've ever seen in which the word *flax* was never mentioned. It was at Smiley's, by the way, that I had enrolled myself in a course called How to Survive in Your Native Land, a course invented by my friend Stan Persky in Vancouver. If it was true that I had little hope of finding out the answer, it was also true that I hoped that as long as I was enrolled I might continue to survive.

Flax is what school is all about. In my own old-fashioned geography books I went to various countries in the company of Bedouin and Greek and Turkish kids and the thing that most remains in my mind now about those imaginary kids is that they always grew flax. I myself put flax on my maps alongside corn and wheat and coal; I wrote down flax to answer questions about the products of countries. I never knew what flax was, but I knew that if I kept it in mind and wrote it down a lot and raised my hand and said it a lot, I would be making it.

Flax is actually a slender erect plant with a blue flower, the seeds of which are used to make linseed oil. Linen is made from the fiber of the stalk. I know this now because I've just looked it up in the dictionary. It is quite possible that it does grow in all those countries like the book and my test papers said. But beyond that, a thing like flax has an important place in a school. Unlike corn, say, which in L.A. we could drive out and see in fields and buy from roadside stands and take home and eat, unlike wheat or cotton or potatoes, I think you could live your entire life in America and never see or even hear of flax, never know about it or need to know about it. Only in the school, only from the geography book, only from the teacher, could you learn about flax.

It showed you how smart the school was, for one thing. For another, it showed you what Learning was; corn, for example, wasn't Learning precisely because you *could* go out and see it in the fields and buy it from roadside stands and take it home and shuck it and eat it and your mother and father could tell you about how they used to grow corn and how to tell fresh corn and about names of corn like Country Gentleman, which my father preferred. You could do all that without ever going to school and so it didn't count. Finally, it showed the school who among the students was willing and able to keep flax in mind, to raise his hand and say it aloud, to write it down, and put its name on maps. So that in the cumulative records of each child the teacher could write down for the next teacher the information that

Child reads flax, writes down flax and says flax.	*Leader.*
Child sometimes remembers flax.	*Nice kid.*
Child can't remember flax.	*Child is black and/or deprived.*
Child digs flax, but inadvertently says "chili-dog" instead.	*Brain-damaged?*
Child don't dig flax a-tall.	*Reluctant learner.*

I think you could make up an entirely new Achievement Test, doing away with expensive and tedious vocabulary and graphs and reading comprehension, doing away with special pencils for IBM scoring and doing away with filling in all those rows. Just pass out a sheet with the word *flax* printed on it in big letters and count the seconds it took for a kid to raise his hand. That would tell you everything that an Achievement Test is designed to tell you.

Even in the Victory Gardens of 1942 America (where such an outlandish name as *Swiss Chard* became part of my experience, growing non-stop in the back yard), no one was ever known to grow flax, no one saw flax sprouting under the eucalyptus trees, no newspaper articles were written about anyone raising flax in the vacant lots, no war hero mentioned flax as contributing to the war effort. It remained, like Learning, a monopoly of the schools.

THE
CRITICS
OF
COMPULSORY
EDUCATION

EDUCATING
CONTRA
NATURAM

THEODORE ROSZAK

Theodore Roszak is a vital spokesman for to-day's counter-culture. He rejects the compulsory public school as a product of the rigid social orthodoxy of industrial society. As for students, he counsels, "Let them go. Help them to escape, those that need to escape." He suggests "talking up the natural rights of truancy and the educational possibilities of hooky."

Theodore Roszak is Professor of History at California State University at Hayward. He is the editor and a contributor to The Dissenting Academy (*New York: Pantheon Books, 1968*) *and the author of* The Making of a Counter Culture (*Garden City, N.Y.: Doubleday Anchor Books, 1969*), *and* Where the Wasteland Ends (*New York: Doubleday, 1972*).

Suppose—instead of applauding, praising, but inwardly insisting that we know better—we heard and affirmed what the poet proclaims: that "heaven lies about us in our infancy," that the child comes to us shaped by nature's hand, a

From Theodore Roszak, "Educating *Contra Naturam*," in *A Man for Tomorrow's World* (Washington, D.C.: Association for Supervision and Curriculum Development, 1970), pp. 12–27. Copyright 1970 by Theodore Roszak. Reprinted by permission of the author.

> Mighty prophet! Seer blest!
> On Whom those truths do rest
> Which we are toiling all our lives to find. . . .

Well then . . . what would education be but the fine art of watching and waiting, and in good time, of summoning forth from the child all that abides within: kingdoms, powers, glories . . . ? So—the task of the teacher would be that of fire-minder: keeper and feeder of the indwelling flame.

Yet if—believing this—we look about us at the world of men which is the result of our labor, what can we do but echo Wordsworth's lament?

> Whither is fled the visionary gleam?
> Where is it now, the glory and the dream?

Our pedagogy deals poorly with these visionary gleams, does it not? How many of us would recognize them if we saw them? In truth, did we ever really believe they were there—within ourselves, as much as in the young?

There is a drawing by William Blake: Age applying the scissors to the wings of Youth. The image tells us what *our* education is all about, *must* be all about in schools financed by church or state and enforced upon the young by compulsion. Tolstoy put the point vividly more than a century ago when, throughout the West, compulsory public school systems were coming into fashion with the unqualified approval of all progressive opinion. He was among the few who saw through this pedagogical fad which was destined to become the iron social orthodoxy of every industrial and industrializing society.

Education [Tolstoy said] is a compulsory forcible action of one person upon another for the purpose of forming a man such as will appear [to society] to be good. . . . Education is the tendency toward moral despotism raised to a principle. . . . I am convinced that the educator undertakes with such zeal the education of the child because at the base of this tendency lies his envy of the child's purity, and his desire to make him like himself, that is, to spoil him.[1]

A harsh judgment. I wince at it as much as you do. For it comes from one who was not only a supreme prophetic spirit, but a gifted teacher of children. And like you I ask, *must* it be so? Is there no other possibility?

Of course there is. There is the possibility Tolstoy himself explored at his own voluntary school for peasant youngsters, Yasnaya Polyana, where, as he put it, "the criterion of pedagogics is only liberty."

"The people," said Tolstoy, "love and seek education, as they love

[1] Leo Tolstoy, *Tolstoy on Education.* Tr. by Leo Wiener. (Chicago: University of Chicago Press, 1967), pp. 110–11.

and seek the air for breathing. . . . Some want to teach and others want to learn. Let them teach as much as they can, and let them learn as much as they will."[2]

That is the other possibility: to teach in freedom, in complete freedom, in response to the native inclination of the student; to be a teacher only when and where and insofar as the student authorizes us to be.

But that libertarian possibility has nothing to do with our schools—our "free" public schools, where "free" refers, not to an existential relationship between teacher and student, but to a budgetary arrangement for the financing of a coercive institution.

"*Let* them learn," said Tolstoy. He did not say, "*Make* them learn," because he knew that true education satisfies a natural appetite. Why then resort to force-feeding?

And yet, how much of our educating proceeds from the assumption that the young must be *made* to learn? Made to learn . . . tricked into learning . . . charmed . . . inveigled . . . cajoled . . . bribed . . . as if in truth education were *contra naturam* and required clever strategies.

If we do not work from that assumption, then why is education ever anywhere a "problem"? A "problem" requiring, mind you, professional, specialized, full-time, and Herculean attention . . . and prodigious amounts of money?

WHY THE COMPULSION?

If we do not work from that assumption, then why the compulsion? And I do not refer only to the legal compulsion of our lower grades, but to such forms of compulsion as military conscription, which has given us a male college population largely made up, not of young scholars, but of refugees seeking sanctuary in draft-deferrable occupations: the coercive process General Hershey once referred to as "choice under pressure." I speak too of the more subtle compulsions: the lure and the goad of jobs, status, licenses, and credentials.

Now it cannot be unknown to any informed person that in so-called primitive societies, as in many pre-modern civilizations, the whole of vast and profound cultures was easily and naturally transmitted from generation to generation without the intervention of an educational establishment. Rather, the burden of cultural continuity rested on what Paul Goodman has recently called "incidental education": learning in the home, on the job, especially at play, by way of observation and imitation, now and then, here and there, from whoever happens to know, as and when the spirit moves . . . above all, without fuss and bother. The pedagogical theory of all this has been neatly summarized by George Dennison in his book *The Lives of Children*.

[2] *Ibid.*, p. 5.

These two things taken together—the natural authority of adults and the needs of children—are the great reservoir of organic structuring that comes into being when arbitrary rules of order are dispensed with.

The child is always finding himself, moving toward himself, as it were, in the near distance. The adult is his ally, his model—and his obstacle (for there are natural conflicts, too, and they must be given their due).[3]

"Incidental education" . . . how precarious this must sound to us. And yet each generation of Eskimos or Bushmen has stepped forth into life in full possession of the culture. This is not because the culture of primitives is "simpler" than our own: a preposterously ethnocentric assumption. What we mistake for the "complexity" of our culture (when we are not simply confessing to our own sad confusion) is really its technical and academic specialization—the correct measure of which is quantity, not complexity. Quantity is a blunt measure of disorganized amount; complexity measures the richness and integrity of the cultural whole within which all things known and valued should properly find coherence.

In this respect—with reference to coherent moral, religious, aesthetic, mythological, and ritual content—primitive cultures are often far more complex than the down-at-the-heels, *Reader's Digest* and Sunday-supplement version of Western civilization most of our fellow citizens are carrying about haphazardly in their heads. There is even a vast store of purely technical know-how every Eskimo and Bushman must learn—a much greater store than most of us need learn who undo the technical snags in our lives by looking in the Yellow Pages and dialing seven numbers.

I grant you, there have been primitive groups in which harsh forms of indoctrination existed; but I call your attention to the others where little of this has been necessary because the culture, after its own fashion and style, gracefully gave expression to the many dimensions of human personality: the workaday practical, the metaphysical-speculative, the sexual, the communal, the creative, the visionary. Oddly enough, the single aspect of primitive culture many civilized people find least palatable is the often grueling rites of passage—especially those that transpire at puberty. But even these rituals have had at least a natural sanction: they have been the culture's way of dramatizing and illuminating an irrepressible constant in the nature of man—and so of integrating it into the personal and communal pattern of life.

How ironic and revealing it is that in our schools we permit children to be hurt, bullied, and browbeaten if they display too much healthy animal energy in the classroom, or if they fail to revere what the school authorities pose as the social orthodoxies. These conformist demands that arise outside the child's experience may be severely enforced. But

[3] George Dennison, *The Lives of Children* (New York: Random House, Inc., 1969), p. 25.

as for the biological imperative of puberty which arises mightily within the child . . . of this hardly a candid word may be whispered in many schools. Either teachers play dumb, assuming a comic and unbecoming chastity; or the so-called "problem" is treated by way of the most fastidiously anti-erotic sex instruction.

Our schools would be chagrined to graduate a student who did not know the ritualistic pledge of allegiance to the flag; but they feel no shame whatever to graduate adolescents who would be (for all their schools had taught them) sexual ignoramuses. And is this not in itself heavy evidence of how pathetically little our own culture knows of the nature of man: that we take a superficial national emblem to be more worthy of ritual elaboration than the deep demands of erotic experience?

Thus, even where primitive cultures have tended to be far more physically brutal than you or I would approve, they have by and large been true to Tolstoy's dictum: "Every instruction ought to be only an answer to the question put by life."

Water finds its level, the swallows fly south in winter, children learn. It is just that simple. That is what Tolstoy knew; that is what the primitives knew. And so they could say, "Let them learn." Societies that trust their culture can let nature take its course, knowing that in their own good time—and usually very promptly—the children will come round and learn what it looks interesting and important to learn; that indeed, their young lives, unless stunted or sidetracked, are nothing but the inquisitive unfolding of potentialities.

But when a society begins to fear that its culture is not interesting or important to the young—that indeed its culture violates nature—then it concludes that education must be *made* to happen: must be organized strenuously into existence and enforced by professionals. And then we have much heavy talk about methods, discipline, techniques, discipline, incentives, discipline, inducements, discipline, the "crisis in our schools" . . . and discipline. We also have blue-ribbon committees, top-level conferences, exhaustive surveys, bold reforms, daring experiments, courageous innovations . . . and the educational establishment grows and grows and grows.

Let us postulate a law: the less secure the culture, the larger the educational establishment. All of us readily recognize that a society in need of heavy policing must be in serious trouble—for the laws have surely lost their power to command respect. Similarly: a society that professionalizes and anxiously aggrandizes its educational establishment —its cultural cops—is also in serious trouble—for the culture has surely lost its capacity to command interest and involvement. The now chronic top-to-bottom state of emergency in our schools does not exist because the educational establishment is not good enough and needs repair. The crisis is that the culture is not good enough. The educational establishment, with all its compulsions, its disciplinary hang-ups, and

—yes—even with its constabulary forces patrolling the corridors—all this only exists in the first place because of the insecurity of the culture.

Once we realize this, we can perhaps see that the feverish efforts of even good-hearted educators to inspire and motivate their students are as pathetic as the belated efforts of our Special Forces in Vietnam to win the hearts and minds of the very people they have degraded and brutalized. Within the context of coercion all efforts to ingratiate are vitiated from scratch. As Tolstoy observed with respect to teachers who seek to achieve "greater freedom" in the schools,

> Those gentlemen . . . resemble a man who, having brought up some young nightingales and concluding that they need freedom, lets them out of the cage and gives them freedom at the end of cords attached to their feet, and then wonders why the nightingales are not doing any better on the cord, but only break their legs and die.[4]

Now if the law we have postulated is true, it leads us to an ironic conclusion about modern Western civilization. If there has ever been a civilization obsessed with what we call "free, public education," it is ours. We invented this quaint institution and we invest a special historical pride in it. We take it as an indisputable sign of social progress that we have built such colossal, affluent, and broadcast school systems. Until, at last, we begin to anticipate that education will soon become our largest "industry"—the major preoccupation of the society. Far from perceiving in this prospect the advanced cultural insecurity it betokens, we feel this is not only right, but ideal. How better to use our wealth, our leisure, and our know-how than to train more teachers, build more schools, process more students?

AN ADJUNCT OF NATIONAL POWER

Why does industrial society do this? Tolstoy's contemporary, Bismarck, knew why. "The nation that has the schools," Bismarck observed, "has the future."

Education as an adjunct of national power: a shrewd insight . . . one worthy of such a grim broker in blood and iron. But one did not have to be a Prussian autocrat and militarist to accept the hard-bitten logic of Bismarck's argument. William E. Forster, who led the good fight for compulsory public education in Great Britain, was a solidly bourgeois Quaker: an industrialist and a self-denying public servant. And here, very revealingly, is how Forster sized things up in 1870 in presenting his successful elementary education bill to Parliament:

> Upon the speedy provision of elementary education depends our industrial prosperity. It is of no use trying to give technical teaching to our artizans

[4] Leo Tolstoy, *op. cit.*, p. 130.

without elementary education; uneducated labourers . . . are, for the most part, unskilled labourers, and if we leave our work-folk any longer unskilled, notwithstanding their strong sinews and determined energy, they will become over-matched in the competition of the world. . . . Civilized communities throughout the world are massing themselves together, each mass being measured by its force; and if we are to hold our position among men of our own race or among the nations of the world, we must make up the smallness of our numbers by increasing the intellectual force of the individual.[5]

Note the tell-tale imagery of the argument: energy . . . force . . . power . . . mass. Education as mental steam engine; the school as brain-production factory. No doubt today the metaphors would draw upon computer technics or information theory. But the argument would nonetheless be the same. "Knowledge is power" said Francis Bacon more than three centuries ago at the dawn of the scientific revolution. And from Bismarck to Project Apollo, that fateful dictum has been the ensign of public policy throughout the developed and developing countries.

Tolstoy, whose healthy anarchist instincts were quick to sense which way the power-political winds of our time were tending, gauged the situation shrewdly. This time he speaks of higher education, but the criticism strikes at the same authoritarian-utilitarian vice which was for Tolstoy the curse of all state-supported education:

No one has ever thought of establishing universities on the needs of the people. . . . The universities were founded to answer certain needs, partly of the government and partly of higher society, and for the universities was established all that preparatory ladder of educational institutions which has nothing in common with the needs of the people. The government needed officials, doctors, jurists, teachers, and the universities were founded in order to train these. . . . It is generally said that the defects of the universities are due to the defects in the lower institutions. I affirm the opposite: the defects of the popular . . . schools are mainly due to the false exigencies of the universities.[6]

The words are as telling in the age of the multiversity as they were a century ago. Yet how easily we have come to accept the assumption—almost as if it were printed on every dollar our schools receive (for in effect it is)—that education exists, not to debate, but to serve the preordained national priorities. How nicely it simplifies everything to define the good student as he who gets the grades that get the job—a deferential simplification that, incidentally, takes on no greater ethical complexity even if the pigmentation of the students who are pressed into service becomes as various as the rainbow.

[5] J. Stuart Maclure, ed., *Educational Documents: England and Wales, 1816–1967* (London: Chapman & Hall, Ltd., 1965), pp. 104–105.
[6] Leo Tolstoy, *op. cit.*, pp. 30–31.

In the dim and dismal past, there was indeed a time when aristocratic and feudal elites jealously defended a deep vested interest in the plain brute ignorance of peasant masses. Those days are gone forever. Industrial society requires, not illiterate serfs and peons, but trained workmen and trained consumers, bound together in the tight coordination of urban life. As rural routines break down before the thrust of modernization, the well-adjusted citizen must be capable of rapidly assimilating new stores of data; he must respond snappily to the myriad signals, commands, instructions of a changeful new world. The peasant guides his conduct by custom; the industrial worker by information. The peasant lives by tradition; the industrial worker by the news of the day. This is what accounts for industrial society's peculiar obsession with literacy: its facile and unexamined assumption that someone who cannot read is, of necessity, "backward," "underdeveloped."

THE "ROYAL ROAD TO PROPAGANDA"

In 1968, while I was in London, Granada Television produced a documentary film on the civil war that has been raging in Portuguese Guinea for the past several years: an embryonic African Vietnam being contested by Portugal (armed by the United States via NATO) and the Guinean National Liberation Front. The report was presented wholly from the NLF side and it captured much of the idealism of these youthful rebels who are out to free themselves from the dead hand of the imperialist past and to usher their society into the modern world.

At one point, we were shown an NLF jungle school where guerrilla teachers were drilling away at children from the bush—and at students considerably older too. One guerrilla, we were told, had only learned to read at the age of 30—and this was now his proudest achievement. We saw the man poring laboriously over a sheet of paper, ponderously shaping out each word with his lips as his finger underlined it, and smiling broadly as each sentence of the text was conquered. It might have been an image out of our own American past: the familiar picture of the Polish or Italian immigrant learning his letters in night school, making the great leap forward into literacy and citizenship.

But what was it our night-school immigrants went on to read once the breakthrough had been made? Legend has it that they all went on to Shakespeare, Tocqueville, and John Stuart Mill. Surely some did. But mostly they went on to the local Hearst press . . . the *Police Gazette* . . . Horatio Alger . . . the Sears catalog. And what was the text our proud Guinean guerrilla was draining of all its insight? Of course: a party bulletin—especially prepared for the feebly literate. It was all his formal education allowed him to cope with. And it was, in any case, about all the party was prepared to give him . . . though perhaps he will eventually graduate to the *Thoughts of Chairman Mao*.

Thus, for the peasant revolutionary as for the vast majority of our own more affluent youngsters, literacy is the royal road to propaganda. Why does industrial—or would-be industrial—society crusade so fanatically against illiteracy? It is hardly because illiterate people are necessarily stupid. They *may* be. But not necessarily so. Recall that high civilizations have been reared on this earth without the aid of the written word. It is hardly because literate people are necessarily smart. They *may* be. But not necessarily so. And to judge by what most of our almost universally literate citizenry patronizes in the way of newspapers, magazines, political oratory, and television entertainment—to judge especially by its gullibility in the marketplace—literacy would seem to bear about as much relationship to intelligence in our society as a Presidential convention bears to a town meeting. It is little wonder then that as of the year 1970, our political leaders come to the convenient conclusion that, in the arena of social controversy, the voice of the universally literate people is . . . a "silent majority."

The simple truth is: industrial society has no use for unschooled people, because unschooled people are too difficult to organize. Lacking the sense of discipline and responsibility the schools provide, lacking the minimal literacy they purvey, people will not pay what they owe, buy what they ought, report for work on time, appear for induction when summoned, dial the right number, sign on the dotted line, fill out the form correctly. They will not know what the advertisement says, they will not know where to put their mark on the ballot, they will not know why the war is necessary, they will not know wherein lie the genius and honor of their leaders. Unless equipped with a good, practical education—"an education for life"—they may even revert to employing the sense they were born with, put two and two together, and *not* come up with a good solid official five.

Of course I know there are exceptions to the standard: exceptional teachers, exceptional students. But let us be honest about our history: the free public school system is a product of industrial necessity within the context of the nation-state. I am not unaware of the genuine idealism that has been and still is entrusted to this institution. Idealism is often planted in barren earth. Believe it or not, in the high days of the French Revolution, the conscripted citizen army—the *levée en masse*—was regarded as a shining expression of liberty, equality, fraternity. Ask our youth today what they think of this great democratic institution. Institutions have such a tragic way of devouring the ideals they exist to foster.

The function of the educational establishment in industrial society is to treat industrialism and all that it demands as "given": necessary, good, inexorably so . . . a veritable force of nature toward which one must be "practical," not "critical." The schools are built because they produce the skills that will turn the populace into interchangeable, socially serviceable units of a productive economy: at the least, reading, writing, ciphering—but also the sophisticated technical skills necessary for elaborating the industrial plant.

In addition, the schools enforce the virtues of what is called "citizenship": meaning eager acquiescence in the national mystique, patriotic resolution, docility before official superiors, well-developed resignation before externally enforced discipline. In collectivized economies, the schools inculcate a deep and automatic appreciation of ideological inanity; in privatized economies, a profound piety for the privileges of property.

In brief, the elites of all industrial societies take their strength from technicians so narrowly proficient that there is no room in their busy consciousness for a single moral scruple, and from masses so minimally literate that nothing intellectually larger than a commercial advertisement or an official political stereotype can wedge itself into so abbreviated an attention span.

What, then, is the measure of the success of the educational establishment? Let me suggest two examples that vividly represent the excellence the establishment was in reality created to achieve. I could have chosen other examples, but I choose these two because they strike me as having required a superhuman effort in dealing with recalcitrant human material and, obviously, because they give us much to ponder.

"THE BALANCE OF TERROR"

The first of these is the gargantuan Russo-American weapons system we call "the balance of terror." It is hardly a secret that, since the end of World War II, the building of this juggernaut has been public business number one for both the U.S. and the U.S.S.R. Nothing in either society—no matter of social justice or humanitarian need—has received more trained manpower or money than these weapons have. Yet there is no system of social ethics—excepting those of Tamerlane, Al Capone, and Joseph Paul Goebbels—which offers a breath of support to this major international enterprise.

Translated out of the official casuistry which covers their true character, these weapons represent an institutionalized commitment to the doing of genocide—perhaps on a global scale. They exist to kill children. Among others, to be sure. Yet I call attention to the children because we are teachers and perhaps this does the most to tear the heart. These weapons are aimed at children, not by accident or unavoidable necessity—but directly, specifically, intentionally, with painstaking malice aforethought, and without apology or guilt. That is what "terror" means. So they have been designed; and so they will be used—when the time comes. They are, as Thomas Merton has called them, "the original child bomb."

Now consider how efficient an educational establishment is required to produce the scientists and technicians who will sell their necessary talents to such a project. Consider how carefully a curriculum must be designed to bring these specialists through 16, 18, 20 years of education without ever once unsettling their conscience. Consider how delicately their acquaintance with the religious and ethical traditions of their culture must have been arranged in order not to preclude their service-ability. Consider with what ingenious cunning they must have been maneuvered through the study of what we call "the humanities." Consider how diligently every inborn trace of moral inquisitiveness had to be surgically removed from their nature, along with every remnant of a sense of humanitarian service, pity, fellowship, or sheer existential disgust—until at last we had specialists whose only remaining ethical reflex would be, "What they do to us, we do to them—worse!" And how many of these men, one wonders, have come from schools which have fiercely defended their right to have the words of Amos, Isaiah, and Jesus read in class?

The second example I offer is an event now much on the public mind. I refer to what happened in the Vietnamese village of Songmy on March 16, 1968. What has followed from that event has led to a great deal of controversy—though I learn from one public opinion poll, taken at Christmas-time 1969, that 51 percent of those questioned refuse—like the Saigon government—to believe that anything untoward ever occurred in Songmy. But let us assume that the U.S. Army and its Commander-in-Chief know better and can be believed when they tell us that an atrocity there took place. In what grotesque sense of the word can that savage act be called a "success" of our educational establishment?

Once again, consider what a labor it must have been to produce the young Americans capable of such a deed. Such ordinary, such stolidly ordinary young men . . . a few years before they turned their guns on these women and children and shot them, they were perhaps going out for the high school basketball team, planning heavy weekend dates, worrying about their grades in solid geometry. No moral degenerates, these: no more so than Adolph Eichmann was. But given the order to kill, they killed. Not because they were monsters, but because they were good soldiers, good Americans, doing as they had been taught to do. Given the order to kill, they killed—the obviously innocent, obviously defenseless, crying out to them for pity.

Later, one of the men is reported as saying that he has bad dreams about the deed. Did he ever learn in school that there are such dreams? Was he ever asked to decide for himself what his duty is to the state? to his own conscience? to his innocent fellow man? Did he ever hear of the Nuremberg trials? Did he ever have a class dealing with the subject "orders one must consider *never* obeying"? Would any board of education, any PTA now demand that such a class be offered? Would the U.S. Department of Health, Education, and Welfare encourage it?

Would the U.S. Department of Defense suggest it? Would the local Chamber of Commerce and American Legion permit it?

Well then: what respect has our culture for the moral nature of our young? Again to quote Tolstoy, our school system "trains not such men as humanity needs, but such as corrupt society needs."

I have said that the great problem with education in our time is that the culture it exists to transmit—the culture of industrial society—is largely worthless and therefore without inherent interest to lively and unspoiled young minds. Worse still, much that industrial society requires degrades all natural humanity. It trespasses against reason, gentleness, and freedom with a force that is plainly homicidal in intensity. That is why the schools, in their eagerness to advance the regimenting orthodoxies of state and corporation—property, power, productivity—have had to distort education into indoctrination. That is why so much is incurably wrong with the schools—all the things keener critics than myself have raised to the level of common knowledge. I need not discuss here what writers like John Holt, Edgar Friedenberg, Jules Henry, Paul Goodman, Jonathan Kozol, and James Herndon have so well analyzed: the compulsion of the system, the tyranny of "right answers," the surrealistic charade of lesson plans, methods, and learning resources, the obsession with discipline, above all the mercenary manipulation of competitive favors—grades, gold stars, good opinions, awards, jobs, status, power.

END TO INDUSTRIALIZATION?

Nor do I have the time here to persuade those of you who do not already feel it in your bones like the plague, that the West's 150-year experiment in industrialization is approaching a disastrously bad end. Our collective nightmares are available for all to consider: the bleak landscapes of the Brave New World and of 1984, hallucinations of thermonuclear extinction or total environmental collapse. If the bomb does not finish us, then the blight of our habitat very likely will. If not the atom's fire, then the poisoned air, water, earth: the very elements pronounce their sentence of death upon industrial society. Surely they will serve even for the least religious among us as the voice of God.

Whatever health remains in a corrupted culture gathers in the gift of prophecy or also perishes. And woe to the people who fail to recognize their prophets because they come in unlikely forms . . . for prophets are in the habit of so doing. The best and brightest of our young go barefoot and grow shaggier by the day; they scrap the social graces; they take despairingly to the streets to revile and cry doom; they abscond to the hinterlands in search of purity and simple dignities; they thrust themselves upon us in our public parks and on the stages of our theaters stripped naked and imploring us to "let the sunshine in." We can hardly be so ignorant of our own tradition that we do not recognize—for all the frequent zaniness and gaucherie—the gesture, the presence, the accusatory word that is here reborn before us. The prophet Micah, wild-eyed and wailing in the streets of Jerusalem:

> Arise and go, for this is no place to rest;
> because of uncleanness that destroys
>   with a grievous destruction . . .
> Your rich men are full of violence;
>   your inhabitants speak lies . . .
> Their hands are upon what is evil
>   to do it diligently;
> the prince and the judge ask for a bribe,
> and the great man utters the evil desire of his soul;
> thus they weave it together. . . .
> For this I will lament and wail;
>   I will go stripped and naked;
> I will make lamentation like the jackals,
>   and mourning like the ostriches.[7]

In the finest moments of their outrage and anger, what the young are demanding is what every prophet has demanded of his people: that they too strip away the defiled garment of society, turn away and inward toward the first principles of the conduct of life. The great question is always the same. It was asked of King David, of Imperial Rome, and now of Imperial America, playing self-appointed policeman to the nations and conquering hero to the whole of nature. "What shall it profit a man if he gain the whole world and lose his soul?"

For those of us who teach, the return to first principles means a return to Tolstoy's critique of compulsory, public education: an honest admission that what our existing pedagogical machinery is programmed to produce is the man that industrial society in its benightedness thinks it needs; and what industrial society in its benightedness thinks it needs of us is but the shriveled portion of our full humanity—how small a portion one must almost weep to say.

But lest we despair, we must remember that for Tolstoy this bleak fact was only a minor blemish on the face of an abidingly beautiful truth; that the spontaneous splendors of the human personality return to us whole in every child and will struggle fiercely to be educated in accordance with their nature. Because he believed this, Tolstoy was prepared—indeed, compelled—to sweep away the state's claim to all educational authority, which could only be the authority to pollute the wellsprings of learning. There can be no more precise way to frame the

---

[7] *The Holy Bible*, Revised Standard Version (New York: Thomas Nelson & Sons, 1952), pp. 723–24, 726–27.

matter than as he did in raising the question: *who has the right to educate?* His answer:

> There are no rights of education. I do not acknowledge such, nor have they been acknowledged nor will they ever be by the young generation under education. . . . *The right to educate is not vested in anybody.*[8]

It was out of this clear perception that authentic education derives only from the need of the child, not from the right of the adult, that Tolstoy appealed for that which presently animates campus rebellion throughout the Western world—now in the colleges; but soon enough I suspect our high schools too will be ablaze (not only figuratively) with the demand: "freely formed institutions, having for their basis the freedom of the learning generation."

A steep demand. A demand that is bound to seem unthinkable to those who mistake a proper sense of adult responsibility for automatic submission unto the higher powers of the social order and to the bizarre necessities that come down to us from these obsessive profit- and power-mongers. Such resignation in the name of responsibility can only drive us to cling to the established way of things as if it were all the deck there is and everything beyond, the cruel, cold sea. Nothing to do then but clap the would-be mutineers in irons, rearrange the cargo, patch up the leaks, and continue the cruise to oblivion.

But the deck is afire, while the sea, if not benign, is yet filled with a multitude of inviting islands: the possibilities of culture on the far-side of industrial necessity and nationalistic idolatry. The possibilities are there, though I think the diminished consciousness to which we are—most of us—beholden will see them only as mirages or not at all. That is why the expertise and technician-intelligence to which we habitually turn for solutions—as if with the reflex of duty well-learned—are really no help to us: more statistics, more surveys, more professional shoptalk and hair of the dog. As if there could be no knowledge of man that did not wear the official uniform of research.

But the poet Shelley tells us there are and have always been "unacknowledged legislators of mankind" whose age-old gift it is to "bring light and fire from those eternal regions where the owl-winged faculty of calculation dare not ever soar." A word from them does more than all our science and its dismal train of imitators to reclaim the wasted dimensions of our identity: the buried erotic powers, the truths of the imagination that yield meaning to song, dance, or ritual gesture, but which common literacy will never touch but to kill. Astonishments of the spirit . . . gods of the heights and of the depths . . . thrones and dominions that only the lamp of prophecy reveals . . . and all these inborn glories of our nature useless, useless for achieving what the nations would achieve. We deal here in vistas of experience in which the

[8] Leo Tolstoy, *op. cit.*, pp. 111, 114.

orthodox ambitions of our society shrivel to nonentity. Yet what else would we have the education of the young be but such an adventure in transcendence?

So the demand is for "freely formed institutions": education beneath the sway of the visionary gleam. From where we stand, a revolutionary demand. And I can hardly be sanguine that many of us here who belong to the establishment will prove to be effective revolutionaries.

Should I be asked, however, "what then are *we* to do?" perhaps, for those having ears to hear, I can offer one minimal suggestion (since the maximum one can do is obvious enough): not a program, not a policy, not a method, nothing to be worked up into a research project or the grist of the conference mill—but only a silent commitment to be pondered in the heart and practiced with unabashed guile when opportunity permits. And it is this: might we not at least let go of our pretensions . . . and then simply let go of the students?

Let them go. Help them to escape, those that need to escape. Find them cracks in the system's great walls and guide them through, cover their tracks, provide the alibis, mislead the posse . . . the anxious parents, the truant officers, the supervisors and superintendents and officious superegos of the social order.

At least between ourselves and the young, we might begin talking up the natural rights of truancy and the educative possibilities of hooky—which is after all only matriculating into the school without walls that the world itself has always normally been for the inquisitive young.

And who knows? Once we stop forcing *our* education on the children, perhaps they will invite a lucky few of us to participate in *theirs*.

DESCHOOLING SOCIETY

IVAN ILLICH

Illich contends that for most people the right to learn is hindered by the obligation to attend school. He believes that universal education is neither feasible nor desirable, and that the dispossessed members of society would be better served if schooling were not confused with education. He suggests that in order to disentangle schooling and education, we must disestablish the schools.

Ivan Illich served as a Catholic priest in New York City, Puerto Rico, and South America; he permanently resigned his priestly functions in 1969. He founded the controversial Intercultural Center of Documentation in Cuernavaca, Mexico, in 1961. His book, Deschooling Society, *was hotly discussed in the United States after its publication.*

Neither learning nor justice is promoted by schooling because educators insist on packaging instruction with certification. Learning and the assignment of social roles are melted into schooling. Yet to learn means to acquire a new skill or insight, while promotion depends on an opinion which others have formed. Learning frequently is the result of instruction, but selection for a role or category in the job market increasingly depends on mere length of attendance.

Instruction is the choice of circumstances which facilitate learning. Roles are assigned by setting a curriculum of conditions which the candidate must meet if he is to make the grade. School links instruction—but not learning—to these roles. This is neither reasonable nor liberating. It is not reasonable because it does not link relevant qualities or competences to roles, but rather the process by which such qualities are supposed to be acquired. It is not liberating or educational because school reserves instruction to those whose every step in learning fits previously approved measures of social control.

Curriculum has always been used to assign social rank. At times it could be prenatal: karma ascribes you to a caste and lineage to the aristocracy. Curriculum could take the form of a ritual, of sequential sacred ordinations, or it could consist of a succession of feats in war or hunting, or further advancement could be made to depend on a series of previous princely favors. Universal schooling was meant to detach role assignment from personal life history: it was meant to give everybody an equal chance to any office. Even now many people wrongly believe that school ensures the dependence of public trust on relevant learning achievements. However, instead of equalizing chances, the school system has monopolized their distribution.

To detach competence from curriculum, inquiries into a man's learning history must be made taboo, like inquiries into his political affiliation, church attendance, lineage, sex habits, or racial background. Laws forbidding discrimination on the basis of prior schooling must be enacted. Laws, of course, cannot stop prejudice against the unschooled —nor are they meant to force anyone to intermarry with an autodidact —but they can discourage unjustified discrimination.

A second major illusion on which the school system rests is that most learning is the result of teaching. Teaching, it is true, may contribute to certain kinds of learning under certain circumstances. But most people acquire most of their knowledge outside school, and in school only insofar as school, in a few rich countries, has become their place of confinement during an increasing part of their lives.

Most learning happens casually, and even most intentional learning is not the result of programmed instruction. Normal children learn their first language casually, although faster if their parents pay attention to them. Most people who learn a second language well do so as a result of odd circumstances and not of sequential teaching. They go to live with their grandparents, they travel, or they fall in love with a foreigner. Fluency in reading is also more often than not a result of such extracurricular activities. Most people who read widely, and with pleasure, merely believe that they learned to do so in school; when challenged, they easily discard this illusion.

But the fact that a great deal of learning even now seems to happen casually and as a by-product of some other activity defined as work or leisure does not mean that planned learning does not benefit from planned instruction and that both do not stand in need of improvement. The strongly motivated student who is faced with the task of acquiring a new and complex skill may benefit greatly from the discipline now associated with the old-fashioned schoolmaster who taught reading, Hebrew, catechism, or multiplication by rote. School has now made this kind of drill teaching rare and disreputable, yet there are many skills which a motivated student with normal aptitude can master in a matter of a few months if taught in this traditional way. This is as true of codes as of their encipherment; of second and third languages as of reading and writing; and equally of special languages such as algebra, computer programming, chemical analysis, or of manual skills like typing, watchmaking, plumbing, wiring, TV repair; or for that matter dancing, driving, and diving.

In certain cases acceptance into a learning program aimed at a specific skill might presuppose competence in some other skill, but it should certainly not be made to depend upon the process by which such prerequisite skills were acquired. TV repair presupposes literacy and some math; diving, good swimming; and driving, very little of either.

Progress in learning skills is measurable. The optimum resources in time and materials needed by an average motivated adult can be easily estimated. The cost of teaching a second Western European language to a high level of fluency ranges between four and six hundred dollars in the United States, and for an Oriental tongue the time needed for instruction might be doubled. This would still be very little compared with the cost of twelve years of schooling in New York City (a condition for acceptance of a worker into the Sanitation Department)—almost fifteen thousand dollars. No doubt not only the teacher but also the printer and the pharmacist protect their trades through the public illusion that training for them is very expensive . . . .

TEACHERS AND PUPILS

By definition, children are pupils. The demand for the milieu of childhood creates an unlimited market for accredited teachers. School is an institution built on the axiom that learning is the result of teaching. And institutional wisdom continues to accept this axiom, despite overwhelming evidence to the contrary.

We have all learned most of what we know outside school. Pupils do most of their learning without, and often despite, their teachers. Most tragically, the majority of men are taught their lesson by schools, even though they never go *to* school.

Everyone learns how to live outside school. We learn to speak, to think, to love, to feel, to play, to curse, to politick, and to work without interference from a teacher. Even children who are under a teacher's care day and night are no exception to the rule. Orphans, idiots, and schoolteachers' sons learn most of what they learn outside the "educational" process planned for them. Teachers have made a poor showing in their attempts at increasing learning among the poor. Poor parents who want their children to go to school are less concerned about what they will learn than about the certificate and money they will earn. And middle-class parents commit their children to a teacher's care to keep them from learning what the poor learn on the streets. Increasingly educational research demonstrates that children learn most of what teachers pretend to teach them from peer groups, from comics, from chance observations, and above all from mere participation in the ritual of school. Teachers, more often than not, obstruct such learning of subject matters as goes on in school.

Half of the people in our world never set foot in school. They have no contact with teachers, and they are deprived of the privilege of becoming dropouts. Yet they learn quite effectively the message which school teaches: that they should have school, and more and more of it. School instructs them in their own inferiority through the tax collector who makes them pay for it, or through the demagogue who raises their expectations of it, or through their children once the latter are hooked on it. So the poor are robbed of their self-respect by subscribing to a creed that grants salvation only through the school. At least the Church gave them a chance to repent at the hour of death. School leaves them with the expectation (a counterfeit hope) that their grandchildren will make it. That expectation is of course still more learning which comes from school but not from teachers.

Pupils have never credited teachers for most of their learning. Bright and dull alike have always relied on rote, reading, and wit to pass their exams, motivated by the stick or by the carrot of a desired career.

Adults tend to romanticize their schooling. In retrospect, they attribute their learning to the teacher whose patience they learned to admire. But the same adults would worry about the mental health of a child who rushed home to tell them what he learned from his every teacher.

Schools create jobs for schoolteachers, no matter what their pupils learn from them....

GENERAL CHARACTERISTICS OF NEW FORMAL EDUCATIONAL INSTITUTIONS

A good educational system should have three purposes: it should provide all who want to learn with access to available resources at any time in their lives; empower all who want to share what they know to find those who want to learn it from them; and, finally, furnish all who want to present an issue to the public with the opportunity to make their challenge known. Such a system would require the application of constitutional guarantees to education. Learners should not be forced to submit to an obligatory curriculum, or to discrimination based on whether they possess a certificate or a diploma. Nor should the public be forced to support, through a regressive taxation, a huge professional apparatus of educators and buildings which in fact restricts the public's chances for learning to the services the profession is willing to put on the market. It should use modern technology to make free speech, free assembly and a free press truly universal and, therefore, fully educational.

Schools are designed on the assumption that there is a secret to everything in life; that the quality of life depends on knowing that secret; that secrets can be known only in orderly successions; and that only teachers can properly reveal these secrets. An individual with a schooled mind conceives of the world as a pyramid of classified packages accessible only to those who carry the proper tags. New educational institutions would break apart this pyramid. Their purpose must be to facilitate access for the learner: to allow him to look into the windows of the control room or the parliament, if he cannot get in by the door. Moreover, such new institutions should be channels to which the learner would have access without credentials or pedigree—public spaces in which peers and elders outside his immediate horizon would become available.

I believe that no more than four—possibly even three—distinct "channels" or learning exchanges could contain all the resources needed for real learning. The child grows up in a world of things, surrounded by people who serve as models for skills and values. He finds peers who challenge him to argue, to compete, to cooperate, and to understand; and if the child is lucky, he is exposed to confrontation or criticism by an experienced elder who really cares. Things, models, peers, and elders are four resources each of which requires a different type of arrangement to ensure that everybody has ample access to it.

I will use the words "opportunity web" for "network" to designate specific ways to provide access to each of four sets of resources. "Network" is often used, unfortunately, to designate the channels reserved to material selected by others for indoctrination, instruction, and entertainment. But it can also be used for the telephone or the postal service, which are primarily accessible to individuals who want to send messages to one another. I wish we had another word to designate such reticular structures for mutual access, a word less evocative of entrapment, less degraded by current usage and more suggestive of the fact that any such arrangement includes legal, organizational, and technical aspects. Not having found such a term, I will try to redeem the one which is available, using it as a synonym of "educational web."

What are needed are new networks, readily available to the public and designed to spread equal opportunity for learning and teaching.

To give an example: The same level of technology is used in TV and in tape recorders. All Latin-American countries now have introduced TV: in Bolivia the government has financed a TV station, which was built six years ago, and there are no more than seven thousand TV sets for four million citizens. The money now tied up in TV installations throughout Latin America could have provided every fifth adult with a tape recorder. In addition, the money would have sufficed to provide an almost unlimited library of prerecorded tapes, with outlets even in remote villages, as well as an ample supply of empty tapes.

This network of tape recorders, of course, would be radically different from the present network of TV. It would provide opportunity for free expression: literate and illiterate alike could record, preserve, disseminate, and repeat their opinions. The present investment in TV, instead, provides bureaucrats, whether politicians or educators, with the power to sprinkle the continent with institutionally produced programs which they—or their sponsors—decide are good for or in demand by the people.

Technology is available to develop either independence and learning or bureaucracy and teaching.

FOUR NETWORKS

The planning of new educational institutions ought not to begin with the administrative goals of a principal or president, or with the teaching goals of a professional educator, or with the learning goals of any hypothetical class of people. It must not start with the question, "What should someone learn?" but with the question, "What kinds of things and people might learners want to be in contact with in order to learn?"

Someone who wants to learn knows that he needs both information and critical response to its use from somebody else. Information can be stored in things and in persons. In a good educational system access to things ought to be available at the sole bidding of the learner, while access to informants requires, in addition, others' consent. Criticism can also come from two directions: from peers or from elders, that is, from fellow learners whose immediate interests match mine, or from those who will grant me a share in their superior experience. Peers can be colleagues with whom to raise a question, companions for playful and enjoyable (or arduous) reading or walking, challengers at any type of game. Elders can be consultants on which skill to learn, which method to use, what company to seek at a given moment. They can be guides to the right questions to be raised among peers and to the deficiency of the answers they arrive at. Most of these resources are plentiful. But they are neither conventionally perceived as educational resources, nor is access to them for learning purposes easy, especially for the poor. We must conceive of new relational structures which are deliberately set up to facilitate access to these resources for the use of anybody who is motivated to seek them for his education. Administrative, technological, and especially legal arrangements are required to set up such web-like structures.

Educational resources are usually labeled according to educators' curricular goals. I propose to do the contrary, to label four different approaches which enable the student to gain access to any educational resource which may help him to define and achieve his own goals:

1. Reference Services to Educational Objects—which facilitate access to things or processes used for formal learning. Some of these things can be reserved for this purpose, stored in libraries, rental agencies, laboratories, and showrooms like museums and theaters; others can be in daily use in factories, airports, or on farms, but made available to students as apprentices or on off-hours.

2. Skill Exchanges—which permit persons to list their skills, the conditions under which they are willing to serve as models for others who want to learn these skills, and the addresses at which they can be reached.

3. Peer-Matching—a communications network which permits persons to describe the learning activity in which they wish to engage, in the hope of finding a partner for the inquiry.
4. Reference Services to Educators-at-Large—who can be listed in a directory giving the addresses and self-descriptions of professionals, paraprofessionals, and free-lancers, along with conditions of access to their services. Such educators, as we will see, could be chosen by polling or consulting their former clients.

THE
CRITICS
OF
THE
CRITICS

JOHN
DEWEY
AND
HIS
BETRAYERS

SIDNEY HOOK

Sidney Hook has written extensively on John Dewey's educational philosophy. For instance, he wrote John Dewey: An Intellectual Portrait *(New York: John Day, 1939) and edited* John Dewey: Philosopher of Science and Freedom *(New York: Dial Press, 1950), republished in 1967 (New York: Barnes and Noble).*

In this article, Hook admonishes the progressive critics of education for what he regards as their misinterpretations of Dewey's thought. Hook believes that in attempting to support their ideas, contemporary critics of education distort Dewey's position on such issues as freedom and authority, education and experience, the child and the subject matter, need and desire, democracy and education, and schools and politics.

Often in the forefront of action for academic freedom, Hook in the late 1960s organized the University Center for Rational Alternatives. Among his recent books are American Freedom and Academic Anarchy *(New York: Cowles, 1970) and* In Defense of Academic Freedom *(Indianapolis: Bobbs-Merrill, 1971). He is now professor emeritus of philosophy, New York University.*

During the last few years there has been an open season on the American school system from the most elementary to advanced levels. It has been indicted not only for its failure to teach the rudiments of the traditional disciplines, but for its repressive attitude towards the spontaneous activities and the outreaching natural curiosity of the child and student as learning animals. The schools have been compared to penal institutions not only because of the physical conditions that exist in some ghetto areas but even more so because of the manner, spirit, and methods of instruction.

Such criticism comes from those who regard themselves as libertarians and humanists and who either profess themselves inspired to some degree by the thought of John Dewey or are commonly regarded as continuing his influence—writers like Paul Goodman, Ivan Illich, John Holt, Jonathan Kozol, George Dennison, Edgar Friedenberg, George Leonard. Their criticisms are exercising a surprising influence on educators and teachers: they are partly responsible for a phenomenon observable in liberal arts colleges from one end of the country to another, viz., the abandonment of required courses and even area distribution studies as unendurable forms of faculty paternalism and violations of the "student's autonomy, his moral freedom and responsibility." Since the student, in this conception, is the best judge of his own educational needs, it is a tyrannical imposition from without to require him to take any courses that he thinks he does not need.

I am concerned here with the ways in which such views misinterpret the thought of John Dewey. It is an open question whether Dewey's educational philosophy has been more flagrantly distorted in the accounts given of it by some of his latter-day disciples than by the criticisms of his vociferous detractors. Both, it seems to me, have been intellectually irresponsible in disregarding his plain and easily available texts. But the moral failings of the professed followers of Dewey are graver than those of his critics: first, by the very virtue of their allegiance, which should impose a greater conscientiousness upon them, and second, because the fundamentalist critics of Dewey have as a rule seized upon *their* formulations, as professed followers of Dewey, as evidence of the validity of their fundamentalist reading of him.

The first misconception of John Dewey's philosophy stems from the notion that because he stressed the importance of freedom, he was therefore opposed to authority. Nothing could be farther removed from his true teaching. "The need for authority," he wrote, "is a constant need of man." (*Problems of Men*, p. 169) It is a constant need because conflicts, differences, incompatible desires, perspectives and possibilities are ever present features of existence and experience. Some authority is therefore necessary, and for Dewey the supreme authority is intelli-

Reprinted with the permission of author and publisher from the November, 1971 issue of *Change* Magazine, pp. 22–26.

gence. It is "the method of intelligence, exemplified in [but not identical with] science, [that should be] supreme in education." (*Experience and Education*, p. 100) Intelligence recognizes that not all forms of conduct are possible or desirable, that restriction and negation are as central to any discipline as affirmation, and that the growth which prepares the way for further desirable growth can be achieved only through a limitation of possibilities. Freedom outside the context of the authority of intelligence is the license of anarchy. The democratic idea of freedom, Dewey tells us again and again, is *not* the right of each individual to do as he pleases; instead the "basic freedom is that of freedom of *mind* and of whatever degree of freedom of action and experience is necessary to produce freedom of intelligence." (*Problems of Men*, p. 61) Far from being an anti-intellectualist, he is more vulnerable—but only on a first glance—to the charge of intellectualism.

The second misconception of Dewey's philosophy—one more fateful because of its educational corollaries—is the equation drawn between education and experience. From this equation it is inferred that experience itself is educative, and that any series of experiences—the more direct and dynamic the better—can be substituted for formal schooling, which is often disparaged as an artificial experience. Experiences of travel and living away from school are often considered as appropriate substitutes for study. In short, *having* an experience is identified with knowing or understanding it.

Dewey, however, makes a central distinction between experiences that are "educative" and experiences that are "non-educative" or "mis-educative." The first are those that result in increased power and growth, in informed conviction, and sympathetic attitudes of understanding, in learning how to face and meet new experiences with some sense of mastery, without fear or panic or relying on the treadmill of blind routine. The second may give excitement but not genuine insight, may result in a mechanical training or conditioning that incapacitates individuals when the situations encountered in life change and must be met by intelligent improvisation.

But is it not true, some critics counter, that Dewey believes that we learn by doing? And does not that mean that anything a child or student desires or decides to do inside or out of school is *ipso facto* educational? No, emphatically, no! Doing is a part of learning only when it is *directed by ideas which the doing tests*. Doing in Dewey's sense is the experimenting that is guided by an hypothesis, not the blind action that never reaches the level of an experiment. It is true that we learn by doing: it is not true that all doing is a form of learning.

The fallacy that converts Dewey's statement that "all genuine education comes about through experience" into the belief that "all experiences are genuinely educational" is reflected today in two kinds of curricular abuse in our liberal arts colleges. The first is the tendency to assume that any subject matter is as good as any other subject matter for educational purposes and that all intellectual standards or hierarchies or grades of achievement and excellence merely reflect traditional prejudices that must be swept aside from the standpoint of the egalitarian ethic of a democratic education. This is a point of view held unfortunately not only by students eager to reform or reconstitute the curriculum but by some members of the faculty. One recent college reader titled *Starting Over*, apparently making a fresh start to get away from the prejudices of the past, declares in its preface to these selected readings: "We don't rule out the possibility that Lenny Bruce may have more to teach us than Alfred North Whitehead." They do not indicate *what* we can learn from Lenny Bruce that is of such moment that it dwarfs the many things that one can learn from Whitehead. Dewey, on the other hand, insists that "the central problem of an education based on experience is to select the kind of present experiences that live fruitfully and creatively in subsequent experiences." (*Experience and Education*, p. 17)

Dewey has two basic principles which still provide the direction for continued criticism not only of existing practices but of any proposed reforms: first, an equal concern that *all* children in the community develop themselves by appropriate schooling to the full reach of their powers and growth as persons; and second, a reliance upon the best available scientific methods in the psychology of learning to discover the means, methods and materials by which this growth can best be achieved in the case of each individual child.

It should be obvious how absurd it is to attribute to Dewey a belief that *only* the child is important in the teaching process and not the subject matters that he is taught, and that therefore it is relatively unimportant what he is taught or what his present experiences are so long as they are enjoyed. What Dewey is saying simply is that unless we take into account the "powers and purposes of those taught," their needs, capacities, attention spans and related phenomena, we cannot rely on the alleged inherent educational value of any subject to become meaningfully acquired in the child's present experience. Enjoyment, of course, is an aid, not a drawback to learning, but it should come from interest and growing absorption in the tasks and problems to be mastered. He does not believe we can substitute for a sound psychology of learning a set of hunches, intuitions and impressionistic anecdotal accounts of what has occurred in teaching highly selected children in special circumstances without any objective controls. But the latter constitute the stock in trade of much of the recent writing of our school critics, who totally disregard the danger of extrapolating techniques and methods from episodic learning situations to a public school system that must provide structured and sequential courses of study. Their familiar assertion that because children learn to speak and walk without formal schooling they can learn almost anything else they need to know in the same way, is evidence of how dogma can put out the eyes of common sense. It is not even true in most cases for learning how to read and write, divide and multiply. There are some skills which if not acquired when young by formal schooling are rarely completely mastered in later years.

The greatest damage of the new dogmas that equate experience and education is apparent not only in what students are offered in the way of courses, and materials within courses, but what they are often permitted to do in fulfillment of their academic responsibilities. Much of this is covered by the euphemisms of "field work" or "independent study." These must be sharply distinguished from the clinical experience that is essential to the acquisition of knowledge and skills in many scholarly and professional areas. Genuine clinical experience is related to a definite body of knowledge or set of techniques that the student tests or applies in concrete situations continuous with those he will subsequently face; it is carefully supervised, the student's progress checked and evaluated so that he knows in what direction to continue. "Field work" today often means no field except what the student professes an interest in, and work means whatever he chooses to do.

The New York Times (April 26, 1971) revealed the kind of "field work" done at the New York State University College at Old Westbury under the presidency of Harris Wofford. According to this uncontested report, the independent study which students were allowed to pursue embraced:

Almost any project that was neither illegal nor hazardous. Among selected topics were 'Migrant Camps and Workers,' 'Liberation of the Ghetto Through Economics,' 'Film Study,' 'Guitar—Country Blues,' 'The Craft of Sewing' . . . One student's project was called 'Creative Candle-Making—learning how to (appreciate) and making candles.' The professor's role in this five credit project was 'to look at my candles when I make them and receive several as gifts' . . . The project of one woman student, for five credits, was called 'Poetry of Life.' Her project description reads as follows:

Now I hear beautiful music. Then I paint a mind picture. Later I walk in the wood. Reverently I study my wood, know it. Converse with a poet meaningful to me. Make Love.

These oddities undoubtedly are not representative of all institutions that offer "field work," although the chief architect of this curriculum was rewarded by being offered a post at a more prestigious educational institution. But Old Westbury marks a growing tendency to substitute a period of mere lived experience for a period of academic study. Unless undertaken in connection with a structured course of study and intelligently supervised by faculty it would be far better to terminate academic study at the point where the student is ready "to do his own thing," and hopefully earn his own living.

The issues I am discussing are raised in a fundamental way when any general requirements are proposed for educational institutions. The new critics of education are against all requirements on the ground that needs are personal and that students are the best judges of their educational needs. I find a threefold confusion in this point of view: the tendency to assume that, first, desire and impulse are synonymous with need; second, when not synonymous, desire is an unfailing index of need; and third, because needs are personal, they are unique and necessarily subjective.

Impulse and desire may sometimes be an expression of need, and desire is often a consequence of frustrated impulse. But our common experience shows that we sometimes desire things we don't need and that we sometimes, especially in an educational context, discover what we really need only when we have ascertained what our purposes are. One may need to acquire certain skills and knowledge in order to achieve a purpose. Therefore as Dewey puts it, "the crucial educational problem is that of procuring the postponement of immediate action upon desire until observation and judgment have intervened." (*Education & Experience*, p. 81) Like Hume, Dewey believes that desires are the ultimate moving springs of action, but unlike Hume, he holds that we need not be enslaved by our desires, that they can be governed, modified, sublimated.

If this is true, desire is not always an unfailing index of genuine need. It depends on how and when the desire is expressed and whether our intelligence has disclosed the price to be paid in present and future for acting on it.

Finally, even if it is true that human needs are personal and individual, it doesn't follow that the student is the best judge of them or is even always aware of the needs required by his purposes. One can draw an analogy here with the medical needs a person has who wishes to live a healthy life. It does not follow that because they are *his* needs, they may not also be common to others. Nor does it follow that he necessarily is the best judge of them. They are objective needs even if they are personal needs, and the physician is usually the better judge of them than the patient.

Let us apply this to the educational scene, particularly since the new progressive critics of education encourage the present student generation to assert itself against its "exploiters." Students demand the right to select their own courses on every level, and with a kind of democratic belligerence inquire: "Who are *you* to tell me, a grown person of 16 or 18 years of age, what my educational needs are? How can you prate about democracy in education? After all, I am neither an infant nor an idiot!" To which I believe we can reasonably answer:

We are qualified, professional educators who have been studying the educational needs of our students and our culture for many years. We gladly indicate what we believe your educational needs are and are prepared to set forth the grounds on which we select them, inviting your critical response. For example, we believe that you and your fellow students have a need to communicate clearly and effectively, to acquire a command of your own language oral and written, no matter what your subsequent educational experience or career will be. You have that need whether you are presently aware of it or not. We believe you have a need to understand the essentials concerning the nature of your own bodies and mind, for what you don't know about these matters—as the current drug culture indicates—may hurt you, even kill you. Again, we believe that you have a need to understand something of the history of your own society, the political and economic forces shaping its future—all the more so because you have already indicated that you are aflame with reformist and revolutionary zeal to alter society.

Surely you must understand the conditioning social, political, and technological factors of any social change that hopes to improve on the past. Your unwillingness to learn about these crucial matters would cast doubts on the sincerity of your professions. It was Karl Marx who pointed out to William Weitling that ignorance is not a revolutionary virtue. We believe that you have other intellectual needs that are requisite to the proper performance of your function as a citizen, especially now that you are or will soon be of voting age. These needs you have in common with all other students, and the courses we require are those designed to meet them. We welcome your suggestions. Of course, you have other educational needs that are not common but personal and reflect your own special aptitudes, interests and aspirations. Here we are prepared to guide you, and help you fashion your own educational purposes and curriculum. Gradually you must take complete responsibility for your own education. When you do, your decisions are more likely to be sensible if they are informed.

Most of the criticisms the new progressive critics make of the educational establishment have been launched from what they declare to be democratic and humanist premises. I want to say a few things about the roles proposed for students and teachers in the democratic reconstitution of institutions of higher learning. Does a commitment to democracy require or justify the recent demands that students have almost as great an influence as the faculty in deciding the curriculum and operating the university?

We must make some crucial distinctions. In the first instance democracy is a political concept. In a political democracy, however, it does not follow that all the major social institutions can or should be run on politically democratic lines according to which each individual counts for one and no more than one, and where a numerical majority makes a decision that binds the entire community. In a political democracy the army, the church, the museum, the orchestra, the family and the school cannot be organized in a *politically* democratic manner if these institutions are to perform their proper specific functions. There is, to be sure, a sense in which we can speak of a democratic family, of a democratic army, orchestra or university. This is the moral sense. This requires in the family, for example, not that children have an equal vote on all questions affecting them but that they be treated with respect, listened to, given rational answers to their questions and not humiliated by arbitrary decisions. In a school or university the spirit of democracy can prevail, without students functioning as citizens do in the larger political community, by devising modes of participation that will make their educational experience more meaningful and without establishing a preposterous equation of intellectual authority between the learned and the unlearned, the mature and the immature. Such an equation is never drawn between masters and apprentices in any field, and in the field of education the overwhelming majority of students, except on advanced graduate levels, cannot be realistically regarded as apprentices.

Without vesting students with educational power equal to that of the faculty, they are always to be treated as persons, always consulted, always listened to, and given responsibilities commensurate with their growth and maturity in those areas where they have competence until they can take over their own education.

This brings me finally to the role of the teacher in education. Only those unfamiliar with Dewey's work can believe that he rejects the active role of the teacher in planning the classroom experience by properly organized subject matters. The teacher must have, he writes, "a positive and leading share in the direction of the activities of the [classroom] community." (*Experience & Education,* p. 66) Because he eschews the role of a drill master and refrains from imposing adult demands upon the growing child, the teacher's task is more difficult, requiring more intelligence and consequently more subtle and complex planning than was required in the days when pedagogues ruled with loud voice and big stick.

Some of the recent critics of education give the impression that all that is required for good teaching is a loving heart, that most courses in preparation for teaching are a waste, and that not only in teaching, but in all other vocations and professions, individuals learn best by the apprentice method or on the job. That anybody can teach something is probably true, but that anybody can become a *good* teacher merely by teaching on the job is demonstrably false. We may not be preparing teachers properly, but the remedy is not the abandonment of preparation and greater reliance upon volunteers and paraprofessionals but in the improvement of that preparation.

In assessing and selecting teachers, whatever other qualities and skills are sought, one should look for a sense of concern on the part of teachers, especially on the lower levels of instruction, and a sense of mission on all levels. By a sense of concern I mean something stronger than interest and less than affection. A teacher cannot love all children, and most children, except those that *are* genuinely preferred and loved, can see through the pretense of the profession, for they know that genuine love is discriminatory. Paul Goodman asserts that one must either love students or resent them, but this is typical of his false disjunctions. The good teacher respects all of his students, is concerned about them and recognizes his equal responsibility for the educational growth of all of them.

The teacher's sense of mission is troublesome, because it can easily be transformed into an indoctrinating zeal that uses the classroom for purposes foreign to the process of learning. Dewey was unalterably opposed to indoctrination, political or otherwise. He was aware of the great social reforms and reconstructions that were necessary in order for the schools to realize the moral ideals of the democratic society, and as a citizen he was always in the forefront of the battle for reform. But all the schools could legitimately do was "to form attitudes which will express themselves in intelligent social action." This, he says, "is something very different from indoctrination" (*Problems of Men*, p. 56) because intelligence, alone of all virtues, is self-critical. Only those indoctrinate who are unable or unwilling to establish their conclusions by intelligent inquiry. Dewey was confident that if his views about men and society had merit they would be recognized as valid by those whom the schools—in the proper exercise of their educational function—had taught to study and deal with the social world and its problems responsibly, i.e., intelligently, scientifically, conscientiously. He would have regarded any attempt to indoctrinate students with his own doctrines and proposals as an arrant betrayal of his educational philosophy.

The effort today to politicize schools and universities from within is foolish for many reasons, the most obvious being its counter-productive character. For nothing is more likely to bring about the politicizing of the university from without, and from a perspective extremely uncongenial to that of the new progressive critics of education. In combatting this internal politicizing, one of the most formidable problems is coping with the teacher who regards his class as a staging ground for revolutionizing society or for disrupting the local community if its norms of social morality fall short of his notions of the good society. In pursuit of a political commitment, he is often led to abandon elementary principles of professional ethics, and sometimes to deny in an apology for his political mission that any distinction can be drawn between objective teaching and indoctrination.

The following passage appears in a publication of Teachers College (*Perspectives in Education*, Fall, 1969), where John Dewey formulated the principles of education for a free society:

It is the task of the teacher to educate—to educate for change—to educate through change. To educate for orderly planned revolution. If necessary to educate through more disruptive revolutionary action.

John Dewey would have been the first to repudiate this travesty of the role of a teacher in a free society. The task of the teacher is to educate students to their maximum growth as perceptive, informed and reflective persons so that they can decide intelligently for themselves *what* is to be changed, *where* and *how*. It is not the teacher's function to indoctrinate his students in behalf of any cause no matter how holy, to brainwash them into becoming partisans of revolution or counter-revolution. To declare as this teacher does—and unfortunately he is not alone—that students are to be educated for and through "disruptive revolutionary action" is to declare oneself morally and pedagogically unfit to inhabit the academy of reasoning.

John Dewey's philosophy is not understood in many of the places where he is honored as well as in many of the places he is denounced. He is not the father of permissiveness, nor the prophet of life adjustment. We can still learn from him without assuming that he said the last word about our problems in school or out. For him democracy was not merely a set of political mechanisms but a way of life in which we use all the arts of intelligence and imagination in behalf of human freedom.

WHO NEEDS SCHOOLS?

JOHN H. FISCHER

John H. Fischer is a highly experienced schoolman. He began his educational career as a teacher in the Baltimore public schools and twenty-three years later became superintendent of schools in the same city. His support for desegregation in public schools during his administration was widely recognized and hailed. He became dean of Teachers College, Columbia University, and has been president of Teachers College since 1962.

In calm and reasoned terms, Fischer sets forth the case for improvement rather than abandonment of public schools. He concludes that for a variety of practical and theoretical reasons public schools are definitely needed.

For all the turmoil of the Sixties—the excitement, the demonstrations, the revolutionary rhetoric—the decade now ended has brought little actual alteration in most schools. To be sure, the atmosphere has changed. Students' hair is longer, their clothing scruffier, and their language less inhibited. The teachers, too, seem different. They are more outspoken, better organized, and less compliant than they were. But the institutional character of schools—their purposes, forms, and functions—look in 1970 much as they did in 1960.

What has happened during these ten years is that pressures of the sort that produce and usually must precede institutional change have accumulated to the point where significant reforms are not only possible but inevitable. Whether or not, recalling George Counts's query of the 1930s, the schools will dare now to build a new social order, the social order appears ready to rebuild the schools.

Predicting the schools of tomorrow has long been an attractive pastime for scholars, pundits, and prophets, but today the ordinary citizen is coming into the act. Although agreement on the kinds of schools we need is still something less than unanimous, parents, taxpayers, and voters do seem to agree that the schools are less effective than they ought to be. The current dissatisfaction is more than the chronic criticism to which schools and teachers are normally subjected, for it reflects a growing sense that the whole system needs overhauling. However widely they may differ in their premises and purposes, conservative elders and radical youngsters alike insist that American education, as it now operates, is not responding as it should to the problems of modern society.

The most impressive evidence of the new attitude is an increasing willingness to consider solutions that heretofore would have been unthinkable—among them the abandonment of public schools. Middleclass city families began some years ago to express their preferences; by the thousands they are removing their children from the public schools and competing desperately and at high cost for the limited places available in private schools. Ghetto parents, sick and tired of condescending and recalcitrant school officials, are battling them for control of the schools in their own neighborhoods. Minority groups are organizing store-front centers and street academies to give their children a better chance of making it. Some of the alternatives, such as the Job Corps and the Neighborhood Youth Corps, take the form of programs to rehabilitate the casualties of the school system. Many aspects of the educational activities of the armed forces, industry, and the unions are merely extensions, under other auspices, of functions that a properly conducted school system could and should be expected to provide.

Even the affluent suburbs that have long supported elaborate and expensive public school programs are now rejecting bond issues and higher budgets. The shortage of money is obviously one factor, but another, clearly, is a growing disbelief that the schools are giving proper value for the money put into them. And in Washington, the White House insists that before more federal funds are committed to education, ways must be found to get more for the taxes already being spent.

One result of the complaints is the proposal that alternative schools be established to compete with public institutions. A particularly bold venture is the so-called "voucher plan," which, ideally, would enable every child to attend whatever school his parents choose for him. With the pupil would go a voucher entitling his school to the amount of money appropriated per pupil in the local school budget. By thus expanding the options available to parents, the proponents of vouchering mean to stimulate creation of new independent schools, free of the inertia of public school bureaucracies and not inhibited by the traditional constraints of existing private schools. A major consequence envisioned by the proponents of this plan is the rapid reform of public institutions. The hope is that public school authorities would be persuaded by the pressure of competition to change their ways—or else, "else" meaning a precipitate loss of pupils and, with it, the money to pay teachers and administrators. A pilot program in vouchering will shortly begin under the auspices of the Center for the Study of Public Policy at Harvard and with the support of a grant from the Office of Economic Opportunity. It will be watched with interest by many observers and with more than a little apprehension by public school people.

Despite the enrollment of a sizable minority of children in nonpublic schools, elementary and secondary education in the United States is, for all practical purposes, a public monopoly. Aside from the 10 or 11 per cent whose parents prefer religious schools or can afford the tuition fees of independent schools, the sole course available to most families is to send their children to the public school designated by the local school board. Nor in most school districts and particularly in large cities can a parent exercise any effective influence on what his child learns, how he is taught, or how he is treated as a person in the public school he is required to attend. One need not be an enemy of public education to agree that the stimulus of real competition might produce more responsiveness and faster responses than years of public discussion and political pressure have so far achieved.

The issue whether schools should be publicly or privately controlled, competitive or monopolistic, is overshadowed, however, by a prior and more basic question: Are they necessary? While a flat negative answer would be as irresponsible as it would be shocking to most people, the question cannot be dismissed out of hand. For some children, schools of the types now most common are simply not appropriate institutions. The radical question must be raised, for it deserves a well-considered response. Extremist critics argue (usually, however, within a narrow context) that existing schools are so damaging to the development of children that no child should be required to attend them. Instead, they say, he should spend his time acquiring whatever he needs to learn directly from the culture in which he lives. Such participation, they argue, would be superior to current pedagogy and less harmful to the child's growth and personality. Technologists press the claim that teaching machines, television, and tape recorders are more effective than most teachers, and that the best arrangement of all would be a computer console in every home.

Others, skeptical about schools but still hooked on humans, advocate a system of child-care centers extending from age two or younger to the upper primary level and providing every child with a combination of services integrated to assure optimum physical, mental, emotional, and social development. Intellectual development is presumed to follow as a consequence of a suitably nurturing environment in which the child finds opportunity, stimulation, and reward. And unintentionally augmenting the company of those who deny the necessity for formal schooling are the teachers and administrators who endorse the contention that some children don't need schools. These are the people who every year suspend from school substantial numbers of children. They act on the ground that exceptional behavior, which demonstrates to some observers a clear need for competent instruction and intensive care, is really evidence that the public interest, if not the children's, is best served by excluding them from school.

Approaching the question from a somewhat different viewpoint are the advocates of "schools without walls." This group sees the process of schooling as more important than the place and holds that learning comes most profitably from experience in a variety of circumstances, exposures, and involvement. The community becomes the school, and whoever knows what the pupil wants to learn becomes his teacher. This is, of course, precisely the way most of us have learned the greater part of what we know. While estimates of the community's power to teach may divide the theorists, that power is a fact of life, and one too often ignored by school people in general and curriculum planners in particular.

The numerous proposals for replacing schools with less restrictive opportunities for learning include sound and promising ideas, a number of which are already being used and others of which might well be. But for attaining the goal of universal education they fall far short of the possibilities of a well-conceived and properly managed system of public education.

In the face of the sheer magnitude of the schoolgoing population, total conversion from public to independent sponsorship of education becomes impracticable. Moreover, every reform proposal that has been offered assumes that the cost, whether to support private schools through vouchers, provide electronic gadgetry in homes, or furnish transportation to museums, shops, offices, or zoos, will be borne by the public purse. The funds required, we may be sure, will not be distributed in the absence of public authorization, control, and accountability. Where public money goes, the public auditor inevitably follows, with guidelines, deadlines, and multicolored forms in quadruplicate.

If the target population remains, as obviously it must, "all the children of all the people," we shall continue to be involved in *public* education, together with the inescapable restraints of public policy and the customary controls on the use of tax funds. It does not necessarily follow, however, that the public is educable only through the public school system in its traditional and familiar form. The options already available—and others easily imaginable—are not limited to mutually exclusive choices between the public school as it now stands and the recently devised alternatives. The more promising possibility and one that could give genuine validity to the concept of community control is that we might develop varied—and readily changeable—institutions, programs, procedures, and schedules.

Any notion that the American people would consent, at the local level or on a broader scale, to liquidating the public school system is not what one could confidently call a betting proposition. It is wholly within the bounds of reality, however, that responsible proposals for opening out the schools to build reciprocal relationships with a wider world would be welcomed and supported. The current dissatisfaction with the existing system is exactly that: It is focused on the system. By no means does it imply to any significant degree a general rejection of education. On the contrary, there is convincing evidence that criticism of schools and teachers, among both youngsters and their parents, stems mainly from a pervasive desire for better, not less, education.

Possibly the most realistic projection of what had happened during the Sixties is that while only a few of the innovations may continue as alternatives to the public schools most of them will generate new and stronger pressures to compel change in the purposes, policies, and practices of the institutions we now possess and which, with alterations, we shall probably retain.

Out of the welter of irate demands, visionary campaigns, and authentically creative ideas for reforming education, certain recurring emphases are beginning to emerge with reasonable clarity. Through them run the dual threads of unifying purpose that have long characterized humane education: that every young person should find the means to make the most of whatever he has it in himself to become, and that simultaneously he should come to understand the world of man and nature deeply enough to want to live in it with responsibility and grace. The schools' most serious failing is not that they achieve these purposes imperfectly; they are, after all, only human agencies. The fault is, rather, that they deny so many young people even minimal opportunity to pursue the goals, much less to reach them.

To correct the weaknesses and close the gaps in present arrangements for educating our young people, it will not be enough to create a few exotic substitutes for public schools. The massive size of our youth population—of the disadvantaged minority alone—cannot be accommodated in a handful of exciting centers staffed by a small corps of dedicated enthusiasts. The response must be commensurate with the magnitude of the problem. What we need are not so much alternatives to the school system as fundamental alterations in that system. And these must begin with changes in the assumptions underlying present policy and practice.

The first assumption to be abandoned is the view that the schools' principal function is to screen and classify students. Ever since the acceptance of universal education as a valid social concept and a viable political commitment, educators have been caught on the horns of a dilemma. They have found it easy enough to agree that at the lowest academic levels schools should be open to all. But as soon as differences among pupils become evident, the question arises whether the schools' proper business is to promote learning among all or, having offered a common opportunity, to concentrate on those who respond most readily to standard instruction. The classic procedure for resolving the conflict has been to obscure it, arguing that the graded reward system by which most schools are managed is in any case the best stimulant to learning. Once that premise is accepted, it becomes eminently logical to reinforce the inducement of a more estimable future status by the threatened penalty of being "left back" for not making the grade. For a system intended, at least in principle, to be *both universal and educational,* a less effective—or efficient—scheme would be hard to contrive. The result is an institution that while educational for many is universal only in the sense that it permits all children to submit themselves to screening. The evidence is plentiful and conclusive that by using schools as sorting mechanisms we reject, psychologically and physically, vast numbers of children whose potentiality is neither determined nor developed. For others, who do manage after a fashion to survive, the overriding lesson learned in school is that education is a meaningless waste of time.

Yet, in all fairness, it must be conceded that as long as the public interest and private well-being both could be served by a low standard of common literacy and by the preparation of a small minority for the more demanding intellectual tasks, the sharply narrowing pyramid offered a workable model for an educational system. That such a model makes no sense today has become embarrassingly plain.

The question is how to do it, for the central issue is not so much one of techniques or policy as of definition—*the* definition, to put it most simply, of a good school. Learned disquisitions on the matter are legion, but for all the rhetoric the most widely held view is old and simple: A good school is a school full of good pupils—that is to say, pupils who, for whatever reason, could survive successive screenings. By the same token, when one found a class of such pupils, one was entitled to assume that he had also come upon an effective teacher. Whether the pupils' performance was due to heredity, fortunate homes, good health, or compliant dispositions was irrelevant. Accountability was easy and direct: Schools and teachers were given straightforward credit for the gross performance of their pupils and few other questions were asked.

Now we can no longer delay coming to grips with the essential queries: What kinds of difference should the school be expected to make in the learning, growth, and development of children? What factors in the school induce such differences? How can they be discovered? How are they best introduced, cultivated, recognized, and rewarded? It is to such problems that we must now direct attention, not to create a scattering of shining exceptions, but to revise the character of the entire educational system.

We could, however, fall into another fallacy were we to embark upon a search for the effective school in the hope of arriving at some optimum pattern that might then be replicated in ten thousand places. Long since, we should have learned that equality of opportunity—or of any other humane value—is rarely achieved through uniformity. The misconception that uniform treatment of people respects or promotes equality plagues in many situations. It persists with impressive vigor in public schools. Despite contrary protestations for the record, conformance with standard operating procedure remains more the rule than the exception in school management. In the design of buildings, the certification and selection of staff, the fixing of salaries, the construction of curriculums, the classification of pupils, and even the wording of diplomas, schools in general and the schools of any single district in particular are disconcertingly alike. Such differences as do distinguish schools reflect less often the planning and procedures instituted by staffs than the cultural backgrounds of children and the indigenous qualities of communities.

A fundamental problem all school policy makers confront is to get beyond the conventional platitudes in praise of individuality and to set up policies and supportive administrative schemes that truly facilitate originality, inventiveness, and initiative in the classroom and the school. One hardly needs to say that such changes do not come easily. The chief difficulty is not simply the hidebound behavior of superintendents, for a looser structure not only opposes assumptions long held by professionals and the public alike, but denies teachers and principals the support and comfort of the remote authority on which many of them habitually depend. Once the power of decision, together with equivalent responsibility and accountability, lodges in the school, the dynamics of control and criticism takes on a new format.

The current trend in large cities toward decentralized administration and community control may prove to be steps in a useful direction, but at best they will be only partial solutions. While these reforms are understandable and logical responses to present pressures, expecting too much of them could lead to disappointment and frustration. A school board and central administration responsible for thirty schools— or ten—may be less remote, but it can be just as restrictive as a central authority directing five hundred schools. Sooner or later we shall have to learn that what counts most in education is always what happens to the pupil in the school.

The development of collective bargaining, despite its power to enhance the status and improve the working conditions of teachers, could also become a threat to the freedom of individual schools to adapt to the requirements of local situations. What is called for, however, is not less bargaining or weak teacher organizations, but more imaginative contracts. The standard procedures and objectives of negotiation will have to be revised as radically as the outmoded practices of school boards and administrators.

The distinctive and attractive qualities of the alternative schools that have appeared recently are due in virtually every case to the broad latitude their teachers and directors enjoy in collaborating with community people and responding to children's needs. If, now, the means and the will can be found to give the faculty of every public school a substantial measure of such latitude and a similarly close identification with their clientele, while maintaining at the same time the stability of public financial support, we could be on our way toward the schools we need.

But while the education of the public cannot and should not be considered exclusively the province of the public school system, neither can it be left to the uncertain enthusiasms of voluntary enterprise. If we have learned anything about promoting the general welfare of the American people, it is that a fundamental factor in that effort is the power of education. The wise use of that power through humanely conceived and administered institutions must have first rank priority on the agenda at every governmental level. There is no more important segment of the public business. Yet, with due concern for the dangers of uniformity and monopoly, and with full appreciation of independent initiative, we must nonetheless insist that whatever else happens in education, the public schools be reformed, strengthened, and preserved.

CRISIS IN THE CLASSROOM

CHARLES E. SILBERMAN

Charles E. Silberman is a distinguished journalist and a first-rate scholar. His first major book, Crisis in Black and White (*New York: Random House, 1964*), *predicted and brilliantly analyzed some of the trends in black-white relationships which were currently emerging in America. His vigorous book,* Crisis in the Classroom, *is a spectacularly ambitious attempt to deal with American education as a whole.*

Silberman is critical of some of the compassionate critics. Yet they would endorse the overwhelming majority of the elementary school practices, and many of the secondary school procedures, that Silberman approves. However, he is fearful that the child-centered compassionate critics may oversimplify basic educational issues. One such issue which he repeatedly calls to the attention of his readers, as the excerpt which follows indicates, is the need for centrality of purpose and philosophy in education. He argues that the failure of the recent curriculum reform movement, which focused on rebuilding the separate academic disciplines, was related to the inability of scholars to recognize the central importance of the questions raised by the leaders of the progressive movement in education. He supplies a thoughtful epilogue to the decade of the 1960s which began with the subject reformers and ended with the compasionate critics—while the inescapable questions of the progressive persisted.

Silberman was on leave from Fortune *magazine while he directed the Carnegie Study of the Education of Educators.*

It is one thing to say that education must be purposeful; it is another to say what those purposes should be. The fashion in contemporary American writing about education holds that talk about purpose is a frightful bore. Dr. James B. Conant, probably the most prestigious and influential contemporary student of education, has confessed that "a sense of distasteful weariness overtakes" him whenever he hears someone discussing educational goals or philosophy. "In such a mood," he writes, "I am ready to define education as what goes on in schools and colleges"—a definition that has prevented him from asking whether what now goes on should go on. Martin Mayer, an influential educational journalist, is equally disdainful of talk about goals. "It is well to rid oneself of this business of the 'aims of education,'" he states flatly in his book *The Schools*. "Discussions on this subject are among the dullest and most fruitless of human pursuits."

But philosophical questions neither disappear nor resolve themselves by being ignored. Indeed, the question of purpose kept intruding itself throughout the course of the research, and even more, through the course of the writing. Writing is always painful, for it is a continuous process of dialogue with oneself, of confrontation with one's thoughts, ideas, and feelings. "As is true of any writing that comes out of one's own existence," Lillian Smith has said—and no serious writing can entirely avoid that source—"the experiences themselves [are] transformed during the act of writing by awareness of new meanings which settled down on them . . . the writer transcends her material in the act of looking at it, and since part of that material is herself, a metamorphosis takes place: *something happens within:* a new chaos, and then slowly, a new being." [Emphasis hers]

It was not until I was well into the writing, therefore—not until I had, over a summer, completed and abandoned a first crude draft— that I began to realize what a metamorphosis had taken place in me and in my thinking about education. In struggling to find my theme, I discovered that my views had changed profoundly. I had not thought hard enough about educational purpose until the agony of writing forced me to; I thought I *knew* what the purpose of education should be: namely, intellectual development. "The United States today is moving away from progressivism," I had argued in 1961, and still believed when I started the study, "not because it is 'false' in some absolute sense, but because it badly serves the needs of our own time. The growing complexity of organization and the explosive pace of technological and social change are creating an enormous demand that is without historical precedent. Society has always needed a few men with highly developed and disciplined intellects; industrial society needed masses of literate but not necessarily intellectual men. Tomorrow requires something that the world has never seen—*masses of intellectuals.*" [Emphasis in the original][1] . . .

. . . I am indignant at the banality of the mass media: no one concerned with the quality of American life can avoid a sense of sickening disappointment over the Vast Wasteland that public as well as commercial television has turned out to be. Nor can much more satisfaction be derived from contemplating the rest of the mass media. I am indignant, too, at the narcissism of so many college professors and admin-

[1] Charles E. Silberman, "The Remaking of American Education," *Fortune*, April 1961.

istrators who, at least until prodded by student rebels, refused to think about the nature and content of liberal education, particularly about the ways in which knowledge may have to be reordered to make it teachable to a new generation. And I am indignant at the smug disdain with which most academicians view the problems of the public schools.

Most of all, however, I am indignant at the failures of the public schools themselves. "The most deadly of all possible sins," Erik Erikson suggests, "is the mutilation of a child's spirit." It is not possible to spend any prolonged period visiting public school classrooms without being appalled by the mutilation visible everywhere—mutilation of spontaneity, of joy in learning, of pleasure in creating, of sense of self. The public schools—those "killers of the dream," to appropriate a phrase of Lillian Smith's—are the kind of institution one cannot really dislike until one gets to know them well. Because adults take the schools so much for granted, they fail to appreciate what grim, joyless places most American schools are, how oppressive and petty are the rules by which they are governed, how intellectually sterile and esthetically barren the atmosphere, what an appalling lack of civility obtains on the part of teachers and principals, what contempt they unconsciously display for children as children.

And it need not be! Public schools *can* be organized to facilitate joy in learning and esthetic expression and to develop character—in the rural and urban slums no less than in the prosperous suburbs. This is no utopian hope; as I shall argue and demonstrate in the chapters that follow, there are models now in existence that can be followed.

What makes change possible, moreover, is that what is mostly wrong with the public schools is due not to venality or indifference or stupidity, but to mindlessness. To be sure, teaching has its share of sadists and clods, of insecure and angry men and women who hate their students for their openness, their exuberance, their color or their affluence. But by and large, teachers, principals, and superintendents are decent, intelligent, and caring people who try to do their best by their lights. If they make a botch of it, and an uncomfortably large number do, it is because it simply never occurs to more than a handful to ask *why* they are doing what they are doing—to think seriously or deeply about the purposes or consequences of education. . . .

If mindlessness is the central problem, the solution must lie in infusing the various educating institutions with purpose, more important, with thought about purpose, and about the ways in which techniques, content, and organization fulfill or alter purpose. And given the tendency of institutions to confine day-to-day routine with purpose, to transform the means into the end itself, the infusion cannot be a one-shot affair. The process of self-examination, of "self-renewal," to use John Gardner's useful term, must be continuous. We must find ways of stimulating educators—public school teachers, principals, and superintendents; college professors, deans, and presidents; radio, television, and film directors and producers; newspaper, magazine, and TV journalists and executives—to think about what they are doing, and why they are doing it. And we must persuade the general public to do the same. . . .

One need only sit in the classrooms, in fact, and examine the texts and reading lists to know that, with the possible exception of mathematics, the curriculum reform movement has made a pitifully small impact on classroom practice. The criteria for deciding what should be in the curriculum, Jerome Bruner of Harvard, one of the chief architects of curriculum reform, has suggested, should be to ask "whether, when fully developed, [the subject or material] is worth an adult's knowing, and whether having known it as a child makes a person a better adult. If the answer to both questions is negative or ambiguous, then the material is cluttering the curriculum."[2]

The answer is negative to both questions for an incredibly high proportion of the elementary and secondary school curriculum. There is a great deal of chatter, to be sure, about teaching students the structure of each discipline, about teaching them how to learn, about teaching basic concepts, about "postholing," i.e., teaching fewer things but in greater depth. But if one looks at what actually goes on in the classroom—the kinds of texts students read and the kind of homework they are assigned, as well as the nature of classroom discussion and the kinds of tests teachers give—he will discover that the great bulk of students' time is still devoted to detail, most of it trivial, much of it factually incorrect, and almost all of it unrelated to any concept, structure, cognitive strategy, or indeed anything other than the lesson plan. It is rare to find anyone—teacher, principal, supervisor, or superintendent—who has asked why he is teaching what he is teaching. . . .

What happened? Why did a movement that aroused such great hopes, and that enlisted so many distinguished educators, exert so little impact on the schools?

A large part of the answer is that what was initially regarded as the curriculum reform movement's greatest strength—the fact that its prime movers were distinguished university scholars and teachers—has proven to be its greatest weakness. In part because the movement was based in the scholarly disciplines, in part because it grew out of the scholars' revulsion against the vulgarization of progressive education and against the anti-intellectualism that that vulgarization in turn had spawned, the reformers by and large ignored the experiences of the past, and particularly of the reform movement of the 1920s and '30s.

[2] Jerome S. Bruner, *The Process of Education* (Cambridge: Harvard University Press, 1960). Bruner's book was perhaps the most important and influential to come out of the curriculum reform movement.

They were, therefore, unaware of the fact that almost everything they said had been said before, by Dewey, Whitehead, Bode, Rugg, etc.; and they were unaware that almost everything they tried to do had been tried before, by educators like Frederick Burk, Carleton Washburne, and Helen Parkhurst, not to mention Abraham Flexner and Dewey himself.[3]

One result of this failure to study educational history, particularly the history of progressivism's successes and failures, was that the contemporary reformers repeated one of the fundamental errors of the progressive movement: they perpetuated the false dichotomy that the schools must be *either* child-centered *or* subject-centered. Ignoring the warnings of men like Dewey, Boyd Bode, Harold Rugg, and Carleton Washburne, the progressive reformers had opted for the former; their preoccupation with child-centeredness made them content, in Dewey's phrase, "with casual improvisation and living intellectually hand to mouth." It was this "absence of intellectual control through significant subject-matter," Dewey wrote, "which stimulates the deplorable egotism, cockiness, impertinence and disregard for the rights of others apparently considered by some persons to be the inevitable accompaniment, if not the essence, of freedom."[4]

The reformers of the 1950s and '60s made the same mistake, except that they opted for the other side of the dichotomy. They placed almost all their emphasis on subject matter, i.e., on creating "great compositions," and for the most part ignored the needs of individual children. As Dewey wrote of the progressive educators whose onesidedness he deplored, the new reformers "conceive of no alternative to adult dictation save child dictation." Reacting against the banality that child-dictated education had become, they opted for adult dictation. They knew what they wanted children to learn; they did not think to ask what children wanted to learn. Some of the reformers, however, now realize their error. Thus it was Zacharias, at the 1965 White House Conference on Education, who made a passionate plea that educators think about children and their needs.

Because the reformers were university scholars with little contact with public schools or schools of education, moreover, and because they also neglected to study the earlier attempts at curriculum reform, they also tended to ignore the harsh realities of classroom and school organization. The courses they created were, and are, vastly superior to the

[3] Cf. Lawrence A. Cremin, *The Transformation of the School* and *The Genius of American Education*: John I. Goodlad, "Curriculum: A Janus Look," *Teachers College Record*, November 1968; J. Stuart Maclure, *Curriculum Innovation in Practice*, Third International Curriculum Conference, Oxford (Her Majesty's Stationery Office, 1968); Patricia A. Graham, *Progressive Education: From Arcady to Academe* (New York: Teachers College Press, 1967); Harold Rugg and Ann Shumaker, *The Child-Centered School: An Appraisal of the New Education* (New York: World Book Co., 1928).
[4] John Dewey, "How Much Freedom in New Schools?" *The New Republic*, July 9, 1930.

tepid and banal fare most students now receive. But without changing the ways in which schools operate and teachers teach, changing the curriculum alone does not have much effect.[5]

To some degree, this error reflected the reformers' innocence and naïveté. Because they had so little firsthand experience with the elementary or secondary school classroom (in contrast to most of the great figures of the progressive movement), they somehow assumed that students would learn what the teachers taught; that is, if teachers presented the material in the proper structure, students would learn it that way. Thus, they assumed implicitly that teaching and learning are merely opposite sides of the same coin. But they are not, as we have seen in Chapter 4.

The error reflected academic hubris as well: not content with ignoring the classroom teacher, the reformers, in effect, tried to bypass the teacher altogether. Their goal, sometimes stated, sometimes implicit, was to construct "teacher-proof" materials that would "work" whether teachers liked the materials or not or taught them well or badly. "With the kind of casual arrogance only professors can manage, when they conceived of lower schools," Dean Robert J. Schaefer writes, the curriculum reformers' goal was "to produce materials which permit scholars to speak directly to the child." They viewed teachers, if they thought of them at all, as technicians, and they conceived of the schools, Schaefer suggests, as "educational dispensaries—apothecary shops charged with the distribution of information and skills deemed beneficial to the social, vocational, and intellectual health of the immature. The primary business of a dispensary," Schaefer continues, "is to dispense—not to raise questions or to inquire into issues as to how drugs might be more efficiently administered, and certainly not to assume any authority over what ingredients should be mixed."[6]

The effort was doomed to failure. For one thing, the classroom teacher usually is in an almost perfect position to sabotage a curriculum he finds offensive—and teachers are not likely to have a high regard for courses designed to bypass them. For another, many of the "teacher-proof" curricula have turned out to be more difficult to teach than the courses they replaced; certainly the "discovery method" makes far more demands on the teacher than does rote drill or lecturing. But insofar as they thought about in-service education of teachers, the reformers tended to assume that the problem was to get teachers to know—to really know—the subject they were teaching. This was crucial, of

[5] Cf., for example, Blythe Clinchy, "School Arrangements," In Jerome Bruner, ed., Learning About Learning: A Conference Report, U.S. Office of Education, Cooperative Research Monograph No. 15. The Clinchy essay is one of thirty in this volume; it is the only one directly concerned with the ways in which schools and classrooms operate.

[6] Robert J. Schaefer, The School as a Center of Inquiry. (New York: Harper & Row, 1967).

course, but experience with National Defense Education Act Institutes and the like have made it painfully clear that mastering the subject matter does not begin to solve the problem of how to teach it.

The failure to involve ordinary classroom teachers in the creation and modification of the new curricula, moreover, tended to destroy, or at least inhibit, the very spirit of inquiry the new courses were designed to create. Curriculum designers are not likely to attract students to the life of the mind if they fail to entice the students' teachers as well. "How can youngsters be convinced of the vitality of inquiry and discovery," Dean Schaefer asks, "if the adults with whom they directly work are mere automatons who shuffle papers, workbooks, and filmstrips according to externally arranged schedules?" Since the spirit of inquiry "necessitates a live sense of shared purpose and commitment," the teachers *must* participate in the scholar's search if the effort is to succeed.

The most fatal error of all, however, was the failure to ask the questions that the giants of the progressive movement always kept at the center of their concern, however inadequate some of their answers may have been: What is education for? What kind of human beings and what kind of society do we want to produce? What methods of instruction and classroom organization, as well as what subject matter, do we need to produce these results? What knowledge is of most worth?[7]

---

[7] Cf. especially Lawrence A. Cremin, *The Genius of American Education*, and John I. Goodlad, "Curriculum: A Janus Look."

PART TWO

CURRICULAR
ALTERNATIVES

*In American education, books and articles are
sometimes written advocating and defending
certain educational positions. Sometimes such
books and articles are read and discussed, yet
the basic ideas advanced are not put into
practice. Consequently, the authors'
contentions have little effect; sometimes they
must await rediscovery by later generations.*

*However, this was not the case with the
writings of the compassionate critics included
in Part One of this book. In part because of
the persuasiveness of their views, in part
because of the wide dissemination of their
ideas through the mass media, and in part
because of favorable surrounding social
circumstances, their views were acted upon by
implementers in the late 1960s and early
1970s. Therefore a new part, "Curricular
Alternatives," is included in this revision of*
Curriculum: Quest for Relevance.

Across the country in the later 1960s there

grew up schools variously termed "free," or "alternative," or "open," or "informal." In a wide variety of physical and geographical surroundings, individual educators or small groups of committed people attempted to bring about their versions of what the compassionate critics were advocating and what the nature of society and the individual human person seemed to require.

At first the experimentation with alternatives took place almost exclusively in the private sector of American education. A variety of ingenious approaches were used to initiate small and often short-lived private alternative schools.

In the 1970s, however, there came a development in the growth of alternatives in education which as yet has scarcely been recognized. Some of the public schools which had been under the vitriolic fire of both the compassionate critics and the critics of compulsory schooling began to adapt to some of the new demands. With surprising resilience for so veteran and harassed an institution, the public school system in America began to co-opt some of the basic ideas of its hostile critics. The public sector of education did not go so far as to join a crusade against compulsory public education—obviously, no institution is likely to support its own abolition! But some public school systems began to compensate for the meaninglessness experienced by some students through the development of "schools without walls," individualized programs, mini-courses, etc. True, the new developments were relatively infrequent, and some of them had an air of tokenism about them; yet it was obvious that all public school systems were not about to passively accept the blasts of the critics. Some school systems began to offer alternatives.

Meanwhile, open education was becoming increasingly accepted in American public education. The idea of open education is close kin to the idea of alternative education. Open education stems in part from the progressive tradition in education discussed by this editor in the first article of this anthology, "Is Progressive Education Obsolete?" The rediscovery came about partially through the compassionate critics and partially through experimentation in British Infant Schools. Surviving the transatlantic crossing, open or informal education returned to America via scholarly reports and Charles E. Silberman's book, Crisis in the Classroom, *which popularized its British practice and its American beginnings. Open education was encouraged in its growth by educational and psychological leaders who stressed the need for humanized education and by educational organizations such as the Association for Supervision and Curriculum Development.*

So a movement to develop alternatives to conventional and traditional education in American schools has been relaunched in recent years. The movement is still so new that it has not yet settled upon a single name, as the varied vocabularies of our authors graphically demonstrate. Though all agree on sharp dissatisfaction with the status quo in education, the proposed approaches are as varied as their sponsors' ideologies. It is reasonable to expect that some alternatives will break genuinely new ground and others will simply naively reproduce errors of past infantile ventures. For instance, it is probable that the better of the programs, such as Philadelphia's Parkway School approach, will probably be given a black eye by the worst, even as well balanced programs of progressive education from the 1920s through the 1940s were given a black eye by sentimental and inadequate programs which were purportedly "progressive."

Consequently, it is healthy that some leaders who are respected in the movement toward alternatives and openness are speaking up with cautions and reminders. This is not an easy role to play, for such critics are sometimes regarded by their fellows as betrayers of the faith. Friendly criticisms, too, are sometimes borrowed by hostile critics for purposes of total condemnation. However, just as John Dewey during the 1930s in Experience and Education criticized his colleagues in progressive education, today in education self-criticism is expressed by supporters of alternative or open education.

The implementation of criticisms of education through the development of alternatives is chronicled in the completely new Part Two of this second edition of Curriculum: Quest for Relevance, along with some friendly cautions and reminders.

"Curricular alternatives" begins with an account of the rise of free schools as perceived by a highly competent freelance writer. As Bonnie Barrett Stretch points out, "They turn up anywhere—in city store fronts, old barns, former barracks, abandoned church buildings, and parents' or teachers' homes. They have crazy names like Someday School, Viewpoint Non-School, A Peck of Gold, The New Community, or New Directions—names that for all their diversity reflect the two things most of these schools have in common: the idea of freedom for youngsters and a humane education."

Even now, when alternative schools are discussed, the educational community thinks largely in terms of schools marked by private control and funding. Yet, conceivably, the most exciting development with respect to alternatives is the attempt at adaptation by American public school systems. The development is important not because the adaptation is as yet widespread but because of the potential of alternatives in the public school sector embracing millions upon millions of students in contrast to the limited enrollment of the private alternative schools.

By 1973, some chroniclers of the nonpublic free schools were recognizing that "when compared with the 50 million kids still in public schools, the 13,000 free school students comprise much less than 1% of all school-age children, and that's far from the dreams that started this *whole effort,"* as Robert D. Barr, co-director of the Educational Alternatives Project at Indiana University, put it. Barr sees promise in the development of options in public education. He calls for selection of learning experiences from a wide variety of educational options both in the public schools and in the free schools.

Mario D. Fantini, currently Dean of the Faculty of Education, State University College, New Paltz, New York, sees promise in what he terms *public schools of choice,* as an approach to alternatives in education. In *"Alternatives within Public Schools"* he argues for *"expanding the framework of public education to include a wide range of legitimate educational alternatives [as] the most feasible route to reforming our schools."* Fantini describes contemporary promising alternatives within public schools and suggests a strategy for legitimizing alternatives under the public school framework.

In Portland, Oregon, a group of experimental-minded educators created the program of John Adams High School. The first hundred days of the school are described by Trudy M. Johnson in The Teacher Paper *included here* (and by Allen L. Dobbins in an equally interesting article in Phi Delta Kappan, May 1971, *"Instruction at Adams,"* not reproduced here because of space limitations).

Recently Jerry Conrath, director of Quincy School, which is a school-within-a-school at John Adams High School, reported on present developments at John Adams. He describes the evolution of his own rejection of free schools and deschooling and his acceptance of a radical reform approach within the public school system.

In New York City, the John Dewey High School offered a program which had the combined support of two groups which have often been in opposition to each other: the New York City Board of Education and the United Federation of Teachers. The *"adventure"* of this school, as principal Sol Levine calls it, is reported here. The perceptive reader may be interested in examining the John Dewey High School program in the context of the later remarks made by Alexander Frazier concerning the new freedom and the new fundamentalism. He may wish to speculate on whether the John Dewey High School reconciles both of these approaches or tends in one or the other direction.

The Philadelphia public schools have experimented with two equally innovating and yet quite different approaches to alternatives within a public school system. The *"school without walls"* concept developed under the leadership of John H. Bremer is not included in this book of readings because it has been widely disseminated. Perhaps less well known is the venture into affective education; co-director Terry Borton describes this and similar programs in the pages which follow.

Chicago, too, has experimented with the *"school without walls"* concept, as the article by principal Nathaniel Blackman (included

here) indicates. Perhaps the widest variety of experimentation with
alternatives, however, has taken place within the Berkeley, California,
public school system. The 24 types of schools described by freelance
writer Diane Divoky are bewildering in their variety and apparently
diverse in their effectiveness.

Open education has many dimensions, including space and time
utilization. Here we are particularly concerned about its curriculum
manifestations and we have chosen Alexander Frazier, who combines
both reportorial and analytical skills, to examine open education
programs.

We also have selected for your consideration five cautions and
reminders on alternative and open education by authors whose
credentials are impeccable and who are sympathetic to the new
movements. Jonathan Kozol, one of the original compassionate critics,
has given much of his time to the establishment of free schools, which
he describes and advocates in his article from Psychology Today. Lou
LaBrant is a perceptive, progressive, and scholarly teacher and a close
observer of trends and tendencies in contemporary education. Sylvia
Ashton-Warner is widely known for her classic description of the
education of Maori children in New Zealand, in Teacher. Joseph
Featherstone, through his articles on British education, was largely
responsible for calling open education to the attention of American
educators. H. C. Sun, of Hampton Institute, who also reminds the
advocates of open education of earlier reform efforts, calls attention to
the insights of John Dewey which question the adequacy of a child-
centered school that does not take into account additional important
considerations. Each of these writers has helpful cautions and reminders
for the educator who sees promise in some of the alternatives reported.

FREE, ALTERNATIVE, AND OPEN SCHOOLS

THE
RISE
OF
THE
"FREE
SCHOOL"

BONNIE BARRETT
STRETCH

Bonnie Barrett Stretch, a freelance writer, provides an excellent overview of the alternative or free school movement. Her article in Saturday Review *was one of the first comprehensive attempts to convey the meaning of the movement to a wide reading public. Although instruction and curriculum in the alternative or free schools vary, a common sense of individual freedom pervades the entire movement. The emphasis is upon creativity and individual choice. As Stretch shows, the movement began outside the public school system and in reaction against the traditionalism of many schools.*

For the past five years, critics have been telling parents and teachers what is wrong with the public schools. Such writers as John Holt, Herbert Kohl, Jonathan Kozol, George Dennison, and Paul Goodman have described the authoritarianism that structures many classrooms, the stress on grades and discipline at the expense of learning, and the suppression of the natural curiosity and instincts of the young. Many parents and teachers have begun to see for themselves the boredom, fear, and grievous lack of learning that too often accompany schooling—not only for the poor and the black, but for suburban white youngsters as well—and they have begun to ask what can be done about it.

The revolt is no longer against out-dated curriculums or ineffective teaching methods—the concerns of the late Fifties and early Sixties. The revolt today is against the institution itself, against the implicit assumption that learning must be imposed on children by adults, that learning is not something one does by and for oneself, but something designated by a teacher. Schools operating on this assumption tend to hold children in a prolonged state of dependency, to keep them from discovering their own capacities for learning, and to encourage a sense of impotence and lack of worth. The search is for alternatives to this kind of institution.

In the past two years, increasing numbers of parents and teachers have struck out on their own to develop a new kind of school that will allow a new kind of education, that will create independent, courageous people able to face and deal with the shifting complexities of the modern world. The new schools, or free schools, or community schools —they go by all these names—have sprung up by the hundreds across the country. Through a continuous exchange of school brochures and newsletters, and through various conferences, the founders of these schools have developed a degree of self-awareness, a sense of community that has come to be called "the new schools movement."

The new schools charge little or no tuition, are frequently held together by spit and string, and run mainly on the energy and excitement of people who have set out to do their own thing. Their variety seems limitless. No two are alike. They range from inner-city black to suburban and rural white. Some seem to be pastoral escapes from the grit of modern conflict, while others are deliberate experiments in integrated multicultural, multilingual education. They turn up anywhere— in city storefronts, old barns, former barracks, abandoned church buildings, and parents' or teachers' homes. They have crazy names like Someday School, Viewpoint Non-School, A Peck of Gold, The New Community, or New Directions—names that for all their diversity reflect the two things most of these schools have in common: the idea of freedom for youngsters and a humane education.

As the Community School of Santa Barbara (California) states in its brochure: "The idea is that freedom is a supreme good; that people, including young people, have a right to freedom, and that people who are free will in general be more open, more humane, more intelligent than people who are directed, manipulated, ordered about. . . . "

The Santa Barbara Community School is located in a converted barracks on a hill above the town. The fifty or so children (ages three to fourteen) almost invariably come from wealthy, white, fairly progressive families who want to give their children "the nicest education possible," as one teacher put it. Inside the building are a large meeting room; some smaller rooms for seminars, discussions, and tutorials; a wood and metal shop; classrooms for the younger children; and a small library. Classes for the younger children are based on the Leicestershire model. Rooms are organized by activity centers—a math corner here, a reading corner there. Parents' money has helped provide a remarkable amount of creative learning materials. Children are free to move from one thing to another as their interest shifts, and children of all ages frequently work and play together. For the older kids, the method is largely tutorial: one, two, or three youngsters working with a teacher. Although there is a "core curriculum" of literature, science, and social studies, the classes follow the interests and preferences of the students.

Outside and behind the building is enough space for a large playground, a pile of wood and lumber, a large pile of scrap metal including bicycle and car parts, and an old car, whose motor the older children are dismantling as a lesson in mechanics or physics (depending on whom you talk to). Children of all ages use the wood and metal to carve or weld into sculpture, as well as to fix bikes and build toys. "It's important for kids to learn about tools," explained a teacher. "Most kids don't know how things work. You really have to see a six-year-old in goggles with a welding torch to appreciate what it means."

The parents like the school, although they sometimes worry about how much the children are learning. By "learning" they mean the three Rs, social studies, etc. Parent pressure has led the Community School to place more emphasis on traditional subject matter than many free schools do. Teachers, on the other hand, are more concerned about another kind of learning. They would like to help these white middle-class youngsters develop a better sense of the world, to expose them to styles of life and work besides those of their families. There are frequent trips to ranches, factories, local businesses, and other schools. But these experiences, being interludes, remain essentially artificial to children. What are real are the comforts and concerns that inform their daily lives and that are shared with their friends.

In contrast to this isolation is the Children's Community Workshop School in New York City. Situated in an economically and racially integrated neighborhood, the school makes a conscious effort to keep its enrollment one-third white, one-third black, and one-third Puerto Rican. Because it is intended specifically as an alternative to the public schools, the Community Workshop charges no tuition. It is supported primarily by foundation grants and private donations, but the scramble for money is a continuous one that taxes a great deal of the energy of the school's director, Anita Moses.

Like the Santa Barbara Community School, the Community Workshop bases its structure on the Leicestershire method. And, again like Santa Barbara, it does not hold strictly to that method. There is a great deal of emphasis on the children's own interests, and new directions and materials are being tried all the time. A visitor to the school may find one group of children at a table struggling to build arches out of sugar cubes; another two or three children may be working with an erector set, others with tape recorders and a typewriter. In the midst of all this independent activity may be found one teacher helping one child learn to write his name.

Except for the use of Leicestershire techniques, there is little similarity between the Children's Community Workshop and the school in Santa Barbara. The heterogeneity of the student body makes the educational and human problems far more complex. Where achievement levels and cultural backgrounds vary widely, there is a great deal of accommodation necessary on the part of teachers and parents. At the same time, there can be no question that the children are learning more than the traditional three Rs.

Both the Community Workshop and the Santa Barbara Community School, however, have more structure than many free schools. The tendency in these schools is not to stress conventional intellectual training, to offer it if and when the children want it, and in general to let the youngsters discover and pursue their own interests. The new schools agree fully with Piaget's statement that "play is the serious business of childhood," and a child may as easily spend whole days in the sandbox as in the reading center. The lack of structure, however, leads to a lot of noise and running around, and all this activity may seem like chaos to a visitor. Often that's exactly what it is. It is a difficult skill to attune oneself to individual children, and to build on their individual needs and concerns, and few teachers have mastered it. Often, too, older youngsters, suddenly released from the constraints of public school, will run wild for the first few weeks, or even months, of freedom. But gradually, as they work the pent-up energy out of their system, and as they learn that the adults really will allow this freedom, they begin to discover their own real interests and to turn their energy to constructive tasks.

"The longer they've been in public school, and the worse their experience there is, the longer it takes for them to settle down, but eventually they all do," says Bill Kenney, who has taught at Pinel School in Martinez, California, for ten years. Pinel is an essentially Summerhillian school where classes in subjects such as reading and arithmetic are offered, but the children are not compelled to attend.

Based on his experience at Pinel, Mr. Kenney believes that in a school that is solidly middle-class it can be expected that any happy, healthy child will eventually learn to read, write, and do basic arithmetic, whether or not he is formally taught. The experience of other middle-class free schools tends to corroborate this assumption.

The appeal of this philosophy is enormous, judging from the number of students and teachers applying to the new schools—all these schools report more applicants than they can handle—and from the constant flow of visitors who come to watch, ask questions, and sometimes get in the way. A few schools have had to set up specific visiting days in an effort to stem the tide. Three major conferences on "alternatives in education" took place this spring—in Cuernavaca, Mexico; in Santa Barbara, California; and in Toronto, Canada—and people flocked to them by the hundreds to talk to such "heroes" as John Holt and George Dennison, and to talk to one another and learn who's doing what and how. Representatives from foundations, universities, and the U.S. Office of Education also came, eager to know whether the critics' ideas can be given life.

Through the conferences and through correspondence and exchanges of school newsletters, a self-awareness is developing among the new schools, a sense of themselves as part of a growing movement. Much of this increased consciousness is due to the work of the New Schools Exchange, an information clearinghouse that grew out of a conference of 200 schools a year ago. During its first year, the exchange set up a directory of new schools, put teachers and kids in touch with schools, and schools in touch with teachers, kids, materials—and even, occasionally, money. In that year, too, 800 new names were added to the exchange list, and the exchange helped many through the labor pains of birth by offering nuts-and-bolts information about how to incorporate a school, and ways to get through the bureaucratic maze of building, fire, and health regulations.

But the mortality rate among these new schools is high. Harvey Haber of the Exchange estimates about eighteen months is the average life span. This includes those that endure for years and those that barely get off the ground. Money is universally the biggest hassle and the reason most commonly cited for failure. Even those schools that endure are seriously hampered by the constant struggle for fiscal survival that too often must take precedence over education. Most schools are started by people who are not rich, and charge little or no tuition, in an effort to act as an alternative for the common man (the rich have always had alternatives). Teachers work for pennies, when they are paid at all. "How do I survive?" one teacher laughed a bit anxiously. "I found a nice landlord who doesn't bug me about the rent. I dip into my savings, and get my parents and friends to invite me to dinner—

often. Then, there are food stamps, of course. Mostly we rely on each other for moral support and help over the really rough places."

This kind of dedication, however, is too much to ask of anyone for any length of time. Working with children in an open classroom with few guidelines makes tremendous demands on teachers, Anita Moses of the Children's Community Workshop points out. Furthermore, teachers must often give their time for planning, for parent conferences, or for Saturday workshops with new teaching techniques and materials. There are intrinsic rewards for this, of course, but extrinsic rewards are also necessary, Mrs. Moses stresses, and those rewards should be in terms of salary.

There are other hurdles besides money—red tape, harassment by various state and city bureaucracies, and hostility from the community at large. In Salt Lake City, for example, a citizens' committee tried to close a new Summerhill school on the grounds that the school was immoral and the teachers were Communists.

But perhaps the most fundamental factor for survival is the degree of commitment on the part of the teachers and parents. For brochures, newsletters, and other public pronouncements, it is possible to articulate the concept of freedom and its importance to the emotional and intellectual development of the child. But basically the appeal is to a gut-level longing for love, joy, and human community, and often the schools are run on this romantic basis. "If you stop putting pressure on the kids, the tendency is to stop putting pressure on the staff, too," one teacher observed. Schools that fail within a few months of opening tend to be those begun by people merely interested in trying out a new idea. When the idea turns out to be more complex, and its implementation more difficult than anticipated, the original good feeling evaporates and a deeper determination is required.

Parents and teachers who have worked out their ideas together, who have similar goals, who know what they want for their children and why, have a better chance of keeping their school alive. Nonetheless, almost every school follows a similar pattern. If they make it over the physical hurdles of getting money, finding a building, and meeting bureaucratic regulations, they run into the spiritual struggle. Usually, somewhere in the first three to six months, according to Harvey Haber, comes the first great spiritual crisis: "structure" vs "nonstructure." Having experimented with the idea of freedom, and having discovered its inherent difficulties, many parents and teachers become impatient and anxious. Are the children learning anything, they wonder, and does it matter? Frequently there is a slowdown in the acquisition of traditional academic skills. Children, it turns out, would rather play than learn to spell, and the blossoming forth of innate genius in a warm, benevolent atmosphere fails to occur. Anxious adults begin to argue for more structure to the school day, more direction for the kids, more emphasis on the familiar three Rs. Others insist upon maintaining the freedom, and upon learning to work with children on a new freer basis that really tests its limitations and possibilities.

As Robert Greenway, whose sons were enrolled in the Redwood Association Free School in Sonoma County, California, wrote:

> It seems to me that this anxiety that gets aroused about "what's happening to our kids" is understandable and inevitable. In a public school, we turn our children over to the wardens; there is no illusion about the possibility of influence to torture us. . . . But a truly cooperative venture arouses every possible hope about involvement in the growth of our children—and probably every latent frustration about what we think *didn't* happen to us as well. . . . I suggest that, unless we find a way of dealing with the real anxieties and concerns that this type of enterprise arouses, then we'll fail before we've hardly started (I'm responding to my own growing sense of frustration and anxiety, and to the sign of sudden and/or premature withdrawals from the school, and to the growing hue and cry for "more organization").

The Santa Fe (New Mexico) Community School went through this crisis in the middle of its second year, a bit later than most. Parents were willing to go along with the school as long as the teachers seemed confident about what was happening with the children. But when one teacher began to articulate the fears many parents had tried to suppress, the situation came to a head. There was a period of trying to impose more order on the kids, and the kids rebelled and refused to take it. Some staff members were fired, and parents demanded more teachers with bachelor's and master's degrees, but found they could not get them for a salary of $200 a month. There were endless pedagogical debates, and finally some of the parents simply took their kids back to the public school. "Unfortunately, those who left were the ones with the most money," sighed one teacher. "We're poorer now, but the people here are here because they're dedicated."

After the crisis, the school was reorganized. Previously ordered by age clusters, it is now divided into activity centers, and children of all ages move freely from one center to another. On a bright Southwestern day a visitor may find a couple of boys sitting in front of the building, slumped against a sun-warmed wall, eating apples and reading comic books. Inside, in the large front room, a group of children may be painting pictures or working with leather or looms. In a quiet, smaller room, someone else is having a guitar lesson. A room toward the back of the building is reserved as the math center; a couple of teachers are math enthusiasts, and many of the older children pick up from them their own excitement for the subject.

In the playground behind the building is an Indian kiva built by students and teachers learning about the culture of local Indian tribes. The Southwest is a multicultural area, and the Community School has tried to draw on all these cultures. There are Indian and Spanish children enrolled, as well as white, and each is encouraged to respect and learn from the cultures of the others.

But despite its efforts to reach into the Indian and Spanish communities, the Santa Fe Community School remains essentially a white middle-class school. The Chicanos and Indians, mainly poor or working-class, tend to shy away from such experiments, partly because their cultures are traditionally conservative with highly structured roles for adults and children, and partly because the poor cannot afford to take a chance on the future of their young. Middle-class whites can always slip back into the mainstream if they choose. But for the poor, neither the acquisition of such intellectual tools as reading and writing nor a place in the economy is guaranteed.

These fundamental differences show up clearly in the community schools operated by and for black people. Black people on the whole bring their children to these schools, not merely because they believe in freedom for self-expression or letting the child develop his own interests, but because their children are not learning in the public schools, are turning sullen and rebellious by the age of eight, and are dropping out of school in droves. The ideology in many of these schools is not pedagogical, but what one school calls "blackology"—the need to educate the children in basic skills and in pride of race. In the black schools there is much more emphasis on basic intellectual training and much more participation on the part of parents. By and large, parents are the founders of these schools; they are the main source of inspiration and energy. They have the final say in selecting both teachers and curriculum, and their chief criterion is: Are the children learning?

As in the white schools, classrooms for the younger children are frequently patterned after the Leicestershire model. But the approach is deliberately eclectic, providing closer guidance and more structured activities for youngsters who need it. The academic progress of the children is carefully observed and quietly but firmly encouraged. "We want teachers who will try a thousand different ways to teach our children," said one mother.

Equally important is a teacher's attitude toward race. Although some schools would like to have all-black faculties—and in a number of cities, parents are in training to become teachers and teacher aides—they must still hire mainly whites. "When I interview a teacher," said Luther Seabrook, principal of the Highland Park Free School in Boston, "I always ask, can you think of a community person as an equal in the classroom?" Many teachers cannot, either because of racial bias, or because of notions about professionalism. Even after a teacher is hired, the going is still rough where feelings run high on the part of blacks and whites, but there is a determination to confront these problems directly through open discussion and group sessions.

The same approach applies to daily work in the classroom. Teachers and aides are encouraged to talk openly about their successes and problems in weekly planning sessions, to admit mistakes, and to try out new ideas. Such sessions are frequently the keystone of the teaching process in these schools. They are the times when teachers can get together and evaluate what has been happening in the classroom, how the children have responded to it, and how the teachers have responded to the children. "It's a tremendous place to grow," one teacher remarked. "You're not tied to a curriculum or structure, and you're not afraid to make mistakes. Everyone here is in the same boat. We get support from each other and develop our own ways of handling things."

There is little doubt that the youngsters prefer the community schools to traditional schools. The humane and personal atmosphere in the small, open classrooms makes a fundamental difference. The children work together writing stories or figuring math problems, working with Cuisenaire rods or an elementary science kit. They are proud of their work and show it eagerly to visitors. There is virtually no truancy, and many youngsters hate to stay home even on weekends, according to their mothers.

But perhaps the greatest achievement of these schools is with the parents. They develop a new faith, not only in their children but in themselves. "Now I know," said a New York City mother, "that, even though I didn't finish high school, it is possible for me to understand what they are teaching my child." In changing their children's lives, these parents have discovered the power to change their own lives, as well. Parents who are not already working as aides and coordinators in the classrooms drop by their schools often to see how Johnny is doing. At the East Harlem Block Schools in New York, stuffed chairs and couches and hot coffee put parents at ease, while teachers talk with them as equals and draw them into the education of their children.

Nonetheless, black schools share many of the problems with the community that white schools have. People are suspicious of new ways of teaching, even though their children obviously are failing under the old ways. Parents who enroll their children out of desperation still grow anxious when they see the amount of freedom allowed. In integrated schools, like Santa Fe or the Children's Community Workshop, there is the added problem of race and class, as middle-class parents learn that all the children are not necessarily going to adopt middle-class values and life-styles, that cultural differences are valid and must be accepted.

Some schools are fed up with "parent education"; it takes too much time away from the children. A number of schools already are taking only children whose parents are in sympathy with their aims, parents who won't panic if the child doesn't learn to read until he is eight or nine.

But as a school grows more homogeneous, it faces the danger of becoming an isolated shelter against the reality of the outside world. Instead of educating kids to be strong and open enough to deal with a complex world, the schools may become elitist cloisters that segregate a few people even further from the crowd.

Once again the free schools must ask themselves what they are all about. If one assumes (as many free schools do) that any healthy, happy youngster will eventually learn to read and write, then what is the purpose of school? Is it enough simply to provide one's children with a school environment more humane than the public schools, and then stay out of nature's way?

At a California high school in the Sausalito hills, teachers and students think that that in itself is quite a lot. After going through a typical cycle of kids getting high on freedom and doing nothing for six months, getting bored, and finally facing the big questions—What am I doing? Where am I going?—students and teachers think they have learned a lot about themselves and each other. But as the youngsters return to studying and start to seek answers to those questions, they find the teachers have little to offer besides a sympathetic ear. Some kids return to the public school feeling better for their experience with freedom. (Feeling, too, perhaps, that it didn't work, that they really do need all the rules and discipline their parents and teachers demanded.) Gradually, those who remain have forced the teachers back to the traditional textbooks as the chief source of knowledge.

The humane atmosphere remains, but missing is a curriculum that truly nurtures the independence of thought and spirit so often talked of and so rarely seen. It takes extraordinary ingenuity to build on students' needs and interests. A few brilliant teachers, such as Herbert Kohl, can turn kids on, meet them where they are, and take them further—can for example, take a discussion of drugs and dreams and guide it through the realms of mythology, philosophy, and Jungian psychology. But what do you do if you're not a Herb Kohl? According to Anita Moses, you "work damn hard." There are other things, too: You can hire a master teacher familiar with the wide range of curriculum materials available. Little by little you can change the classroom, or the school itself, to make it do the things you want it to do. And little by little, through working with the children and hashing out problems with help from the rest of the staff, you begin to know what it is you want to do and how you can do it.

But even this does not answer the deeper questions—questions that are implicit in every free school, but that few have faced. Is it only a new curriculum or new ways of teaching that we need? Or do we need to change our ideas about children, about childhood itself, about how children learn, what they learn, what they need to learn, from whom or from what kinds of experience? It is clear that our ideas about teaching are inadequate, but is it possible that they are simply false? For example, children can often learn to read and write without any formal instruction. This is not a miracle; it is a response of an intelligent young being to a literate milieu. It is also clear that children learn many cognitive as well as social abilities from their peers or from children but a few years older than themselves. What, then, is the role of the adult in the learning of the child?

In simpler times, children learned from adults continually, through constant contact and interchange, and through their place close to the heart of the community. Today, the society has lost this organic unity. We live in times when children often see their fathers only on weekends. We live in a world that separates work from play, school from the "real" world, childhood from personhood. The young are isolated from participation in the community. They seem to have no integral place in the culture. Too often schools have become artificial environments created by adults for children. How is it possible to forsake these roles?

Young people are trying. Many will no longer accept without question authority based solely on tradition or age. They are seeking alternatives to The Way Things Are. But the venture into unfamiliar territory generates enormous anxieties. The young are painfully aware of their own inexperience; they lack faith in themselves. But who can help them in their conflicts both within themselves and with the outside world? Surely, this is a function of education. But in today's world there are few adults who can do this for themselves, far less for their children. For who can respond with assurance to the anxieties of young people over sex, drugs, and the general peril in which we live? Who knows how to deal with others when the traditional roles are gone?

And yet it should be possible for adults to relate to young people in some constructive way. It must be possible because the young, in their alienation and confusion, and the culture, in its schizoid suffering, demand it. In the words of Peter Marin, former director of the Pacific High School, a free school in California:

Somebody must step past the children, must move into his own psyche or two steps past his own limits into the absolute landscape of fear and potential these children inhabit. . . . I mean: we cannot *follow* the children any longer, we have to step ahead of them. Somebody has to mark a trail.

Is this what the free schools are all about? Few of them have asked these questions. Few will ever want to. But the questions are implicit in the movement. The free schools offer alternatives—alternatives that may be shaped to meet new needs and aims. At least they offer a first step. At least the possibility is there.

WHATEVER
HAPPENED
TO
THE
FREE
SCHOOL
MOVEMENT?

ROBERT D. BARR

Robert D. Barr looks back at the free school movement almost three years after Bonnie Barrett Stretch's article on the rise of free schools outside the public school systems. He believes that the free school movement failed to become the wave of the future and probably never will achieve substantial dimensions. He argues that there is no one best way for all people to learn and he calls for fostering options in public schools as well as the development of free schools.

Robert D. Barr is associate professor of education at Indiana University, Bloomington, where he is co-director of the Educational Alternatives Project. He is the editor of Changing Schools, *a newsletter of the National Consortium on Educational Alternatives.*

In 1969 a couple of hundred radical educational reformers met in California to hold the first conference on free schools. In the process they invented a "movement." As Harvey Haber would say later, "We were quick to discover that all that is necessary to have a movement is to declare it as such, which we did. It was as simple as that. An old hand-crank mimeograph and a typewriter and the New School Movement was defined."

Haber continued, "So, a couple of dozen new schools with pretentions no greater than wanting to save a couple of hundred kids from the death of public schools found themselves part of a national movement."[1] The reformers also set up the *New Schools Exchange Newsletter*, which they called the "first grass-roots national educational reform tool," and the "movement" was on its way.

A year later a skeptical George Dennison admitted that "there are

[1] Sallie Rasberry and Robert Greenway, *Rasberry Exercises* (Freestone, Calif.: The Freestone Publishing Co., 1970), p. 107.

Reprinted by permission from *Phi Delta Kappan*, March 1973, pp. 454–457.

no signs that a movement exists, but there are many that one might." And signs there were. People were hard at work setting up new schools and holding conferences and writing and generating excitement and enthusiasm. The writings of Holt, Kozol, Illich, Friedenberg, Goodman, and a host of others provided, if not a blueprint for reform, at least a constituency of ideas and a legitimacy of effort. And in an era of depressing educational research and general professional pessimism, the movement began to attract skeptical interest from some in the U.S. Office of Education, universities, and major foundations. It also began to draw heavy fire from conservatives.

Exhilarated by their own daring, a number of free school advocates turned to newsletters, newspapers, periodicals, and clearinghouses as a means of spreading the word. There was a flurry of activity. Borrowing heavily from the style and format of counter-culture "underground newspapers," the *New Schools Exchange* was joined by *Outside the Net, EdCentric, The Teacher Paper, This Magazine Is About Schools,* and dozens of regional and local papers of lesser quality that began to crank out, in sporadic fits of affluence, an uneven assortment of typo-mangled calls for support and subscriptions.

Like reformers everywhere, many forsook the kind of self-restraint demonstrated by George Dennison; projections of massive growth in the movement (we'll drop the ironic quotes around "movement" now) became quite common. In 1970 Harvey Haber, writing in *Rasberry Exercises,* boasted of 2,000 schools "surging the movement across all 50 states."[2] He was followed by Mike Rossman, who maintained that free schools will quickly become a major alternative to the public system and drain from it more and more of its innovative teachers; responsive kids, and certain classes of parents, hip-liberal in the main."[3] Rossman went on to make a number of theoretical extrapolations which he felt were "fairly safe bets." Claiming that there were already 60,000 students in 1,600 free schools in 1971, he predicted 340,000 students in 7,000 such schools by 1973 and 1,400,000 in as many as 25,000 to 30,000 schools by 1975. Free schools seemed to be riding the crest of history.

Unfortunately, it wasn't so. Despite the dramatic projections and the proliferating press of the free schools, recent indications suggest that the movement is really rather small and the future far from the promised predictions.

In October, 1971, Peter Marin, who did so much to put life and style into the movement, admitted that it was not all he had hoped. "The truth is," he said, "that there isn't, at the moment, as much of a

2 *Ibid.*
3 Michael Rossman, "Projections on the New School Movement," *New Schools Exchange,* No. 52, p. 8.

free school movement as we would like to think."[4] He compared the number of free schools with the number a year earlier and concluded: "There hasn't been much change." His calculations put the movement at somewhere between 350 and 450 free schools. "Unintentionally but inevitably," Marin continued, "we construct what looks like a 'movement,' something put together from small descriptions and rhetoric, and what is lost within it is precisely what free schools were meant to restore: a devotion to what is truthfully human."[5] Marin's "honesty" had broken the faith, and a number of the free school "true believers" came forward to redefine their movement and explain why Marin was wrong.

Allen Graubard, currently of MIT and the *New Schools Exchange*'s man in the East, had just completed a free school directory for the U.S. Office of Education and was startled by Marin's calculations. Feeling it to be "his duty" to correct an "erroneous impression" about the rate of growth in the free schools, he set out to put the matter straight.[6] Follow, if you can, his argument:

Graubard maintained that Marin was incorrect and the free school movement was not "about the same" but actually increasing. He blamed part of the confusion on the "enormously inflated" estimates that had been made by some of his colleagues. He then set about proving his point. By going through earlier *New Schools Exchange* directories and supplements, Graubard counted 324 "possible" schools in the fall of 1970. But he explained that he "knows" (without telling us how) that one-third of these schools "are not in any way to be counted as free schools." So he figures that *really* there were only around 200 free schools in the fall of 1970, of which he said some "are quite likely not properly included." As of fall, 1971, Graubard estimated the number of free schools to be in the 400–500 range, including schools started that fall. But his own directory included only 346, some of which were likewise "brand new." But he admitted (again without telling us why) that there are "many more new ones [free schools] we don't know about." He also admitted he missed some in his count and guessed that number to be around 30–50 at most. Now, he figured, if you didn't count the "new schools" and used a reasonable definition for a free school, there would have been around 330–350 in the fall of 1971. "So," he concluded, "there is very substantial growth [in free schools], and their growth continues."

Now we have a question for you: Not counting schools you don't know about and the schools you know about that aren't, and eliminating those you would "guess" are out there and, of course, those just

[4] From a letter by Peter Marin, *New Schools Exchange*, October 31, 1971, p. 3.
[5] Peter Marin and Vincent Stanley, "Exchange Exchanged," *New Schools Exchange*, October 31, 1971, p. 3.
[6] From a letter by Allen Graubard, *New Schools Exchange*, February 1, 1972, p. 8.

starting or just deceased, how many free schools do you think there are? The right answer, unfortunately, is that no one knows for sure.

Reporting recently in the *Harvard Educational Review*, Graubard still argued that the number of free schools has "increased dramatically" during the past five years and that the increase suggests the emergence of a movement between 1967 and 1971.[7] Let's look at his movement. In the early 1960s he counted fewer than five free schools. He claims the rise of free schools began in 1966 and 1967. Around 20 free schools were founded between 1967 and 1969 and another 60 in 1969. By 1970 the number was 150, even more in 1972. His final count of 346 schools was estimated to be serving between 11,500 and 13,000 students. The average school size was 33 students, with two-thirds of the schools having fewer than 40 students and over 20% having fewer than 20 students. Even for a free schools enthusiast, such numbers must be disappointingly small. For when compared with the 50 million kids still in public schools, the 13,000 free school students comprise much less than 1% of all school-age children, and that's far from the dreams that started this whole effort. Closer examination of Graubard's figures proves even more depressing. He explains that a "considerable number" of free schools close after one or two or three years of existence. And although he admits that "existing data do not present an entirely accurate picture," his "sense is" that at most one out of five new schools closes before the end of its second year, though perhaps the number is not more than one out of 10. But as he admits, he does not really know. Others have argued that most free schools have no more than an 18-month life span. Sallie Rasberry and Robert Greenway wrote in 1970 that "most of them fail before the end of the first year."[8] With no accurate data available, and with approximately half of Graubard's schools being less than two years old, his whole argument as well as his movement are called into question. And given the difficulties he has had arriving at an accurate count of existing schools, it is evident that it would be impossible ever to discover how many free schools have come and gone, starting and failing. Without such information, Graubard's claim of "dramatic increases" is hollow indeed.

Following the matter a step further, yet another provocative question arises. As Graubard's "numbers" are analyzed, one's curiosity is aroused. Are these 346 schools *really* all free schools? Or more important, What are free schools anyway? The answer again is hard to find.

While the free school movement has always included a wide assortment of very different kinds of schools, they have always been held together by two common characteristics: All the sponsors were attempting to escape public education and create something new and better,

[7] Allen Graubard, "The Free School Movement," *Harvard Educational Review*, August 1972, pp. 351–73.
[8] Rasberry and Greenway, *op. cit.*, p. 3.

and all endorsed the "idea" of freedom. But from the beginning there were two basic kinds of free schools, each with a conception of freedom that was at best contradictory. On the one hand were the predominantly white middle- and upper-class free schools in which the coercion, regimentation, and authoritarian atmosphere of the public schools was replaced with the free learning environment of "do-your-own-thing" pedagogy. The other group of schools, usually poor, black, and inner-city, might better be described as community-control schools. Related historically to the earlier civil-rights freedom schools, these free schools typify the larger struggle of minority groups against racist institutions and have been set up by parents to liberate their children from the "indoctrination and destruction" of the public schools. These community schools are the antithesis of the "classical" free school, usually having a good deal of structure, required classes, and intensive drill in basic skills.

In his new book, *Free Schools*, Jonathan Kozol carefully delineates between the two kinds of schools just described and lays out quickly and clearly that he believes the inner-city community school is the true "free school."[9] He writes with a bitter rage about the "hippie"—middle- and upper-class kids—"off in the Vermont woods" shuttling their hand-looms, basket weaving, and making Iroquois canoes that even Indians no longer need. He summarizes his point with cutting directness: "In my belief, an isolated upper-class free school for the children of the white and rich within a land like the United States and in a time of torment such as 1972 is a great deal too much like a sand box for the children of the SS guards at Auschwitz."[10] If Kozol could define the parameters of the free school "movement," Graubard's "dramatic increases" might be far less than anyone would care to calculate.

The whole matter is further complicated by a recent directory published by the *New Schools Exchange*.[11] At first glance there seems to be a fairly large discrepancy between the figures in the NSE directory and those published by Graubard, for the former lists 801 schools. A quick examination, however, while further confusing the free school issue, does at least explain the difference in totals. The NSE directory is not just a listing of free schools; it is a "continuing directory of new and innovative schools in the U.S. and Canada." The directory not only includes schools planning to open but lists a surprisingly strange group of "bed-fellows," including tutoring projects, junior colleges, day-care centers and nursery schools, summer camps, boarding schools, parochial schools, Montessori schools, and community "evening"

9 Jonathan Kozol, *Free Schools* (Boston: Houghton Mifflin, 1972).
10 *Ibid.*, p. 11.
11 "Continuing Directory of New and Innovative Schools in the U.S. and Canada," *New Schools Exchange*, June 30, 1972, No. 81, pp. 3–34.

schools. Most surprisingly, it lists 130 public schools. For a movement that set out to escape public education, such an inclusion is, I think, significant. Also notable is the fact that the NSE directory lists private free schools as only one kind of alternative, along with dropout centers, multicultural schools, advancement schools, magnet schools, learning centers, schools-without-walls, open schools, and Montessori schools—both public and parochial. Herein lies a point well worth considering.

It appears that the movement, by focusing solely on "free schools," has been defined much too narrowly, for something far bigger seems to have been occurring, namely, the diversification of education into a wide variety of learning options. I think it can be argued persuasively that free schools are not for everybody; they may be best for only a small percentage of people. The trouble is that a basic assumption of the free schools movement has always been that most *everyone* would be *happier* and *learn better* in an atmosphere of freedom; that is one of the particular points that Kozol was arguing. The answer to the cultural dilemma of Kozol's black, poor, mistreated students is not so much "freedom" as it is hard work, drill, dedication, and political awareness. But if Kozol proposes his kind of school for all kids, he is making the same error as the other free-schoolers. For, obviously, everyone doesn't need and wouldn't accept the intensive learning environment of the black inner-city free school.

Not everyone should be in a free school, just as not everyone should be in conventional public schools. I don't believe that all the school children in North Dakota should be in open schools, any more than I believe all the students in Philadelphia should be in the Parkway School-Without-Walls. The point I am arguing is that there is no one best way for all people to learn, and this assumption seems to be borne out by the wide variety and diversity of schools being organized and operated at this time throughout the country.

We are a pluralistic nation, with very different kinds of people; we have different personalities and values, goals and aspirations; different talents and different skills, different life-styles. And we may each learn best in very different environments. Some may learn best by having no structure; others may need a rigid structure. Some may not need a "teacher"; others may learn best with programmed materials or computer-assisted lessons, or even in conventional classrooms. If the assumption that people learn best in different ways is right, then we should work to provide a wide variety of distinctly different learning environments, and give parents, students, teachers, and administrators the opportunity to shop around in a diversified educational marketplace, making decisions about their own best interests.

Surprisingly enough, much more of this sort of diversification is now occurring within public education than in the free school movement. The Berkeley, California, public schools now have 24 alternative schools: everything from free schools to bilingual schools to environmental studies schools to conventional education. The Seattle, Washington, public schools have complemented their "regular" school program with over 30 alternative schools: schools-without-walls, dropout schools, and reentry programs that have attracted over 3,000 students back into the public schools. In Grand Rapids, Michigan, any student can leave his regular school to attend—for one course, or for his entire program—an alternative school located in a downtown office building. Grand Rapids also has an "independent learning center" and even offers students the option of leaving public schools to attend college while getting credit in both places. The district has an "alternative education center" where poor, racially different students work through program learning packages and are actually paid for the learning they do. Free schools like those in Berkeley are now being operated by public schools in Minneapolis and Ann Arbor; open schools are available in St. Paul and Louisville; and there are schools-without-walls in operation in at least six major districts in the U.S.

Other public schools have established continuous progress schools, learning centers, vocational programs, career internships, social internships, community-based learning experiences, and all sorts of options and alternatives. Sometimes the options are schools-within-schools; at other times they are housed in old hotels, office buildings, warehouses, storefronts, churches, libraries, and even in refurbished homes.

This situation can be found in hundreds of public school systems in 33 states and Canada. What is truly significant is that these schools have been developed by community efforts, as a local response to educational problems. *But in each case they have not only diversified public education, they have democratized it as well. For in each case students, parents, teachers, and administrators have the freedom to choose their education from a variety of learning options.*

This idea of providing free choice in education is not only a significant breakthrough but one that is uniquely American. In the past, educators have always picked and placed students via diagnostic testing or on some arbitrary basis like geography, student behavior, or administrative whim or bias. In an increasing number of public schools this situation is now changing.

As in the free schools, these public school options have all been started by dedicated, concerned people conscientiously striving to bring a richer educational experience to their children and students. Unlike the free schools, they are backed with tax money, and per-pupil costs are figured. The teachers have salaries, yet there is no tuition.

Some observers think much of the reform activities now going on in the public schools result primarily from the work of individuals formerly involved in free schools. While there is some evidence to support this idea, in most situations it is not the case. In a few instances free schools have developed outside public education and, after demonstrating success, have been incorporated into local public schools. Herb Kohl's Other Ways School in Berkeley is probably the best-known free school to make this transition. But it seems to be the exception rather than the rule. Most free school proponents are still adamant about keeping their movement "free" from public education. They have always worried about the public schools "co-opting" their movement or about being "re-absorbed into the dominant system." "The free schools," says Mike Rossman, "will cause the mainstream to adapt competitively, in the classic way—by modifying and adopting the lesser pieces of radical programs, as fragments stripped of their broader implications. Thus we see already some loosening of curriculum, schedule, learning-group size; some fuzzing of the grading system; expansion of teaching into affective domains; and so on."[12] But cause and effect are probably not that direct. All too often, developments in public education have been made in spite of the free schools rather than because of them. A public school teacher recently complained to me about his difficulties in working with school administrators and the local board of education. "No matter what I say or do, they inevitably see me as a 'free school freak' and pull out a whole catalog of nightmare stories about local free schools that have started and failed. My most difficult problem is to get people to forget about free schools and deal with the realities of our kids' educational programs and needs."

Far from being an outgrowth of the free school movement, the development of options in public education has come from a different source and has a different history. The people most influential in this development have been superintendents of schools, classroom teachers, relatively straight parents, and a variety of Establishment types. People like Mark Shedd, John Bremer, Larry Wells, Mario Fantini, Wayne Jennings, Don Glines, and a host of others, who were calling for public school options and developing them long before Harvey Haber announced there was a free school movement. The development of options in public education has been slow and steady work, for success has demanded the reeducation of many boards of education, parents, and administrators. Public school options have been held accountable for their efforts, and a growing body of evaluation data is becoming available that demonstrates their success. The "idea" is growing more acceptable, but rather than declare their work a new movement most public school reformers worry that the idea of options will become a fad and lose the promise this development holds for far reaching reform. At present public school options are still small indeed. With the exception of a half-dozen school districts that have developed clusters of

[12] Michael Rossman, "Crystal Balling," *New Schools Exchange*, February 1, 1972, No. 71, p. 2.

diverse options, few public schools have more than one, and too often it involves only a few students. Such schools are often under attack from their colleagues in conventional programs, from conservative school boards, and from insecure administrators. At best they can only be called a beginning, but it is a beginning that holds promise of the day when all American youth may be able to select learning experiences from a wide variety of educational options both *in* public school and *without*, and from the cradle to the grave. In such a dream the free school movement, and learning networks and parochial schools, and public school options would all enrich one another as components in a democratic educational mosaic.

The free school movement failed during the sixties to become the wave of the future, and, if we are honest, I think we must all now admit that it probably never will. The movement has, however, managed an impressive accomplishment in developing and maintaining so many free schools "outside the system." The movement has demonstrated that dedicated, creative people, with much courage and little money, can achieve significant goals. In the long run such vitality and energy and anger and sacrifice should only help to diversify and enrich education for American youth.

ALTERNATIVES WITHIN PUBLIC SCHOOLS

MARIO D. FANTINI

Mario D. Fantini has been in the forefront of recent reform movements in public schools. Among the books he has co-authored or co-edited are: Decentralization: Achieving Reform (*New York: Praeger, 1973*) *and* Community Control and the Urban School (*New York: Praeger, 1970*). *He has been a successful innovator in his work with the Ford Foundation. Currently he is Dean of the Faculty of Education, State University College, New Paltz, New York. The concepts in this article are drawn from his current writing on "public schools of choice," an approach to alternatives in education which he favors.*

Fantini traces the growth of alternatives within public schools and suggests some criteria to be applied before an alternative can be legitimized under a public school framework. He describes several current ventures and concludes with his reasons for advocating expansion of the framework of public education to include a wide range of educational alternatives as an approach to school alternatives.

Fifteen percent of American families have always had alternatives to public schools. Diverse private schools, from Montessori to prep, Summerhill to military, religious to secular, ethnic to multicultural, have provided choice for those who could afford it. For the masses, however, the only choice was and is a rather uniform public school system.

For the most part, "alternatives" within our public schools presently take the form of vocational education, special education, general education, dropout prevention, unwed mothers program, etc. These alternatives often carry with them ego-bruising stigmas. They are based on a status system of human classification—ranging from fast to slow learners, from academic to general education—that is often dysfunctional for the growth and development goals of the school. Moreover, the mainstream of students, parents, and teachers have not yet been affected by optional education.

A 1971 Gallup Poll reported that 60% of those using public schools were satisfied with them. A critical mass of about 40% are dissatisfied. It is members of this latter group who are most responsive to the move for alternatives within public schools. While no statistics are available, one might hypothesize that approximately the same percentage of

Reprinted by permission from *Phi Delta Kappan*, March 1973, pp. 444–448.

132

teachers are dissatisfied with the standard approach and would support alternatives. Educational alternatives can become a major force for constructive reform of public schools if we can take heed of certain lessons already learned from our early experiences.

Our experiences with the civil rights freedom schools, the counter-culture free schools, and the British open classroom have provided evidence that there are other ways of educating than the pattern found in public schools.

However, while these surfaced as alternatives in education, they were not necessarily based on consumer choice. They usually became alternatives *to* public schools and outside of its jurisdiction. Whatever the form an alternative took, it was usually accepted by those dissatisfied with public schools—a mere handful in comparison to the large numbers who could be affected within public schools. For those who tried to introduce alternatives within the public schools, the problem was different. Open classrooms, for example, were developed by teachers and were often imposed on the students and parents, on the ground that this form of education was better than the standard. While many parents and students responded to this alternative, a significant number did not, and they questioned their forced participation.

Further, proponents of many alternatives, in order to establish their legitimacy, waged a fierce attack on the established educational offerings. In short, they made the standard school look bad by comparison. This naturally made those who were content with the standard—professionals and laymen alike—upset and resistive. A political tug-of-war developed which fragmented educational communities and disturbed the instructional climate for both camps.

Moreover, because alternatives had emerged from a background of specialized needs like overcrowded schools or nonadjusting students, i.e., since alternative forms of education were necessary to help children who were having problems, the entire initial public conception of alternative education was cast in an atypical light.

To complicate the situation, some minority communities resisted alternatives because they were different from the normal forms of education. The resentment was expressed by such remarks as, "Why are you giving us something different? Aren't we normal like others? We want what the whites have—not something different." In short, those accepting an alternative would be admitting that something was wrong with them—a verdict already rendered by white society. Moreover, a mood of fiscal austerity vis-à-vis rising school expenditures gripped the mainstream and the public policy makers, including school boards. The natural question became, "Will alternatives cost more money?"

When alternatives were first introduced to the mainstream, the bulk of the samples came from urban settings with minority children or with the counter-culture folk. Both groupings carried preconceived images with the mainstream. Educational programs for blacks are seldom perceived as models for whites. The attitude is almost the same with those programs for "long-haired hippie-type" youth. The first response of the mainstream to alternatives was a resounding "If this is what you're calling alternatives, fine for them but not for us."

However, since the need for alternatives cut across social class lines, it soon penetrated the most prestigiously perceived school systems— the ones looked up to by the mainstream. When descriptions of alternative education are made from such school districts as Newton (Massachusetts), Scarsdale and Great Neck (New York), Webster Groves (Missouri)—and when alternative schools are linked with successful college entry—then the mainstream is more likely to respond. The mainstream, the majority who use public schools, need to feel that alternative forms of education do not compromise their sense of quality. Unless an alternative school can give assurance that the student will be equipped for further learning, will succeed in college, the option is doomed.

Yet another problem is that those embracing alternative forms of education have been too quick to use labels. For instance, when a group proposing an option refers to it as "open," "individualized," or "humanistic," then those in the standard program rightfully respond: "When you use the term *open, individualized, humanistic,* are you implying that what we do is closed, non-individualized, dehumanistic? Obviously, our programs are also open, individualized, and humanistic, but we resent the implication."

The psychology of labeling may seem like a minor point in the legitimization process, but it can result in bitter conflict extending beyond semantic differences. Since most of the mainstream are products of the standard alternative, they know it best and tend to feel more secure with it. Proposed alternatives that appear dramatically different are often viewed with extreme caution. Certain conceptions of open education, where students are given considerable freedom, may be viewed as overly permissive and chaotic. Further, mainstream parents will reject alternatives that do not convince them that the educational objectives they have come to value are being emphasized. Thus, even when the open classroom is initially appealing to parents, they may soon lose their enthusiasm if children do not bring home school books and homework (symbols of academic legitimacy to parents who have gone through public schools) or if the basic skills, including reading, are not handled in the structured ways that parents have come to expect.

Those who are connected with alternatives sometimes not only lose sight of the importance of parent and public education, but expect parents to learn the whole thing after a few hours of exposure. It is difficult for mainstream parents to accept a child development point of view, which explains that their child will eventually learn to read—

perhaps as an adolescent or when he is most ready. Most parents have been oriented to a normal-abnormal view of child growth and development. They are eager to know how well their child is doing vis-à-vis other children his age. They want their child to progress according to age, not by some theoretical notion of development. After all, argue these parents, aren't most schools age-graded?

Mainstream parents may have various motives for considering alternatives, some of which cannot be sanctioned under a public school framework. When the notions of alternatives and choice are packaged together, some may want to use this plan as a way of maintaining or reattaining racial or socioeconomic exclusivity. Why can't an alternative be for all white or all black students? The answer, of course, is that public school alternatives cannot be used to circumvent the law. The concept of alternatives within the framework of public schools involves enhancing the comprehensive goals of human growth. They are tied to the noblest ideals of a free society. Deliberate exclusivity cannot be condoned and is a criterion for determining whether a public school alternative is legitimate.

The lessons seem to add up to this: Before an alternative can be legitimized under a public school framework, the following criteria must be applied:

1. The alternative must be made available to students, teachers, and parents by choice. It cannot be superimposed.
2. It cannot claim the capacity to replace existing alternatives like the standard school. Premature claims of superiority, belittling the worth of other alternatives, tend to create a negative political climate. The option being advanced is just that: an option for those students, parents, and teachers who are *attracted* to it. The existing alternatives are just as legitimate as those being proposed.
3. It must give evidence of being geared to the attainment of a comprehensive set of educational objectives, those for which the public school is accountable and not merely selected ones. Public schools are responsible for intellectual and emotional development. They include development of basic skills such as reading, writing, speaking, and appreciating; learning-to-learn skills such as critical thinking, planning, problem solving; talent and career development; citizenship preparation; a positive feeling of self-worth; and the like.

An alternative which emphasizes only the intellectual or only the emotional is suspect. For example, if a free school embraces only the educational objective of joy or "ecstasy" (however viable this is), it is doubtful that such an alternative could be legitimized as a public school. The other range of educational objectives must be also guaranteed to the consumer. If such alternatives were legitimized, it is possible to have a student who is happy while in school but unable to read, write, or otherwise qualify for the economic survival needs of modern society. Public schools cannot shortchange the learner because of the limited nature of the public school alternative he may have chosen. The public must be protected from consumer fraud.

4. It is not designed to promote exclusivity—racial, religious, or socio-economic. Equal access must be guaranteed.

5. It is not dependent on significant amounts of extra money to implement and does not increase the per-student expenditures beyond those of established options. The idea is to utilize existing resources differently—perhaps more effectively.

The ground rules for legitimizing alternatives within our public schools are critical. Without common ground rules, playing the alternatives ball game will be not only difficult but politically dangerous. Without ground rules, alternatives may spring up, get out of hand, and require enormous after-the fact expenditures of energy, creating additional ill feelings and conflict. Such setbacks may be irrevocable for an alternative schools movement.

For instance, some alternatives begin by default. That is, the educational need is so great, the demand so strong, that a group may create an alternative and control it before a school district has a chance to prepare itself. Later, when the school district wants to bring the alternative back into the fold, it may find that the process is much more complicated than expected. When the school system has lead time, where there is not the overt demand for change from the public, it can begin to set in motion the cooperative procedures for establishing alternative schools. In fact, now is the time for professional educators who have been delegated the responsibility by the public to implement effective education to assume such leadership. Alternative schools can produce a more effective learning environment for students in any community. The process for developing alternatives should be as natural a professional undertaking as considering a new reading program. If professionals wait for the problems to deepen, they will be responding to an often angry public.

The most prevalent pattern is the separate school alternative. Under this model, the alternative is housed in separate quarters from the established public schools. This format has advantages. For one thing, those involved can start from scratch and not be subjected to any restraints, including the politics imposed by an established school culture.

The Village School in Great Neck, New York (housed in a church basement), Brown School in Louisville, Kentucky (located in a downtown office building), Nike School in Long Beach, New York (located in a building of an abandoned Nike base), and scores of others fit this separate-school framework.

Almost equally prevalent is the school-within-a-school approach. In this pattern an established school building hosts two or more alternatives. Sometimes it is called the "minischool" format.

Schools-within-schools also have advantages. For instance, they do not have to look for new space and they can utilize the established resources, e.g., physical education, music, health, etc. Further, since most school districts have gone to great lengths to have the community pay for new school buildings, it may make political sense to utilize these modern facilities for alternatives.

Haaron High School in New York City has 14 minischools within a single building. Jefferson Elementary School in Berkeley has three distinct alternatives within its boundaries. There are many other such schools at various stages of development.

Another pattern is the alternative classroom. A teacher or group of teachers of the same or differing grade levels create an alternative such as the open, behavior modification, or Montessori classroom. Thus, if there are four teachers teaching in the first grade, then perhaps three will be standard and one will offer the alternative. Such designs enable a school to start slowly on the alternatives journey. Alternative classrooms allow teachers, parents, and students to seek evaluation on a small basis before expanding. Some alternative classrooms become schools within schools. Others remain as single classroom options.

Slowly, the alternative movement is beginning to focus more sharply on teaching and learning styles. The hope is to develop alternatives that will provide a better productive match between the two. Some schoolmen, parents, and students favor matching teaching-learning styles within the standard public schools. A teacher who considers her style to be "open," for instance, finds great satisfaction in having an "open classroom" legitimized by the school. Before there were alternatives, she found it necessary to "sneak" her style into the classroom. Further, she was forced by the uniform school not only to restrict her style but to impose it on a group of students who had not necessarily chosen it. Oftimes, this mismatch caused problems.

Proponents argue that if a student can choose the teacher who is most compatible with his own style, then a major educational problem is solved and we do not need to create alternative schools. Further, since the classroom and the teacher are really the heart of the school anyway, a fruitful match at this level would achieve as much as creating an elaborate school-within-a-school. Why can't a student choose a compatible teacher at any grade level? If there are four sixth-grade teachers, for example, why can't each student in sixth grade choose the teacher with whom he learns best? Of course the teacher would have to make his own teaching style public, but this should not be a difficult task. Teachers know how they teach. For example, teachers could reveal whether they generate a competitive or noncompetitive classroom environment, whether they maintain a formal or informal structure, where they employ a deductive or inductive approach to learning, whether they attempt to integrate knowledge around problem areas or cover each discipline separately and systematically, etc.

Other allies of optional education view a cluster of teachers with similar styles as forming the core staff of each alternative. Different alternatives attract different teachers. Such alternatives as standard, open, prep, behavior modification, etc., each with its own educational diet, cater to those teachers who feel most comfortable working with any one of them. The promise of dealing more basically with teaching-learning styles is enhanced by the alternatives movement.

Several public school systems either have embarked upon or are planning a districtwide approach to alternative education. The most advanced user of alternative schools is the Berkeley Unified School District, which has developed 25 options (with the help of the Ford Foundation and the federal government) that fall into four distinctive program categories: multiculture schools, community schools, structured skills-training schools, and schools-without-walls.

The Quincy Public Schools in Illinois have developed an Education-by-Choice Plan for its secondary schools. With the help of a Title III planning grant, several workshops were held to consider alternatives. With extensive faculty, student, and community participation, a range of alternatives were sketched that seem to fall in three broad styles. The Education-by-Choice planning team depicts these three options with diagram and purpose as shown in Figure 1.

Figure 1. Education-by-Choice Model

$T = teacher$
$S = Student$

1. This option could provide a learning environment which is primarily teacher-controlled. A school incorporating some of the ideas of the Classic School or the Structured School with Student Input could create this environment.

2. This option could provide a learning environment which would receive direction from both teacher and student, but for the most part would be teacher-controlled. A school incorporating some of the ideas of the Modular School or the individualized Instruction School might create this environment.

3. This option could provide a learning environment where teachers and students together would plan the learning experiences. A school incorporating the ideas of Project To Individualize Education or the Open School could create this environment.

Education-by-Choice Project, Quincy Public Schools, Title 111, ESEA, Illinois Grant No. 312-1-72.

The Office of Economic Opportunity has recently made a grant to the Rochester School District in New York to study the feasibility of an alternative educational system. Having established an Alternative Schools Study Office, the Rochester City School District will proceed to contact parents, students, teachers, and administrators on the feasibility of developing viable educational alternatives based on choice.

The OEO has also funded an experiment in education vouchers with the Alum Rock School District in San Jose, California. After an initial feasibility study grant in February of 1971, resulting in general acceptance of a voucher experiment, a demonstration was mounted in 1972. Parents in this pilot project receive vouchers worth about $680 for children in elementary school and about $970 for those in the seventh and eighth grades. Six schools and about 4,000 students are involved. Each of the six schools offers at least two alternative programs. If the evaluation of the first year proves positive, then the demonstration will expand during the second year.

Alternatives run along the entire pedagogical continuum. The labels try to reveal the flavor of each alternative—e.g., "open," "community school," "individualized," and "multiculture"—but there is still a fuzziness surrounding the instructional process itself. How are alternatives different? What does a student do in the alternative? What does the teacher do?

One way to consider alternatives is to place them on a continuum according to how much freedom or independence a student has to choose the elements of learning, i.e., how much freedom the student has to choose the teacher, content, methodology, time, and place for learning. At one extreme the learner selects what he shall learn, with whom, when, where, and how. At this end of the continuum the learner is most "free." At the other end he has little or no choice of teacher, content, methodology, time, and place. At this end he is most dependent on the institutional procedures and requirements, i.e., the institution predetermines the conditions of learning for the student: who his teacher will be, how the teacher will teach, what the subject matter will be, how much time is spent on each subject, and when and where this learning takes place.

Between these extremes there is a range of possibilities. The learner can be free to choose certain content areas; others are required for everyone, e.g., reading, writing, arithmetic, physical education, health. He may have some freedom in how he wishes to approach these content areas, e.g., by reading a book, by viewing video tapes, by doing research, by listening to a lecture, by discussion with others, etc. He may have some freedom to choose the time and place to learn, e.g., he may enter into a "contract" with the teacher to complete a project by a certain time. He may decide to spend most of his school time for the first week on art but devote considerable time after school hours on science. He may have access to resources in the community which he wishes to utilize: libraries, museums, artists, writers, television and radio studies, etc. Such an educational continuum is charted in Figure 2.

In the overlapping continuum model, we can see that the free school alternative enables each learner to orchestrate his own education. He has complete freedom to select and use his own resources (of which the teacher is only one), whether these are in the school or not. He could choose not to study mathematics or science and instead spend most of his time pursuing his own interests, e.g., art, drama, etc.

There are obviously different types of "free" school alternatives, ranging from an Illich-Reimer mode, which deemphasizes schooling and makes the individual learner the orchestrator of his own learning, to a Summerhill model, which uses school as a type of permissive self-governing unit. At this time free school alternatives are the most difficult to legitimize under a public school framework and will likely remain outside, as private alternative schools. They appear to run counter to the emerging ground rules for alternative public schools; e.g., they may not emphasize the full complement of educational objectives for which the public schools are responsible (basic skills, citizenship, careers, talents, self-concept, etc.).

The open phase of the continuum obviously overlaps with the free, but limits the learner's range of choice. Thus, while a student can choose when and how he will learn science or math, and while no subject is forced, subjects are nevertheless still "required." Such schools may feature "learning centers," i.e., areas that contain the resources for learning a particular subject area. But content is still largely predetermined by the teacher, who helps guide students in various subject matter areas.

The British infant schools, Montessori schools, and schools-without-walls could be examples of the "open" category. Schools featuring ungraded continuous progress, modular scheduling, and behavior modification are possible alternatives in the "modified" category. Formally organized, age-graded schools, and uniformly regimented academies tend to fall into the standard option category.

Alternatives also enable a more humanistic process of education to evolve. Smaller structural units replace the mass production, factory-like nature of today's schooling. Education options assume their own sense of community. Both teacher and student assume a new identity as part of a common, often more personalized, social system.

The small size of alternatives, together with the right of choice, takes us a giant step closer to humanizing our public schools.

Expanding the framework of public education to include a wide range of legitimate educational alternatives seems the most feasible route to reforming our schools for the following basic reasons:

1. EDUCATIONALLY The introduction of alternatives enhances the capacity of the school to tailor or individualize. Students can match

Figure 2. Alternatives on a Freedom to Prescription Continuum

Free	Open	Modified	Standard
Learner-directed and -controlled. Learner has complete freedom to orchestrate his own education. Teacher is one resource.	Learner has considerable freedom to choose from a wide range of content areas considered relevant by teacher, parent, student. Resource centers in major skill areas made available to learner.	Prescribed-content is made more flexible through individualization of instruction; school is ungraded; students learn same thing but at different rates. Using team teaching; teachers plan a differentiated approach to the same content. Teacher and-programmed course of study are the major sources of student learning.	Learner adheres to institution requirements uniformly prescribed: what is to be taught— how, when, where, and with whom. Teacher is instructor-evaluator. Student passes or fails according to normative standards.
Opening of school to the community and its resources.	Opening of school to the community and its resources. Teacher is supportive guider.		
Noncompetitive environment.	Noncompetitive environment.		
	Teacher-student planning.	Competitive environments.	Competitive environments.
No student failure Curriculum is viewed as social system rather than as course of studies.	No-student failure Curriculum is viewed as social system rather than as course of studies.	School is the major instructional setting	School is the major instructional setting
Learner-centered.	Teacher-centered.	Subject-matter-centered.	Institution-centered.

themselves with a range of differing educational environments. If one is not compatible, there are others. Alternative schools adapt to the learner, not the other way around.

A teacher connects with the alternative that best enhances his style and talent. He is more nearly matched with students who prefer his approach. This should increase educational productivity, one of the major concerns of the American public at this time, and should reduce conflict between teachers, parents, and students.

Alternatives also have a renewing effect on the school as a major institution. That is, as certain alternatives prove to be more productive than others, they will be increasingly demanded. Other alternatives will be introduced as the less effective schools fail. Those that produce will be retained, triggering a continuous cycle of renewal.

Optional education gives priority to staff development, which is now clearly tied to helping professionals retool for "their" alternative.

Alternatives deal with the very substance of education. By creating a range of education environments, they also break down the impersonal system of education. Alternatives provide the basis for creating more intrinsic, humane units within our schools.

2. POLITICALLY   Alternatives reduce intra- and extra-institutional political conflict. Since alternatives are a matter of choice, none is imposed on any party—teacher, parents, or student. Further, since the rights of the *individual* (teacher, parents, student) are made salient by alternatives, group-oriented politics are reduced, e.g., the politics of parent bodies, teacher associations, etc. Since parents, teachers, and students connect by choice and together help develop the alternatives, a new spirit of cooperation can emerge. Consumer choice and satisfaction in alternatives respond directly to the call for educational accountability.

3. ECONOMICALLY   Alternatives do not depend on large inputs of additional money. Rather, they are based on a reutilization of existing resources. For example, existing teachers have more opportunities to regroup themselves according to the preferred alternatives. Space is utilized differently, as in schools-within-schools. Federal and state funding now used for compensatory, add-on programs can be converted for use as seed capital for alternative education.

ADAMS HIGH: THE FIRST HUNDRED DAYS

TRUDY M. JOHNSON

Trudy M. Johnson, who lived through the first hectic days as a teacher at John Adams High School, provides an understandably sympathetic and warmly human portrait of the first hundred days in the life of this innovative high school in Portland, Oregon. Her optimism and enthusiasm are tempered with a realistic appraisal of the problems the school faced during its inception. This article contains a vivid description of the programs which set Adams apart from the mainstream of American public education. Trudy M. Johnson is associate editor of The Teacher Paper.

"What Kind Of A Nut House Is This?" Thus John Guernsey, education editor for the Portland *Oregonian*, titled an article on John Adams High School last August, a week before

Reprinted by permission from *The Teacher Paper* (Spring 1971), pp. 5–8.

the new school was to open in Portland. Now, after fifteen weeks of operation, a lot of people have asked themselves this same question in tones ranging from scorn to horror to delight. A sampling of comments from the press:

Parents of John Adams High School students who believe the new experimental school has become "an undisciplined monster" gathered Friday night to form an organization to help combat problems which have beset the school since it opened nine weeks ago. (*Oregonian*, November 15, 1969)

My son is a student at John Adams and he is proud of his school. I am pleased at his increased interest in the problems of our modern society and increased understanding of the problems of the minorities and underprivileged. I am proud that the Portland School Board invited the innovation of John Adams to come to Portland. (Letter to the Editor, *Oregon Journal*, November 14, 1969)

The conditions that exist at John Adams High School are in my opinion appalling and very disturbing . . . I'm very concerned about young people who have such bad manners to refuse a flag of their country, regardless of the donor. In fact, I believe any excuse would have served their purpose, and in my opinion they are not interested in our flag from anyone. They condemn the establishment, but what are they doing to improve things? (Letter to the Editor, *Oregonian*, November 10, 1969)

[Robert] Taylor [Director of Admissions at Portland State University] called the liberality "reasonable experimentation, a groping to find a way to make education relevant. I think it will win," he predicted, "and if it does, your young people here will have an education far superior to that of the students coming out of many high schools and colleges." (*Oregon Journal*, December 17, 1969)

What kind of nut house indeed? What kind of weird school would dare refuse a flag presented by the Daughters of the American Revolution (D.A.R.)? Where else do students control their own student body funds? Where else do teachers and students have veto power over the principal and a voice in the hiring of new teachers? And what other place could provoke the comment that "what you've got at Adams is a community, not a school"?

How did we get from being an "undisciplined monster" to being a "community"? Much of it has to be the work of the kids. All last spring and during a six-week institute in the summer when the staff was involved in planning, we kept talking about the concept of community—that Adams was going to be a cooperative effort of administrators, teachers, students, and parents. A Parent-Teacher-Student Association was organized early last spring, and forums were held at all schools from which Adams students would be coming. A government structure was proposed that would allow for much greater student and teacher voice in making basic policy than ever before in a public high school. Students were around in the summer, talking to the staff and working on committees dealing with things like grading and government. But still ... what would happen when all the kids showed up in the fall? Would they groove with the idea of a community? Or would this turn out to be another liberal idea destined to die because of its idealism?

Someone remarked ironically that during the summer the only unlocked door was the one farthest to the left at the front of the building. On September 8, all the doors were opened, and Adams became its own particular microcosm of the world with attendant problems.

The first few weeks were ones of testing the system. Teachers, students, and administrators tested themselves and each other. Adams drew students from three other Portland high schools—Grant, Jefferson, and Madison—representing a range of socio-economic groups, and students from those schools needed to find out where the power and influence lay. We had fights. We had kids from outside who came to Adams to do their own kind of testing. We had racial problems, particularly with outsiders and kids from Madison who had had virtually no contact with blacks before. (The student body is about 25% black.) And we had no real way of distinguishing between our own students and outsiders until I.D. cards were issued later in September.

This situation would be a perfect excuse for repression. After all, if kids won't behave "rationally" and "correctly," the usual solution is to tighten up fast and hard, because control tends to come first in most schools. But Adams doesn't work that way. There have been virtually no policy pronouncements from the Top. Problems at Adams are solved by everybody working together, which is, again, an idealistic notion. Perhaps the Adams staff read the headline in the A.C.L.U. paper last spring about the Tinker armband case: "Kids Are People." Kids are certainly first-class citizens in the Adams Community.

At any rate, a group of about forty students formed a Human Relations Committee that first week to try to solve some of the problems. They held student-planned and student-run assemblies to try to get it together. A lot of kids began to show that they cared about making Adams work.

But there also had to be an atmosphere, a feeling, a mood at Adams to make the kids care enough about a new school right after its opening to work hard to overcome problems. This atmosphere was created by a rather incredible staff with a personal commitment to Adams and the "Adams dream." On the second day of school, Bob Schwartz, the principal, sent a memo to the faculty stating: "I have placed in your box a letter addressed principally to the students concerning the Adams dream and yesterday's trouble. I would like this letter to be read and discussed in *every* first period class today. Please allow the students to vent their feelings about yesterday to the extent they wish. Stress that for Adams to succeed we have to have their support." This is part of the letter:

Adams High School represents a dream that many people have worked to bring about—a dream of a school where students and teachers from different backgrounds could work together toward common goals in an atmosphere of freedom and trust. Many people have told us that our dream was an impossible one, that students could not handle the freedom we wanted them to have, that black and white students could not really work together, that students and teachers could not trust one another.

This dream began in the fall of 1967, when seven students in the Harvard Graduate School of Education got to talking about the direction of education and how they could work to get the school to be the central unit for educational change, somehow putting into practice current educational theories that often seem to be so far away from the realities of a school setting. Figuring that they had a better chance of getting things done as a group rather than individually, they wrote a proposal for a "clinical high school," modeled after the concept of the teaching hospital. The clinical high school combines quality education for students, pre- and in-service training programs for teachers, and a research and development component. Portland was one of the districts around the country that expressed an interest in their proposal, and they decided that Portland was a good place to try their program. Four of the seven—Bob Schwartz, principal; Trish Wertheimer, coordinator of social services; John Parker, coordinator of Education Professions Development Act projects; and Al Dobbins, coordinator of teacher training—spent the 1968–69 school year in Portland, planning, recruiting a staff, and trying to make the dream a tangible reality. A fifth member of the group, Jerry Fletcher, who is coordinator of research and evaluation, came to Portland last summer.

The staff of about 100 came primarily from the Portland area. It is difficult to generalize about such a diverse group, but a few observations can be made. Quite a few members of the faculty are politically left of center, and there are a number of people active in local politics. Some faculty members took part in local Moratorium Day activities, either by turning the Moratorium into an educational experience at school or by activities undertaken outside of school and forfeiting a day's pay. On the whole, the faculty is quite independent and is not submissive, like the faculties in the two other schools in Portland in which I have taught. Lots of staff members work many extra hours helping work out policy for the school and generating curriculum which will be appropriate to Adams. There are also more people interested in current educational theories than in the average school. Copies of *Teaching As A Subversive Activity* (editors' note: see book reviews this issue) circulated last summer. Terry Borton, co-director of the

Affective Education Research Project, Philadelphia Public Schools, spent time at Adams during the summer and for several days in December, conducting workshops in his curriculum, which combines affective and cognitive education. A group of teachers has been working with this process curriculum this fall. And, finally, there are more people who really *care* about kids and teaching than in any other school I've ever seen.

That caring comes out in the relationships in the school. Most teachers gave their students the option of calling them by their first names or using the more formal form of address—whatever the kids felt most comfortable with. Many students have adopted the first-name calling, and the results are not a lack of respect, but rather a closer relationship, better classroom rapport, and, ultimately, perhaps, a more genuine respect. A student said, "A big factor here is that teachers are more like friends. They work with you kind of like your parents do. They're both teachers and friends. You don't just see them in class and talk to them about studies. You see them all over the school. You talk with them about all kinds of problems. With this kind of relationship you feel you owe the teacher something."

And teachers feel they owe students something, too. A good example of this is the way class cutting is handled. There are no cut slips. Suspending students from school for not coming to school is a little absurd. So, many teachers have taken it upon themselves to call or otherwise contact those kids not coming to class regularly to find out why and what can be done to make things more interesting, attractive, or relevant enough to get them back in class. In a number of cases, this has been very effective. Students have made a commitment to come to class and have kept it; teachers have been able to work with specific individual problems that the students might be having, such as family trouble, skill deficiencies, and so forth.

The structure of the school lends itself to increased personal contact. Each of the 1300 students was assigned to one of four "houses" by a process of "stratified random sampling," which insured that there would be a cross-section of the student body in each house. The houses act as sub-schools, each with its own administrator-teacher (curriculum associate), counselor, teams of teachers, and aides. Each student spends about half his time in the houses, taking General Education, which is organized on a non-graded basis (no tracking by grade levels) with completely heterogeneous grouping. The houses are beginning to be more than just arbitrary administrative units; students are identifying with their houses and forming house governments, and parent advisory groups and being organized by houses. The houses were originally named for the four curriculum associates: P.O. (Pat) Marsubian, Ed Mitchell, George Flittie, and Ed Gottlieb. Marsubian house has been renamed Shabazz House (Swahili for "self-educated"), and Mitchell House is now Harambee House (Swahili for "let's pull together"), as a result of student votes.

The General Education Program is the core of the curriculum. It incorporates English, social studies, basic math, and general science in a three-period block of time (a little over two hours). GenEd is supposed to be a problem-oriented course that draws together elements of the four areas listed above, and over the period of the first fifteen weeks of school, each house has developed its own model of GenEd, ranging from large group/small group activities to choices of "selectives." The latter model has been described ironically as "enlightened traditionalism." We're still experimenting with models that can work, given the problems of teaching untracked groups of students without regular textbooks (since these don't deal with current and future problems in ways that cut across traditional subject matter lines) within the usual constraints of space and time. But whatever the model, the focus is on contemporary problems, like pollution, population, how to deal with rapid change in society, racial conflict, and so on, and making the course relevant to the kids' lives and experiences.

In addition to GenEd, students have a wide range of electives (both semester and year-long) to choose from. These include a number of vocational courses, like graphics technology, electronics, automotive technology, and wood technology. In addition, six-week mini-courses are available, covering most things imaginable: bachelor cooking, silk screening, driver ed., poetry of rock music, beginning swimming, Russian History, basic piano, Afro-American art, heavy sounds, and on and on. Students may propose and teach their own mini-courses.

All classes are offered on the basis of a credit-no credit system, but the students also have the option of receiving A B C-no credit in semester or year courses if they wish. By getting "no credit" instead of a failing grade, a student still has the option of making up the work necessary for credit. We're trying to get kids to experience success for a change. At the end of the first grading period, written evaluations (with circles and arrows and a paragraph on the back . . .) were sent home on each student. These indicated progress in the course, and the student's work was judged satisfactory or unsatisfactory. This is an excerpt from such an evaluation:

René has done work of satisfactory quality in General Education this grading period. Her journal was kept up to date most of the time and shows that she is concerned about her education and is willing to work, but not always on her journal. She completed most of the other written work. In class discussions, she participated easily, but not as much as we had hoped . . . René is capable of doing better work and could be more responsible for getting work in. What she does do is thoughtful and of good quality most of the time . . .

Attendance—Excellent (two absences)

Class Work—Satisfactory

This method of evaluation increased the rapport between kids and teachers and also made a number of parents feel better.

There has been much parent criticism of the Adams idea. A group of seventy-five parents presented a nine-point letter to the superintendent and school board in October, objecting to a number of things about the school. These points included their belief that the atmosphere of Adams was one of "confusion and disorder," that we were not preparing students for college, and that they felt some teachers were undermining parents by indicating that parents who disagreed with the Adams idea were "squares" (their word). This had several effects. First, a lot of students united behind the program and tried to convince our detractors that Adams was a good school. Petitions in support of Adams were circulated by students and sent to the superintendent. And the kids understood the political pressures from outside and worked even harder to pull things together. A junior remarked, "We have the best school that was ever put together, if a lot of parents will just lay off and give it a chance to work."

Second, the criticism had the effect of forcing us to evaluate our program constantly, which is something most schools never do. And there have been changes so that programs speak more now to individual needs. Also, we've tried to turn the criticism into something constructive by instituting parent advisory councils. A letter from the principal sent to all Adams parents in mid-November said, in part:

Some Adams parents have publicly expressed the view that the school is failing, that it is an "undisciplined monster" altogether lacking in direction and control. If you share this view, we certainly want to hear from you; for we will make every effort to respond honestly to constructive criticism and to adjust our program to meet the needs of individual students. If, on the other hand, you are basically satisfied with our program and feel that our direction is sound, it is imperative that we hear from you as well . . .

As a consequence of all this, the group of seventy-five seems to have decreased considerably in size and intensity.

Some parents still oppose the freedom their children have at Adams. I can't help but think of George's comment in *Easy Rider* that those who aren't free feel threatened by those who are, and they will strike out against those who threaten them. One parent even commented that "kids have had too much freedom ever since the Warren Supreme Court went into effect." Bob Schwartz, the principal, has a slightly different view of this:

I think the real problem now is that many parents fear freedom—the freedom their children have in educational pursuit. I am confident we can win the support of most parents if we get the other issues resolved. The school is designed to make learning interesting—not try to pound in education with the discipline of a military operation. But many people still think that learning should not be fun. One parent actually complained to me that he was sure his son wasn't learning anything at Adams—"because he likes the school and never gripes about it. Some parents even come here and tell the teachers how sorry they feel for them. I recognize that the transition to dependency on yourself may take a little time for some students, but the students are actually taking the lead in solving some of the problems."

Solving these problems at Adams is done in as democratic a way as possible. The Adams Community Government roughly follows the federal model, with an Administrative Cabinet, Student Senate, and Faculty Senate. A judicial branch is to be included as soon as procedural details can be worked out for the Appeals Board. Each branch checks and balances the others, and students and teachers have a great deal more power than ever before. The model was proposed by Schwartz last spring, but teachers and students wrote their own constitutions. Students and teachers will be interviewing prospective teachers this spring and will make recommendations to the Cabinet about hiring them. Joint committees from the Student and Faculty Senates deal with such things as grading policy, curriculum, evaluation of courses, and community relations. They may pass legislation, subject to executive branch approval, but the principal's veto may be over-ruled by a simple majority vote of the faculty and a two-thirds vote of the student body. (The two-thirds vote was the students' idea.)

A good example of the democratic process in action is the celebrated D.A.R. flag incident. Earlier this fall, the Adams community was faced with the problem of whether to accept a flag from the Daughters of the American Revolution. Two years ago, the D.A.R. was given permission to present an American flag to the new high school when it opened. But when the presentation ceremony occurred, Kathy Tinnon, a black student chosen to accept the gift on behalf of the student body, refused the flag on the grounds that it was a gift from a racist organization. A number of students—black and white—walked out of the assembly, and Mr. Schwartz accepted the flag for the school. There were strong feelings over this issue. A petition circulated demanding immediate return of the flag. The local branch of the N.A.A.C.P. supported the refusal. Letters in the newspapers reflected some public feeling that Adams was unpatriotic. One lady suggested that the administration had been "cowed" and "coerced" by students during the flag incident. Some students then investigated the D.A.R.'s membership policy and came to the conclusion that it really is still a racist organization. The issue was presented to the Community, and a vote was taken. A majority of those students and teachers who voted favored returning the flag, and it was done. Since then, students have raised money by selling suckers and other goodies to buy two flags, one for the auditorium and one for the gym.

How is Adams different from every other school? Where else would you find about twenty members of the staff (including three administrators) with beards . . . no sign-in policy for teachers . . . a school television station named KWAP (Kids With A Purpose) as a result of a student contest . . . signs in the halls for students which say "please" . . . a remark by a kid that since he's been at Adams he misses school on the weekends . . . and a head secretary with her own personal copy of The *Teacher Paper*'s Guerrilla Manual who keeps wondering when we're going to plant grass in the chalktrays?? That's what kind of a nut house Adams is. Right on!

GETTING SERIOUS ABOUT RADICAL SCHOOL REFORM

JERRY CONRATH

Jerry Conrath works at John Adams High School in Portland, Oregon. He is now the director of a school-within-a-school, the Quincy School. His article is useful not only in bringing the reader up to date on the school described in the prior article by Trudy M. Johnson. He also supplies insight into the thinking of an educator who supports a radical education and who has concluded that neither the free schoolers nor the deschoolers have the answers. His commitment is to change within the public school system.

Now that it is becoming acceptable for members of the "free school" movement to take a look at the destruction it is bringing down on the lives of many of its member students, it is well past time to get serious. For too long we have rearranged jargon, tampered with curriculum innovation, fled from the reality of the system, and substituted our fantasies for a kid's chances for a decent life. I use the word "our" out of kindness. I am not, have not been, and do not intend to become a "free schooler." I will confess that when I was

Reprinted by permission from *The Teacher Paper*, October 1972, pp. 10–11.

teaching in one of the most restrictive and authoritarian high schools in Oregon I was, in my frustration and lack of wisdom, attracted to the notion. Happily I did not join. I grew a beard instead. And then, after changing jobs, I got serious.

When one is serious it is quickly discovered that certain things are simply not radical. Nor are they worthy alternatives to the present educational system. Private schools, for example, cannot be radical. What is bad for an economic system is bad for a school. Competition, prices of admission, exclusivity, and lack of pluralism are just not worth doing. Elitism is not radical. In my observation, most "alternatives" are based on some kind of elite: economic, intellectual, or hip. Elitism may not be the goal, but that seems to be how it ends up. Deschooling schemes would most certainly result in this, for we have not yet designed a system where market-place choices do not create a brutal class structure. Curriculum "innovation" without structural change is not radical. Happier sounding course titles with happier students pursuing happier objectives is keen. It is usually, however, a cover for an unwillingness or inability to restructure how students and teachers spend their day together: the same old oppressive stuff in new clothes. Finally, and articulated by other writers, telling kids that they don't need credentials, that they don't need to know how to read, write, and figure, and telling kids that we are all one big family of learners skipping merrily after lofty objectives (e.g. "ecstacy," etcetera, etcetera) is a vicious hoax. It is also not radical.

What then is radical? As I see it, to be radical is to strike at the heart or guts of a system, to turn things around. A radical school would impose upon itself the political agenda of changing the course or direction of education. At the same time it would have as its moral agenda the teaching of skills, competencies, and understandings that would enable participating students to join in the work of turning things around if they would so choose, and to help the students uncover choices in the system that would lead toward a decent life, career, and sense of self-merit. This was the agenda we had when we planned Quincy School. To the extent that we have kept to this agenda, we are radical. Even when we do things poorly (which we sometimes do) we are, I hope, radical.

The truth is that education is part of the culture, and in America it cannot avoid operating within a competitive, capitalist system. It cannot avoid operating within a culture dominated by the work-ethic, authoritarian procedures, democratic rhetoric, competition, and violence. It is also a culture in which political and business leaders actually believe that 4% unemployment is a good thing. And it is a culture in which business, political, and education leaders actually believe that a full employment economy and sound ecology are incompatible and that poverty will always be with us. Education that does not examine the sources and consequences of these absurdities, that does not teach the necessary skills for survival, *and* does not propose alternatives is fake. A school that does not help students realize the hazards and reality of operating within such a system, and a school whose leaders, because they run a public service and not a business, do not function first as political beings and as budget experts second, is foolish. To be foolish and fake also is not radical.

As indicated, I work at Quincy School. It is a school-within-a-school at John Adams High School in Portland, Oregon. When we planned Quincy we wanted to be radical reformers. We understood some important concepts. We understood that to be something other than an attractive extension of our egos, Quincy had to be a model for reform of the public school system. Anything short of that could never touch the lives of the thousands of teachers and millions of students who presently are being anesthetized and neutered by the nation's school systems.

We understood that we had to build a constituency for what we were doing. We were not willing to hold out groovy experiments to kids and their parents and say, "cross our line into our vision of the glorious future and we will love you." We crossed their lines. We had many students whose expressed needs were very different from our theory. We went to them, met their needs, and hence gained enough credibility with them and their parents to teach them our theory. That cannot be done if you, as a teacher, are viewed by your students as a kindly, friendly, loving fraud. We understood that all our students, all their parents, all of our colleagues, and all members of the community have the right to expect us to explain what we are doing, with logic and evidence. In short, we comprehended the necessity to be openly and honestly held accountable.

We also understood that we were not at Quincy because we were good people, because we liked kids, or because we were "with it." We were there because we had a job to do. We were intellectually competent and we viewed students that way. We also were political agents of the state empowered to grant certificates of citizenship: credentials. We were in a position to manipulate the hell out of the system to help our students, but we were in this position because we were in the system.

We understood that as educational leaders we had an obligation to clarify goals, propose strategies for pursuing those goals, and do our homework so that we had exciting, reasonable, and effective tactics for the day-by-day operation of the school and classes. We had an agenda each day. The agenda was always negotiable, and sometimes it was a miserable flop. But we came in with it; we were ready, for better or for worse, for school each day.

We understood that success in learning and teaching was essential to our growth as individuals and as a school. That success, therefore, had to be planned, arranged, structured, and then examined. Only the luxurious can afford the luxury of letting success fall where it may. Our kids needed it day by day. So did we.

We understood that as a school-within-a-school we were a satellite school and not an alternative school. If we could pull off an effective operation with 150 kids, a teaching staff with a student-teacher ratio no more favorable than the rest of the district, and offer high quality education, then we could hold ourselves up to Adams, the Portland School District, and the world as a model for reform.

Most of all we understood that a team of teachers and students must make the essential decisions of allocating resources. No longer can such decisions be made from a quiet office. Space, time, and personnel must be allocated each day by those who are consuming the resources. Quincy was offered as a model for decentralizing the educational and decision-making process. It worked.

There's a lot more to say about Quincy. I should write about our curriculum, about our specific goals (heavily borrowed from Art Pearl—read his new book, *The Atrocity of Education*), about the fun and frustration we had, about the mobilization of our parents into a political group who knew how they wanted their tax dollars spent, about our setbacks that came from our own inadequate planning, and about our attempts to make career education something more than the old vocational education tracking wrapped in new jargon. Some of the evidence is in. This year Adams has four more programs operating on our model. One down, two to go: the Portland system and the world. I should also add that I have spoken of Quincy in the past tense. That is misleading. This is our second year; we are alive and well. Since we really are serious about radical school reform something should be written in the future tense. Until that time, come visit us.

THE
JOHN
DEWEY
HIGH
SCHOOL
ADVENTURE

SOL LEVINE

*John Dewey High School provides a
significant departure from the traditional public
high school. As described here by principal Sol
Levine, the New York City public school is
attempting to provide an alternative through
"an adventure in education." The innovations at
Dewey include: modular scheduling, cyclical
programming, Dewey Independent Study Kits,
and a wide range of course offerings from the
"literature of protest" to "marine biology."*

"Modular scheduling." "Schools without
walls." "Schools within schools." A new jargon indicative of administrative tinkering—or substantive change in the process of secondary education? Proponents of reform search earnestly for answers to the all-too-evident problems of our schools: disruption, racial conflict, tuned-out students, and curriculum irrelevance. Nationwide, there has been a mushrooming of educational experiments designed to provide answers. John Dewey High School, located in the borough of Brooklyn, is one such experiment. Or, as the school brochure hopefully describes it, John Dewey High is "an adventure in education."

THE DESIGN

When it opened in September of 1969, John Dewey High represented a major departure from the traditional New York City high school. The blueprint for Dewey, drawn up by a committee of New York City educators with educational savvy and foresight, included the basic concepts of flexible modular scheduling, cyclical programming, learning for mastery, and independent study. The committee envisioned a new school with distinctive characteristics:

It abolishes grade levels, discontinues the Carnegie Unit as a measure of progress, breaks the five-period-per-week lockstep, abandons the distinction between major and minor subjects, provides instruction in practical arts for college-bound as well as work-oriented youngsters, incorporates extraclass activities into the curriculum, involves the classroom teacher in guidance, utilizes new methods and modern technology to supplement conventional instructional procedures, and makes use of a longer school day.

This blueprint became the basis upon which the educational program of the school was structured. Inherent in the program are some of the goals of the school:

Reprinted by permission from *Phi Delta Kappan*, October 1971, pp. 108–110.

1. Enabling students to learn at their own rate.
2. A vast array of course offerings designed to meet the needs and interests of students of all ability levels.
3. Individualization of instruction and a serious attempt to avoid the impersonalization of large, overcrowded schools.
4. The development of a sense of self-reliance and independence among students and an ability to learn on their own outside of the formal classroom.
5. Teacher and student involvement in the development of the educational program.

IMPLEMENTING THE DESIGN

The goals and ideals are lofty. To what extent has the philosophy been translated into program?

One parent, making her way uncertainly through knots of students relaxing on campus grounds, commented, "This looks like Woodstock." She saw students strumming guitars, playing frisbee, and otherwise relaxing. But after a tour through the building she sat down and wrote a letter expressing admiration for the school's relaxed and open atmosphere.

Student reaction is typified by one who said, "It's unbelievable. I'm experiencing the kinds of things no other school could give me." As part of his high school program, this student works one day a week helping a professor at the New York University Dental School. John Dewey's planners believe that learning can take place outside of the formal classroom.

All students *elect* to attend John Dewey High School. There is no special examination for admission into the school. Students need only apply for admission. Every effort is made to maintain an integrated school (approximately one-third of the students are black and Puerto Rican) and to have a broad spectrum of student ability levels. The school population is typical of Brooklyn academic high schools.

The teaching staff is young and exciting. By agreement with the United Federation of Teachers (the union has been superlative in its cooperation with this experiment) 50% of the school staff is chosen by the principal without regard to seniority status. All remaining teachers transfer into the school voluntarily. Teachers new to the school are required to attend a summer orientation institute. Much of the time in the summer program is spent in developing curricula and teaching materials. The overall success of this orientation program is reflected in the staff's dedication to and enthusiasm for the experiment.

From an organizational point of view the essential ingredients in the Dewey program include the following:

1. AN EIGHT-HOUR DAY   Teachers and students alike have an eight-hour day to enable students to learn at their own rate. Approximately 25% (varying with the daily schedule) of the student's day is spent on independent study. Students can accelerate in all subject areas by taking DISKs: Dewey Independent Study Kits. DISKs are self-contained courses taken outside of the formal classroom. Department advisers are available to help and guide students working on DISKs. Students can get course credit by passing examinations (written, oral, or laboratory) designed to determine mastery in a DISK.

2. INDEPENDENT STUDY   The independent study program is non-directive. That is, the student need not account for this time. Students have the option of going to department resource centers, using the school library (generally packed to capacity), involving themselves in club activities (built into the school day), or relaxing on campus grounds. Resource centers are a vital focal point of the independent study program. The centers are equipped with all sorts of software and hardware related to individual subject areas. Moreover, teachers are always available at the center to help students having difficulty or to assist those who are advancing more rapidly than the average. Each teacher spends approximately one hour and 40 minutes a day in his departmental resource center.

3. FLEXIBLE MODULAR SCHEDULING   The eight-hour day is broken into 20-minute time periods, better known as modules. Courses can be programmed to meet for two, three, or more modules. For example, social studies classes generally meet on a 2-3-2-3 basis four times a week. That is, they meet for 40 minutes on Mondays and Wednesdays and for an hour on Tuesdays and Thursdays.

4. CYCLICAL PROGRAMMING   The Dewey year is divided into five seven-week cycles with an optional sixth summer cycle. Students are reprogrammed every seven weeks. (The school programming is done in affiliation with the Brooklyn College computer center.) A Dewey term generally ends on a Friday, and on Monday students receive their new programs and start the new term. Despite the fact that officials are very liberal with program changes, a total of fewer than 500 changes (out of a possible 16,000) were completed in three days. The efficiency of the programming system is astounding. Courses are designed to last for one, two, or more cycles. This "mini-term" concept has enabled Dewey to help students avoid the "long corridor of failure" associated with annual or semi-annual organization.

5. A BROAD ARRAY OF COURSE OFFERINGS   The mini-terms facilitate the development of an unusual number of course offerings in all subject areas. By way of illustration, the English department offers well over 35 courses to students. E.g., Introduction to the Novel, The American Dream (an interdisciplinary course), The Bible as Literature, The Generation Gap in Literature, Literature of Protest, Literature of

Science Fiction and Fantasy. Thus a student can select, cafeteria style, those courses of interest to him. To assure a "balanced diet," Dewey students must meet the minimum requirements established for all New York City high school students. However, Dewey has one of the highest curriculum indices (number of subjects taken per student) in the city; most students take between seven and eight subjects in each cycle. This means that students will graduate early or will be in a position to take additional electives. A Dewey student's program might include: transportation (the automotive shop is one of our six shops), sculpture, the modern novel, consumer economics, brass ensemble, typing (all students must show proficiency in typing), marine biology, and algebra.

6. AN EXTENSIVE GUIDANCE PROGRAM There are seven full-time guidance counselors with a student load of 300 each. This enables counselors to provide omnibus counseling—educational, vocational, and college counseling as well as "crisis" counseling. We also have the part-time services of a psychologist and social worker.

7. LEARNING FOR MASTERY Dewey students do not receive numerical grades, inasmuch as an underlying concept of the school program is that students learn to achieve mastery. Students receive four basic grades: M (for mastery), indicating sufficient mastery to move into the next phase of work; R (for retention), indicating need to repeat the course due to a failure to achieve mastery; MI (for mastery in independent study), indicating mastery in the DISK program; MC (for mastery with condition), indicating marginal mastery with specific areas of weakness. This grade enables us to provide for "prescriptive teaching." All students receiving MC or R have an educational prescription form sent home which explains specific areas of deficiency. These prescriptions are available to the new teacher and are also available in the resource center. Teachers can help students overcome deficiencies in both the classroom and resource center. The language department requires students to take supportive DISKs (with teacher assistance) where a student has received an MC.

The question most frequently asked concerning the John Dewey grading system is, Will it permit students to be admitted to the colleges? Extensive meetings and communication with college admissions officers have yielded an overwhelmingly favorable response. College admission will represent no serious problem for our students. In fact, at this writing one of our 10 graduates (graduating after two years in our school) has already been accepted by a private college.

8. INNOVATIONS IN TEACHING TECHNIQUES The area where the most work remains to be done is that of teaching methodology. Dewey rooms have folding walls, permitting us to operate a number of team-teaching programs. We are hopeful that this program will be expanded. The marine biology program (an extensive and exciting one) makes full use of the surrounding beach areas and the Coney Island Aquarium.

Interdisciplinary courses are being developed. For example, a metal sculpture class is a combined effort of the fine arts and industrial arts departments.

One of the more exciting programs we have instituted on a pilot basis is our "4-1 Program." This involves students in an educational experience outside of the school one day a week. As of last March, Dewey students were studying anthropology in the Museum of Natural History, art students were studying in the Brooklyn Museum, science students were working in a number of medical fields at the Brooklyn Downstate Medical Center, and a number of other students were pursuing projects in areas of their particular interest. For example, one student was working as a free-lance reporter for a local newspaper. Students receive course credit for work done in this program.

ELIMINATING THE GENERAL TRACK

"Tracking" or homogeneous grouping does not exist in John Dewey High School. We hope thus to come to grips with the glaring inadequacies associated with the "general diploma"—a course of study which is essentially a hodge-podge of courses leading, in my view, to few educational or marketable skills. In English and social studies students who receive an R can opt for an alternative course, thereby avoiding the failure syndrome associated with repeating courses. In sequential skill subjects, such as mathematics and foreign language, we have provided for a series of attenuated courses. That is, students can take algebra in the normal five-phase span (one year), in a seven-phase span (one and one-half years), or in 10 phases (two years). There is frequent movement within the 5-7-10-phase courses, depending upon teacher-counselor recommendations.

SUCCESS OR FAILURE?

It is obviously too early to evaluate the success or failure of the Dewey program definitively. Ongoing formal and informal evaluations will continue. Yet there are certain basic indications of apparent successes and problems.

Do students use their independent study time productively? While one can quibble over the meaning of the term "productively," there is evidence that most of the students do use their study time in an educationally positive manner. The school library is generally filled to capacity (a beautiful sight when one considers the underutilization of many high school libraries), and the resource centers are used on an average of 75% of capacity. The sight of teachers working with students on a one-to-one basis or in small groups is a delight to an educator's eye.

The DISK program is extremely popular. During the first three cycles, 559, then 1,138, and finally 1,174 students signed up for DISKs. The completion ratio during Cycle II averaged approximately 40%, while approximately 30% of the students received credit for courses on DISKs. Our experience indicates that the highest rate of passing (in the DISK program) is among those who have taken out multiple DISKs. There have been obvious problems with the DISK program, however. As might be expected, the overwhelming number of subscribers for DISKs are advanced students; relatively few students who receive R's are involved.

"Coming to Dewey was like moving from a prison to freedom," remarked one student. While he was doubtless overstating the case, nevertheless his comment reveals a problem. Students coming from traditionally structured school environments often find it difficult to adjust to the large blocks of independent study time. A relatively small percentage of students spend too much time in the cafeteria, failing to avail themselves of the school's superb facilities. Continued counseling, parent consultation, and ongoing orientation have led to some limited success with these students.

Has the generally relaxed atmosphere led to an improved student-teacher and student-student relationship? We believe it has, although atmosphere is hard to measure. Nearly all the visitors to Dewey cite the "excellent tone" within the school. The frequent reprogramming of the school has led to an improved teacher-student relationship. During the course of a year, teachers meet many students and form strong educational associations. A very small percentage of the students can still be classified as alienated, but the overwhelming number get along quite well.

A long list of pluses and minuses would, at this point, serve little purpose. A formal evaluation is being developed with faculty, student, and parental assistance. John Dewey High School is experiencing all of the growing pains and excitement associated with a new educational undertaking. While many of the innovative aspects of the school program can be found in other experiments throughout the country, what makes it particularly exciting is the commitment of one of the largest educational systems in the world—the New York City schools—to this venture into educational alternatives. It is my own view that *one* of the answers to the problems of large urban school systems is the development of an increasing number of educational alternatives for students. When students can *elect* to go to the school of their choice, a major step forward will have been taken. I look forward to the creation of additional John Dewey High Schools located in each of the five boroughs of New York City.

REACH, TOUCH, AND TEACH

TERRY BORTON

The supporters of education of the emotions are not revolutionaries; they call attention to an aspect of learning which they think has been grossly undervalued. They believe that affective education is needed in American schools and that cognitive learning should not be granted the dominance called for by most of the advocates of study of the disciplines (with the notable exception of the psychologically oriented Jerome S. Bruner).

The Philadelphia public schools sponsored the Affective Education Research Project. Terry Borton, as co-director of the project, helped teachers to deal with psychological as well as logical processes. In "Reach, Touch, and Teach" he reports on classroom experiences and teacher training techniques, and discusses the problems of becoming accepted which affective education encounters.

The article reproduced here was adapted from Borton's book, Reach, Touch, and Teach: Student Concerns and Process Education (*New York: McGraw-Hill, 1970*).

There are two sections to almost every school's statement of educational objectives—one for real, and one for show. The first, the real one, talks about academic excellence, subject mastery, and getting into college or a job. The other discusses the human purpose of school—values, feelings, personal growth, the full and happy life. It is included because everyone knows that it is important, and that it ought to be central to the life of every school. But it is only for show. Everyone knows how little schools have done about it.

In spite of this, the human objectives describe the things all of us cite when we try to remember what "made a difference" in our school careers: the teacher who touched us as persons, or the one who ground out our lives to polish our intellects; the class that moved with the strength and grace of an Olympic team, or the dozens of lessons when each of us slogged separately toward the freedom of 3 o'clock. What we learned, and what we became, depended to a significant degree on how we felt about ourselves, our classmates, and our teachers. The schools were right—the human purposes *were* important. But with the

Reprinted from *Saturday Review*, January 18, 1969, pp. 56–58, 69–70. Copyright 1969 Saturday Review, Inc. Reprinted by permission of the author and publisher.

exception of those teachers who were so rare we never forgot them, the schools did little to put their philosophy into practice.

Recently, however, a variety of programs have begun to build curricula and teaching methodology that speak directly to the human objectives. These programs, stemming both from within the schools and from various branches of psychology, point the way to a school practice which not only recognizes the power of feelings, but also combines academic training with an education directly aimed at the student's most important concerns. Schools may soon be explicitly teaching students such things as how to sort out and guide their own psychological growth, or increase their desire to achieve, or handle their aggressive instincts in nonviolent forms.

The new impetus has a variety of names: "psychological education," "affective," "humanistic," "personological," "eupsychian," "synoetic." Some of these names are a bit bizarre, and none has yet gained wide acceptance. But taken together their presence indicates a growing recognition that in the world's present state of social and moral turmoil, the schools' traditional second objective can no longer be for show. Riots, poverty, war, student rebellion, swollen mental hospitals, and soaring crime rates have involved an enormous number of people. They have generated a broadening conviction that society is as responsible for the psychological well-being of each of its members as is each individual. And that conviction has created a receptive audience for new kinds of educational critics.

The new critics do not simply attack the schools for their academic incompetence, as did the Rickovers of a decade ago. They are equally concerned with the schools' basic lack of understanding that students are human beings with feelings as well as intellects. Jonathan Kozol has given a gripping sense of the "destruction of the hearts and minds of Negro children" in his *Death at an Early Age*. In *How Children Fail* John Holt has shown that even in the best "progressive" schools, children live in constant fear which inhibits their learning, and Paul Goodman's *Compulsory Mis-education* has made a powerful case for his contention that "the present school system is leading straight to 1984." The intuitive warnings of these "romantic critics" have been backed up by statistical evidence from the largest survey of education ever conducted, James Coleman's *Equality of Educational Opportunity*. This survey correlates academic achievement with attitudes such as a student's self concept, sense of control over his fate, and interest in school. The study concludes that these attitudes and feelings are more highly correlated with how well a student achieves academically than a combination of many of the factors which educators have usually thought were crucial, such as class size, salary of teachers, facilities, curriculum.

The pressure to deal more directly with student feelings (increasingly a pressure from students as well as critics) has given rise to dozens of different projects. None of the three examples which I will discuss here has yet reached the size or influence of the giant curriculum centers (such as the Educational Development Corporation) which grew up as a result of the post-Sputnik criticism. But in the long run they may be much more important. For the post-Sputnik curriculum reforms were essentially attempts to find better ways to teach the traditional disciplines of math, science, or social studies—often with the effect of moving the college curriculum into elementary and secondary schools. The programs I am describing not only operate with different techniques, but also begin to define and develop new curriculum subjects and a new school orientation toward practical and applied psychology. If expanded, they will make a profound change in American education —hopefully a change toward a more humane educational process, and a more human student.

The project which I co-directed with Norman Newberg, the Philadelphia School Board's specialist in "affective education," is an example of such a curriculum. It is being developed from within the schools— in this case by a group of urban teachers trying to find a philosophy and method which would work with the students they were asked to teach. The program is based on the assumption that every person handles massive amounts of information, and needs to be taught both logical and psychological processes for handling it. Two semester-long courses, one in communications, and one in urban affairs, isolate such processes as symbolization, simulation, dreaming, and deescalating pressure, and teach them in an explicit fashion. At the same time the classes are designed to tie these processes to the amorphous undercurrent of student concerns for self-identity, power, and relationship.

I dropped into a high school communications class one hot day during last summer's field testing, when the teacher was working on "taxonomy of process," or a way of looking at what, why, and how behavior occurs and changes. The purpose of the class was to show the students a simple technique for analyzing their own habitual forms of processing the world around them, and then to show them how they could develop new responses if they wanted to. The class was working in groups of twos, filling in "What Wheels" for each other. One boy in the back was without a partner, so I joined him, and we agreed that I would make a What Wheel for him, and he would make one for me. I drew a circle, filled in the spokes, and wrote down my first impressions of him: "strong, quick, Afro, shy, bright."

The teacher asked us to read each other our What Wheels, select one adjective which interested us most, and ask our partner to draw a "Why Wheel" to explain *why* that adjective was meaningful to him.

Charlie read me his What Wheel—he was perceptive, as students usually are about teachers. Then I read him mine.

"Why'd you write 'shy'? I ain't shy."

"Well, I just met you, so I can't fill out a whole Why Wheel about it. But when I first sat there, I noticed you looked down at your desk instead of up at me. So I just guessed you were shy with strangers—maybe just with strange teachers."

Charlie took his What Wheel from me and looked at it. "You know, that's the truth. I thought nobody, except maybe my mother, knew that about me, but well, it's the truth anyhow."

The murmur of the class's conversation quieted while the teacher told us how to make up "How Wheels" with our partners. We were supposed to write down the range of actions which would either increase or decrease the trait we had been discussing.

"Aw, man, it would be easy to increase being shy," laughed Charlie. "I just wouldn't look at nobody."

"And decreasing it?"

"I'd look at you like I'm looking at you right now," he said, looking me straight in the eye. "And more than that, I'd look at you like that when you first came in here. Teacher, or white man, I wasn't afraid of you; no reason why I should act like I was."

We talked for a while—about my wheels, about the effectiveness of the what, why, how process questions for looking at behavior, and about school. When the bell rang, we shook hands. "See ya around," he said.

"See ya around," I said.

While many teachers have been experimenting with techniques similar to ours, research psychologists usually have been rather disdainful of messy problems in the schools. Increasingly, however, psychologists such as David McClelland of Harvard are beginning to work on problems of motivation and attitude in schools. The progression of McClelland's study is a good example of how basic research may be applied to problems in education. McClelland began working on problems of measuring the motivation of rats deprived of food, performed a series of experiments to measure hunger motivation in humans, and then devised a system for measuring "achievement motivation" in men by counting the frequency of its appearance in fantasy images. He defined the need for achievement (n-Ach) as a pattern of thought and fantasy about doing things well, and discovered that those people who had such a pattern were characterized by a preference for moderate risk goals, a desire for immediate feedback on their performance, and a liking for personal responsibility. McClelland reasoned that if a society had a great number of such individuals, the society itself should show outstanding achievement. Twenty years were spent in a mammoth research effort to substantiate his claim that achievement research provided a "factual basis for evaluating theories that explain the rise and fall of civilizations." The next step was to devise educational methods for increasing the achievement motive in people who did not have much of it, and to test out these methods in this country and abroad.

Dr. Alfred Alschuler, director of the Harvard Achievement Motivation Development Project, which is one result of McClelland's research, is in charge of a federally funded five-year research project to assess what factors lead to effective achievement training. The project has devised many classroom techniques for increasing achievement motivation in students, most of them involving experiential learning that takes place in a game situation. I visited one training program for teachers in a nearby city, and sat in on a session that used a contest in making paper airplanes to demonstrate to the teachers how achievement motivation affects their students.

There was a lot of joking around the table, as everyone was a little nervous.

"Now they're going to use the old carrot on us," cracked a little physics teacher sitting on my right.

The head of the math department, an enormous man, smiled broadly, first at the physics teacher, and then at me. "Feeling cutthroat?" he asked.

I didn't say so, but I was, and he knew it. My "n-Ach" was way up. We eyed each other while we set our own quotas for the number of planes we would make.

Dr. Alschuler gave us the start sign. I was making planes feverishly; out of the corner of my eye, I could see the math department head moving more slowly, but doing a better job—the quality control check at the end of the game might go in his favor. The physics teacher was using mass production techniques, making one fold at a time.

At the end of five minutes the game was up, and we were all laughing at the tension it had produced. The physics teacher had more planes than any of us, but his mass production assembly had failed—all the planes were missing one wing. I had the second largest number of planes, but several had sloppy folds and were disqualified.

"Nuts to this," said the physics teacher. "I'm not going to get another heart attack over a bunch of paper airplanes. Next time I'm dropping my quota in half. I'm only going to make six."

I was swearing at myself—I should have been more careful. Next time through the game I would set a slightly lower quota and do a better job.

The math teacher was smiling broadly. He had won.

Later we all talked about our experience in the game and how our own behavior did or did not reflect the characteristics of a high achiever. Did we set moderate risk goals? Did we utilize information on our success or failure? Then we began to dig into the more fundamental value issues that were involved. Suppose that we could use games like the paper plane construction to teach students the characteristics of a high achiever, and through a variety of such exercises could actually train him to think and act as one. Was that a good thing? Did we want to subject our students to the pressure that we had felt? Could we decide that achievement training was good for some students who were not achieving up to our standards, and bad for those who were too competitive? On what basis?

Just as researchers are becoming involved in the practical questions of education, so clinical psychotherapy is getting up off its couch and finding ways to add its skill to solving school problems. Dr. Carl Rogers, founder of client-centered therapy, is presently working with Western Behavioral Sciences Institute and a group of Catholic schools to devise ways to use "sensitivity groups" in the schools. (A "sensitivity group" or "T-group" is composed of about a dozen people who meet for the purpose of giving feedback on how each person's behavior affects the other people in the group.) The National Training Laboratory, an associate of the National Education Association, is now running a year-round series of T-groups and related experiences for teachers and administrators. And in San Diego, child psychiatrist Dr. Harold Bissell and educator Dr. Uvalo Palomares have set up the Human Development Training Institute which has written a two-year sequence of lesson plans to improve a primary school child's self-confidence and awareness, and has trained 1,000 teachers to use it.

One of the most eclectic approaches in the clinical tradition is the project run by Dr. George Brown of the University of California at Santa Barbara. Brown's project, sponsored by the Ford Foundation through the ebullient Esalen Institute, utilizes many different approaches, but particularly the theories of Gestalt therapy which attempt to get youth in touch with how they are feeling in the "here and now." With such theoretical orientations in their background, the teachers in Brown's project are encouraged to devise their own techniques to integrate academic with affective or emotional learning in order to achieve a more "humanistic education."

I joined the teachers at one of the monthly meetings where they learn about new ideas, and share with each other the techniques they have developed. Gloria Siemons, a pretty first-grade teacher, was describing an exercise that she had first conducted with the entire class, and then used when one child became angry at another. She lined the class up in two rows on the playground, had them find a partner, put their hands up facing each other, and push.

Push they did, laughing all over the field, especially at their teacher, who was being pushed around in a circle by several of the bigger kids.

Later, when two kids got into an argument at recess, Mrs. Siemons simply asked them: "Are you angry now? Would you like to push?"

"Yes, I'm angry. I'm angry at him."

Both agreed to the contest, pushed for a minute as hard as they could, and then collapsed into each other's arms giggling. Their anger was worked out, but without hurting each other.

"What would happen," I asked Mrs. Siemons, "if one kid pushed another hard enough to hurt him?"

"We have a rule about that. 'It's OK to be angry with someone, and it's OK to push, but it's *not* OK to push him into the rosebush.' "

Good teachers, particularly good first-grade teachers such as Mrs. Siemons, have always responded to the emotional side of their students' lives, and it is precisely this intuitive gift which Dr. Brown is capitalizing on. By systematizing such techniques and relating them to a general theoretical framework, he and the teachers of his staff have begun to generate hundreds of ways to integrate the feelings of students with the regular curriculum taught from kindergarten to high school.

The techniques being developed, the dozens of programs, and the various theories differ in many respects, but they have several features in common. First, and most important, all of them deal in a very explicit and direct way with the student's feelings, interpersonal relations, or values. It is the fact that they are so explicit and direct which sets them apart from the vague protestations that schools have usually made about this area. While schools were concentrating on math, science, or English, they often ignored or actively suppressed feelings. The new programs make what was covert behavior the subject of overt discussion; they make the implicit explicit. They legitimize feelings, clarify them for the student, and suggest a variety of behaviors which he can use to express them. They do so on the assumption that these feelings exert a powerful effect on a student's behavior, both in the present and in the future. If schools want to influence behavior, then it makes sense to deal directly with its major sources, not just with the binomial theorem, the gerund, or the Seventeenth Amendment.

A factor in the new field which often causes misunderstanding is that most of the programs use non-verbal experiences, either through physical expression and involvement, or through art, sculpture, or music. For the most part, this involvement with the *non*-verbal is not *anti*-verbal or *anti*-intellectual. Non-verbal educational techniques are based on the obvious but little-utilized fact that a child learns most of his emotional response patterns at a very young age—before he can talk. His knowledge of love, rejection, anger, and need does not come through words, but through his physical senses—touch, a flushed face, a gnawing in his stomach. Even later, when he begins to talk, the words he learns are "Mama," "doggie," "see"—words for things and actions, not feelings. Indeed, many children seem entirely unable to give a name to their current feelings—they have been taught how to say "I am bad," but not "I feel bad." Education that deals with feelings is often facilitated by skipping over the verbal labels which have been learned relatively late in life, regaining the other senses, and then reintegrating them with verbal thought and new behaviors.

Another common technique which causes confusion is the reliance of many of the programs on games, dramatic improvisations, and role-playing. Again, though those utilizing the techniques believe in fun and use games, few of them are simply advocating "fun and games." Their interest stems from an insight into the learning process of small children. By playing games—house, fireman, office, war—little children learn what it will be like to be an adult, and begin to develop their own style in that role. But our culture provides few such opportunities for older children or adolescents, even though the society is changing so fast that many of the response patterns they learned as a three-year-old may be no longer relevant, or even dangerous. Games and improvisation allow a simulation of the self. While they are real and produce real emotions, their tightly defined limits provide a way to try out new behavior without taking the full consequences which might occur if the same action were performed in ordinary relationships.

There are answers for questions about non-verbal and gaming emphasis, but there are many other questions which the programs raise for which there are no answers. At best, solutions will come slowly, and that is bound to produce tremendous strain in a time when events wait for no one. Many of these problems are already developing. Though Dr. Alschuler at Harvard and Dr. Willis Harman at the Stanford Research Institute are both engaged in large surveys to find out what techniques and philosophies are presently being employed in the field, there is still no common theoretical base for the programs, and very little research on their effectiveness. The Achievement Motivation Development Project has by far the most extensive research program, and Dr. Alschuler's experience with it has made him feel strongly about the need for additional evidence before program expansion:

We have very little hard evidence that programs in this new field accomplish much more than natural maturation. We have claims, promises, and fascinating anecdotes. But we should not institute these programs without first using the most sophisticated research techniques we have to improve them and explore their consequences.

In addition to unanswered questions about effectiveness, there are practical limitations to all of the programs. Few have done an adequate job of integrating their material with the usual skills and knowledge that everyone recognizes the schools must continue to teach. No attempt has yet been made to work together with the free-flowing academic programs (such as the Leicestershire movement) which seem natural complements. Though all of the projects I have discussed here stress their responsiveness to student concerns, it is not yet clear how they can do that and yet not be heavily dependent on the skills and personalities of a few teachers like Mrs. Siemons who can both legitimize anger and make the rosebush out of bounds.

Politically, programs with both the potential and liabilities of these are obvious hot potatoes. It is unclear as yet how projects designed by psychologists will fit in with current efforts toward more community control and what seems to be the resulting concentration on "teaching the basics." Even a mode of politics that is in consonance with the ideals and methods of the new programs is unknown, for the vision they present is often as utopian as that in George Leonard's exciting new book, *Education and Ecstasy*. How to get from here to there without waiting until 2001 is a complex political problem. Suppose, for instance, that a school district decided to adopt an entirely new curriculum and school organization based on the concepts I have been discussing. Would the teachers be able to change? Great care would have to be taken with their feelings and concerns, for not only are they as human as the children, but—as recent events in New York have indicated—they will strike if they feel they are being treated unfairly.

The most fundamental problem, and the one which is likely to get people the most upset, is the ethical question caused by changing the expectations of what schools are for. At present, students go to school to "learn stuff," and though they may expect schools to provide information, they do not expect schools to change them in any fundamental way, or even to offer that opportunity. As long as schools continue to have relatively little explicitly acknowledged impact on the students' values, attitudes, and behaviors, no one is likely to worry much about ethical issues. If schools consciously begin to make important changes in students' lives, people will suddenly become very concerned about what is happening to immature minds that are forced to accept this kind of education for twelve years. They will begin to ask whether there should be compulsory education, or whether students should be free to accept or reject schooling. And they will begin to ask hard questions about what should be taught, and how it should be presented.

If, for instance, all children should be motivated, should they also be "achievement motivated"? At what age? Who decides? And who teaches? What is to stop teachers from working out of their own needs rather than for those of their pupils? Should teachers who share an important confidence have the same legal privilege which a lawyer or a minister has? How can parents and children be assured of the privacy which is their right?

The ethical problems are likely to be compounded by the reporting of the mass media. The new field is peculiarly open to parody ("HARVARD PROF TEACHES PAPER AIRPLANE CONSTRUCTION") and to easy association with the exotic and erotic. (*Life* recently stuck a single misleading paragraph on Brown's project into a long article on Esalen Institute. By far the most arresting thing in the article was a two-page picture spread on a nude sensitivity group that had nothing to do with either Brown's project or Esalen.) Sensational publicity is not what the new field needs. It does need the time, the careful research and planning, and the critical reporting which will allow it to grow or decline on its merits. The alternative is a series of fads, created by ignorance and publicity, and death—after a short and enthusiastic life—in disillusionment.

The new programs are too important to allow that to happen. They are delicate, and they are moving into an area which is fundamentally new, so they can be expected to suffer from the attention they attract, to make mistakes, and to run into blind alleys. If it takes the big curriculum development corporations a million dollars and three years to build a single course in science or social studies, it will be even more difficult to build a fully developed curriculum in a new field. But the effort should be encouraged. For while it may not be novel to assert that a man's feelings are a crucial determinant of his public behavior and private well-being, there is no question about the novelty and significance of school programs that explicitly educate both the feelings and the intellect. Such programs raise many of society's basic questions about purpose and meaning—tough questions which will not be easy to answer. But they also offer a possibility for building a saner world—a world where people are more open about their feelings, careful in their thinking, and responsible in their actions.

METRO: EXPERIMENTAL HIGH SCHOOL WITHOUT WALLS

NATHANIEL BLACKMAN

Cities other than Philadelphia are also developing community oriented schools. Chicago's Metro appears to be successfully utilizing the educational environment of the city as its classroom. In this "school without walls," educative encounters are directly experienced by students, not just described by teachers. Physiology is taught at a school of medicine, a lawyer teaches "how a lawyer works," and changes in the city are studied in a course called "Halsted Street." Nathaniel Blackman is principal of the Chicago Public High School for Metropolitan Studies.

Metro High School is an experimental four-year school without walls; it has no conventional school building. Students are participating in learning experiences all over the city of Chicago—all hours of the day and night and on weekends.

Metro opened in February, 1970, with 150 students who applied because they were unhappy with the regimentation of their traditional high schools. The students come from every high school in the city and reflect the diversity of Chicago's population in ethnic backgrounds, interests, and previous school achievements. Some 3,000 students applied when enrollment was expanded to 350 students in September, 1970. Students who were admitted were selected at random by a lottery system, so that a cross section of the city would be represented.

The format of the school program reflects five innovations in education which staff members are attempting to develop:

1. The possibilities for meaningful education are enhanced when such education occurs in real life situations such as businesses, cultural institutions, and neighborhoods of Chicago.

   Examples: We find students studying the human body at the Abraham Lincoln School of Medicine and telescope making at Adler Planetarium. The American Civil Liberties Union is teaching a course called "Dissent in America," slide-tape production is being taught at the Art Institute, French is being studied at the Belgian consulate office. Through the Board of Health, students were placed at a state hospital to work with emotionally disturbed preschoolers. One of the city's daily newspapers has provided personnel to teach a creative writing course.

2. Students can learn from people with varied skills and interests:

Reprinted by permission from the *National Association of Secondary School Principals Bulletin*, May 1971, pp. 147–150.

lawyers, artists, scientists, electricians, etc. A skilled teacher can utilize the talents of these people to provide a greatly enriched educational experience for the students.

Examples: A stock broker is teaching a course on the stock market; a lawyer has a course called "How a Lawyer Works"; a correctional officer is teaching a course called "Penal Justice"; a professional artist is teaching a course in studio art and a professional actress is teaching a course called "Improvisational Theater."

3. An educational curriculum for modern urban youth should grow out of the realities of the city. A new interdisciplinary curriculum is necessary to tap both the physical and human resources for learning what the city has to offer.

Examples: County Hospital gives student placements for our core courses. A local community organization teaches a course on politics. The city filtration plant is a meeting place for the ecology class; the utility companies provide instructors; our students are learning the history of Chicago by taking a course called "Halsted Street" (which requires students to travel the length of the city noting the changes that have taken place over a period of years).

4. An urban secondary program must be developed with student involvement in decision making. Students should become independent learners by helping to make decisions about how the school will be structured and how their own education will proceed.

Examples: Students are involved in teacher selection, curriculum development, and governance of the school. They are accountable for their own educational goals. There are no grades or standardized tests. However, students are involved in the evaluation of their courses. There are very few established rules and regulations; common sense is the dominating factor in control.

5. The diverse backgrounds of students provide a resource for educational guidelines that become an integral part of the school program.

Examples: Students having knowledge of certain courses because of their background are utilized as teachers. There are students teaching multimedia, photography, rug making, ballet and dance, black pride, consumer education, karate, and a course in independent reading and discussion.

What have these innovations done for students? They are changing socially and finding the daily routine of attending school more acceptable. Parents are saying they no longer have to get their children up in the morning for school. Students arrive at school at 7:30 A.M. for 9:00 A.M. classes.

The students are put out of the building at 6:00 P.M. in order that the staff may go home. Parents say that for the first time in years they are communicating with their children. Students are going home telling parents how they have spent their day and where they have been. Last summer, students did not want school to end; approximately 75 of them returned voluntarily to attend a four-week summer teacher workshop.

We are trying to teach motivational qualities that will make students want to go out and learn. Students at Metro are concerned about getting educated and they recognize that learning is up to them; that they must assume the responsibility of their education, with proper guidance from the staff. The adult world will have to recognize that assuming responsibility for one's own education is an education in itself.

BERKELEY'S EXPERIMENTAL SCHOOLS

DIANE DIVOKY

Of all contemporary American public school systems, Berkeley, California, has been most vigorous in setting up alternative schools within the public school framework. At the time that Diane Divoky wrote in 1972, Berkeley had no less than 24 experimental schools. The development is attributable in part to Berkeley's unusual social orientation and to the willingness of superintendent Richard L. Foster to encourage experimentation. Diane Divoky looks at Berkeley as a freelance writer and reports the characteristics of many of the alternative schools within the Berkeley system.

The world's biggest Afro whizzes by on a ten-speed bike. A skate-boarder figure-eights his way down the street, and a frizzy-headed woman in white opaque pajamas tries to hitch a ride. Other hitchhikers stand, sit, and lie near the intersection, holding signs asking to be taken to Oregon, Texas, Maine, East—anywhere. I'm on University Avenue, heading into Berkeley, California. I park for a look around. Over an old poster of a smiling black politician, words have been scrawled in lipstick: "Tom, outrageous Tom." Back in my car I find fistfulls of handbills stuck under the wipers: "Support African

Liberation Day," "Protest GM and ITT's involvement in South Africa."
"Sign up for a new alternative school, family and community-oriented
—multi-ethnic . . ."

Berkeley, California, pop. 116,716. Berkeley, California, pop. white
university professors and white dropouts, black welfare mothers and
black executives, superfreaks and superstraights. Once home of the
Free Speech Movement, the Yippies, the People's Park. Still home of
the University of California—probably the best public system of higher
education in the world. In the rich and pretty hills overlooking San
Francisco Bay, Berkeley has many fine homes and one of the nation's
first cyclotrons. Down in the flatlands of the Bay shore it has a new
participatory politics that works, sometimes—an elected City Council
that on some issues fields a radical majority.

Berkeley: It's different here, some say. Berkeley's public schools—
45 percent black, 44 percent white, and 11 percent Chicano and Asian
—sure are different. The system was desegregated, voluntarily, a full
four years ago when 3,550 elementary school pupils were bused all over
town (SR, Dec. 21, 1968). Today, the schools thrive on variety and
controversy. Where else could one group of parents charge that Snow
White is a racist story, while another argues that a Malcolm X comic
book is sexist? This fall the Berkeley public schools are probably the
most diverse and experimental in the country.

Most of Berkeley's experimental schools got under way last year as
part of a five-year project sponsored by the U.S. Office of Education,
although the Ford Foundation had started underwriting some alternative schools a few years before that. The federal Experimental Schools
Project also made grants to school systems in Tacoma, Washington
(to test individualized instruction), and in Minneapolis, Minnesota (to
test autonomous administration), but the Berkeley project—designed
to challenge all the old assumptions about how public schools operate
—is by far the most ambitious. "It's everything you always wanted to
know about change but were afraid to ask," says Richard L. Foster,
Berkeley's superintendent of schools.

The experiment in Berkeley centers on twenty-four alternative public
schools. All told, they enroll approximately 4,000 elementary and secondary school students—more than one-fourth of the city's entire school
population. Some of the new alternative schools are on the grounds of
the regular public schools; others are in former factories, homes,
churches, and storefronts. Some are deliberately intimate, with a limit
of fifty students; others are larger than the traditional schools from
which they've drawn their students. Some emphasize multicultural
studies; others are racially exclusive. In some, parents are required to
participate; in others, they aren't even courted. All twenty-four experimental schools, however, say that they share two priorities: the elimination of institutional racism and the delivery of basic academic skills.

Whatever the neat phrases mean, they capsule Berkeley's heightened sensitivity about race. In the school system, it seems, every act has racial implications. When ten out of eleven students signing up for a dramatics group at one experimental elementary school are white, the staff grows a bit edgy: Why don't the black students want to participate? At another alternative school the black principal notes that white parents feel free to criticize white teachers but make no comment about a weak black teacher. The very alternative schools that were designed for alienated white students anguish over their inability to attract blacks.

The fact of race overrides considerations of social class, economic status, and individual differences. It also creates a new set of stereotypes, peculiar to Berkeley. If a white is on welfare, it must be "by choice." On the other hand, a black teacher, a third generation of college-educated bourgeoisie, describes herself as "just another Third World person."

The day before a school holiday to honor Malcolm X, thousands of black and white elementary school pupils—from both the experimental and the traditional schools—come to the high school theater for a special program. Inside the huge, darkened auditorium a man in a green dashiki introduces an ensemble of black fourth-, fifth-, and sixth-graders who play African drums. With none of the awkwardness common to most elementary school performers, they start to play. They are very good; rhythm flows through the audience.

The master of ceremonies takes over. With some contempt he says that white girls have to go to finishing schools to become ladies and learn how to walk, while black African girls have a natural, graceful walk because they must balance heavy loads on their heads.

After another drum number he introduces the audience-participation section of the program, explaining that an audience simply listening to a performance is a white, European kind of entertainment, while in African entertainment everyone joins in. He leads the audience through a fast-moving chant. After each phrase the kids shout "black" louder and louder, sassier and sassier.

Whatever their success in living up to their labels, Berkeley's alternative elementary schools are brighter, more intense, more interesting institutions than the "experimental schools" in most other communities. The hall displays, for example, include photographs taken by students, pictures illustrating a spring dream ("I wish to be a horse, and kind, and a sun"), stories of a field trip ("Tripping to Santa Cruz"). Teachers have the sophistication to provide all kinds of materials—records of Leadbelly wailing and Indians whooping, chemistry kits and origami packages, terrariums and tape recorders, Spanish readers and science centers. In Berkeley it's all there. Last spring I visited most of the experimental schools. Here are some impressions—and some tentative conclusions—about them:

JOHN MUIR: So many parents opted for the open classroom alternatives in John Muir's lovely, old Tudor-style building that only a few rooms remain organized in the traditional way. Outside, in the playground, a young black man in tight, purple pants and a felt hat closes down a recess basketball game: "Okay, you guys, back to class." Inside, students go about their business in classroom after classroom—reading, cooking, drawing, measuring, counting, typing, pounding, painting, using clay and dictionaries and aquariums and blueprints and counting rods and workbooks. In a bungalow the primary students do a spontaneous choral reading for the visitors.

LINCOLN: This is the home of the Environmental Studies Program, an alternative for some 200 fourth-through-sixth-graders with a predominantly black staff. The school is trying out trips to the beach, explorations in the community, music, dance, karate, dramatics, photography, almost anything, to get "unteachable" kids to learn.

"We get pushouts and lots of problem kids," says Mrs. Robbie Burke, the mother of six who has been with the alternative for a year. "We get Johnny already turned off by school. We let him act out, if it's not destructive to other students. But there are no sympathy trips. We expect as much from black kids as from whites, and we keep a tight watch on progress. If Johnny's folder shows he's not doing long division now, and two weeks from now he's still not doing it, we talk to the teacher and then deal with it at the staff meeting.

"The rewards are very small—maybe just a child completing a paper or smiling some morning. With one child, who came here very withdrawn and scared, my reward was watching the first time he went up and punched another boy. I was well pleased."

The assignments can be unusual, too. In one math project a student wrote the school superintendent to find out why he earned more than a teacher.

KILIMANJARO: If Berkeley has a counterculture elementary school, Kilimanjaro—in a residential area just north of the university campus—is it. The buildings are being renovated by the People's Architects. The school, limited to fifty elementary pupils, attracts white "welfare-by-choice" parents.

Michael Cohen, Kilimanjaro's co-director, greets visitors in the school's charmingly scruffy basement office, wearing a thermal undershirt. "There is a strong contingent of single mothers," he says. (To indicate diversity in the student body, teachers point to one student whose father works in the post office.)

The school is run by parents, and all decisions are made by consensus. There are no attendance rules, no grades. Kilimanjaro began with a rule that all parents had to participate five hours a week, but this proved unrealistic. So did a nonstructured approach. "The kids ran around and screamed for three months," Cohen says, "and then they and their parents requested more structure."

The curriculum is heavy on crafts, humanizing, and physical contact. "Sometimes I'm a human tree," Cohen says. A few moments later kids came into the room through windows and doors to hug a teacher or sit on her lap.

The staff believes that basics—such as reading—depend not so much on methods or materials as on a child's sense of himself. "Reading has to do with the environment and self-concept," Cohen says. "I never knew a kid who couldn't learn to read if he believed he was worth something."

A boy, the kind of tense fidgeter who is labeled disruptive in many schools, breaks up a math game that three girls are playing and announces, "I want to stay in here and make trouble." Cohen takes him away. Elsewhere a handful of kids work on individual projects, but others seem to be roaming around, looking for something to do.

Most of the alternatives for high school students are at Berkeley High, a massive institution with 3,000 students, including 1,200 enrolled in one or another of the six alternative schools on its six-block campus. Three of these are: Model A, which emphasizes basic skills; On Target, geared to "job awareness experiences;" and the School of the Arts, heavy on drama, music, and dance. The others:

COMMUNITY HIGH (GENESIS) Actually, Community High started three years ago—before the federal experimental schools program—as a free-flowing school for middle-class kids who were turned off by the routine and impersonalization of the big high school. José Romero, its former director, says it "was founded with the idea of lots of humanization and personal contact. It was the school with the flower power staff, the Spock generation of teachers. It worked for a few years, but it's a long shot from working now. Staffs have come and gone. The new black staff has provoked the black kids, helped polarize all the students, and the whites are over-compensating. The racial thing still isn't worked out. The tribes—the working units of students—dissolved, and everything's at a point of real apathy."

Last spring the vibes around Community High no longer felt right to many people in Berkeley, and they wondered how long it would take for things to change. Why should there be a school for alienated white kids when black kids still aren't learning to read? Is there something wrong with a school that suits whites better than blacks? The good feelings about free schools and kids doing their own thing that flowered in the late Sixties made Community High an exciting proposition three years ago; now it is worried about finances and racial balance and motives.

At a staff meeting a black student representative asks that the school's name be changed from Community High to Genesis. The motion carries with no discussion. The student then puts in his own name as director of the school for the coming year; the self-nomination is accepted. Then the real business at hand gets under way—money and autonomy. Because of a budget cut at Berkeley High, Community High is faced with cutting its staff from eight to three teachers.

"The more we compromise, the more we become a department of Berkeley High and not an alternative school."

"Maybe we should go up to 225 students, if we can get enough blacks."

"Who's going to recruit?"

The talk is tired, and over the room hangs the question of whether Community High will—or should—continue to exist. Some students explain that they will return to Berkeley High this fall. "Going to Community High involves more of a commitment than going to the regular school," says one, "but not enough people will make that commitment. I've decided that school is something I just want to get through."

A black student defends Community High's approach. "Here you learn what's really going on, and teachers and students learn from each other. They don't treat you like a child, and they don't grade as hard." But a girl, about to graduate after two years at Community High, has some reservations. "I can't stand classes where the teacher comes in and asks the students what they want to do," she says. "They're supposed to have the expertise. My best class here was the most formal. I used to think kids could learn without structure or pressure, but I don't anymore."

AGORA: Designed to teach an appreciation of racial differences, Agora keeps its staff and enrollment balanced at one-quarter each white, black, Chicano, and Asian, promising a structured multicultural experience for its 120 students. The courses run from Egyptian hieroglyphics to sailing but all carry an overlay of cross-cultural studies. Each student, as part of a class that is racially mixed, is required to take four sections of multicultural experience, each from the perspective of one of the four racial groups and taught by an instructor of that race. At the end of the rotation the students go off in separate racial groups to evaluate the courses freely, and then come together again for an integrated evaluation.

The black and Chicano courses, according to some staff members, have fared better than the others. In fact, Agora has emphasized black and Chicano unity, showing how the two groups have been pitted against each other in the past, and how the similarities between them might be used for cooperation. "We've really been getting Third World people together, academically and socially," a teacher says.

Not surprisingly, the white multicultural courses such as "white psyche" have turned into heavy guilt trips for many white students. So now the teacher of the white studies courses tries to use materials that show that whites, too, can be down-and-out (readings on immigrants), isolated (Appalachia), and tortured (*Death of a Salesman*).

COLLEGE PREP: Started in the middle of last year for 150 students (almost all black), College Prep carries a firm structure—and imparts even firmer basic skills to students who have the ability to go on to college but probably wouldn't get there without some extra help. It enrolls tenth through twelfth graders, and is designed to motivate, counsel, and drill them on to higher education.

Ronald Fortune, College Prep's young black director, talks about teaching kids what he calls "college survival skills"—how to take standardized tests, use reference materials, study. A set of review notes are part of the program, he says, so students will know how to pass a test on Shakespeare for example, without actually having to read very much Shakespeare. The content of the curriculum is fairly traditional, but it is taught from an "Afro-American oriented approach."

WEST CAMPUS WORK STUDY: Here, Director Arnold Lockley holds the hands of fifty or more ninth-graders who already are in trouble. He finds the losers, the dropouts, the pushouts, the first offenders at Juvenile Hall and offers them a half-time school program, gets jobs for them in the afternoons, and, in effect, shadows their lives.

"We do a kind of brainwashing here," says Lockley, a black former science teacher. "We tell the kids we don't want to hear about their past; we want them to take each day one at a time. But there will be no excuses here. They have to be in class, every day, every period, and they have to be polite. If a kid's having a problem in a class, we go and sit through it with him. If a teacher's ripping him off, we'll move him out. But we push the kids. We come down on them now rather than have them get killed two years from now. And they will get killed, the way they're going when we get them. Right now eleven of our kids aren't making it, but eleven others are on the honor roll."

EAST CAMPUS: Started five years ago when a group of liberal teachers decided to remodel what used to be merely a continuation school, East Campus now is one of the system's most stable alternatives, offering students a last chance to pick up a diploma. East Campus is housed in an airy mesh of sunny classrooms and raised outdoor runways across town from Berkeley High.

On one ramp two students are locked in a dramatic embrace as others move by to classes. In an English class two boys earnestly debate whether the right clothes can get someone a job as a *Playboy* photographer. Next door students read paperbacks silently until Tom Parker, the director, enters with visitors. "Who didya bring, Uncle Tom, the FBI?" asks a bereted student. Much laughter and shouting. East Campus students must enroll voluntarily—and there is a waiting list. The program emphasizes individualized work on basic skills. Students must go to class—or face dismissal. "Kids can't get away with jiving or running down games like they did at other schools," Parker says.

CASA DE LA RAZA: At first glance Casa seems the shabbiest of the alternatives. Classes are held in a series of old wooden sheds at the far end of a stark parking lot behind a junior high school. But some of Casa's 150 Chicano students, as part of an Aztec art project, have painted joyful revolutionary scenes and slogans on a high fence outside the bungalows. The two outdoor toilets have been covered with red, white, and blue stars and labeled, "This is America." Inside, Casa has a sense of humor, a warm camaraderie that flows through the school; indeed, Casa has a reputation in Berkeley as a warm, child-oriented, Chicago-flavored open school that is particularly strong at the primary level. (It houses pupils from kindergarten through the twelfth grade.)

Casa, a family-style bilingual institution, is run by a parent-teacher-student governing board; it is open all year. At the start of summer school a film teacher, taking some time off from Stanford, greets mothers coming to register their children. The science teacher arrives with an armful of material, eager to explain his program—the telescope and rockets students have made, the laser in progress, the kitchen physics, the ham radio, the Mayan and Aztec astronomy, the "whole bunch of electronic projects" the kids have completed. Whatever its exterior, a lot is going on inside Casa.

BLACK HOUSE: While Casa is open only to Latinos, Black House is open only to blacks. As a result, both institutions are in constant negotiations with the U.S. Office of Education about possible violations of the Civil Rights Act. Its teachers are all black, its courses are taught from "the black perspective." Horace Upshaw, the bearded, young black director of Black House, says its goal is to make its sixty students "responsible to the black community."

It is difficult to learn what is happening in Black House; representatives of the "white media" are not allowed in. Second-hand reports indicate that the classroom style is traditional, except that the guiding philosophy is that the teacher himself is the course and not just a conveyor of information.

The style of Black House—a racial consciousness raising, an independent assertion of identity—holds a good deal of appeal to other minority people in Berkeley. Another alternative school, Black Perspective, has opened along the lines of Black House, but with enrollment open to all races. The Marcus Garvey Institute, which author-teacher Herb Kohl started several years ago as Other Ways, has become overwhelmingly black in enrollment and tone, and has become a "survival center" next to Black House. An all-Asian school, New Ark, also has emerged. Now New Ark, Black House, Odyssey House—

a multiracial alternative for junior high kids—and Casa have combined in a loose federation to try to satisfy civil rights requirements. But separatism seems to be a growing phenomenon in Berkeley.

At a central staff meeting for all of Berkeley's experimental schools, people are talking—with deep feeling—about how they are going to talk to each other. Define, lay it out, replay, communicate, rap, respond, relate. Input, output, dynamics, data, structure, restructure, manage, organize, implement. The language of computers straining to make sense in the ill-defined world of children and learning. Finally, the decision about a staff crisis falls to Larry Wells, director of the experimental schools project. Silence holds the room as everyone waits for his opinion. "My honest response is a nonresponse," he says with great seriousness. Why can't anyone in Berkeley say he doesn't know the answer?

It is difficult for anyone to find the answers in Berkeley. Technically, the experimental schools are a research model, not a demonstration project. The U.S. Office of Education has awarded a $748,000 "out-of-house" grant for an evaluation of the Berkeley schools due next year.

After only one year the existential questions are still coming: How can you test uniqueness? What is progress? What is success? What do you test? Five alternative schools—the ones committed to delivering basic skills—flatly refuse to use any standardized tests on their students, saying the tests are racist, culturally biased, and/or inconsequential. As replacements, they offer alternative instruments such as teacher evaluations, attitudinal surveys, and audio tapes.

The Experimental School staff has formed an evaluation team to devise some tests to measure the delivery of skills. But even they are having trouble with Berkeley's ambiguity. "No one here will agree on what basic skills are," says one researcher. "For some people it means reading well enough to get a job. For others it means reading well enough to understand Franz Fanon." And any evaluation of a school system that is changing as fast as Berkeley's is delicate at best. "We're trying to paint a moving train in about four colors," says another staffer. "And suddenly we're on the train, not in the railroad station."

In Washington, Cynthia Parsons, program director for Berkeley's experimental schools in the U.S. Office of Education, will buy none of the line that Berkeley is a unique place. "In spite of its hip educational image," she says, "the Berkeley public school system is like any other. It's a big mess. The poor old system reflects the rest of the country. It doesn't teach minority kids as well as it teaches middle-class kids.

"Once you cut through the verbiage, the experiment is relatively uncomplicated. Can you give parents and students a clear, viable choice of schooling? We've asked them to select certain experimental schools that they'll really test over the next four years. I don't blame the schools for having problems living up to their rhetoric. They've made grandiose claims, and yet in new situations people tend to do what they were taught in the past. There's a real gap between the rhetoric and the ability to deliver. But they've got four years."

At the end of June Berkeley's experimental school staff submitted a progress report to the Office of Education. It listed nine ways the alternative schools had positively affected the local school system, but more than balanced them by also listing twenty-eight problems—ranging from frustration, intolerance, inflexibility, and paranoia to lack of community information and teaching materials. Every problem that school people could find to complain about was laid out, plus some that only school people in Berkeley could find.

By contrast, consider the experimental school project in Tacoma in which everything is neat, controlled, predictable. Tacoma isn't going to make any big mistakes, and Berkeley is making them all the time. But Tacoma isn't asking any of the big questions either and isn't likely to make a major change.

For all its rhetoric and self-importance, Berkeley is bold enough to question a lot of the assumptions that have kept American public schools going for so many years. Berkeley is looking for a new direction —and some better answers. It isn't going to find all of them in the next four years. But if it finds a few, it will be way ahead of the same old game the public schools are playing out for children in most other cities.

OPEN	*The Association for Supervision and*

OPEN
SCHOOLS
FOR
CHILDREN

ALEXANDER FRAZIER

The Association for Supervision and Curriculum Development has long been in the forefront of efforts to humanize education and to foster reasoned experimentation in schools. Therefore it is natural that the ASCD would authorize one of its past presidents to prepare an incisive and thoughtful booklet on open education. Alexander Frazier is professor of early and middle childhood education at Ohio State University. In his pamphlet he combines accurate descriptions with careful analysis of programs of open education. One of his most significant insights is the recognition that open education lends itself not merely to what Frazier calls "the new freedom" but also to "the new fundamentalism." The selected excerpt from his pamphlet centers about this particular contrast.

FREE AS FREE CAN BE

To the most severe contemporary critics of the curriculum, the term itself has a kind of epithet of disgust and disapproval. "Curriculum" is taken to represent much that is restrictive and irrelevant about life in schools. Why should boundaries of any kind be imposed on what can be learned? "Instruction" may be included in the litany of damnation. Direct teaching constricts or diverts or dampens the flow of natural energy that can impel young learners to try to make sense out of their world and find satisfaction in it if they are given free rein.

We may be tempted to try to straighten out the despisers of "curriculum" and "instruction" by helping them find broader meanings for the terms. After all, would they not be comfortable with the idea that whatever the child experiences under the auspices of the school can be called curriculum? Or that instruction may be defined to take in all the circumstances that support and affect learning in the school? They might be. Yet if we succeed in educating our critics to use words our way, we may lose the essence of their message. And they would seem to be saying something we need to hear. Let us contend, if we wish, that their picture of authoritarianism comes in part from limited or uniquely poor experience. Even then, we ought to be able to listen and learn. Critics can be right for the wrong reasons.

Frankly, we may need to be aware that the wrong reasons could include the fact that several now veteran spokesmen for an open curriculum based their early critical reports on their own ghetto teaching. What they saw to be the problem led to proposals that go far beyond the ghetto, of course. But their image of black children and what they need may seem less insightful now than it did in the early or mid-sixties. Certainly today many black parents and leaders would reject the notion of a totally "free" curriculum for their children as irresponsible if not insulting.

May we turn, then, to look as clearly and generously as possible at some of the main ideas of the critics who would have the curriculum become as free as free can be?

Life: The Unstructured Curriculum What would happen if schools just closed their doors for good? Children would be returned to the community to learn through living. Participants with their parents in the work of the world, they would profit from the ultimate of openness. They would go to school to life itself.

Strange as this kind of thinking may seem to us, life is still the school to which most people have had to go around the globe. One out of four South Americans is illiterate, three out of four Africans, half the Asians. The idea that formal schooling is right for everybody and everybody's right is a relatively recent notion and plainly one that even yet is not worldwide in acceptance or application.

Yet in every society children who survive infancy do grow up to become reasonably effective human beings, capable of enjoying life and active in contributing to and maintaining the ways of living into which they have been born. Schools may play a role central to this process or they may not.

Is it possible for schools to interfere with the process of becoming a fully functioning human being? This question is not unfamiliar historically. It was asked as women began to be educated and as schools were being built for members of the working class. Today it is being asked by critics who fear the school as the source of several kinds of possible distortion.

Schools may serve to teach children repression of life instincts, substituting subservience to routines and authority for exercise of the freedom and self-direction basic to becoming happy and creative persons. Schools may serve as agents of an economic system that thinks of people mainly as replacements for its worn-out parts or as a market for unneeded and unwanted products; such schools will tend to turn out unthinking automatons rather than self-determining free men. Or—

more plainly and perhaps even more grimly—schools may be so concerned with overtaught trivia and so lacking in genuine stimulation that children will be put to sleep, never to wake up.

Living fully ought to be the goal, and living freely thus has to be the means. This seems to be the message. Suburban parents who are banding together to establish Summerhill-type schools, commune dwellers in the mountains of New Mexico who are trying to teach their own children as they grow, some inner city schools for older youth that are letting them slip out into the urban arena in larger numbers for both work and study—all seem to be trying to say that life itself, unstructured and too much as it may be, has to come first.

Dependence on Quality Experiences Occasionally we may wonder whether some critics who rail against the schools really care to think about curriculum making on any terms, open or otherwise. Trying to decide what needs to be made sure of in the education of children may strike them as both unnecessary and boring. Everybody knows the child has to learn to read and write and add and subtract. What is the problem?

Such critics may have opposed the school largely in terms of its psychological impact as an institution without much real interest in or knowledge of what is intentionally taught there. Pressed, they may agree that they would expect basic learnings to be got—but on the run, so to speak, without interfering with the child's experiences in living. Also, some of the critics would seem to be willing to talk about the quality of one experience in living as against another and may thus come to be engaged in curriculumizing after all.

We may agree then that we would like children to have varied experiences worthwhile in themselves. Life as it goes on will provide some such experiences. Yet a school that is open to making the most of life for children will try for more than chance experiences.

Other persons are a part of every child's experience. In school, however, children and adults too are likely to be more varied and numerous than elsewhere and experiences in living and working together can thus add new dimensions to home and neighborhood experience.

The arts are everywhere. Yet in school the child may hear more kinds of music than he may outside and possibly learn to respond to music in new ways, perhaps to make music, even to compose it.

The world is all about us. Still, children may come to see some of it with new eyes as they return from a walking trip to a nearby park or greenhouse or try to sort out together their impressions after talking with a helicopter patrolman.

The choice of quality experiences for children does suppose that some structure will be applied to life. Yet openness to the real and the vital remains a key concern. What we may wish to ask ourselves is the extent to which room for such experiences can be found in the curriculum we now have.

Partnership of Children and Teachers A most familiar position among the advocates of openness is that of insistence upon freedom for teachers to plan with children as they see fit, untrammeled by the expectations or constraints of a preplanned curriculum. Of course, this is the classic posture of progressive education, maintained by many teachers of young children and revived in part by the new British progressivism.

As partners, children and teachers build on and extend the needs and interests that arise out of their ongoing experience in the school. Goals for learning are defined and experiences selected by those involved. Within the plans, room is made for children to work on their own and in small groups as well as to function as a total group. The concerns and problems for exploration are kept open to admit new interests and to honor the full range of children's ideas.

The program that develops under this kind of partnership will be unique to its members. Such an approach is thought of as child-centered rather than task-centered, although the amount of work accomplished and its quality may go far beyond what is envisioned by most preplanned programs. Continuity is counted on to come from the exercise and development of the powers and purposes of the child, to use Dewey's language, and from the guidance of teachers who know not only how to help children get the most out of their current experience but also how to move children ahead into ever more adventurous experiences in learning.

Persons writing today in behalf of such freedom for children and teachers are likely to speak of the open or unstructured classroom and may combine elements of what we have called open structure in their proposals, especially freedom from time schedules and from inflexible staffing patterns. Their major emphasis, however, goes to the relevance and liveliness of the school experience that develops under partnership planning. As in the reports of earlier progressives, they propose to include more opportunities for children in the expressive and creative arts and in environmental exploration. Children compose and create, discover and experiment; teachers arrange and guide, listen and participate (see Figure 1).

The freest proposals for an open curriculum, then, include the return of children to the community or to new learning situations set up there to foster learning through living, and also the provision of quality experiences selected to make the most of experiences good in themselves. They include the concept of the open classroom that would maximize the partnership of children and teachers to plan a curriculum in terms of the powers and purposes of learners. Trust is the ultimate issue—trust in the children and in the adults around them, trust

Figure 1. What Children and Teachers Do in Task-Centered and in Child-Centered Schools (Representative Language)

Kind of School	What Children Do		What Teachers Do	
Task-Centered School	begin	perform	check	monitor
	carry out	practice	coordinate	organize
	complete	pursue	develop	plan
	correct	reach	diagnose	prescribe
	execute	respond	govern	present
	follow	satisfy	keep track	schedule
	move on	succeed	maintain	test
Child-Centered School	choose	mess with	advise	observe
	compose	organize	arrange	participate
	create	plan	enable	question
	discover	play	encourage	share
	experiment	solve	guide	stimulate
	hypothesize	talk	listen	support
	manipulate	work	move around	watch

in the lessons to be learned from living as meaningfully and richly as possible. Has such trust been lost in some of our schools for children today?

FREEDOM WITH CONTROL

What may surprise us more than anything else about the proposals of anti-curriculum critics is the familiarity of much of their language. Whether they always know it or not, they sound very much like the early progressives.

Some of them—those most vehement against authoritarianism—may seem to sound a new note as they inveigh against schooling as an instrument of a sick or suspect society. For some of these critics, there appears to be a growing conviction that all present institutions must be opposed if a new and less exploitive society is to be helped to emerge. Yet even this kind of talk may remind us of the thirties. An enduring point of conflict within the Progessive Education Association was whether schools should serve society or recreate it. Of course, the activists of that era never doubted that the schools had a choice. Perhaps this is where a real difference may be found to exist between them and today's most radical critics. The latter seem to have little respect for education as a force for change, and indeed they may regard the idea as just one more fiction or trick that an obsolescent society uses to prevent change.

Most of today's opponents of the structured curriculum do have faith in education. They might be willing to see some schools closed, but not all. And they would hope that closed schools, once reopened, would be possessed of a new commitment to staying open, truly open—

open to life-centered experiences good in themselves, experiences planned and selected by those involved in learning.

The familiarity of the language the new progressives use is matched for many of us by the familiarity of the doubts that assail us. Will children's experiences under a free-as-free-can-be kind of curriculum have the balance they ought to have? Will children develop the skills and concepts they need for the effective exercise of their powers or capacities? How can we ever know that it all adds up?

Thus, we may examine two of the new approaches to a more open curriculum for children that seem to represent an effort to guard against loss of control over outcomes.

The New British Progressivism   Part of the attraction for us in the new British progressivism is the apparent control that exists in the midst of so much more freedom than we are accustomed to in most of our own classrooms. We may suspect and hope that a way has been found to make sure of learning and reduce or offset the formlessness thought to have been the major problem of the old progressivism.

The question of order has not been altogether resolved, it is clear. Most of the accounts of what goes on in the British Primary School lay heavy stress on the acceptance by teachers of responsibility for close and continuous assessment of progress. No doubt critics of the new education in Great Britain serve to simulate this profession of vigilance. Yet it also seems to come out of an awareness new to progressivism that "checking on" children's development is facilitated by an open environment; indeed, that the ease of working to guide individual growth is among the major gains or goods of the integrated-day program.

We do know that planning in the British schools goes beyond the restructuring of floor space and the de-structuring of the timetable. We are interested, for example, in the similarity of activities reported from one school to the next. Children are measuring the width of the corridor, the length of the playground, and the circumference of their teacher's head in Birmingham and York as well as in London. Recipes are collected and tested and inscribed in hand-bound books in village schools and city schools. Bejeweled Elizabethan costumes, scale models of Tudor houses, and clock candles half burnt show up in reports of group studies from all over the kingdom. We will want to know how this replication comes about under free choice education. Agreement on a range of valued activities would seem to promise relief from the threat of chance and whim as determiners of an open curriculum.

And, more important, is there something to these agreements that goes beyond the accumulation or conventionalization of interesting learning activities that have been found good in themselves? The puzzled American teacher may have been helped over a weekend to rearrange the furniture and been reminded to take down the daily schedule posted by the door. But bereft of the guidance that comes from textbooks and curriculum guides and the assurance derived from successful experience under more formal conditions, where does the teacher turn? Teaching informally has to involve more than watching and waiting.

The likelihood is that progressive education in Great Britain has learned how to prepare teachers so that they carry about in their own heads all that is needed to impose order on the rich and varied activities of their classrooms. They come to understand that many kinds of activities can be employed to help children learn the skills and concepts they need to know in such matters as measurement or proportion.

British teachers do have guides to help them. The Nuffield mathematics materials are a case in point. Teachers-to-be may also have active experience in schools from their first months in teacher education and thus learn at first hand how varied experiences may be used to ensure wanted learnings—and also how a given experience such as a group study of Elizabethan times may yield learnings in several fields of knowledge. Much attention in both preservice and in-service education goes to principles of learning, particularly those derived from the work of Piaget, that may be related to guiding and keeping track of children's intellectual development.

Schools are small, too. Teachers of older children may come to know their prospective pupils beforehand, and under family-type grouping may be assured of several years in which to guide learning. Head masters or mistresses work directly with teachers in assessing what children know and in helping shape experiences for them. Open structure assists the provision and pursuit of ordered learning in the open curriculum.

If there is a secret of how the British combine freedom with control, it may well be found, then, in the education of teachers to be genuine curriculum makers on their own—to hold clearly to ends that they fully understand and accept as they arrange for and with children the most rewarding school experiences possible.

Options and Alternatives   One way being developed to provide freedom with control in our own schools is the planned provision of options and alternatives within the curriculum we now have. Several versions of this approach can be identified.

Perhaps the openest is the setting aside of a time or band of time for children to use more or less as they like. The assumption is that given free time, children will differ in what they choose to do with it. Interest will lead some to work on science activities, others to become involved in art projects, still others to search out books that will help them answer their questions or provide personal enjoyment. If several wish to work together, that may lead to an experience which meets social as well as intellectual needs.

Such free time is identified as time for exploration or questing or personalized study. Behind the practice may be a concern for bringing into balance the possible overdirection of children under some programs of individualized instruction in which everything is carefully laid out and independence limited to rate of progress through the study sequences.

Another use of options and alternatives comes in cases where content to be learned is organized or reorganized as a series of short units, mini-units, or learning packets for individual study. Sometimes the units will be divided between those to be completed by all children and those from which choices may be made. Presumably the common learnings being sought will be covered by the required units, and personal interests and individual needs will be provided for by the exercise of option among the rest.

A third use of options and alternatives may be found to be incorporated in the preparation of the new-type individualized study units themselves. Following a pretest, the child is confronted by a variety of avenues by which he may fill in the gaps he has become aware of in what he already knows. He may consult one or more textbooks, listen to a recording, see a filmstrip, work with a piece of programmed material, or ask for a sheet of teacher-prepared information. His exercise of option is in the choice among alternative ways of reaching an established goal. When ready, he takes a post-test to find out whether he chose wisely among the alternatives. This use of option is supported by the belief that children differ in learning styles and will discover that one kind of material is more useful to them than another.

Such new approaches to making room for choices in what is to be learned would seem to belong in any discussion of providing greater openness in the curriculum, even though some appear in situations that have a good deal of formality about them. Teachers who have operated under a program of large-scale unit teaching or group studies may feel that the value of older ways of providing for choice ought also to be included in the arena of options and alternatives. The process of defining questions or problems for study did make it possible to bring into group plans the interests and ideas of many children even though an area of study might have been set by a curriculum guide. Organizing into small groups for getting needed information or "answers" offered some degree of option. Within the small groups, individuals might find still further room for the pursuit of their own most pressing concerns.

The value of giving children opportunity to choose what to study has been with us since *Emile*. However, our concern for making sure that openness results in experiences that add up must remain as a major element in our definition of adult responsibility in the school, as it did for Emile's tutor. The appearance of new plans for organizing to include more options and alternatives is a recognition that we do still hope to find better ways to combine freedom with control.

FREEDOM FOR NEW KINDS OF FORMALISM

Openness in curriculum is also being advocated by some persons today in behalf of freedom to replace the old program with another different in design but no less formal in structure. Closure in curriculum planning is what is under attack. Room needs to be made to develop and test out competing programs that may have more to offer. Formalism, in short, is not itself the issue but whether the schools can accommodate new kinds of formalism. Structure is accepted as essential in school programs. The question to be answered is whether the conventionally structured curriculum really does what needs to be done.

The developments in open curriculum we have discussed thus far have been concerned with lifting restrictions on what can be learned in school and maximizing the role of children as participants in planning and selecting their learning experiences. Openness of this variety is not the concern here. Adults are assumed to be engaged in the proper exercise of responsibility when they plan the curriculum for children. Indeed, the selection of what is to be learned is seen as a task requiring a high level of professional competence that could hardly be delegated to children. Perhaps not even teachers are competent to make basic curriculum decisions. So advocates of the new formalism might contend.

The persons who are proposing formal substitutes for present programs may seem, then, to be different in intention from the others with whose ideas we have been dealing. Their attitude toward attempts to provide a free-as-free-can-be environment for learning might well be that such schools are misreading all the social signposts as well as indulging in sentimentalism about children. The British model of combining freedom with control might be taken to represent an undeveloped sense of accountability, attributable in large part to differences between national cultures. As to the idea of options and alternatives, the formalists would probably be suspicious of how much children can gain from free time for personal exploration. They would feel more comfortable, no doubt, if choice were confined to specified options within a closely structured curriculum.

The New Fundamentalism Conflict between curriculum proposals rooted deeply in a desire for more freedom for children and those arising out of the drive for a new kind of formalism will certainly increase in the immediate years ahead. The strongest campaigners from among the formalists may be those committed to preplanned programs of individualized instruction.

These new fundamentalists, if we may be permitted to call the individualizers that, seem to have everything going for them. The movement toward open space has given them a push because open space invites or even compels teachers to reduce group instruction and move toward independent study. The inclusion of easily accessible learning materials centers in open space schools forwards the use of a greater variety of materials than could be housed in the classrooms of old. The developments under open structure also support individualization. Classification into large groups and optional and flexible internal grouping dispose of barriers to individualization, as does the loosening of the time schedule. Staffing by teams or substaffs makes it possible to try for new and supportive teaching roles and functions that help programs of self-directed study work well.

In addition, all the diverse developments under way during the past 15 years or so in the preparation of study materials seem to have coalesced into one fairly sophisticated body of know-how in support of individualized instruction. The undreamed of as well as the unlikely are now found possible. We can state our goals in terms of highly specific behaviors, diagnose need more precisely, select or prescribe learning sequences that have been proved more or less failure-free, and evaluate progress with greater accuracy against a wider spectrum of possibilities than we ever could before. To forward the steps of this process, materials can be organized as packages or systems of one kind or another, some with computer-assisted sequences and others with elaborate multimedia episodes. When all else fails, we can fall back on what we are learning from reinforcement theory and contingency management.

The new fundamentalism can also count on support by powerful community forces. Teaching results from the new preplanned programs are more accessible. The increasingly reluctant taxpayer wants his money's worth and may demand proof that he is getting it before responding to the pleas of school systems in danger of going out of business. State legislatures, moving slowly if surely to the rescue of local districts, are in the mood to hold teachers newly accountable. And racial and ethnic minorities whose older children came through school largely untaught are vitally interested in the prospect of successful learning. Teachers in Gary may not care much for the performance contracting setup at Banneker School. But the school board and the parents of children in the school have high hopes.

The goal of mastery is back in the picture again. Effort still goes to trying to discover more about the learning disabilities and deterrents that may exist in the child or his circumstances. Yet more and more, the energy of investigators is being redirected to find out what can be done to improve teaching. The conviction is growing that most children can learn what they need to if they are well taught.

Can the two movements—the one toward more freedom and the other toward a new fundamentalism—be joined in some way that may enable us to hold onto and strengthen the best in both? This may be historically the major curriculum challenge of the seventies.

Figure 2. Two Major Educational Movements of the Seventies:
The New Freedom and the New Fundamentalism

The New Freedom	Elements	The New Fundamentalism
Walls in the school pushed out Learning areas equal in floor space to several classrooms Expansion out of doors—field trips Use of public facilities as study space Community-centered study projects Some space may be structured as interest or work centers	1 Space	Large study areas—may be several classrooms opened up to form study space Smaller spaces for discussion groups Specialized facilities such as studios, laboratories, workshops Provisions for individual study: carrels, stations, computer terminals
Larger units—like 75 to 125 May be called learning communities, schools within schools, subschools Grouping may be interage, vertical, family-type Children may remain with same teacher or teachers several years	2 Classification of pupils	Pupils handled as individuals Grouping as such not regarded as too important Grouping for instruction on basis of achievement or need level Regrouping for instruction in basic skills
No bells—few fixed time divisions Work going on in many aspects of study at same time Individual pupils planning own use of time within some limits Relatively few occasions for work in large groups—mostly small group and individual or independent study	3 Time schedules	Flexible scheduling related to needs Regular attention, however, to major skills and content areas Individual pacing in progress through study sequences Large amounts of time devoted to individual study
Many resources of all kinds—may have media center easily available Live animals—garden—pond Junk or nonstructured stuff Few textbooks in sets—more trade and reference works in or close to wherever study takes place	4 Resources	Boxes, programs, learning packets, multimedia packages: super textbooks Diagnostic devices Assignments highly explicit in terms of study materials to go through Much testing of progress

The New Freedom	Elements	The New Fundamentalism
May plan and teach together May be assigned to large group of children as a staff rather than to 25 or 30 Paid and volunteer lay workers part of mix	5 Staff	Paraprofessionals to handle routine tasks High level of accountability for getting desired results Teachers coached to ensure greater effectiveness (increased in-service education)
More emphasis on learning than on teaching Teacher as guide and helper Planning done by children Emphasis on learning by doing—centered on activities Stress on satisfaction and sense of growth in personal competence	6 Instruction	Mastery the goal Individualized instruction seen as ideal Ends exemplified in behavioral terms—highly explicit Tutoring relationship valued Much small group target teaching Remediation continuous concern Prescriptive teaching
Many options and choices for children Use of unexpected incident to lead into group undertakings Much attention to interest, sense of need, current concerns Emphasis on large or global goals Structure for learning exists chiefly in heads of teachers, not on paper	7 Curriculum	Carefully worked out lessons in basic skills and content areas Stress on scientifically determined placement of content Sequences of work very carefully planned Evaluation geared to specific content and its learning
Free and easy Children treated as partners Movement from one place to another informal Noise and messiness seen as likely products of meaningful activity Friendly—good humored	8 Environment as a whole	Busy and industrious atmosphere Quiet and orderly Everybody buckling down to work No nonsense Children expected to be where they are supposed to be Formal—firm but concerned with success and good adjustment

CAUTIONS
AND
REMINDERS

FREE SCHOOLS FAIL BECAUSE THEY DON'T TEACH

JONATHAN KOZOL

In a social movement, the excesses of initial enthusiasm are sometimes modified by constructive reflective second thoughts. Here, one of the most vigorous proponents of the alternative school movement expresses concern about the educational value of the curriculum of some alternative schools. Throughout his book, Free Schools *(Boston: Houghton Mifflin, 1972), Kozol identifies the two overwhelming problems of these schools as "the terrible anguish about power and the paralyzing inhibition about the functions of the teacher." He warns that the power needed by the poor and black to survive rests in the acquisition of complex and intricate knowledge that cannot be learned through the spontaneous and ecstatic education which the free schools are so adept in providing. He believes that teachers must provide adult direction; teachers make a grave mistake in the free schools by reducing themselves to ethical and pedagogical neuters.*

Jonathan Kozol, a leader of the free school movement in the Boston area, is a former Rhodes Scholar and the author of Death At An

194

Early Age. *The following portion of his book*
Free Schools *appeared in the April 1972 issue of*
Psychology Today.

The average life span of the free schools has
been nine months. Why do they fail so often?

Unfashionable and unromantic as it may appear, the major cause for
failure in the free schools is our unwillingness or inability to teach the
hard skills.

This is the kind of square and rigorous statement that you do not
often encounter in the free-school literature. It is something that we
had better speak about, however. If we do not, these schools will not
survive.

In the free schools, as in the public schools, there are always a certain
number of children who learn to read in much the same way that they
learn to tell time, navigate the streets of their own neighborhood or
talk and play games with each other. For these children, formal reading
methods are a waste of time. They tend merely to mechanize and to
devitalize the child's own creative power. In most cases, however, it is
both possible and necessary to teach reading in a highly conscious,
purposeful and sequential manner.

Teach I believe today as strongly as I ever did that all education
should be child-centered, open-structured, individualized and unoppres-
sive. This point of view inspired me and others in our struggle for
reform within the Boston public schools, and it led eventually to the
creation of the free schools. There is no question now of going back
to a more circumspect position. There *is* a question, however, about
the naive, noncritical acceptance of the unexamined notion that you
cannot *teach* anything. It is just not true that the best teacher is the
grownup who most successfully pretends that he knows nothing or has
nothing to suggest to children. It is not true, either, that the best
answer to the blustering windbag teacher of the oldtime public school
is the free-school teacher who attempts to turn himself into a human
version of an inductive fan.

Some of the young white persons who came new into the free-school
situation are surprisingly dogmatic and, ironically, manipulative in
their determination to coerce the parents of poor children into accepting their notions about nonmanipulative education. In his book about
Bill Ayers and Diana Oughton, *The Making of a Terrorist*, Thomas

Powers tells the history of one of the original free schools, established in 1966 in Ann Arbor, Michigan. The school went under for a number of reasons, but Powers notes: "The single most important failing of the school, and the one on which it foundered in the end, was the fact that no one learned to read there."

Collapse   In the jargon that pervades part of the free-school movement, *the child will ask someone to teach him to read as soon as he really wants to read.* Powers observes that, in the three-year history of the school, "that time never seemed to arrive." The school ended on a bitter note. The participants claimed that harassment by public officials caused the school's collapse. In fact, however, it collapsed because parents were taking their children out of it. The founders of the school were committed to helping black children, but according to Powers, they "rejected the terms on which the black parents wanted their children to be helped." In turn, the parents rejected the school.

This is a classic sequence. White men and white women who come in to teach and work alongside black and Spanish-speaking people in the intense, committed atmosphere of the urban free school have to learn to exercise their ideologies and their ideals with great sophistication. Poor people will never reach political consciousness and power by adopting the values of the upper-class elite. These elite ideologies and ideals do not meet the actual needs of the specific, real and nontheoretical children who are sitting here before us.

Weave   It is a bitter pill for many young white persons to swallow, but in many cases the very rewards and skills that we—who possess them—now consider rotten and corrupt are attractive and often irresistible to poor people. Often enough it is not material greed that motivates them—it is the more immediate matter of survival. There's not much that a poor, black 14-year-old can do in cities like New York or Boston if he cannot read and write enough to understand a street sign or to read a phone book. It is too often the rich college graduate who speaks three languages with native fluency, at the price of 16 years of high-cost, rigorous and sequential education, who is most determined that poor kids should make clay vases, weave Indian headbands, play with Polaroid cameras, and climb over geodesic domes.

In the matter of reading, there is no reason why the free school must adhere to either of two irresponsible positions. It is as much an error to say that learning is never the consequence of conscious teaching as it is to imagine that it always is. The second error belongs most often to the public schools; the first to many of the free schools. The truth of the matter is that you *can* teach reading. Lots of people do. I have taught children to read in many situations in which they very likely would not have learned to read for several years if I had not taken a

clear initiative. George Dennison has done the same. So too have the
people at the New School for Children in Boston. It is true, as I have
mentioned, that it is not always necessary. When it is not necessary, it
obviously is ill-advised. When it *is* necessary, but when, in the name of
joy and freedom, it is not undertaken, the parents have very good
reason to be angry.

Shock Frequently, a child who comes into the free school after a
number of years in public school will associate the printed word with
pain and intimidation. He is shell-shocked and numb, afraid of anything that has to do with books and with black ink. If he is ingenious
and sophisticated, as many 14-year-olds in Boston's South End are, he
may be able to disguise his fear of words and, in this way, deceive the
young white teacher.

"He's beautiful," the young utopian volunteer will say. "He just likes
cinema and weaving more than books . . . When he's ready for books
. . . when he senses his own organic need . . . he'll let us know."

The horrible part of this is that the young volunteers really mean this
and, moreover, often believe it with a dedication that precludes any
possibility of self-correction. It is too much like looking into the windows of a mental hospital and making maniacal observations on the
beautiful silence of the catatonic patients. Children who are in psychological shell shock over reading are not beautiful and are not in the
midst of some exquisite process of organic growth. They are, in the
most simple and honest terms, kids who just can't do a damn thing in
the kinds of cities that we live in. There must be a million unusual and
nonmanipulative but highly conscious ways to free children from this
kind of misery. There is only one thing that is unpardonable. This is
to sit and smile in some sort of cloud of mystical, wide-eyed, nondirec-
tive and inscrutable meditation—and do nothing.

How do we teach reading? George Dennison offers many good ideas
in *The Lives of Children*. Sylvia Ashton-Warner, James Herndon and
Herbert Kohl also recommend a number of specific approaches.

I have had the most success with a mixture of approaches; in one
case I even made profitable use of a sequential, rather rigorous, old-
fashioned phonics method, but tying it in with a lot of good, intense,
uninhibited dialogue with students. In dialogue, the children could
find words that carried high intellectual voltage or great sensuality.
Certainly, words like *sex* and *cops* and *cash* and *speed* and *El Dorado*
are far more likely to stir the passions of the 14-year-old children that
I know than *postman, grandmother* or *briefcase*. I also find that many
children who think they cannot read, and who are afraid to begin from
zero, are excited to find that "GTO," "GM," "GE" or even "CBS-
TV" are at the same time words and letters that they already under-

stand quite well. They do not think they have the right to call this reading.

Some of the most intelligent and inspired writing on this subject has been done by the Brazilian scholar, Paulo Freire. The heart of his method has to do with the learner's recognition of a body of words that are associated with the most intense and potentially explosive needs and yearnings of his own life. Freire calls these words *generative*, because they generate thirst, consciousness and motivation in the learner, and also because they can be broken down and reassembled to generate new words. Freire's methods are inherently political. I doubt, therefore, that they can be applied in public schools without immediate repercussions. They are, however, ideal materials for use and application in the free schools.

Impose The issue of reading opens up the larger question of the purpose and function of a free school in the neighborhood that is economically cheated and politically disenfranchised. In my belief, it is unwise for young white teachers to attempt to impose their version of the counter-culture upon poor children and their families. It is especially dangerous if they do this while they neglect certain obvious survival matters.

Frequently a young newcomer to the free-school movement refuses to recognize that to a very considerable degree his own risk-taking attitudes and antisystem, antiskill, anticredential confidence is based upon the deep-down knowledge that in a single hour he can put on shoes, cut his hair, fish out an old but still familiar piece of plastic from his wallet, go over to Brattle Street, go into Brooks Brothers, buy new clothes, and walk into a brand-new job.

Some of us do not like to admit that we have this sense of intellectual and financial back-up. The parents of poor children, however, recognize this sort of thing quite clearly. They also recognize, with equal clarity, a) that their own children do not have this kind of protection, b) that, if they do not adapt to the real conditions of the system they are fighting, they will not survive, and c) that much of the substance of the white-oriented counter-culture is no real help in that struggle.

I have twice visited Cuernavaca to talk with Ivan Illich and Everett Reimer. Twice I have returned to Boston to confront the hard realities that still must shape decision-making here. It is a luxury, at 2,000 miles' distance, to consider an educational experience that does not involve credentials or curriculum or long-term sequential labor. In immediate terms, in cities such as Boston and New York, it is unwise and perhaps destructive to do so. Instead, we must face up to the hard truth that these credentials and measured areas of expertise and certified ability constitute, *as of now*, the irreducible framework for our labor and our struggle.

In speaking of this issue, I find myself in the difficult position of one who admires Ivan Illich and respects Everett Reimer, but who also lives in Boston in the year of 1972. I try to find the meeting place between these widely separated points of reference in something that I think of as waging guerrilla warfare with credentials.

I would like to join in court suits as co-witness or co-plaintiff, to confront the racist, stupid, pernicious character of College-Board Examinations. I would like to join in obstructive, meddlesome and—wherever necessary—illegal civil disobedience in the offices of the men who govern and control the Educational Testing Service. I would like to join in the campaign of words that John Holt and Ivan Illich are waging against illegal job-discrimination—not just on grounds of race, religion, sex, or years, but also on grounds of previous years of certified domestication and indoctrination in the public schools. I would, moreover, like to go beyond the war of words and take specific action that would make people aware of how unjust this credential apparatus is.

There are also some less-public, but no less-important guerrilla activities. The most obvious way to show up the flimsiness of the 12-year public-education interlock is to short-circuit these sequential obligations. Twelve years of lock-step labor in math or language manifestly waste a child's learning energies. Freire teaches basic literacy in 40 days. Few children need six years to learn to write 10 consecutive, reasonable, cogent and powerful sentences. Ivan Illich and the U.S. State Department both have developed methods by which students can master three years of high-school French or Spanish in three months. Several free schools now are thus short-circuiting the accepted sequences of public school. This is, however, a very different thing from turning our backs and acting as if the system of credentials will just go away. The citadel does not need to be revered or loved in order to be stormed and conquered. It is insane, however, to behave as though it were not there.

Scorn Many of the poor parents I know are anguished, angry or uneasy when they are with young white women and white men who appear to scorn the credentials-curriculum interlock. Too often, these teachers do not recognize the real needs and the specific agonies that poor people in this country must cope with.

Social insult, hunger, sickness, physical alarm, the siren's scream and the blue light spinning in the neon sky, the desperation of a mother in the back-street clinic of a miserable urban slum—these are the metaphors of truth and pain that still must shape our judgments and decisions.

In my neighborhood, one family of four, who have been my friends now for six years, live on an annual income of 3,000 dollars. Another family, to which I have been drawn through friendship with two of the oldest children, has survived some recent 12-month periods on 1,800 dollars (there are 10 children in the family). Men and women who are locked into such lives will inevitably be unsettled by white persons who tell them that their children do not really need degrees, do not need math or English, do not need to find out how to psych-out an exam, do not need college, do not need money, do not need ugly, contaminated, wicked, middle-class success. The issue for these children is not success. It is survival.

Lag Black and Puerto Rican children in this neighborhood of Boston live in a medical, economic and educational disaster area. Children whose basic competence is the equal of any child in Palo Alto or in the wheatfields of Nebraska are, statistically, by fifth-grade level, at least one year behind their white suburban counterparts in such basic coding and decoding skills as math and reading; by seventh-grade level, they are two years behind; by ninth-grade level, three years; by 12th-grade level (if they ever get there), four or five years.

Ninety percent of the Puerto Rican kids in Boston drop out of school before they get into the 10th grade. Their odds, first on surviving the attrition-rate, then on being able to go on to higher education, are one 20th the odds of kids in ordinary white suburban schools, one 30th the odds of kids in places such as Evanston and Greenwich, one 50th the odds of kids at St. Paul's, Exeter and Groton.

Decree The medical odds with which these children live are even more alarming. On the national average, 20 children out of 1,000 die during the first 12 months of life. In all-white neighborhoods outside the cities, the figure is much closer to 15 per 1,000. In black communities like Harlem, Watts and Newark, the figure seldom runs lower than 30 or 35 and often runs as high as 50. Northern liberals like to remind each other that some of the most catastrophic health conditions still exist primarily in rural sections of the Deep South. In the event that we feel smug, however, H. Jack Geiger of Tufts University points out that there are a number of Northern ghetto census-tracts in which the infant-death rate exceeds 100 deaths for every 1,000 children. In these sections of the United States we have come very close to the level of the Biblical plague in the Book of Exodus.

For poor black, poor white and poor Puerto Rican people, the risk of death before age 35 is four times greater than the average for the nation as a whole. In certain neighborhoods of the United States the childbed death-rate for black women is now six times the rate for white women. The excess mortality figure for poor people in New York City is 10,000 to 15,000 yearly. The figure for newborn infants nationwide is estimated to be as high as 40,000. These infant-deaths occur primarily in the rural slums and in the Northern ghettos. These 40,000 infants are the victims of social, professional and institutional murder.

Poison Those children who survive the hour of imperfect birth encounter equally formidable dangers in the first few years of life. The crumbling plaster in many slum dwellings is covered with sweet and sticky lead paint that poor children eat or chew as it flakes off the walls. The lead paint poisons the brain-cells of young children. Infants become blind, are paralyzed, undergo convulsions, and sometimes die, if they chew it over a long time.

The forces of the law in Boston do not compel a landlord to replace, repair or cover over the sweet-tasting crust of paint that paralyzes children. The law *does* allow a landlord to take action to evict a family if the mother or father misses one rent payment by as much as 15 days. Even in those cases in which the letter of the law supports the tenant, judges often will not penalize or publicly embarrass rich and powerful owners of slum properties who are their friends or are financial benefactors of politicians to whom the judges owe their court appointments.

Rage It is in this context, then, that sane and sober parents, in such cities as New York and Boston, draw back in fear or anger at the condescending, if often idealistic, statements of young teachers who tell them to forget about English syntax and the Mathematics College Boards, but send away for bean seeds and for organic food supplies and get into grouptalk and encounter.

It seems to me that the parents of poor children are less backward and more realistic than some of their white co-workers are prepared to recognize. Survival skills are desperately important for the children of the powerless and the poor within this cold, efficient nation; they must not be sarcastically and ignorantly scorned by rich young white boys in blue jeans and boots with good degrees from Princeton, Oberlin and Yale.

Harlem does not need a new generation of radical basketweavers. It does need radical, strong, subversive, steadfast, skeptical, rage-minded, and power-wielding obstetricians, pediatricians, lab technicians, defense attorneys, building-code examiners, brain surgeons. Leather and wheat germ may do the trick on somebody's radical estate 10 miles east of Santa Barbara or 16 miles south of Santa Fe but it does very little good on Blue Hill Avenue in Boston on a Sunday night when a man's pocket is empty and his child has a fever and the buses have stopped running.

I cannot draw a perfect blueprint for passionate, angry, realistic education. I know, however, that it is within our reach and that some of the free schools come extremely close. I also know this is the kind of goal that is most worthy of our pursuit. There has to be a way to find pragmatic competence, internal peace, and ethical passion all in the same process. This is the only kind of revolution that can possibly transform the lives of the people in the land in which we live and in the time in which we are living.

A WORD OF PROTEST

LOU LABRANT

Lou LaBrant, who contributes "A Word of Protest," is an outstanding teacher who taught for years at the high school level in the Ohio State University School prior to teaching at the college level. She reminds the sponsors of alternative and open education that there is a substantial body of teaching experiences that have been reported by progressive teachers in earlier decades. She suggests that the reformers do their homework and read about the successes and the failures of the progressive movement.

After her contribution to education as a professor at New York University, Lou LaBrant continued teaching at Dillard University in New Orleans, one of America's largely black colleges.

Nowhere are the contradictions of our age more evident than in the field of education. We have continued emphasis on use of visual and auditory aids and a lessening of dependence on print, but no lessening in the spate of books and articles advocating changes in education. If no one reads, why write? Experts deal at length with individualizing education, the open school, a school without walls, the English plan, informality in general, better communication, and closer pupil-teacher relations. Titles vary and programs overlap in design, but while the advocates continue to write many pages, they themselves appear hesitant about reading. A little more time spent with other people's pages would surely tell them that many procedures they offer as new and experimental were (under slightly different captions) not only advocated but put into operation, tested, sometimes proved good and sometimes rejected—all of this during the twenties and thirties of the present century. No one would ask them to go as far back as *Emile*.

Perhaps present-day writers are frightened by the label "progressive" which was attached to much of those twenty years of experimentation. With the advent of World War II, the end of those twenty years, our nation suddenly turned to old-time procedures. We were, of course, dominated by the military, and were too busy with the war to read the careful evaluations which were just being completed. Moreover, the new programs were (and would still be) more expensive than formal instruction attached to sets of texts, with large classes and minimal equipment. A further factor was the drain of young people (essential to a new movement) into the war effort. The McCarthy era gave a final blow. The "progressive" movement became associated with a lack

Reprinted by permission from *Teachers College Record*, December 1972, pp. 167–169.

of responsibility, sometimes dubbed "permissive" treatment, and hence the whole movement was either lost or discredited.

Whatever the causes of the return to conformity, serious educators today should go beyond labels, for there is abundant literature dealing with the processes and plans they advocate. It is unfortunate that some of our more prominent writers seem to have assumed that significant literature is restricted to their own period—a natural but not too encouraging attitude.

Today's writers do, of course, refer frequently to John Dewey and his philosophy. They seldom mention—indeed they seem not to have discovered—the scores of classroom teachers who made practical application of these theories. Many elementary schools introduced projects in which children helped to plan, execute, and evaluate undertakings of significance to them and to their society. I recall one junior high school group that studied its own small town, found a serious situation, and persuaded the city fathers to extend the sewage system to an underprivileged area.

Usually the projects were not without some direction or suggestion, but the specific undertaking, its level of interest, and the formulation of questions came directly from the students, and the resulting work offered them not only development of specific skills in reading, writing, numbers, and social responsibility, but gave them the additional highly important experience of thinking critically (on their mental level) about what they had accomplished and how one goes about learning anything. The general movement of involving students in planning their own education concerned all ages, and not the elementary school only. New programs ranged from those at the Bank Street School to curricular approaches at Sarah Lawrence College.

A number of journals and yearbooks of national organizations are informative. On the secondary level, the most elaborate of experiments was known as The Eight Year Study or sometimes The Thirty School Experiment. There were also The Stanford Language Arts Investigation, The Southern Study, and a host of smaller but thoughtful attempts at basic change. Many private schools joined the movement; a few continue to be experimental today. Many universities sponsored experimental summer programs for teacher observation.

Periodicals which might be consulted include the *Teachers College Record, Elementary English Review, Educational Method, Educational Review,* and *Progressive Education.* Gray's annual (University of Chicago) reports on research during the period include some significant studies. The Eight Year Study was given elaborate evaluation under the sponsorship of the Progressive Education Association. Results include a record of the students' college success or failure. Reports were published in a series of books, pamphlets, and articles.

Many writers contributed, but search might begin with the following names: Harold Alberty, Elsie Clapp, Orville Brim, Harold Fawcett, Harry Giles, Frieda Heller, Alice Kelleher, Holland Roberts, Harold Rugg, William Van Til, Carleton Washburne, Paul Witty, and Laura Zirbes. Boyd Bode wrote extensively on the need to break down subject matter lines (producing, as he said, logic-tight compartments). The Class of 1938, Ohio State University School, wrote its own six-year history and evaluation. Interesting also is a follow-up study of this class by Margaret Willis in 1961.

Books and articles of that period deal with individualizing reading, both in early teaching for all children and in remedial work for those who do not succeed. Washburne's school attempted to discover at what age a child should be taught to read. His findings contradict some present-day emphases. While the selection of particular books has changed with the social scene, the basic methods and the underlying theory were the same as those used in such national programs as Upward Bound.

Obviously, the great body of American schools did not take part in experimentation thirty to fifty years ago, but neither are the majority of schools today undertaking radical change. The schools which did experiment, however, were serious about their efforts, and reported them thoughtfully. Much of their experience might save today's leaders from deadend roads.

Like many of today's reformers and critics, the earlier leaders saw great concern with freedom of both thought and behavior. Educators questioned the lockstep teaching of conventional subject matter, limitations of the material, and formality instead of natural teacher-pupil relations. In their initial enthusiasm for change, however, they overlooked the fact that as group size increases, so the need for some organization grows. (American cities cannot use the town meeting today.) Thus in their zeal for freedom, teachers sometimes produced only chaos. The literature, therefore, soon came to discuss organization as well as freedom: the balance between a program without plan or control of any kind and one where students could express beliefs freely and work on questions important (relevant?) to them with coherence and order.

Since critical thinking was an important emphasis, a number of writers discussed the difference between opinion and proof. Tests were devised for measuring results. This question merits attention, and since experimentation takes time, the available reports have value.

Underlying the issue of freedom, responsibility, order, organization, and their interrelationship was a need to understand human growth. Obviously, ability to choose from an increasingly broad scene grows only gradually and is determined by the extent of the individual's experience. Faced with choices too wide or too vague, the child or adolescent often preferred an immediate and temporary interest, and became disillusioned when his suggestion proved futile. It was for this reason that a more structured set of offerings was developed, with choices among units. This still unsolved problem might be clarified by earlier experiences.

Perhaps an example from a high school situation will illustrate the above question. An eleventh grade class planned a final unit for the year: to read together (they usually read independently) one book, which they described as "a very great and famous one." They would then test their varied approaches to the questions which such a book should raise. The instructor agreed and asked: "What book?" The student response was "How can we choose a book we have not read? Tell about some ten or twelve you have read." The reader may not agree with the students' solution, but their demand poses the question.

Obviously, any serious movement involves a host of problems, problems which are common to any revolution. Specific materials change with the times (there was no TV in the period between 1920 and 1940), but the basic relations of child to adult maintain many common factors. The aims of education continue to be important. Current critics might well compare their ideas with those which preceded their own adulthood. William Allen White once wrote, somewhat inelegantly, that the Lord has "put a hog-tight fence around experience." Maybe he was right, but we just might try to break through.

SPEARPOINT: TEACHER IN AMERICA

SYLVIA ASHTON-WARNER

Teacher (*New York: Simon and Schuster, 1963*), *by Sylvia Ashton-Warner, an exciting account of teaching Maori children in New Zealand, is a book which is highly respected by many of the compassionate critics and the young teachers who are developing free or alternative schools. Therefore, her penetrating description of her experiences in teaching in a free and open school in the United States was read with deep interest by those engaged in current curricular experimentation with free and open education. Since she writes as a sympathetic observer, her questions concerning the meanings of equality and authority in education are taken far more seriously than would be the hostile criticisms of a traditionalist.*

Ashton-Warner's article appeared in Saturday Review of Education *and was adapted from her book* Spearpoint: Teacher in America (*New York: Alfred A. Knopf, 1972*).

One day in the autumn, I go straight from the plane into a foreign school of a culture I thought I knew. I'm agog with confidence in my own work, knowing it like ABC, but not knowing that I, from the tail end of civilization, have descended upon the spearpoint. True I have lived in other countries at varying stages of civilization, so that I know what civilization is and what a stage of civilization is, but here, in no time, the days are a matter of survival and my work is XYZ. There's no time space or mind space to remember romantic conceptions of life about being a wandering exile or to dream about the stars. My comfortable principle of life . . . "Ask of no man but give to all" . . . fails in the face of survival. My new watchword, clumsily assembled, becomes . . . "Adapt and survive."

I can't stand closed doors where children are segmenting the family fluidity, and when I see the door of the math room shut I take the liberty of opening it. I'm not one to intrude or invade if I can help it but, "That's no way for big boys to behave."

"We'll do what we like!" Crash the Cuisenaire rods on the floor.

"Standing on a table hurling things on the floor. That's like babies."

"We have every right to do what we like!" Bang, whiz, spin. . . .

"Not like six and seven," I say. "You're both like little babies standing up there throwing valuable material that other children need. Babies."

"When you say something about someone," he shouts, "it sticks on yourself. It's you like the baby. You, you!"

It's true. They're far cleverer than me. This is a modern open school and I've got to be that too. No pride or anything like that. No hurt. All being equal, he can say what he likes, And do what he likes too. I'm learning that reciprocal respect is not necessary to equality. On the other hand, am I respecting their right to release their imagery; who am I to criticize?

"It's you that's the baby," he repeats.

"Could be too. Me the baby. But in any case you bore me."

"And you bore us."

A jolly good answer. I'm floored again. Like the Cuisenaire rods. I try another way: "What makes you two think you're so clever?"

Flings more rods but he's thinking. "Because" . . . bash! . . . "We *are* clever."

"I agree. But does that make you interesting too?"

No answer from either.

"Why don't you answer?"

The bombs still pound the target but still there is no answer, so I walk toward the door, ashamed of victory.

"Yes, go," they say, "and shut the door. We want to be by ourselves."

I obey. I'm getting the hang of equality and the evils of authority.

I stand in the tunnel-corridor while children run, collide, and wrestle. What would the American teachers have done? I think I know. Without any debate, they might have got down on the floor, collected some rods as they landed and set about making a math pattern illustrating and honoring the function of the rods, so that in time the two might have joined them. But only might have. The rapport between American and American at work. But what did I do? Attacked.

I still stand while the children gambol. The corridor is lit by nylon lighting, the air by my standards overbreathed, overhot, reverberating from some tom-tom beat pulsing from a stereo. Too enclosing the architecture, built for thoughtful men rather than exploding children. Whose life am I living, mine or someone else's? Can't I stop the ship and get off?

I like children's voices, high, wild or low, solo or in unison, but the beat and the boom of stereo and the hitting of the suffering piano in the foyer . . . what is this thing, freedom, supplied to the children in overspilling glassfuls, in tankards, in brimming kegs? Must glorious freedom mean all this? Is this, indeed, freedom? If it is, what good is it? How long is the equipment going to last which they need for learning; the piano, the guitar, the Cuisenaire rods? And, as equipment, how long will I last? Astonishingly the Americans don't notice the noise; you can tell by their faces. They can talk and think along with it. Think and talk *better* along with it . . . with all the dire discords.

Maybe they've made a mistake in summoning me, inviting an alien to them. Alien. There's the word. I should reel from it but I don't. I don't dislike being an alien. An artist must be an alien in life. Art must walk alone, a pariah of the human family.

But can't I get off? Where's a window? It's wide outside, the plain, within the cradling mountains. And still. What I need is a moment of seclusion or two to regroup my faculties. Adapt and survive . . . remember it.

Through the intoxicated children I weave my way, careful not to offend by touching, down the narrow spine of the ship to the storeroom, and plug in the pot for tea. This storeroom might be all trash cans, furnace, dirty mugs, and pets, but it's where big things are said; where you meet everyone who is anyone, which includes guinea pigs and children. True there's no place for one to sit, but you get that kind of rest unrelated to chairs. Confidences are exchanged to the hum of the furnace, revelations to the smell of the trash cans; between teacher and teacher, child and child, between teacher and child; between parent and teacher, between parent and visitor, between everyone and everyone. Everything goes, from educational policy to exacting metaphysics and what happened at the last board meeting. In and out of season, the most important thing in life blossoms in this storeroom: that which passes between one and another, so that when Senta glides in to make some coffee I laugh and say, "My office."

A smile as she cleans a mug.

"I'm trying to work out what you mean by freedom."

"What I mean by freedom, or the kids, or the parents, or the—?"

"Well, I mean . . . there's an intoxication . . . you know, it's not really what children are. It's . . . I don't want to use words like 'license' and 'anarchy,' but. . . ."

"What happened was," from Senta, who is head of the upper school, "the kids were told before we opened they could do what they liked."

"We lost before we started, then."

"No, not quite," accurately, with a steady respect for facts, "but you can't start a school like this on immediate unqualified freedom. Kids coming from structured schools should be given freedoms gradually. They should have brought the structure over to start with, then loosen up in stages. The kids are not used to it, not ready yet."

"Apparently."

And we laugh. "We can recover in time," quietly.

"Time. True. The main things we need are time and privacy. Who're all these people here every day? It's like an air terminal."

"Om . . . parents and visitors to see the school . . . there's great public interest you know, right? Crowds come every day wanting to teach. About nine volunteers walk in each morning. There's a big movement in the country, a breakaway from the traditional. There're thousands of these open schools."

I pour boiling water on the exposed tea leaves. If ever I'm asked to speak anywhere on education in this country, I'll lecture on how to make tea. "Senta. What you're telling me, then, is that our children as they are now are not really normally as they are now. The frightening irresponsibility, the. . . ."

"Oh, no, no. No."

Meaning, I do not voice, that their contempt for me is no more than a transitory symptom?

"The kids are all right," she assures. "When we get settled, when they. . . ."

"At one stage yesterday, the infant room was packed with grownups and there wasn't a child in sight."

"*C'est la revolution*," and we laugh again.

"Senta!" from a pretty girl child, throwing her arms around her slim body, "Senta. I want you to come and see my beadwork and tell me what to do next."

Now I'm talking to someone else. "Time and privacy is all we want really," I repeat.

Conversation, however pointed, however critical, can't last long in the thronged storeroom. Conversations can't last long in the . . . conversations can't last . . . conversations can't . . . conversations . . .

Not unlike a cocktail party.

Carl is a young American whose rapport with the children is as true as the hues on the mountains; no contrivance about it. As casual as the heath at your feet. It is also, at this point, indispensable. His outlook on life is the same as theirs, his values, background, and racial characteristics; his language and even his legs, which he ties in a bow beneath him. That he's also an anthropological graduate I know by accident only.

As a man rolls up his sleeves to a job, Carl takes off his socks to a job, so that his feet are what you notice. There's rarely no smile mixed up with his glasses somewhere inside his whiskers, and our children use him as a commodity, an item of equipment they don't have to put away. As I do too. You seldom see how tall he is, he usually being cross-legged on the floor. Although standing, he swings high like a cottonwood; in ego he swings low like the sage. Self-effacingly.

You can limb all over him if you like, over his back, knees, and head, as you can climb all over his mind . . . through, under, or behind it. You can crawl right through his smile to the storeroom of his knowledge, finger what's there, and help yourself to it whether you put things back or not.

Getting the children to do their jobs is climbing a mountain backward. "We need some children to help the teachers," I say, "to see that everyone does his job. A couple of policemen to. . ."

Outrage from the teachers. "You can't do that!"

"Oh?"

"D'you know what that means, Mrs. H.?"

"Policemen?"

"That means pigs in this country."

"Pigs? It means friends in our country."

Carl reproves. "You can't use that word, Mrs. H."

"Heavens. What'll we use, then?"

"Not *pigs!*" Horror from the teachers.

"Helpers, then?"

"But we're *all* helpers."

I've no doubt you are, I do not say, but in a way not immediately obvious. "Friends . . . can we use that?"

"We're *all* friends."

"I take it," warming up, "that what you're all telling me is that no one is in the position to ask the children, *expect* the children, to help us with the other children?"

Doggedly, "They don't like any one of them to be in authority over any other."

"They 'don't like.' Interesting." The authority terror again. No wonder they go in for the wannadowanna. I'm baffled. I don't know what to do about the terror of authority. New ground. New country to colonize. In some societies, the police are as close to the people as bartenders and butchers. I sit a moment on the floor to think it over while our children careen, carouse, and climb. I'm recalling other children I've known honored to be the policemen, and children who like being policed by each other. If we could get clear of politics, we could get on with teaching. Where the devil has the *substance* of education got to? Ah! I've got it. "Have you got anything against the word 'captains'?"

No one answers at once. No one stops Rocky from standing on the guitar while Monty unscrews the strings.

"You do have captains in this country, don't you . . . in sport?"

Carefully thoughtful, examining it.

"Aren't I allowed to ask a boy to bring in the children, for instance? After all, he's more agile and energetic than I am. I can be preparing their work. I can do things that he can't and he can do things that I can't. Or does it work only one way in an open school—in an open country, if you like: that I do things that he can't but he's too free to do things that I can't? Is this what you mean by equality?" How holy is this equality?

No one answers. I find American graduates most careful about their thinking, sacrificing all for it like a woman in love. I know that when an answer does come it won't be irresponsible.

"Is that guitar of any value to anybody? We've already lost the use of the ukulele."

A soft voice says to Rocky, "Would you like to put the guitar on the table?"

Or would you *not* like? I keep to myself.

"I dowanna."

Another voice says, still soft, "Captains. That's all right."

I may be wrong. Everyone here thinks better than I do with my passion and metaphor. Maybe it's authority to bring in the children at all. Maybe we should sit talking, waiting for some whim to move the children to come inside. A test of our TV entertainment value to lure them in. How can you teach anyone anything at all when all, irrespective of age, knowledge, or experience, are exactly equal? Since democracy is based on envy, presumably equality is too. Whereas I'm here to teach, rather than serve or baby-sit.

The teachers carefully agree to the word "captains" and, having had enough of this will-you-won't-you, will-you-won't-you, will-you-join-the-dance, I choose the captains myself, damn it. I choose three boys who hang together whose leader has a certain charisma. Boys who seem to me interesting people, more bored than the rest, being not extended, more mature. The boys indeed who were throwing the rods with only contempt for me. Zed of seven, leaning in doorways, whose vivid, livid imagination ensures arduous followers . . . Agar and Henry. Zed Zane & Co. Boys who live their lives more in the mind than with hands and legs and who have personal drawing power. It's true that Henry hurts me when he sticks out his tongue and calls me dum-dum, but I realize I am a dum-dum. I've never heard the word before, but its meaning gets through. Who knows? I may soon be American.

"This meeting is too long," states Henry.

"I hate meetings," from Jonathon.

"So do I, Jonathon."

"Can we go to snack now?"

"Those who don't work don't eat. Those who work . . . do. Please yourselves whether you do your jobs or not. But those who have, come and sit by me," cross-legged on the floor. And . . . I might mention . . . within the door.

Authority, Equality, Freedom. Yet someone did use the word "Responsible" one day. Oh, yes it was Carl: each is responsible for his own possessions. Not: each is responsible for all possessions, which is too collective. It makes some sense on paper, but there's far too much paper anyway, with or without sense on it. Take all the paper from North America, and the country would come right in a week. And another thing . . . as child after child comes and sits before me, his work done behind him, and I lay a hand on his head . . . another thing: what in God's name do they mean by teaching? What in Freedom's name, I should say. Adapt and survive or go home.

But it is sweet, oh, so sweet! . . . the little ones sitting before me. So sweet to lay a hand on each head. "This one is here," I murmur. "This one, this one, this one. And here is this one . . . and this one . . . and good heavens here is this one. *Now* you can go to snack. . . ."

TEMPERING
A
FAD

JOSEPH
FEATHERSTONE

As a contributing editor for The New Republic, *Joseph Featherstone has written numerous articles about the education scene in both the United States and Great Britain. On leave from* The New Republic *in 1970, Featherstone wrote* Schools Where Children Learn (*New York: Liveright, 1971*) *about British informal schools. In this article, adapted from his introduction to a series of booklets sponsored by the Ford Foundation, he cautions about faddishness as to open schools.*

Featherstone believes the idea of informal schools alone is no more likely to solve or cancel out the fundamental, recurring problems in education than did the gimmickry of educational technology, abstract versions of progressive education, or the fake distinctions between child-centered and teacher-centered classrooms. "The most pressing American educational dilemma is not the lack of informality in classrooms: it is whether we can build a more equal, multiracial society."

Word of English schools reaches us at a time of cultural and political ferment, and the American vogue for British reforms must be seen as one element in a complex and many-sided movement. Within our schools, there is nearly a pedagogical vacuum. Few reformers have come forward with practical alternatives; even fewer have deigned to address themselves to working teachers. The grass-roots nature of the English reforms, with their emphasis on the central importance of good teaching, has a great appeal for people who

Reprinted from *The New Republic,* September 25, 1971, pp. 17–21. Reprinted by permission of Citation Press, a division of Scholastic Magazines, Inc., from *An Introduction* by Joseph Featherstone, © 1971 by Schools Council Publications. *An Introduction* is the first book in the British Primary Schools Today Series, published by Macmillan Education, Ltd., England.

are victims of the general staff mentality of our school reformers and managers. Blacks and other minorities are interested in new approaches simply because they reject all the workings of the schools as they stand; some of the best of the community control ventures, such as the East Harlem Block Schools, have been promoting informal methods, as have some of the parent-controlled Headstart programs. And there are growing numbers of middle- and upper-middle-class parents in favor of "open" and "informal," not to mention "free," schooling, even though they are vague on the pedagogical implications of these terms.

The most cogent chapters in Charles Silberman's *Crisis in the Classroom* are a plea for American educators to consider the English example. Silberman's book is interesting as a cultural document, as well as a statement in its own right. For it registers an important shift in opinion. Silberman is arguing that too many American schools are grim and joyless for both children and teachers. What was once said by a handful of radical critics is now very close to being official wisdom. Silberman, it should be added, distinguishes himself from many critics of the schools in that he is deeply sympathetic to ordinary classroom teachers and has a clear sense of the crucial importance of the teacher's role in creating a decent setting for learning.

By now I've visited a fair number of American classrooms working along informal lines. The best are as good as anything I've seen in England; the worst are a shambles. In the efforts that look most promising, people are proceeding slowly, understanding that preparing the way for further improvements and long-term growth is more important than any single "innovation." (As I've noted, there are too few entire school environments run along informal lines.)

Understanding the need for slow growth and hard work with teachers and children, many of the informal American practitioners I've talked to are alarmed at the dimensions of the current fad for "open" schools. There are reasons for skepticism. From today's perspective, which is no doubt morbid and too disheartened, it seems that our successive waves of educational reform have been, at best, intellectual and ideological justifications for institutions whose actual workings never changed all that much. At the worst, the suspicion is that past reform movements, whatever their rhetoric, have only reinforced the role schools play in promoting social inequality. The realization that schools alone cannot save the social order—which should have been obvious all along—has prompted some to despair over ever getting decent education.

Added to these sobering reflections is a fresh sense of dismay over the outcomes of the past ten years of "innovation." For we have finished a decade of busy reform with little to show for it. Classrooms are the same. Teachers conduct monologues or more or less forced class discussions; too much learning is still rote; textbooks, timetables, clocks set the pace; discipline is an obsession. The curriculum reform efforts of the '6os brought forth excellent materials in some cases—materials still essential for good informal classrooms—but they took the existing environment of the schools for granted. Perhaps because so many were outsiders, the reformers failed to engage teachers in continuous thought and creation, with the result that the teachers ended up teaching the new materials in the old ways. Being for the most part university people, specialists, the reformers were ignorant of classrooms and children: of pedagogy. They concentrated on content—organized in the form of the standard graduate school disciplines—and ignored the nature of children and their ways of learning. Too often children were regarded as passive recipients of good materials, and teachers as passive conduits. The reformers lacked a coherent vision of the school environment as a whole. It was characteristic of the movement that it ignored the arts and children's expressiveness.

In the philosophical chaos of the curriculum projects, the proponents of precision had a debater's advantage. They were able to state their goals in precise, measurable, often behavioral terms. For a time this false precision encouraged a false sense of security. And for a while the behaviorists and the education technology businessmen were allies: they imagined that a new era of educational hardware was dawning, promising profits commensurate with those in the advanced defense and aerospace industries. Now that the bubble has burst, it seems evident to more and more people that this curious alliance had all along been talking about training, not education. Training means imparting skills. It is an aspect of education, but not all of it. I suggest a reading example: if I teach you phonic skills, that is a kind of training. Unless you go on to use them, to develop interests in books, you are not educated. This ought to be the common sense of the matter, but it isn't. Our technicians conceive of reading as a training problem on the order of training spotters to recognize airplane silhouettes. If a sixth grader in a ghetto school is reading two years below grade level, as so many are, the problem may not be reading skills at all. A fourth grade reading level often represents a grasp of the necessary skills: part of the problem is surely that the sixth grader isn't reading books and isn't interested.

Another reason why some practitioners are dubious about "open" education reflects a further skepticism about the evangelical American mode of reform, with its hunger for absolutes and its weakness for rhetoric. Our "progressive" education movement often neglected pedagogy and the realities of life in classrooms and instead concentrated on lofty abstractions. It will be essential in promoting good practice today to abandon many old ideological debates. Yet the English example is now part of a whole diverse American cultural mood, which means that it is already ranged on one side of an ideological debate. The

American milieu is polarized culturally and politically; this polarization conditions American responses to accounts of informal teaching. The responses tend to fall into the stereotyped categories of a cultural cold war raging between the hip, emancipated upper middle class and the straight middle and working class. It is a class and cultural conflict, and it takes the form of battles between those who see life as essentially a matter of scarcity—and defend the virtues of a scarce order, such as thrift, discipline, hard work—and those who see life as essentially abundant—and preach newer virtues, such as openness, feelings, spontaneity. Hip people like the idea of open classrooms, because they seem to give children freedom; straight people fear the supposed absence of order, discipline and adult authority.

If I portray this conflict in highly abstract terms, it is because it seems to me remote from the concerns of good American and British practitioners actually teaching in informal settings. Take the issue of freedom, for example. Letting children talk and move about is helpful in establishing a setting in which a teacher can find out about students; it helps children learn actively, to get the habit of framing purposes independently, using their own judgment. But this freedom is a means to an end, not a goal in itself. As a goal, freedom is empty and meaningless—"a breakfast food," as e. e. cummings once put it.

There are always those who argue that freedom is something negative —freedom from—and those who argue that freedom is positive. From authoritarians like Plato to libertarians like Kant and Dewey, the second line of argument has linked freedom with knowledge—the free use of reason or intelligence and, sometimes, action with knowledge. Whatever the merits of the positions in this fascinating, perpetual debate, it is surely more appropriate for educators of the young to conceive of freedom in the second sense, not a momentary thing at all, but the result of a process of discipline and learning. Informality is pointless unless it leads to intellectual stimulation. Many children in our "free" schools are not happy, and one suspects that part of the reason is that they are bored with their own lack of intellectual progress. As William Hull remarks in a trenchant critique of the current fad for "open" education: "Children are not going to be happy for very long in schools in which they realize they are not accomplishing very much."

Or take the issue of authority. That it *is* an issue is a mark of deep cultural confusion, as well as a reflection of the frequent misuse of legitimate authority in America. Whatever their politics, good practitioners assume as a matter of course that teachers have a responsibility to create an environment hospitable to learning, that there is what might be called a natural, legitimate basis for the authority of an adult working with children. In his superb little book, *The Lives of Children*, George Dennison outlines some aspects of this legitimate authority:

"Its attributes are obvious: adults are larger, more experienced, possess more words, have entered into prior agreements with themselves. When all this takes on a positive instead of a merely negative character, the children see the adults as protectors and as sources of certitude, approval, novelty, skills. In the fact that adults have entered into prior agreements, children intuit a seriousness and a web of relations in the life that surrounds them. If it is a bit mysterious, it is also impressive and somewhat attractive; they see it quite correctly as the way of the world, and they are not indifferent to its benefits and demands. . . . [For a child] the adult is his ally, his model—and his obstacle [for there are natural conflicts, too, and they must be given their due]."

Disciplinary matters and the rest of the structure of authority in American schools work against the exercise of legitimate authority. And thus, in reaction to the schools, the education opposition movement foolishly assumes that all adult guidance is an invasion of children's freedom. Actually, in a proper informal setting, as John Dewey pointed out, adults ought to become more important: ". . . Basing education upon personal experience may mean more multiplied and more intimate contacts between the mature and the immature than ever existed in the traditional schools, *and consequently more rather than less guidance.*"

If you remove adult authority from a given group of children, you are not necessarily freeing them. Instead, as David Riesman and his colleagues noted in *The Lonely Crowd*'s critique of "progesssive" education, you are often sentencing them to the tyranny of their peers. And unacknowledged adult authority has a way of creeping back in subtle and manipulative ways that can be more arbitrary than its formal exercise.

Another fake issue in the debate on open education is the distinction between education as something developed from within and education as something formed from without, the old, boring question of whether to have, as they say, a child-centered or an adult-directed classroom. There are, to be sure, certain respects in which the best informal practice is child-centered. The basic conception of learning, after all, reflects the image of Piaget's child-inventor, fashioning an orderly model of the universe from his varied encounters with experience. The child's experience *is* the starting point of all good informal teaching. But passive teaching has no place in a good informal setting, any more than passive children do. Active teaching is essential, and one of the appeals of this approach to experienced teachers is that it transforms the teacher's role. From enacting somebody else's text or curriculum, the teacher moves toward working out his own responses to children's learning. The teacher is responsible for creating the learning environment.

Still another confusion on the American scene lies in the notion that liberalizing the repressive atmosphere of our schools—which is worth doing for its own sake—will automatically promote intellectual development. It won't. We need more humane schools, but we also need a steady concern for intellectual progress and workmanship. Without this, it is unlikely that we will get any sort of cumulative development, and we will never establish practical standards by which to judge good and bad work.

Some American practitioners question the utility of slogans such as the "open school," or "informal education." The terms are suspect because they become cliches, because they don't convey the necessary values underlying this kind of teaching, because they suggest a hucksterized package and because they divide teaching staffs into the "we" doing the open approach and the "they" who are not. Some imitate the philosopher Charles Saunders Pierce, who changed his "pragmatism" to the much uglier-sounding "pragmaticism"—in order, he said, to keep his ideas safe from kidnappers. They prefer an awkward and reasonably neutral term like "less formal." A brave few are modestly willing to march under a banner inscribed "decent schools."

This suspicion of slogans can be carried to ludicrous extremes. But at the heart of the evasiveness is an important point: educating children or working with teachers is an entire process. A good informal setting should not be thought of as a "model" or as an "experiment," but as an environment in which to support educational growth in directions that have already proved sound.

Some observers fear the manner in which our schools implement reforms in a way that destroys the possibility for further development of teachers. (There are already instances where principals have dictated "open education" to their staffs.) There is a deep—and I think altogether justified—mistrust of the conventional channels of reform from the top down: pronunciamentos by educational statesmen, the roll of ceremonial drums, the swishing sound of entrepreneurs shaking the money tree. Most of the serious American informal practitioners are self-consciously local in their orientation. They are interested in planting themselves in Vermont, Philadelphia, New York City, North Dakota or wherever, and working at the grass roots. They imagine that it will take a very long time to get good schools, and they do not believe that big-wig oratory or White House Conferences on Education are any substitute for direct engagement with teachers and children in classrooms.

The changes they are starting are small but they have large implications. All teachers, no matter how they teach, suffer the climate of our schools, and every serious attempt at reform will soon find itself talking about lunchrooms, toilet passes, the whole internal control structure of the schools, relationships to parents, relationships to supervisory staff, the ways in which supplies are ordered, the links between an individual school and the central bureaucracies; ultimately issues of politics, power and money.

As schools move in informal directions, there will be an increasing criticism of our system of training and credentialing teachers and administrators. (Here, with the exception of outstanding institutions like London's Froebel Institute, the English do not have examples to emulate: their teachers' colleges are improving, but they have trailed behind the work of the best schools.) The training of administrators will come under attack, and in some places separate training programs for administrators will be abolished. The inadequacy of teacher training will also become more evident, although it is far from clear how to improve it. What we do know is that theory has to be reunited with practice. Without a solid grounding in child development, much of our informal teaching will be gimmickry; and without a sound base in actual practice in classrooms, theory will remain useless.

The enormous variety of the American educational landscape makes it difficult to speak in general terms. In certain areas, education schools willing to restore an emphasis on classroom practice may unite with school systems ready to move in informal directions. In other areas, where the education schools are unable to change their mandarin ways, school systems will have to assume more and more of the responsibility for training and credentialing teachers. Whichever the pattern, a central feature of successful programs will be periods of work in good informal settings. Thus a prerequisite to any scheme of training will be the existence of good schools and classrooms to work in. The single most important task is the reform of schools and classrooms, for good informal classrooms provide the best teacher training sites.

Whether the current interest in informal teaching leads to cumulative change will depend on many things. Two are worth repeating: whether enough people can understand the essentially different outlook on children's intellectual development which good informal work must be based on, and whether our schools can be reorganized to give teachers sustained on-the-job support. I'm somewhat optimistic about the first: the ideas are in the air, and many teachers, on their own, are already questioning the assumptions behind the traditional classroom. The second question will be much harder to answer satisfactorily. In some places, the schools are ripe for change; in others change will come slowly and painfully, if at all; and in others the chances for growth are almost zero. Those promoting informal teaching ought to be wary of suggesting good practices to teachers working in institutional settings where real professional growth is out of the question. In such a setting, all obstacles mesh together to form what people rightly call the System. Right now it seems unlikely that the System in our worst school systems will ever permit teachers to teach and children to learn.

But things may have looked that way to some British educational authorities in the '30s, too.

A final word on the faddishness of our educational concerns. The appearance of new ideas such as the clamor for open, informal schools does not cancel out old ideas. "Open education" will be a sham unless those supporting it also address themselves to recurring, fundamental problems, such as the basic inequality and racism of our society. The most pressing American educational dilemma is not the lack of informality in classrooms: it is whether we can build a more equal, multiracial society. Issues like school integration and community control have not disappeared, to be replaced by issues like open education. The agenda simply gets more crowded. It will be all the more essential, however, to keep alive in bad times a vision of the kind of education that all wise parents want for their children.

THE OPEN CLASSROOM: A CRITIQUE

H. C. SUN

In his examination of the open classroom, H. C. Sun combines sympathy and support with reminders of lessons from the thinking of John Dewey. He points out that Dewey believed that the important freedom is freedom of intelligence, that some experiences are educative and others miseducative, that education based upon living experience cannot be contemptuous of the organization of facts and ideas, and that Dewey believed the teacher has a genuine role as to direction and guidance.

H. C. Sun is a professor of graduate education at Hampton Institute and a long-time member of the John Dewey Society. He contributes frequently to educational journals.

Some critics of public education in search for alternatives have hit upon the concept of "open" classrooms since 1965, otherwise known as "free" schools, "informal" education or "street" school. The growth in number and variety of such schools suggests a need for a critical look at these ventures and their rationale.

Reprinted from *The High School Journal*, December 1972, pp. 134–141 by permission of the publisher, University of North Carolina Press.

Apparently this development is a reaction to the Sputnik-produced educational reform, or discipline-centered approach with emphasis on the cognitive realm. Consonant with the recent "humanizing" education movement sponsored by the NEA, the concept of the open classroom is prescribed as the best antidote for the prison-like public school. Reportedly, in hundreds of tiny, private free schools and in public classrooms in nearly every state, children roam from one study project to another, theoretically following their native curiosity and learning at their own uneven rates through self-discovery. The approach threatens to become a fad.[1]

The open schools, operated in varied set-ups, have two things in common: freedom for the youngsters and a humane education. They are noted for the informal atmosphere and flexibility which characterize each and every aspect of the school—unstructured, undirected and sort of do-your-own-thing classroom scenes. Sound assumptions upon which the new critics of public school build their framework of the open classroom include:

1. Genuine learning takes place when the learners participate actively.
2. A warm and humane climate facilitates learning.
3. The learner is motivated when he sees meaningful relationships between his school work and his goals.
4. The four walls of a schoolroom do not define the boundaries of learning.

Negatively, they may also be right in pointing out most American schools as grim, joyless places with petty and oppressive rules. Too much emphasis has been placed on grades and discipline at the expense of learning. Neglected is the education of the feeling and the imagination; this neglect resulted in an intellectually sterile and esthetically barren atmosphere. Rigidity in program planning and grade organization has led to lock-up situation, which fails to adjust to the individual differences of the learners.

However, in the juggling of the ingredients of the open-classroom recipe, it is not always easy to carry on the educative process in a balanced way. As the Delones[2] well pointed out, how to give the student individual freedom without drifting into anarchy; how to place him at the center of the curriculum without sacrificing other vital curricular bases; how to prepare a student for the "real world" without so adjusting him that his creative impulse and aptitude for change are stifled; how to educate for an uncertain future without throwing out the past; these and other polarities of similar nature are slippery and frequently contradictory ideas and ideals. Silberman came to the con-

---

1 "Education: Sober Chaos," *Time*, January 3, 1972, p. 44.
2 Richard H., and Susan T. Delone, "John Dewey Is Alive and Well in New England," *Saturday Review*, November 21, 1970.

clusion that "finding the right balance is never easy" in his diagnosis of the ills of American education in his monumental study, *Crisis in the Classroom.*

In the free schools,[3] there are no dress codes, no rules about leaving the campus to go to town, no censorship of student publications, no restrictions on student political activity, and no differential treatment of students and adults. A student court has sole power to suspend or expel. The student council makes all non-academic rules, subject to the joint veto of the headmaster and student body president and vice president. This does sound like free schools. However, they stress the distinction between "freedom from" and "freedom to." Students are free from the negative rules to do things which meet certain minimums. At Windsor Mountain, students believe that certain rules are necessary. They rejected "open dorms" during certain hours on the grounds that the larger society upon which the school depends is not ready for it.

Two constraints form the framework on faculty freedom: college admission standards and student interests and welfare. The direction of the school, according to one headmaster, is to draw students, teachers, parents and community together, not toward a free school where everyone does what he wants. It was reported that between 90 and 100% of their graduates go on to college, and they do well on achievement tests no matter where they choose to go.

On the other hand, the kind of free school as described in *The Lives of Children*[4] presents quite a contrast. The children, since they come to school dirty from dirty homes, are not expected to meet any cleanliness standards. The theory is that, if the teachers should try to clean them up, they would alienate the children from their families. The school was, in the words of George Dennison, "dirty and looked awful." But, "it resembled their (the children's) immediate and familiar environment." It was according to the same principle that the teacher handled the field trip. Instead of putting the token given to them for subway fare in the slot, the children crawled in under the turnstile. And the teacher followed suit.

It is interesting to note that the leaders of the free schools "profess themselves inspired to a considerable degree by the thought of John Dewey."[5] In his account of *The Lives of Children* in a school located in Manhattan, George Dennison stated that the school was committed to Dewey's philosophy. The Delones' article on their visit at four free schools in Massachusetts and Vermont bore the title, "John Dewey Is Alive and Well in New England." In a new high school in Brooklyn

[3] *Ibid.*
[4] George Dennison, *The Lives of Children* (New York: Random House, 1969).
[5] Sidney Hook, "John Dewey and His Betrayers," in Jacques Barzun *et al.* (eds.), *Papers on Educational Reform* (LaSalle, Illinois: Open Court Publishing Co., 1971), p. 111.

named after John Dewey, there are no grades or homework, and students are permitted to chart their own courses.

However, Professor Hook, a leading exponent of the philosophy of John Dewey, contends that Dewey's philosophy has been "flagrantly distorted" in the current literature of criticism. "It is also false to claim that its (public school) radical critics today are justified in invoking his ideals for their distinctive proposals."[6]

One of the misconceptions of Dewey's philosophy stems from the notion that because he stressed the importance of freedom, he was therefore opposed to authority. What Dewey does write is: "The need for authority is a constant need for man"—a constant need because conflicts, differences and incompatible desires are ever present features of existence. In point of fact Dewey, upholding social control, does not rule out exclusion if it is the only available measure, although it is admittedly no solution. The supreme authority or the "only freedom that is of enduring importance is freedom of intelligence, that is to say, freedom of observation and of judgment exercised in behalf of purposes that are intrinsically worthwhile."[7] Dewey writes further on freedom and authority:

> There can be no greater mistake, however, than to treat such freedom (external and physical side of activity) as an end in itself. . . . There is no intellectual growth without some reconstruction, some remaking, of impulses and desires in the form which they first show themselves. This remaking involves inhibition of impulse in its first estate.[8]

Another major misconception of Dewey's philosophy is to equate experience with education. The truth is that Dewey makes a central distinction between experiences that are "educative" and experiences that are "non-educative" or "miseducative." In fact, Dewey says:

> Everything depends upon the *quality* of the experience which is had. The quality of any experience has two aspects. There is an immediate aspect of agreeableness or disagreeableness, and there is its influence upon later experience. The first is obvious and easy to judge. The *effect* of an experience is not borne on its face. It sets a problem to the educator. . . . Hence the central problem of an education based upon experience is to select the kind of present experiences that live fruitfully and creatively in subsequent experiences.[9]

The third fallacy is to attribute to Dewey a belief that since traditional education rested upon a conception of organization of knowledge that was almost completely contemptuous of present living experience, therefore education based upon living experience should be contemptuous of the organization of facts and ideas. The new cur-

[6] *Ibid.,* p. 133.
[7] John Dewey, *Experience and Education* (New York: Macmillan Co., 1946), p. 69.
[8] *Ibid.,* pp. 73–4.
[9] *Ibid.,* pp. 16–7.

riculum theory that the content cannot be viewed outside of the learner may, taken literally, lend support to the notion that there is not much subject matter which needs to be taught despite the knowledge explosion.[10] Let us see where Dewey stands.

But as an ideal the active process of organizing facts and ideas is an ever-present educative process. No experience is educative that does not tend both to knowledge of more facts and entertaining of more ideas and to a better, a more orderly, arrangement of them.[11]

The organized subject-matter of the adult and the specialist cannot, writes Dewey, "provide the starting point. Nevertheless, it represents the goal toward which education should continuously move."[12] And he warns that "the basic material of study cannot be picked up in a cursory manner." Occasions unforeseen should be utilized in the teaching-learning situation. "But there is a decided difference between using them in the development of a continuing line of activity and trusting to them to provide the chief material of learning."[13]

To make abundantly clear his stance on the issue, Dewey persists:

Nothing can be more absurd educationally than to make a plea for a variety of active occupations in the school while decrying the need for progressive organization of information and ideas. Intelligent activity is distinguished from aimless activity by the fact that it involves selection of means—analysis—out of the variety of conditions that are present, and their arrangement—synthesis—to reach an intended aim or purpose. . . . Otherwise an activity ceases to be educative because it is blind . . .

. . . But . . . experiences in order to be educative must lead out into an expanding world of subject-matter, a subject-matter of facts or information and of ideas.[14]

Just as two points define a straight line, so the present standpoint of the child and the facts and truths of studies define instruction.[15]

Fourthly, Dewey's philosophy was invoked to justify the "lax, undirected, do-your-own-thing classroom scene," which tends to "proceed as if any form of direction and guidance by adults were invasion of individual freedom." What Dewey does say on the role of the teacher is:

[10] Fred T. Wilhelms, "Design of the Curriculum," in J. Galen Saylor and Joshua L. Smith (eds.) Removing Barriers to Humaneness in the High School (Washington, D.C.: Association for Supervision and Curriculum Development, NEA, 1971), p. 60.
   In a similar vein wrote Ronald Gross and Paul Osterman, the editors of High School (New York: Simon and Schuster, 1971, p. 13): "Equally outdated is the idea that there is a given body of knowledge all students should learn."
[11] Dewey, op. cit., p. 102.
[12] Ibid., p. 103.
[13] Ibid., p. 96.
[14] Ibid., pp. 105–106; p. 111.
[15] John Dewey, The Child and the Curriculum (Chicago: The University of Chicago Press, 1902), p. 11.

On the contrary, basing education upon personal experience may mean more multiplied and more intimate contacts between the mature and the immature than ever existed in the traditional school, and consequently more, rather than less, guidance by others.[16]

It is then the business of the educator to see in what direction an experience is heading . . . In this direction he must be able to judge what attributes are actively conducive to continued growth and what are detrimental.[17]

The educator is responsible for a knowledge of individuals and for a knowledge of subject matter that will enable activities to be selected . . .[18]

It is absurd to exclude the teacher from membership in the group. As the most mature member of the group he has a peculiar responsibility for the conduct of the interactions and intercommunications which are the very life of the group as a community.[19]

The concept of the open classroom rests upon some assumptions which are educationally sound in principle. Its advocates strike at the problems of the public schools with equally convincing evidence. However, at the very heart of the issue is the factor that teaching is the most challenging human art—an art of helping the young become fully human—for which there is no easy answer. Particularly, "dropping conventional constraints makes teaching absolutely more difficult," so stated Lillian Weber, one of the advocates of informal education.[20]

How "open" should a classroom be? How "free" should the children be? That the classroom should be made enjoyable is beyond dispute, but remember Bruner's warning that "Johnny may be happy but he is an idiot." True, love is the most important ingredient of humane education. "All you need to add to Purina Chow is love" makes more sense, however, than "All you need in teaching is love." To let the student learn at his own rate and at his own level is psychologically sound, but it is equally indisputable that the rate of learning is not fixed and the adult's expectation can influence the learning outcome. "When we did badly," so reminisced Bill Cosby about Mrs. Mary Nagle, his fifth grade teacher, "she'd say: 'I think you're worth more than that' . . . You had to do better than yourself."[21]

While juggling for the right balance is hard, the educative process can slip easily into a position, which is child-centered, society-centered, discipline-centered, or something else. It is a deplorable fact that the educational philosophy which professes to be based on the idea of freedom and openness may become as dogmatic as ever was the public school under attack. Ironically, the radical critics in their earnest search

[16] John Dewey, *Experience and Education, op. cit.*, p. 8.
[17] *Ibid.*, pp. 32–3.
[18] *Ibid.*, p. 61.
[19] *Ibid.*, pp. 65–6.
[20] *Time, loc. cit.*
[21] Herbert Kupferberg, "Bill Cosby's Favorite Teacher," *Parade*, February 6, 1972, p. 9.

for educational alternatives have proclaimed with assurance the demise of the school.[22]

In closing, a review of the criticisms of progressive education made by two eminent scholars three decades ago may be refreshing in the appraisal of the current movement toward "open" classroom—a revival of progressivism in education.

Boyd H. Bode, a leader of the pragmatic philosophy of education, wrote in his *Progressive Education at the Crossroads* in 1938:

If progressive education persists in a one-sided absorption in the individual pupil, it will be circumnavigated and left behind.[23]

Walter Lippmann who had praised Dewey's *Democracy and Education* as "the mature wisdom of the finest and most powerful intellect devoted to the future of American civilization," lashed out later against the superficiality and parochialism of the modern school as follows:

There is no common faith, no common body of principle, no common body of knowledge, no common moral and intellectual discipline. Yet, the graduates of these modern schools are expected to form a civilized community. They are expected to govern themselves. They are expected to have a social conscience. They are expected to arrive by discussion at common purposes. When one realizes that they have no common culture, is it astounding that they have no common purpose? That they worship false gods? That in the fierce struggle for existence they are tearing Western society to pieces?[24]

[22] Jack Fields, "Book Review: *School Is Dead*," *Saturday Review*, January 15, 1972, p. 64.
[23] New York: Newson and Co., pp. 43–4.
[24] Quoted by Lawrence A. Cremin in *The Transformation of the School* (New York: Alfred A. Knopf, 1961), p. 326.

PART THREE

CURRICULUM TODAY

Despite the criticisms made of education in Parts One and Two, a commentator on schooling in the mid 1970s can report many good things about American education. Education grows bigger and often takes place in better buildings with better equipment. Aid for governmentally favored fields has enhanced the quality of instruction in some curricular areas. Disadvantaged people begin to participate in the process of curriculum change. Some schools are innovative and experimental.

Yet an honest commentator must also report on problems that beset education in the mid 1970s. General education is inadequate; when it exists, it often fails to illuminate social realities, meet individual needs, and develop humane values. Integration of knowledge through the curriculum is lacking. Compensatory education does not obtain hoped-for results.

227

Inadequate schools persist. Children of the blacks, the other minority groups, and the poor are especially shortchanged. Even young people from privileged backgrounds protest unreality in the curriculum. The disciplines proposal crests and ebbs; yet no socially oriented proposal for humanized education gathers sufficient support to rival subject-by-subject reform. The struggle among forces in society for control of curriculum change grows sharper.

You will find that there is much in common among our authors on curriculum. Notably, they write with a sense of urgency. They know that they live today in a time of crisis. Each in his own way quests for genuinely relevant education. Each seeks a curriculum which makes sense. Yet, naturally, they often support different means for achieving their curricular ends.

My role as editor is to comment on some of the authors' ideas and, in the process, share some of my own convictions on curriculum. If I were you, I would read the articles which constitute Part Three of this anthology before reading further in this editorial. Turn back here later for some comparisons and contrasts.

As a prologue to the section on curriculum today, the editor of this volume, who believes that current compassionate critics, like the child-centered progressives, have some but not all of the answers, supplies a comment. In "The Key Word Is Relevance," which appeared in Today's Education, the NEA journal, the editor reiterates his conviction that if educators are to achieve relevance, there can be no substitute for knowing the learner as an individual. But neither is there a substitute for illuminating the social realities which characterize the total environment, or for a philosophy which gives direction to the educational enterprise by clarifying values through the use of the method of intelligence. Some of the compassionate critics and their supporters may scorn these additional concerns as pretentious, unattainable, or even unnecessary, but the editor regards them as essential to meaningful education.

There is much reflective thought combined with good will in the viewpoints of our authors. There is good sense in each of their proposals. One wishes that he might call for implementation of each proposal and avoid making choices.

Take, for instance, the six encompassing recommendations for the entire curriculum which are grouped in the section, "An Approach to Curriculum." Take Theodore Brameld's advocacy that at least half the curriculum be experienced outside the schoolroom through direct participation and travel. Versions such as Brameld's of community school and social travel proposals—seminal ideas suggested in earlier decades yet largely disregarded—are urgently needed in today's social setting, in which young people struggle to make a difference through participation and seek to build relationships through meeting other

*people in other places. Take Arthur W. Foshay's aspiration for a
synthesis of what is real with what is conceptual, particularly in the
neglected social studies and arts. As Foshay warns, we should not
jettison coolness and logic and settle solely for heat and involvement.*

*Take R. Thomas Tanner's socially sensitive proposal for new science
themes to carry on such unfinished business in an unfinished country as
improvement of the quality of the environment through
interdisciplinary work involving teachers of the social studies and other
educators. Tanner's view is a clear recognition of the folly of any
discipline attempting to go it alone without multidisciplinary programs
and relationships. Take Jerome S. Bruner's proposal for "if not a
moratorium, then something of de-emphasis on matters that have to
do with the structure of history, the structure of physics, the nature of
mathematical consistency." Bruner, who first brought to the educational
world what Foshay calls the disciplines proposal, now suggests "that it
is possible to conceive of a Monday-Wednesday-Friday curriculum
covering the standard topics, and a Tuesday-Thursday and indeed
Saturday way of doing things in which immediate and compelling
concerns are given the central place."*

*Take Lawrence E. Metcalf and Maurice P. Hunt's call for youth to
examine and appraise their rejection of the adult world in order to
clarify their own values and make their own social policies better
grounded and internally consistent. This proposal reflects the
inescapable necessity of using intelligence in human affairs. Take
Edward G. Olsen's espousal of dealing with vital issues and the
fundamental problems of living. Olsen puts social issues at the center of
the curriculum.*

*Such proposals cannot be fully carried through in a curriculum tidily
and tightly separated into discrete subjects. Though supportive of the
achievements and potential of "the disciplines proposal," Foshay
recognizes and defines its limitations in the present crisis which
include: begging the question of the integration of knowledge, not
dealing directly with the relationship between education and life,
failing to take into account the nature and need for teacher education,
being directed to the college-bound rather than all children and
youth, conceiving education as strictly rational, and lacking relevance to
anything but further work in the selected disciplines.*

*There are two forms of curricular organization which might
encompass the following characteristics which these authors recommend:
Brameld's participation, Foshay's integration of knowledge and
relevance of knowledge to the real world, Tanner's neglected
environmental quality, Bruner's activist curriculum, Metcalf and Hunt's
clarification of values and social policies, and Olsen's life-and-death
issues. One possibility is a substantial block of time for interdisciplinary
study focused on the real and pressing dilemmas of human beings and*

supplemented by needed education for diversity in broad curricular fields. The other form of viable curriculum organization utilizes distinct, yet closely cooperating, subject fields in order to teach young people about agreed-upon overarching themes and central concerns of human beings faced by social realities.

Yet the separationist and isolationist forces which prevailed in curriculum development during the 1960s have opposed the use of such forms of curricular organization in the 1970s. In the mid 1970s, cannot the case also be heard for the integration of knowledge relevant to the real perplexities and dilemmas of human beings? Interrelatedness and wholeness in curriculum development have too long been neglected.

Special new problems have emerged for curriculum makers of the mid 1970s. For instance, racism persists in American society. The difficult task which faces American education is how to provide education relevant to the needs of members of ethnic minority groups while also providing an education which is relevant to the American dream of a united nation characterized by democratic human relations. James A. Banks and Robert L. Green have done some hard thinking on the matter and suggest some constructive procedures. Each refuses to oversimplify the problem by depending exclusively on combating white racism or exclusively on building proud self-concepts in ethnic group members. Both call for immediate action by schools and society. Banks warns that such action "is imperative if we are to prevent racial wars and chaos and the complete dehumanization of the American man." Green calls for the educational system to "change its direction and pace" else "schools will continue to be the sources of conflict and turmoil in the community."

Educators of the 1970s have inherited earlier debates over what is the proper work of the school and how the curriculum can be changed. The customary debate over innovation focuses on whether or not team teaching, independent study, the nongraded school, and so forth, have made any real difference. But Fred T. Wilhelms, without quibbling, sensibly accepts innovations that contribute to personalization. He believes that priorities in change efforts must go to helping each young person in his personal becoming, and to dealing with the social agenda of the present. One can do little more than add a fervent "amen" to Wilhelms' eloquent presentation of the genuine priorities as to innovations. It is worth noting that Wilhelms too is concerned about curriculum fragmentation; he calls for interdisciplinary curriculum building in each of his three major "streams": science-math, the social studies, and the humanities.

Complicating the lively controversies over content, organization, media, and methods in current curriculum discussion are problems concerning curriculum change. The supposed "good old days" of leaving all the curriculum decisions to the educators are past—if they *ever actually existed. Now, in the words of the immortal Jimmy Durante, everybody wants to get into the act. As Ronald C. Doll points out, some forces seek power, some control the spending of governmental and philanthropic dollars, some offer knowledge accumulated by scholars, and some foster the needs and concerns of pupils, educators, parents, and community members.*

J. Merrell Hansen, writing primarily to administrators in the National Association of Secondary School Principals Bulletin, *calls for a reappraisal of current curriculum changes. He believes that "all innovation, all the materials and paraphernalia, and all the acclaimed successes are inappropriate unless the teacher behaves more effectively and the student relates to the experiences more meaningfully." He believes that educators must "visualize their objectives, institute experiences which make the curriculum a life experience, and evaluate in terms of their objectives." He calls attention to the fact that change is not necessarily synonymous with improvement.*

Forward-looking educators have long urged that everybody get into the act. After all, the public schools do belong to the people. Consequently, current misgivings by some educators concerning teacher, student, parent, and community demands for participation have a hollow sound. For better or worse, so-called "outside" forces are "in," as our authors point out. We cannot and we should not try to turn back the clock to an educators' monopoly in curriculum change. Yet neither should educators abdicate their roles as participants and as leaders.

The challenge today in regard to curriculum change is to establish a process in which multiple forces will be taken into account, yet reasonable decisions as to curriculum will be made. We cannot afford a paralysis created by endless discussion. Nor can we allow confrontation to prevail as the accepted way of making curriculum change. Today in curriculum change we are close to an anarchic situation in which the forces and agents with the most power reign temporarily in an eternal "king of the hill" struggle. We have to develop new ground rules for a wider sharing in curriculum decision-making which utilizes more effective democratic processes than have yet been devised.

Let us hope that educators and citizens of the future recognize, with many of our authors, the central place that should be occupied by social realities, the needs of individuals, and humane values. If we base our educational programs on social realities, needs, and values, and if we stress integration of knowledge, education may have a fighting chance to make a difference in the quality of the lives of the individuals who inhabit this nation.

PROLOGUE:
THE
KEY
WORD
IS
RELEVANCE

WILLIAM VAN TIL

The editor's prologue is a reminder that the quest for relevance leads through a curriculum based on learners, social realities, and human values. As the compassionate critics rightly insist, the curriculum must be related to the individual learner. A curriculum which ignores the learner's experience will have no meaning for him, and thus relevance will be unattainable.

Yet a child-centered curriculum alone is not enough, despite the eloquence of the compassionate critics. Unless the curriculum illuminates social realities and clarifies values for mankind, it is not sufficiently germane to contemporary society. At least so the editor suggests, citing illustrations of irrelevance and suggesting both fundamental changes and adaptations in the contemporary curriculum.

Let us begin with an admission: Some of the content we teach in American schools is not as relevant as it might be to the lives of the young people we teach, to the society in which they are growing up, or to the clarification of democratic values.

Some illustrations are obvious. For instance, one of the many Puerto Rican schools I visited during a New York University survey of education in Puerto Rico was in a village high in the mountains of the interior. The villagers were very poor and afflicted with the problems that go with poverty—poor nutrition, inefficient agriculture, dilapidated housing, bad health, and the rest.

Only a handful of young people of the village and the surrounding countryside ever enrolled in any kind of educational institution beyond high school. Yet, what were the young people studying in the secondary school in this little mountain village? In a social studies class, they were memorizing lists of products of South American countries. Their mathematics work had no relationship to the problems they might encounter in the school shop or at home or elsewhere. In an English class, students were reading eighteenth and nineteenth century British novels: At the time of my visit one class was dissecting *Ivanhoe*. (This mountain school and community, I hasten to say, was not typical; many other Puerto Rican schools were more relevant to learners, society, and values, and many other communities had higher living standards.)

Recognizing the lack of relevance in education in an exotic, faraway setting is easy. Such was the case when I visited a home economics

Reprinted by permission from *Today's Education*, January 1969, pp. 14–17.

class in a town of mud hovels in Iran: The girls were making scrap-books of pictures (clipped from very old magazines) that portrayed the clothes and foods of prosperous Americans and Europeans.

The closer to home we get, however, the harder it becomes for a teacher to recognize irrelevance. Take Doris Smith and Harry Jones, for instance. She teaches in the suburbs in the Midwestern United States; he, in the slums of a West Coast city. Both of them would quickly recognize the lack of meaning in the two faraway examples cited. Yet, both might have difficulty recognizing that they have their own problems in making the content of their classes meaningful to some students.

Doris Smith teaches social studies in an affluent suburb that is among the first places where new national projects and proposals are tried. A genuine innovator, she uses a variety of methods and materials with versatility. She uses simulation techniques, for example, and has just completed an academic game with her eleventh graders. The game deals with economics; the players adopt roles and the ones who make the most money are the winners.

Margaret, one of Miss Smith's better students, went through the motions of the game but was fundamentally uninvolved. Why? Because, like Benjamin in *The Graduate*, Margaret had painfully learned from the lives of her parents and their friends that affluence did not necessarily result in a good life. Why, wondered Margaret, were teachers blind to what was most relevant to young people? For instance, why didn't the teacher see that the most important thing about this game would be to examine the materialistic goals which were taken for granted as desirable?

During follow-up discussions, Miss Smith raised questions with the class about the strategy of moves made during the game. Margaret's responses were correct but unrelated to her concern for values.

Harry Jones teaches language arts in an intermediate school in a slum neighborhood. Though Mr. Jones is white and most of his students are black, racial differences have not been a barrier to mutual liking and respect. The class is now reading a selection in a new anthology which is quite appropriate to the level of the students' reading abilities. Mr. Jones notices that Jess isn't reading the assigned selection, but instead is simply leafing through the pages. It isn't as though I'd asked the class to read dull, difficult material simply because it's supposed to be an English classic, Harry thinks. I guess Jess just doesn't care.

Jess is thinking: I can't find black men in this book. Where's the brothers? This is Whitey's book. How can a good guy like Mr. Jones be so dumb? Not for me, baby.

"What are you doing, Jess?" asks Harry. "Just lookin'," says Jess.

Good teachers though they are, even Miss Smith and Mr. Jones sometimes attempt to teach content that is unrelated to the lives of learners. Some teachers have even greater difficulty in achieving relevance than do methodologically skilled Doris and well-liked Harry. Classes do exist in your community and mine in which an uninterrupted academic content bores young people. Classes do exist where subject matter is quite unrelated to the dilemmas and struggles and aspirations of many prospective learners.

The teacher who realizes that his content of instruction isn't meaningful has two viable alternatives. He can change his content from the irrelevant to the relevant. Or, if he cannot change the required content, he can teach it in such a way as to give it relevance.

Yes, a third possibility does exist. One can continue with the meaningless content, break his heart trying to teach, and achieve very little.

A teacher does not need extensive instruction in educational psychology to realize that his teaching must be connected with the student's background, drives, and life if any learning is to take place. Experience soon teaches a teacher this axiom.

The obvious and sensible thing to do is to replace the irrelevant with the relevant through changing the content. Remember, for instance, the poverty-stricken Puerto Rican mountain village in which the students were memorizing products, being taught mathematics without application, and reading *Ivanhoe*. Here was a setting characterized by a host of problems in the areas of health, sanitation, housing, nutrition, safety, use of resources, production, and consumption. Here were Puerto Rican youngsters who would face bewildering life problems including those presented by the continuing restless migration from the rural ways of the *barrio* to the urbanized ways of San Juan; from the hospitable island of their birth to the impersonal, tenement-lined canyons of New York City, with its strange folkways and less-than-warm welcome to those regarded as "foreigners."

Reality could be introduced into their education. In social studies, students might well learn of the real problems of the village, the island, the mainland. In mathematics, they might see a relationship between mathematics and the problems they encounter in school shop and in their homes. In English classes, students might well acquire the bilinguality they need by reading English-language newspapers and magazines, as well as books of fiction and nonfiction by Puerto Rican and mainland Americans, plus a sampling of British authors. Fortunately, the better Puerto Rican schools do introduce such realities into their programs.

In mainland America, too, the obvious and sensible approach is to change the content if it is not germane. Most educators will readily grant that a teacher must begin at the actual level of accomplishment of those who are to be educated—not stay there but begin there.

Most will grant that pitching the learning at an unreachable level is an exercise in futility. But additionally we must recognize the vital importance of selecting suitable content.

The curriculum should be made more relevant to the lives of the children and youth for whom the curriculum exists. Through their reading materials, for example, city children must often meet people like themselves, rather than always encounter the legendary Dick and Jane and Spot of suburban life. The world of the city must itself become part of the subject matter if young city dwellers are to improve human relations, develop citizenship, widen horizons, and meet the problems of urban living. In Harry Jones's class, and those of his colleagues, surely the contributions of Negro-Americans should be an integral part of the American literature curriculum for both Negroes and whites.

Nor are the suburbs exempt from the blight of irrelevance. Though some suburban young people have an economic head start in life, they, too, are sometimes cheated. When communities are bland and homogenized and indifferent to reality, the young are sometimes cheated of the opportunity to know people of varied races, religions, nationality backgrounds, and social classes.

When high school students are regarded as college fodder, they are sometimes cheated of sufficient experience in home economics, music, fine arts, and industrial arts. When the only god worshipped is academic success in formal learning, students are sometimes cheated of the opportunity to explore seriously their allegiances to values, their relationships to the adult world, their ways of finding satisfaction, and their participation in political action and social change.

"But," a teacher may say, "I cannot change the required content to make it relevant. I am not a board of regents or a local board of education or a curriculum bigwig attached to the central office staff." He may add, "I am just a humble teacher, a prisoner of the syllabus, the required textbook, and the system in which I am caught. Deviation is not permitted. THEY would not allow it."

Maybe so, but I doubt it. Before the teacher resigns himself to a prisoner's life, he might wish to reexamine his chains. Perhaps they are not as strong as he assumes.

In today's world, more and more educators and laymen are realizing that not all of the answers to the problem of curriculum are in. Since the early 1960's, increasing numbers of educators have attempted to develop curriculums that are more important to the culturally disadvantaged or, in a plainer phrase, the poor.

Now recognition is growing that we are far from having achieved the best of all possible worlds with respect to the education of the economically advantaged. In 1969, still more educators will be looking for curriculums appropriate for young people from affluent backgrounds.

Paradoxically, today's disenchanted young people, including democratic activists and serious and sensitive students as well as hippies and nihilists and revolutionaries, stem mostly from the middle and upper classes.

Possibly the chains of established content are not as binding as assumed. Teacher power grows. . . .

In those cases where, through a variety of circumstances, the chains do prove real and teachers simply must use some prescribed content which is not as relevant as they would wish it to be, how can they make their work more meaningful?

Rather than making fundamental changes in the content, some teachers use the second alternative mentioned and adapt the content to make it more relevant. Illustrations are legion: In literature, teaching *Julius Caesar* in relationship to contemporary dictatorships; in history, preparing and contrasting attitudes toward past American wars with present attitudes on war in Vietnam; in biology, relating the study of human blood to false claims and misleading mythologies as to blood differences between races; in modern languages, teaching the culture as part of the culture's language; in language arts, stressing those readings in anthologies which have most meaning to the particular learners. Miss Smith, for instance, could have discussed with the class the value assumptions behind the economic game that was the required content.

Some readers may ask for the prescription good teachers use for adaptation of content. There isn't any. Sorry about that. If there were a single sovereign remedy, it would have been discovered long ago. The good teacher uses his intelligence in relating the required content to the world of the learner. Good teachers have been doing so for a long time; adaptation is no revolutionary doctrine.

In making content more relevant, there is no substitute for knowing the social realities which characterize the environment of the student. There is no substitute for knowing the learner as an individual. There is no substitute for having a philosophy which gives direction to the educational enterprise. So armed, one can relate much of the content to the learner, the class, the school, and the community.

APPROACHES TO CURRICULUM

A CROSS-CUTTING APPROACH TO THE CURRICULUM: THE MOVING WHEEL

THEODORE BRAMELD

A teacher of philosophy of education and an advocate of social reconstruction, Theodore Brameld proposes a cross-cutting, integrative curriculum in which a minimum of one-half of the entire time devoted to the school curriculum is used outside classrooms. He symbolizes his proposal with a "moving wheel" whose rim represents mankind's predicaments and aspirations, whose hub represents a central question, and whose spokes represent supporting areas or courses.

Brameld is professor emeritus of educational philosophy, Boston University. Author of a dozen books and numerous articles, he is regarded as the leading proponent of the reconstructionist theory of education, which encourages the schools to take an activist position with respect to social and political ills. Recently he has served as a visiting professor at the University of Hawaii and at Lehman College of the City University of New York.

A number of presuppositions must underlie a cross-cutting approach to the curriculum. . . . Let me merely sketch several of these presuppositions.

Reprinted by permission from *Phi Delta Kappan*, March 1970, pp. 346–348.

1. The prime responsibility of the curriculum on any level, but most focally on the lagging senior high school and undergraduate college levels, is the confrontation of young people with the array of severe, indeed ominous, disturbances that now beset the "naked ape" himself.

2. These disturbances are by no means of exclusive concern to the "social studies." Rather, they pervade every aspect of human life across the planet—whether we are thinking either of the political, economic, esthetic, moral, and religious, or of the so-called "objective" sciences and skills of, say, chemistry, botany, and mathematics. Nothing that man has begun to understand or to utilize can any longer be considered as separable from the crucial roles that he now plays, and the extraordinary obligations that these roles entail.

3. The interpenetrating, interfusing, and evolving character of nature, including human nature, compels us to recognize the universality of the critical period through which we are passing. And education in turn, is compelled to create new models of the curriculum that express and dramatize this universality.

4. By the same token, the new curriculum models and applications of them in experimental practice repudiate and supersede the entire conventional structure of subjects and subdivisions of knowledge that, for much too long a time, have reflected a grossly outworn, atomistic model of both the universe and man.

5. The legitimate place that special subjects and skills occupy in transformed conceptions of the curriculum undergoes its own metamorphosis. The part no more remains merely a part than does the heart or the hand when it becomes dissevered from the total human body.

6. To follow the same metaphor another step, the human species requires abundant opportunity to reach inward, outward, and upward toward increasing fulfillment of its ever-developing powers both individually and cooperatively. To the degree that men are denied this opportunity, life becomes a failure for them. When education is not completely geared to this same purpose, it too becomes a failure.

7. The necessarily comprehensive presuppositions that we have made above apply, as norms, to any period of culture and history. But they apply with peculiar urgency to our own period. Fearful warnings, often heard, that the birth of the twenty-first century may never be attended by any historian, because no historian will have survived on our planet 30 years hence, are not warnings that any serious-minded citizen, much less any serious-minded educator, can conscientiously ignore. Unless, of course, he chooses to scoff at such an absurdity.

I am aware that each of these bald statements could be refined and supplemented almost endlessly. Nevertheless, for purposes of discussion, I intend to point directly toward one prospective design for a secondary school curriculum constructed upon the bases that they provide. This is not at all to claim that only one defensible curriculum is possible. It is to claim, however, that models at least comparable to this model should be pulled off the drawing boards and put to the test.

What are the interrelated problems and issues that illustrate the educational agenda inherent in our several presuppositions? I shall state them, again baldly, and without pretense of either order of priority or novelty. They do, however, serve as catalysts for the model to follow.

1. Can the ordinary human being conceivably hope to approach anywhere near optimal fulfillment of his own capacities in the face of accelerated technologized and depersonalized forces?

2. Can the ordinary human being develop a sense of inner personal tranquility and harmony amidst the alienating, divisive, disillusioning experiences by which he is constantly bombarded?

3. Does one (that is, you or I) hold substantial expectations of maintaining any deep sense of relationship with others (that is, with one's mate or family, with one's friends or associates) either amidst chronic instabilities or under the aegis of the folk belief of modern Western culture that self-interest (however "enlightened") still remains the only "realistic" justification for one's daily conduct?

4. Can neighborhoods and other relatively homogeneous communities learn to work together in attacking their own difficulties, in acting concertedly to remove them, and in achieving even a modicum of well-planned, cooperatively organized programs of constructive change?

5. Can racial, ethnic, and other disadvantaged minorities learn to act similarly both among themselves and with other groups of differing backgrounds?

6. Is it actually plausible to expect that human conflicts—for example between the sexes, the generations, and socio-economic classes—can be ameliorated by more humane, viable patterns of living and working?

7. Can religious institutions, with all their rigidities of custom and tradition, still find ways to emulate the same general processes suggested above?

8. Can we reasonably aspire to the expectation that nations will find powerful means to conquer and control the ever-advancing threat of human annihilation?

9. Can the fine arts become a vastly wider, richer experience of unique as well as communal creativity for people across the globe, to be shared freely and openly among diverse cultures?

10. Can communication, in every form (such as travel) and through every medium (such as television), occur without restriction or intimidation not only within but between nations?

11. Can the sciences become equally available to all men, devoted to their welfare and advancement (for example, through the sciences of human health or of the control and growth of natural riches), without depletion and decay?

12. Can economic and accompanying political establishments be rebuilt so that people in every part of the earth have access to and become the exclusive directors of (through their chosen representatives) physical and human resources?

13. Can a converging awareness and unity of mankind as one species— a species with unique, life-affirming, life-controlling powers—be achieved, and will this awareness and unity prove translatable into workable guidelines for political, scientific, esthetic, religious direction and renewal?

14. Can education, finally, direct its attention and energy not only toward the past or toward the present of man's experience, but even more persistently and painstakingly toward man's future as well?

That this agenda is far from all-inclusive is surely obvious. Each question could proliferate into dozens of others; indeed, students themselves, stimulated by mankind-oriented teachers, could and should raise innumerable others. All of these questions, moreover, invite explorations into learning not only by means of books and laboratories; above all, they invite firsthand involvement in the experiences of people in nearby or more distant communities who frequently share the same kinds of questions and seek the same kinds of answers.

To approach the problem somewhat more directly, what does all this mean for the organization and operation of the cross-cutting curriculum? It is possible again to summarize only a number of potentialities. According to this normative model:

1. A minimum of one-half of the entire time devoted to the curriculum is spent outside the classroom—in the laboratory of direct participation with people and institutions, and always with the close support of teacher-consultants equipped to deal with whatever situations or issues have been selected for analysis and prognosis.

2. The circumference of this kind of participation is as wide as the earth, extending all the way from the family and neighborhood outward to the region, nation, and eventually to distant nations. Learning therefore occurs *directly* through intra- and international travel

(let us not be deluded by financial bugaboos; more than adequate funds are available if we insist upon them enough), and *vicariously* through films, the fine arts, and contact with experts such as anthropologists. There are countless other resources.

3. "Team teaching," so often applied adventitiously these days, is supplanted by flexible partnerships of interdisciplinary study, research, and field involvement.

4. The structure of the curriculum may be symbolized (I have developed this proposal at length elsewhere) in the form of a moving "wheel." The "rim" is the unifying theme of mankind—its predicaments and its aspirations. The "hub" is the central question of any given period of learning (perhaps extending over one week, perhaps a semester), while the "spokes" are the supporting areas of concentrated attention that bear most directly upon each respective question. The "spokes" may thus be termed "courses" in art, science, foreign language, or any other pertinent subject or skills. But these are not to be construed as *mere* courses. At all times they are as supportive of the "hub" as it is of them.

5. To the extent that a particular student discovers whatever special interests and talents he may possess, the individual is given every opportunity to develop fields of concentration in his own "spoke." Never is he encouraged to do so, however, for the sake of completing a "major," or passing "college entrance examinations," or other dubious appendages of conventional school systems. Jerome Bruner's truncated concept of structured learning is also of secondary value, for the legitimacy of high-level "excellence" is respected only within the full pattern of the moving "wheel." So, too, Joseph Schwab's cross-cutting but still amorphous schemes for the curriculum are superseded by the theme of post-organic evolution—that is, human evolution—amidst our own age of cultural transformation.

The normative target of this theme is, I contend, far more "practicable" than are most of those advocated in the name of "practicality." This is so because a cross-cutting curriculum of the kind I urge meets the ever more insistent demands of young people for audacious, unconventional, but directly meaningful experiences in both learning and action.

If it is to succeed, students themselves should, of course, share throughout in the planning and implementation of each year's program. Jointly with their teachers, they should decide what issues are most significant to concentrate upon in a selected period. They should help to pre-plan each successive year. They should take heavy responsibilities for all field involvements both in arranging and in following them through. They should support the deviant student who may not always be interested in "problems" at all, but rather in his own "thing" (music, for example). They should engage in the dialogic process of learning that demonstrates (as Martin Buber has so brilliantly urged) how it is possible to face the profound dilemmas of human existence through the mutualities of shared emotion, reflection, and aggressive action.

I suggest, in short, that the time is long overdue when theories of the integrative curriculum should be revived and reconstructed. The trend among influential curriculum experts who have managed during the post-progressive-education period to reverse those theories should itself now be reversed.

In all fairness, nevertheless, let us not pretend that the sufficient cause of anti-integrational and pro-structural curriculum building can be attributed to any such experts in themselves. Rather it is attributable much more fundamentally to imperious demands of the burgeoning industrial-oligarchical order. But, similarly, the causes for curriculum renewal that are now fast emerging become, in one sense, precisely antithetical to this dominant one. More and more independent-minded and future-directed young citizens, not only of America but of other countries, are demanding a radicalization of secondary and higher education. They are doing so both because they are penetrating the facades of conventionality, timidity, and sterility, and because they increasingly want what they rightly deserve: a curriculum that expresses and serves their own time and their own concern. I entirely agree with them.

HOW FARE THE DISCIPLINES?

ARTHUR W. FOSHAY

A researcher and curriculum theorist, Arthur W. Foshay brought the disciplines proposal for curriculum development before the Association for Supervision and Curriculum Development in his 1961 presidential address, entitled "A Modest Proposal." Here he reexamines the advantages and limitations of the disciplines idea in light of experience with the reconstruction of some disciplines in the 1960's and the pressing need for a new curriculum in the 1970's.

Foshay has been connected with Teachers College, Columbia, for many years, beginning as assistant principal of the Horace Mann–Lincoln School in 1946. After a five-year period as director of the Bureau of Educational Research at Ohio State University, he returned to Teachers College as executive officer, then director, of the Horace Mann–Lincoln Institute for School Experimentation. In 1961 he became director and in 1964 associate dean for research and field services at Teachers College. At present he is professor of education there. His writing includes Education in the Elementary School 3rd ed. (New York: American Book Co., 1957 with H. L. Caswell) *and his widely used* The Rand McNally Handbook of Education (Chicago: Rand McNally, 1963).

The idea that the structure, or logic, of each of the scholarly disciplines offers a way of learning the discipline itself was "in the air" during the latter part of the Fifties, and was stated vividly by Jerome Bruner in his *The Process of Education* in 1960. Here, we will call this idea the "disciplines proposal." Bruner's book was surely the most influential bit of educational writing of its time. While the proposal is not very clearly explained in the book, it communicated a fresh insight to a large number of people.

The war between the Progressives and the subject matter specialists had been going on for more than two generations. Within the National Education Association, the departments in the various subject matter fields and the departments dealing with the school as a whole (such as the Association for Supervision and Curriculum Development, the Department of Elementary School Principals and the National Association of Secondary School Principals) had drifted out of contact with each other. Each group—the generalists and the specialists—

Reprinted by permission *Phi Delta Kappan*, March 1970, pp. 349-352.

patronized the other and indicted it on the one hand for being fuzzy and on the other for being too narrowly subject-centered. Bruner's proposal offered a welcome way out of the impasse that had developed. If we could take subject matter as something becoming, instead of as something given, a ground for negotiation would be immediately apparent.

In these pages, I want to discuss what has become of the disciplines proposal since its wide promulgation in 1960, to indicate some of its built-in limitations and possibilities, and to offer certain suggestions for its future.

If anyone had asked the Progressives how they thought subject matter should be learned, they would, as good Deweyites, have responded that all subject matter had to conform to the same general laws of reasoning, and that subject matter ought to be pursued in an active, not passive, way. Of course, the subject matter specialists had the same thing in mind. It is entirely possible that what confused the issue between the generalists and the specialists in the years between 1920 and 1955 was their interpretation of Dewey's notion of the complete act of thought. I myself was present at a highly dramatic faculty seminar at Ohio State in 1956 when a bacteriologist pointed out to one of our principal Deweyites that the complete act of thought did not describe the way he conducted inquiry in his own discipline—that, specifically, it failed to take into account the problem of unknown variables operating in his experiments, and that bacteriologists had long since incorporated a way of dealing with unknown variables into the basic logic of their inquiry.

This was a shocker. The discussion foundered on this rock because, in the last analysis, it called into question the whole core curriculum. The seminar took the position that the function of teaching any given subject matter was to help students to learn how the members of the discipline thought—how they conducted inquiry. Similar discussions must have been going on all around the country. It was because of an audience that had been created by these discussions that Bruner's pronouncement struck fire so quickly.

The idea that the function of instruction is to develop in the student's mind several modes of inquiry is one of the very rare new ideas to have taken root in instruction. The idea has no important background in the tradition of elementary and secondary school instruction. While it probably had occurred to many people at many times, to my knowledge no group had ever coalesced around it before 1960. In the degree that it had any currency, it was found in certain projects within subject matter fields. Harold Fawcett had approached it in the Thirties with a project on mathematics instruction for the Progressive Education Association. No doubt many science teachers had used the idea without naming it during the preceding decades. But the grand tradition of education is not in science and mathematics, both of which are comparatively modern subjects in the curriculum. The grand tradition is in literature, history, geography. The disciplines proposal never had any currency in these fields.

The innovations in instruction of the Progressive era were either technical (like the "unit of work") or policy-oriented (like the "life problems" of the core curriculum). The function of the social studies program during the Twenties, Thirties, and Forties was to teach children how to identify and solve problems, using Dewey's complete act of thought as the means. It was this thrust that separated the Progressives from the subject matter groups.

But if one could take a subject matter as a mode of inquiry, then many of the problems that separated the groups would disappear. One could have an active learner, for he would be actively inquiring. One could have an inquiry-centered strategy which was enough like the "problem-centered" strategy to be recognizable. More important, the approach through inquiry promised a student who would be equipped to persevere in the subject matter he was learning. The older approach to subject matter, whatever its virtues, did not take perseverance as one of its stated objectives. It was, basically, statically conceived. The idea was to make mastery palatable and "meaningful"—but the palatibility and the meaningfulness were to be found through ingenious applications of subject matter to real external life, thus demonstrating its utility. They were not to be found by equipping a student so that he could carry on inquiry independently within the subject matter field. On the other hand, the core curriculum was intended precisely to make the student able to carry on independent inquiry concerning social problems.

The disciplines proposal had developed first in the physics project (PSSC) under Jerrold Zacharias. It was his group which, having found that updating the existing physics curriculum resulted in an impossible load of subject matter, cut through the problem with the notion that the function of instruction physics was not to teach subject matter directly, but to teach it indirectly. Indirect teaching refers to the teaching of styles and methods of thought, as against teaching the myriad of facts that such thought deals with. Not surprisingly, the idea spread rapidly through the several science curriculum projects supported by the National Science Foundation after 1955. This same basic idea also appeared in the new mathematics programs then under development. It appeared in chemistry and biology almost at once.

There has been a substantial evolution of the idea in mathematics and science from that day to this. The new mathematics is said to be in its third generation now. The PSSC program has been followed by

Harvard Project Physics and others. There were at least two prominent chemistry programs, each somewhat differently conceived, and three notable versions of biology.

Interestingly enough, the idea has not fared nearly so well in curriculum projects in other fields, such as literature and history. A distinction perhaps has to be made between fields of knowledge in which inquiry is central and other fields in which something like interpretation is central. One can have disciplined interpretation as well as disciplined inquiry, of course. However, the tradition of disciplined inquiry in literature has had two distinct branches, the historical and the critical; and literary scholars have not traditionally been concerned with the question of the structure of their discipline. In the case of history, although historiography has existed for a long time, writing in the field of historiography has not been nearly so central to historians as has been the writing of history itself. Only recently has a series of books been published to deal with the nature of history as a field of speculation and thought. Perhaps this is why the curriculum projects of the early Sixties in these two fields have not been so concerned with their areas as modes of inquiry as have mathematics and science.

Instruction in foreign language has an independent history that goes back to World War II and the widespread acceptance of the methods of the Army Language Schools. More recently, under the influence of Noam Chomsky, some beginnings are being made to bring contemporary linguistic science to bear on the approach to instruction in this field. Unfortunately, only beginnings are showing; the field is one of the last to respond to this change in the curriculum climate.

The disciplines proposal has suffered the fate of many ideas in education. That is, it has been trivialized, attacked as nothing more than the old enemy, subject-centeredness; it has been misapplied, equated with its opposite (i.e., the complete act of thought), thrown into contrast with creativity (as if there were no such thing as creative inquiry), and so on. We shall not concern ourselves here with this aspect of what has become of the idea. All educational ideas have to survive such pathologies. Rather, let us consider what the built-in advantages and limitations of the idea have turned out to be.

Primary among the advantages of the disciplines proposal is the fact that students are offered subject matter as if it were reasonable. So much of what is offered in school is not reasonable—it is a set of arbitrary codes to be learned, or a set of arbitrary statements to be given back upon demand or recalled when needed—that it is a relief to have subject matter thought of by students as something they can derive out of their own logical processes.

Teachers have wanted students to "understand" subject matter for as long as there have been teachers. We have not had an adequate operational definition of "understanding." The disciplines proposal offers one such. To understand is to be able to give reasons. To inquire is to develop reasons that adequately explain phenomena. The two, understanding and inquiry, finally match each other. The promise of the disciplines proposal is the promise of understanding itself.

Moreover, if pursued in sufficient depth, the approach through the disciplines offers a fresh and enriched view of the nature of general education. At the bottom of every discipline we teach, one may say, is general education. At the bottom, that is, not at the top. A superficial acquaintance with science or mathematics consists only of knowledge of technique. The conceptual material is somewhat deeper. But at the conceptual level the vocabulary of the learned fields turns out to be the intellectual vocabulary of general education. The fundamental concepts of the fields we teach in the lower schools have very wide applicability. *Inverse ratio,* for example, taken from mathematics, can be applied to all sorts of non-mathematical phenomena. There is probably an inverse ratio between the degree of selectivity of the school system and the breadth of knowledge held by the general population in the country. The idea that the more of one thing one has, the less of another, can be learned (it probably is learned) in elementary mathematics. With only slight help, children can see its general value. The notions of *fact, legend,* and *myth,* all from the field of history, have the same general applicability. The notions of *relative motion, the properties of objects, interaction,* and *systems* all arise in one of the better new elementary science programs. I have seen children using this vocabulary in non-science applications, yet with great precision and insight.

The fact that general education has a vocabulary has not been widely recognized. Part of the promise of the disciplines proposal is that the minds of children can be furnished with such a vocabulary, and that the possibility of a real general education is thereby enhanced.

What are the limitations of the disciplines idea? Does it, indeed, have any limitations? There are those who would say that there are none. But there are some.

First, the disciplines proposal begs the question of the integration of knowledge. We must recognize that the integrity of the fields of inquiry—the disciplines—must be preserved if they are to be learned. But this immediately makes it impossible in theory to combine disciplines into multidisciplines for instruction. The subjects have to be taught separately, each in its own way, according to its own logic. To do otherwise is to relapse back into Dewey's complete act of thought, and to resume the old confusions. But to teach subjects separately leaves the problem of integration of knowledge to the student himself to carry out, more or less unaided.

Second, the disciplines proposal does not deal directly with the relationship between education and life—what we call "relevance." One of the oldest questions in education is how education is to be related to real life. The disciplines proposal deals with this question only in terms of the applications of separate fields of knowledge. It does not deal, of itself, with the kinds of life problems the core curriculum used to be concerned with, problems which do not come packaged in disciplines. One could study physics thoroughly and gain very little insight into problems of racial injustice or crime. One could study history— yes, even history—and gain little knowledge of real importance about the problems of poverty in Appalachia, or the nature of the poverty syndrome in our big urban ghettos. To the degree that we allow the school curriculum to be dominated by the disciplines proposal, we fail to offer students the opportunity to become more than superficially acquainted with great public problems.

Third, the disciplines proposal failed to take into account the nature of and need for teacher education. While all of the early science and mathematics programs provided teacher training, the training was brief, suited primarily to those who already had some knowledge of the discipline itself, and not suitable for pre-service education. There was no solid, or even recognizable, conception of teacher education operating in those early projects.

Fourth, the projects as originally conceived did not seek to deal realistically with all the children in the schools. The projects were conceived as suitable primarily for the college-bound, and indeed were mainly intended to improve the education of the college-bound. The 60 percent or so of the population that has no intention of pursuing education beyond high school was simply not taken into account in the early disciplines projects.

Of more fundamental importance is the fact that the disciplines proposal itself is a strictly rational affair. It is naive to assume that all of the problems of the world can be solved by rational men being reasonable with one another. They simply are not. To portray the major fields of knowledge as if they were sufficient is to tell a big lie. The disciplines proposal can be accused of having accidentally committed this grievous error. Man is much more than rational.

The most popular of the criticisms of the disciplines proposal is the lack of relevance of the curricula as developed to anything but further work in the selected disciplines. The projects were too exclusively committed to perseveration as a goal. During the years ahead, it is likely that increasingly sophisticated attempts will be made to show how conceptual knowledge of the kind developed in the disciplines does indeed apply to real problems in the world.

The questions of the integration of knowledge and the relevance of knowledge to the real world will not be denied. They demand a response from the school curriculum, one way or another. If the discipline-oriented curricula cannot respond effectively to these questions, then other responses will be found. It is predictable that we will reinvent the core curriculum, perhaps with some modifications, that a substantial incursion into the regular school day will be made by what were formerly thought of as co-curricular activities, and that students will increasingly refuse to undertake the discipline-oriented subjects. This last has already happened in the case of the physics program, the enrollment having dropped 10 percent during the last 10 years.

We must recognize that the assumptions of values upon which the disciplines proposal is based have come under radical examination during the past few years. Some people reject out of hand the proposal that we improve the present work-oriented system. "If we are foolishly willing to agree that experts are those whose role is legitimized by the fact that the technocratic system needs them in order to avoid falling apart at the seams, then of course the technocratic status quo generates its own internal justification: the technocracy is legitimized because it enjoys the approval of experts; the experts are legitimized because there could be no technocracy without them. . . . Thus, if we probe the technocracy in search of the peculiar power it holds over us, we arrive at the myth of objective consciousness. There is but one way of gaining access to reality—so the myth holds—and this is to cultivate a state of consciousness cleansed of all subjective distortion, all personal involvement. What flows from this state of consciousness qualifies as knowledge, and nothing else does." The above is quoted from a disturbing book, *The Making of a Counter Culture*, by Theodore Roszak (Garden City N.Y.: Doubleday, Anchor Books, 1969, pp. 207–08). It is in the cool, objective, logic-oriented quality of the disciplines proposal that the sensitive and aware young radicals find their greatest challenge. They demand precisely that knowledge be hot, involved, and personal. They would believe the account of scientific inquiry contained in *The Double Helix* before they would believe the account contained in the technical reports on DNA. It is personal knowledge they want, not objective consciousness.

It seems unlikely, given these limitations, that the disciplines proposal of the early Sixties will survive intact into the Seventies. The science and mathematics programs that have emerged out of this period are without doubt more engaging than their predecessors, more respectful of the students' intellectual attainments, less arbitrary, and more sensible. They are also more intellectual in character than the programs that preceded them. It is the quality of this very intellectuality that probably will have to change during the next decade, if the programs are to survive.

I do not mean to propose here that if these challenges are not met, we will go back to what we were doing before. I doubt that we would want to. But we could easily enter into a chaotic period, during which the nature of knowledge would come under fundamental reexamination. What is called for is a change in the spirit of the discipline-oriented curricula and a development of new curricula in the social sciences and in the arts that have something like the power and reach of those in the sciences and mathematics. This latter change is not yet happening in anything like the necessary volume or with the necessary determination.

It is precisely in the social sciences and in the arts that it is easiest to see the connection between education and life. If schooling is to be required to respond to the demand that it be "relevant"—and it seems clear that it has to respond to just such a demand—then the social sciences and the arts would seem to be the curriculum areas in which our efforts should be concentrated in the short run.

Over the long run, it is quite possible that some new version of what a school is and ought to become will be developed. The task is mind-boggling. Without sacrificing the intellectual quality (but at the same time changing its spirit) of the best of the new curricula, we have to find ways of allowing the real problems of the external world to come under searching examination in school. Our secondary school students are rapidly, it appears to me, challenging the concept of adolescence itself. They want to see themselves as participants in the world they live in, not as apprentices for it. They want the world to be in the school and the school in the world.

We cannot meet that requirement satisfactorily by going back to the "problem-centered" curriculum of a generation ago. We have to develop some new synthesis of what is real in the world with what is conceptual, and, as teachers, make all of this suitable for young people who know neither the reality nor the conceptual frameworks.

How fare the disciplines? To me they seem to have become a prologue for a new kind of curriculum theory, a new kind of curriculum organization, a new kind of conception of the meaning of instruction that is likely to come to some sort of fruition during the decade ahead.

THE SCIENCE CURRICULUM: UNFINISHED BUSINESS FOR AN UNFINISHED COUNTRY

R. THOMAS TANNER

R. Thomas Tanner wants to build on past developments in the science disciplines through the inclusion of socially relevant themes. A socially concerned science educator himself, he describes some urgently needed themes related to the quality of our deteriorating environment. These, he argues, are the unfinished business of science education.

Tanner believes a multidisciplinary team approach involving social studies teachers and other educators is essential; we cannot depend upon science teachers alone.

Tanner is a staff member of the Department of Science Education at Oregon State University.

Although the science curriculum has under-gone a major overhaul in the past 13 years, portents of new and needed changes are already blowing in the wind. In this article, I shall 1) summarize the developments of the recent past, 2) suggest some work still left undone, and 3) propose ways in which educators from other curriculum areas may participate in effecting these changes.

In science education, reform movement of considerable dimensions began in the mid-1950s and has achieved fruition in the form of the "alphabet soup" high school courses now familiar to most of us (by name at least): BSCS biology, PSSC physics, CHEMS and CBA chemistry, ESCP earth science, plus a host of elementary school projects. Whereas previous texts were written by individual science educators, the new curricular packages were developed by writing teams in which practicing scientists played a dominant role. The content was not just updated; more important, the curricula were organized around the basic concepts of inquiry and structure.

Inquiry is epistemological. Students were to engage in laboratory work which was genuinely investigative rather than verificational. They were to infer from their own data rather than memorize a rhetoric of conclusions. They were to study the reasoning of scientists in the evolution of scientific concepts rather than commit to memory the associated names and dates. The processes and not just the products of science were emphasized.

Structure is ontological. First, the science course was to represent genuine science and was not to be a catchall for units in alcohol, smoking, narcotics, and the like. Secondly, and more fundamentally, the science course was not to be a hodgepodge of discrete facts or a series of mini-courses in physiology, anatomy, genetics, light, or mechanics;

Reprinted by permission from *Phi Delta Kappan*, March 1970, pp. 353-356.

251

rather, it was to be given unity by a few overarching themes. For instance, the Biological Sciences Curriculum Study claimed nine themes as having guided its work throughout the writing of several texts and supporting materials. These themes include evolution, genetic continuity, and complementarity of structure and function, among others. The Earth Science Curriculum Project chose 10 themes, including universality of change, conservation of mass and energy in the universe, and uniformity of process as the key to understanding the past. The National Science Teachers Association prepared a much-debated list of seven "conceptual schemes" meant to guide future curricular efforts. The schemes are extremely broad generalizations regarding matter and energy; an example is, "All matter is composed of units called fundamental particles; under certain conditions these particles can be transformed into energy and vice versa."

This article is not concerned with inquiry, nor does it question the structures (the themes) which have been developed in the several courses. Rather, I wish to suggest some additional themes. The subject matter developed during the past 13 years may very well constitute a much-improved curriculum in science per se, but it does not go very far beyond science concepts in exploring the societal implications of the scientific enterprise, the interactions of science with society, culture, and human values. Scientists and science educators are beginning to express grave concern over this deficiency in the new status quo of science education.[1, 2, 3] Having long been in complete concurrence with this view, I would like to describe three new themes, which are intended mainly to be suggestive and catalytic. Hopefully, a cross-disciplinary conference of scholars and educators may arrive at a more profound list in the near future.

These three themes all deal directly with technology and thus indirectly with basic sciences upon which technology is founded. (Science is the ongoing pursuit of basic principles of nature; technology is the concurrent application of these principles in developing new products and techniques. The layman often uses the term *science* when in fact he is referring to technology.) The themes:

TECHNOLOGY AND MANKIND: A MASTER-SERVANT RELATIONSHIP

Shall the technological revolution be directed by man for the greatest common good, or shall it sweep us all along toward an unplanned and

---

[1] Fred W. Fox, "A Better Climate for Science" (Eugene, Ore.: Oregon State University, 1968), mimeographed.
[2] Fred W. Fox, "Forces Influencing Education: Present and Future," in David P. Butts (ed.). *Designs for Progress in Science Education* (Austin: Science Education Center, University of Texas), in preparation.
[3] Paul DeHart Hurd, "The Scientific Enterprise and the Educated Citizen: An Unfinished Task." Paper presented at the meeting of the Kansas City, Missouri, Science Teachers, November 17, 1967.

unthinkable brave new world? Will man utilize technological possibilities "just because they are there," or will he weigh their assets against the sociocultural upheaval they instigate? Shall technology be used to aid in uplifting the minds of men, or shall mindless men be used to consume the surplus products of technology? These are the kinds of pressing questions which our students should explore.

The chasm between Snow's two cultures widens; our folkways, laws, institutions, and traditional modes of thought fall further behind our technological advances and their use by industry; social discontinuities proliferate. Automation threatens employability, self-respect, and pride of craftsmanship, while organized labor can respond with little more than feather-bedding and hereditary privilege of union membership. Computers serve the interests of giant corporations while plaguing the individual with incorrect invoices, errorful records, and unresponsiveness to protest. The institutionalized uses of technology have created a populace with wealth, mobility, and free time, but the people are as yet uneducated for use of these benefits. Spaceships and peasants coexist paradoxically within a single nation. Medical technology controls death but laws still do not control birth. The weapons of complete and instant extinction are stockpiled as if they were only spears, rifles, or cannon.

It would appear that if ever we needed a utopia, we need it now. To this end, it is somewhat encouraging to note the birth of futuristics, the study of the future. The Commission on the Year 2000, the World Future Society, and similar organizations are beginning to chart desirable and feasible futures, as answers to the darker dystopias of Orwell and Huxley. Despite the skepticism traditionally accorded utopian thinkers, we must surely place increasing but humanitarian control over the future, if we are to be assured of having one. To continue the practice of brinksmanship in these times is to invite either a bang or a whimper.

TOMORROW'S TECHNOLOGY AND TODAY'S LICENSE

A common excuse for the exercise of greed, irresponsibility, and shortsightedness is that tomorrow's technology can clean up the resultant mess. Once it was easy to turn our backs on the fallacy and go West, leaving the scarred land behind, but now the frontier is gone (although the process is being repeated in "developing" nations). Nevertheless we continue to act as if the frontier were still there. Business equates growth with progress, and the depletion of natural resources is euphemistically referred to as development of natural resources. Population growth causes or intensifies many dilemmas of the day: pollution in all its insidious forms, depletion of natural resources, famine, loss of identity and individual freedom, degradation of the environment, extinction of species, and even war and racism.

Yet technology is optimistically applied to these problems while population growth and economic irresponsibility are accepted or even lauded. Smog devices, desalination plants, floating cities, and high-yield food production methods lull the public into a blind faith in technology, but these are only temporary, stop-gap measures—they are Band-aids applied to a cancer. Similarly, there is a tendency to ascribe to the process of research powers far beyond its capacities. For instance, alarm at the impending extinction of the great whales is assuaged by the assurance that research is being applied to the problem, when it should be obvious that no amount of research will save anything in the absence of strictly enforced international whaling laws.

Implicit in all this is a charge for the educator: A society which has replaced an unquestioning faith in God with a hind-sighted faith in science and technology has not made a very significant intellectual advance. Overfaith should be accorded the same derision as overkill.[4]

MAN IN NATURE, MAN OVER NATURE

American man has traditionally considered nature to be opposed to his progress, and he has endeavored to conquer the natural world and its laws. This attitude, which we have inherited, has deep roots. From Europe's late Renaissance and Age of Reason, Western man brought to these shores the concept of progress through empiricism, in contrast with a former slavish acceptance of the fates. He said, "God helps those who help themselves." Here he found a wilderness which reinforced the attitude by yielding, albeit stubbornly, to his axe, rifle, and plow. At about the time that the frontier was disappearing, along with its opportunities for the common man, social Darwinism became the rationalization for industrial barons who conducted a highly successful "struggle for existence" against nature and against their fellow man. In this century, unionism has spread the wealth to many, and so the many have been cajoled into accepting the industrial revolution's continued battle against the natural world. Now, the technological revolution is succeeding the industrial revolution; it has already contributed to increasing the wealth a hundredfold and decreasing human physical effort by a similar order of magnitude.

This entire period, from Enlightenment to technological revolution, has been marked by a new faith in science as the means of comprehending and thus controlling the environment.

Equilibrium theories such as Festinger's cognitive dissonance give

---

[4] A documented enumeration of our vast ecological problems is not within the scope of this article. These have been detailed at length in the popular press and in technical journals. The reader is referred to such periodicals as *BioScience*, *Natural History*, *Audubon*, and *The Living Wilderness*, and to the *Conservation Yearbooks* of the Department of the Interior. Stewart Udall's *The Quiet Crisis* (New York: Holt, Rinehart and Winston, 1963) and Paul Ehrlich's *The Population Bomb* (New York: Ballantine, 1968) are also recommended.

educators a reasonable explanation of attitudes through this historical progression. The frontiersman wrested his homestead from a resisting wilderness, the captain of industry fought "fang and claw" to the top, and this century's laborers endured wars and depression to claim their share of the bounty. As Festinger might note, they all placed high value on the fruits of their labors because of the effort expended and hardships suffered to obtain those fruits. Thus the concept of a struggle with nature was easily rationalized by all. By the same token, today's restless youth (as epitomized by *The Graduate*) who question the value of great material wealth may be doing so, in part, simply because they themselves did not have to strive for its acquisition. One of our jobs as educators is to bring them to question not just the love of material wealth but also the dangerous concomitant concept of man over nature.

What are the character and the danger of this attitude? Its character is obvious when man boasts of "conquering disease" (but conquers not his procreative urge), when his mineral resources are "ingeniously wrested from a reluctant earth," when he poses proudly with boot and rifle-butt planted atop the carcass of a "savage killer" (unresponsive to the plight of the "killer's" dwindling numbers and insensitive to the ironic self-condemnation of the expression). The attitude is sired by egocentrism and spawned of ignorance. Its danger has already been alluded to under Theme II, above; in brief, an infinitely expanding population can seek infinite material wealth for only a finite period of time, since it exists in a closed system: a planet with finite resources of space and material. Mother Earth is where it is (what's left of it). Those who assume that some day we will find our iron on Jupiter, our water on Mars, or our tranquility in a distant solar system may be asking their posterity to pay the piper an impossible fee. Like it or not, we are *in* nature and it would behoove us to act that way; we can never be *over* nature. We must understand, even more profoundly than did Bacon, that "nature is only to be commanded by obeying her." If we insist upon making a fight of it, we must expect to lose.

A PROPOSAL

As bleak a picture as these themes present, they should not be interpreted as despairing; rather, they represent that enlightened brand of pessimism which anticipates the worst and plans against it, knowing that the only surprises available to the optimist are unpleasant ones, happy surprises being the exclusive delight of the positive pessimist. Furthermore, there is some assurance to be gained when one notes the responsiveness of politicians to the growing grassroots sentiment for conservation issues, and the widespread dismay over the papal position on birth control. Finally, the themes set forth here certainly do not constitute the full range of societal understandings which citizens might appropriately possess; they are only some of the possible candidates for inclusion in the curriculum.

The science teacher is unlikely to possess all of the competencies necessary to deal adequately with these themes or with others dealing with the interplay of science, technology, and mankind. Furthermore, he may require the moral support of others in his school as he deals with possibly controversial issues. This suggests a unified high school course with a multidisciplinary team approach (and that is why this article is being directed to educators other than those in science).

Examples of some possible units and materials are in order. History and science teachers could examine the audacious new way in which man began to view his world during the late Renaissance and the Age of Reason, and the contributions of Copernicus, Galileo, and Bacon to the crossing of the Great Divide. The history teacher might deal with revolutions, the degree to which they are directed by men or, conversely, sweep men along in their course. Sociocultural revolutions such as the pastoral, agricultural, industrial, and technological could be compared and contrasted with political revolutions. The science and social science teacher could contribute to discussion of the technological revolution and its societal concomitants. Teachers of social science, history, and perhaps geography could develop the various concepts of man's place in nature which are held by us and by other peoples, including some of the Indian tribes which preceded us as the human stewards of the continent's resources. Examination of current legislation and government policies would constitute no small part of the curriculum. Political cartoons, such as the conservation gibes of Ding Darling and R. Cobb, would constitute an interesting source of material and a lively vehicle for discussion.

The English teacher could guide the study of contemporary utopian and dystopian novels such as *Lord of the Flies, Walden Two, Fahrenheit 451,* or *Anthem,* as well as brief consideration of earlier utopias such as those of Bacon or More. The University of Southern California film *THX 1138,* by George Lucas, provides a kind of cinematic little *Brave New World* in the light-show, McLuhanish, *cinema verité* form which seems to communicate to many of today's young people. (Incidentally, it was obviously no series of random events which saw these bleak societies conceived of in a century of science rather than in a previous era.) Fletcher Knebel's suspenseful novel, *Vanished,* illustrates the social concern of the scientific community today. Species threatened by the advance of man are considered touchingly in Bodsworth's *Last of the Curlews* and profoundly in Gary's *The Roots of Heaven.* The poetry of Jeffers and the philosophy of de Chardin suggest themselves, among a plethora of possibilities. Even some of the day's popular songs are appropriate.

The construction of such a new curriculum might best be accomplished by the team writing approach used in creating the new science courses. Subject-matter scholars, professional educators, psychologists, school administrators, and classroom teachers would meet together to identify the students they are trying to reach, to state conceptual themes and subsumed objectives, to determine practicable schedules of teacher load and course organization, to effect pre- and in-service teacher training, and to direct the preparation of whatever materials are deemed appropriate—texts, films, exams, etc. The plan not only requires the two cultures to sit at table together, but to be joined there by newcomers from the space, oceanographic, environmental, information systems, and futuristic sciences.

Contemporary educators have often tended to embrace means that were either devoid of ends or connected by illogic to only the fuzziest of ends. The writing group would be charged with keeping sight of ends, both immediate and long-range. Some immediate goals must be the preparation of a curriculum which is resistant to degeneration into dogma, and which will not quickly be made obsolete by the very rapidity of change with which it will be concerned. Consideration of the former goal will necessarily include scrutiny of student evaluation, since objective testing for discrete and trivial facts is temptingly easy and therefore has always been highly contributory to the degeneration process.

A long-range goal is suggested by Max Lerner in an essay written a few years ago: Youth need be instilled with an élan, a "feeling of commitment and of being on fire, a sense of mission . . . of our country still being unfinished, a sense of the authentic revolutionary tradition which is in our history."[5] The youthful unrest which has subsequently become so evident surely constitutes, in part at least, an expression of or search for élan. As a˙ necessary direction for the release of its energies, I submit for consideration the following national purpose: *America should take the lead in establishing and maintaining a varied environment which offers maximum freedom of choice to mankind and to its individual members, everywhere and in perpetuity.* This goal has been discussed elsewhere, along with its implications for our current concepts of economic growth and progress.[6]

This goal should be made explicit for the students in this curriculum. It should be capable of stimulating and directing their élan for some time to come: We are still very far from its achievement.

[5] Max Lerner, "Humanist Goals," in Paul R. Hanna, ed., *Education: An Instrument of National Goals* (New York: McGraw-Hill, 1962), pp. 105, 116.
[6] R. Thomas Tanner, "Freedom and a Varied Environment," *The Science Teacher,* April 1969, pp. 32–34.

THE PROCESS OF EDUCATION REVISITED

JEROME S. BRUNER

In the 1960s Jerome S. Bruner placed much emphasis on the structure of the disciplines. But as the 1970s began, he "revisited" his major book, The Process of Education *(Cambridge, Mass.: Harvard University Press, 1960). In this article, which is derived from a speech he delivered at the annual conference of the Association for Supervision and Curriculum Development in 1971, he suggests a de-emphasis on the structure of knowledge in the disciplines and more concern with knowledge in the context of the problems that face society.*

Bruner was the director of the Center for Cognitive Studies at Harvard University from 1961 to 1972. Now he is the Watts Professor of Psychology at University of Oxford, England.

Ten years have passed since *The Process of Education* was published—a decade of enormous change in the perspective and emphasis of educational reform. I am torn between beginning my account as an archaeologist reconstructing that period by its products, or beginning with a message of revolutionary import. I shall moderate both impulses, begin with a bit of archaeology, and show how my excavations lead me to a certain revolutionary zeal.

Let me reconstruct the period in which *The Process of Education* came into being. Nineteen fifty-nine was a time of great concern over the intellectual aimlessness of our schools. Great strides had been made in many fields of knowledge and these advances were not being reflected in what was taught in our schools. A huge gap had grown between what might be called the head and the tail of the academic procession. There was great fear, particularly, that we were not producing enough scientists and engineers.

It was the period shortly after Sputnik I. The great problem faced by some of my colleagues in Cambridge at the time was that modern physics and mathematics were not represented in the curriculum, yet many of the decisions that society had to make were premised on being able to understand modern science. Something had to be done to assure that the ordinary decision maker within the society would have a sound basis for decision. The task was to get started on the teaching of science and, later, other subjects. They were innocent days. But beware such judgments rendered in retrospect. At worst, the early period suffered an excess of rationalism.

The prevailing notion was that if you understood the structure of

Reprinted by permission from *Phi Delta Kappan*, September 1971, pp. 18–21.

knowledge, that understanding would then permit you to go ahead on your own; you did not need to encounter everything in nature in order to know nature, but by understanding some deep principles you could extrapolate to the particulars as needed. Knowing was a canny strategy whereby you could know a great deal about a lot of things while keeping very little in mind.

This view essentially opened the possibility that those who understood a field well—the practitioners of the field—could work with teachers to produce new curricula. For the first time in the modern age, the acme of scholarship, even in our great research institutes and universities, was to convert knowledge into pedagogy, to turn it back to aid the learning of the young. It was a brave idea and a noble one, for all its pitfalls. It is an idea that still bears close scrutiny, and we shall give it some later.

It was this point of view that emerged from the famous Woods Hole conference on improving education in science (the impetus and inspiration for *The Process of Education*). No curriculum project in the first five years after that was worth its salt unless it could sport a Nobel laureate or two on its letterhead!

The rational structuralism of Woods Hole had its internal counterpoise in intuitionism—the espousal of good guessing, of courage to make leaps, to go a long way on a little. It was mind at its best, being active, extrapolative, innovative, going from something firmly held to areas which were not so firmly known in order to have a basis for test. Of course, everybody knew that good teachers always have encouraged such use of mind. But perhaps good teachers were being driven underground by the prevailing literalism. . . .

At Woods Hole and after there was also a great emphasis on active learning, poking into things yourself, an emphasis on active discovery rather than upon the passive consumption of knowledge. It too derived from the idea that making things one's own was an activity that would get things structured in one's own way rather than as in the book. Some enthusiasts ran away with the idea of the "discovery method," that one should even discover the names of the constellations! It is a modest idea, but with profound consequences, some of which were not understood at the time—and we shall come back to it.

During the early sixties, in various projects, it was discovered again and again how difficult it was to get to the limit of children's competence when the teaching was good. . . . No wonder then that we concluded that any subject could be taught in some honest form to any child at any stage in his development. This did not necessarily mean that it could be taught in its final form, but it did mean that basically there was a courteous translation that could reduce ideas to a form that young students could grasp. *Not* to provide such translation was discourteous to them. The pursuit of this ideal was probably the most important outcome of the great period of curriculum building in the sixties.

With all of this there went a spirit and attitude toward students. The learner was not one kind of person, the scientist or historian another kind. The schoolboy learning physics did so as a physicist rather than as a consumer of some facts wrapped in what came to be called at Woods Hole a "middle language." A middle language talks *about* the subject rather than talking the subject.

I recall a dark day on Cape Cod, the day after the conference ended. It was raining. We, the steering committee, thought surely the whole enterprise had been wrongly conceived. We would end, we feared, by turning the educational Establishment against us and science. Then *The Process of Education* was published. It was acclaimed. I want to tell you about acclaim. Acclaim is very hard to cope with if you have business in mind. For once something is acclaimed it can be ignored in a noble way. The acclaim from which we suffered was that each reader-teacher picked the part he liked best and proclaimed it was exactly what *he* was doing! But the period of being acclaimed into impotence passed as new curricula began to appear.

Producing curriculum turned out to be not quite as we academics had thought. Something a bit strained would happen when one caused to work together a most gifted and experienced teacher and an equally gifted and experienced scientist, historian, or scholar. There was much to be learned on both sides and the process was slow and decisions had to be made about the level at which one wanted to pitch the effort— the college-bound, the "average," the slum kid?

There were aspects of the undertaking that we had not counted on —mostly after the production. One was the problem of bureaucracy in education, the subject of an entire yearbook recently published by the ASCD—the issue of adoption, of distribution of materials, and so forth. A second was an even deeper problem: the training of teachers to use curricula. Both of these remain unresolved—the first constrained by fiscal difficulties, the second by the genuinely puzzling questions of teacher recruitment, training, and supervision. I cannot pretend to competence in this area. . . .

So much for the archaeology. What I should like to do now is shift to other matters more concerned with present and future.

The movement of which *The Process of Education* was a part was based on a formula of faith: that learning was what students wanted to do, that they wanted to achieve an expertise in some particular subject matter. Their motivation was taken for granted. It also accepted the tacit assumption that everybody who came to these curricula in the schools already had been the beneficiary of the middle-class hidden curricula that taught them analytic skills and launched them in the traditionally intellectual use of mind.

Failure to question these assumptions has, of course, caused much grief to all of us. Let me quote from the preface of a book I have just written, *The Relevance of Education:*[1]

This book is built around essays written between 1964 and 1970, years of deep and tumultuous change. They were disturbing years. They had an impact in their own right, amplified by my increasingly strong involvement during the period with very young human beings. These were my "subjects" in experiments and observations. The contrast between the exterior social turbulence and the human helplessness I was studying kept imposing itself.

The period of these essays is the period of the elaboration of youth culture, with its concomitant revolt against "establishment" schooling. It extends from Berkeley to Columbia, through the Harvard bust and the Sorbonne riots, to the Prague spring and summer, and the beginnings of the long and cruel winter that followed. In our own universities we have gone from the salad days of "new colleges" to the present "hard line" of so many faculties. The young began the period in political activism; then there was the sharp fire of a new extremism; now, in . . . early . . . 1971, it is a new disengagement.

Through the turmoil and idealism of these years has run a theme of "naturalness," of "spontaneity," of the immediacy of learning through direct encounter. A distrust of traditional ways has brought into question whether schools as such might not be part of the problem—rather than a solution to the problem of education. American educational reform in the early sixties was concerned principally with the reconstruction of curriculum. The ideal was clarity and self-direction of intellect in the use of modern knowledge.

There were brave efforts and successful ones in mathematics and physics, in chemistry and biology, and even in the behavioral sciences. The faltering of the humanists at this time was puzzling, though it later became clearer. A revision of the humanities involved too many explosive issues, we were to discover.

In the second half of the decade, the period of these essays, deeper doubts began to develop. Did revision of curriculum suffice, or was a more fundamental restructuring of the entire educational system in order? Plainly, the origins of the doubt go deep and far back into the changing culture and technology of our times. But our ruinous and cruel war in Vietnam led many who would have remained complacent to question our practices and priorities. How could a society be so enormously wealthy, yet so enormously and callously destructive, while professing idealism? How wage a war in the name of a generous way of life, while our own way of life included urban ghettos, culture of poverty, racism, and worse?

We looked afresh at the appalling effects of poverty and racism on the lives of children, and the extent to which schools had become instruments

[1] Anita Gil, ed. (New York: W. W. Norton, 1971).

of the evil forces in our society. Eloquent books like Jonathan Kozol's *Death at an Early Age* began to appear.

It was the black community that first sought "free schools," freedom schools. They were to help black identity, to give a sense of control back to the community. Just as the civil rights movement provided models for social protest at large, so, too, the drive for free schools for the children of the black poor produced a counterpart response in the intellectual middle-class community. The revolt against the system very quickly came to include the educational Establishment. Generous-minded men like Ivan Illich and Paul Goodman, inveighing against the deadening bureaucratic hold of teachers and educational administrators, voiced a new romanticism: salvation by spontaneity; "dis-establish" the established schools. It was a view that, as we know, took immediate root in the "in" youth culture.

But if romanticism was solace for some, despair was the order for others. By the spring of 1970, when Elizabeth Hall, one of the editors of *Psychology Today*, asked me what I thought about American education at the moment, all I could answer was that it had passed into a state of utter crisis. It had failed to respond to changing social needs, lagging behind rather than leading. My work on early education and social class, for example, had convinced me that the educational system was, in effect, our way of maintaining a class system—a group at the bottom. It crippled the capacity of children in the lowest socio-economic quarter of the population, and particularly those who were black, to participate at full power in the society, and it did so early and effectively.

It is not surprising then that this little volume, arranged roughly in chronological order, should begin with an essay that bears the title, "The Perfectibility of Intellect," vintage 1965, and end with one called "Poverty and Childhood," a product of 1970.

And so a half decade passed. By 1970 the concern was no longer to change schools from within by curriculum, but to refit them altogether to the needs of society, to change them as institutions. It is no longer reform but revolution that has come to challenge us. And it is not so plain what is the role of the academic in such an enterprise.

What would one do now? What would be the pattern at a Woods Hole conference in 1971? It would not be in Woods Hole, in that once rural, coastal setting. More likely, we would gather in the heart of a great city. The task would center around the dispossession of the children of the poor and the alienation of the middle-class child. In some crucial respect, the medium would surely be the message: the school, not the curriculum, or the society and not even the school. And in my view, through my perspective, the issues would have to do with how one gives back initiative and a sense of potency, how one activates to tempt one to want to learn again. When that is accomplished, then curriculum becomes an issue again—curriculum not as a subject but as an approach to learning and using knowledge.

The rest of what I have to say concerns these issues—of activating a learner, of giving him his full sense of intent and initiative.

Consider first getting people to want to learn something, how to make the learning enterprise sustained and compelling. In a recent article in the *Saturday Review*, I proposed that it is possible to conceive of a Monday-Wednesday-Friday curriculum covering the standard topics, and a Tuesday-Thursday and indeed Saturday way of doing things in which immediate and compelling concerns are given the central place—activism? Let them on Tuesdays and Thursdays prepare "briefs" in behalf of their views, make a case for things they care about. Let them prepare plans of action, whether they be on issues in the school, on the local scene, or whatever. What is important is to learn to bring all one's resources to bear on something that matters to you now. These are the times for the migratory questions that wander on long after their answers are forgotten, just because they are great questions. And there must be more time for the expressive elements— the encounters, the hates, the loves, the feelings. All this need not be antic nor need it all be in the manner of presenting one's case. I have seen experiments using improvisational theater, drama, film, and the like to teach and to question history, projects in which one learns to construe events through different sets of eyes. To what an extraordinary extent do films and plays of the contemporary scene matter in this! Ionesco or Pirandello are not so much concerned with absurdity but with how not to be caught with the obvious. This is not something to be prescribed. But it can surely be explored how it is we are perplexed by the texture of the society in which we live.

An extraordinary, moving book called *Children of Barbiana* is about a contemporary Tuscan hill town in Italy. The children there had failed so many times in so many ways in school that they had given up generation after generation—consigned to unskilled labor. A priest came to the parish. He started a school in which nobody was to fail, a school in which it was expected that everybody had to pass. It was everyone's responsibility to see that everybody in the class mastered the lesson before anybody could go on to the next lesson.

A community is a powerful force for effective learning. Students, when encouraged, are tremendously helpful to each other. They are like a cell, a revolutionary cell. It is the cell in which mutual learning and instruction can occur, a unit within a classroom with its own sense of compassion and responsibility for its members.

These were matters we did not do enough with at Woods Hole. We did not think about mutuality because we were stuck on the idea of curriculum—in spite of the fact that our laboratories and our very curriculum projects were set up rather like communes!

Inevitably, somebody will ask, "Well, how are you going to grade them?" You might also ask, "How in the world are you going to grade all of these distinguished colleagues who write collaborative articles among themselves and their graduate students?"

There is a group of high school girls in Concord, Massachusetts, who are tutoring in the local elementary school. Those who are acquainted with cross-age tutoring will know, as I discovered, the extent to which those who help are helped, that being a teacher makes one a better learner. But should it be such a surprise? Is this not what is meant by passing on the culture?

What we say of the peer group and the near-peer group holds for the different age levels within the society. For in some deep way, what is needed is the reestablishment of a "learning community" beyond formal school, which as now constituted is far too isolating. It is not just by removing the barriers between elementary and high school students or by establishing a lifetime relationship to one's college where one can return for sustenance and become part of a broader learning community again. M.I.T. pronounced a few years ago that an engineer's education is obsolete after five years, so he must be brought back to bring him up to date. Let him come back, yes, but let the price of admission be that he discharge his obligation then to those who are just beginning—teacher, tutor, guide, what?

Finally, I would like to explore, in the interest of relevance, whether we might not recapture something of the old notion of vocation, of ways of life, or to use the expression of so many undergraduates today, of "life-styles." I am impressed with contemporary concern for life-styles. I have just finished a term as master of Currier House, a Radcliffe-Harvard house, and I assure you of the genuineness of this concern. But I am appalled that it is rarely translated into what one *does* with a life-style, the kind of vocation and livelihood in which we can express it. Could it be that in our stratified and fragmented society, our students simply do not know about local grocers and their styles, local doctors and theirs, local taxi drivers and theirs, local political activists and theirs? And don't forget the styles of local bookies, aspiring actresses, or illegitimate mothers. No, I really believe that our young have become so isolated that they do *not* know the roles available in the society and the variety of styles in which they are played. I would urge that we find some way of connecting the diversity of the society to the phenomenon of school, to keep the latter from becoming so isolated and the former so suspicious.

Let me add one last thing not directly connected with *The Process of Education*, but a problem of the first order today. One cannot ignore it in talking of education. We shall kill ourselves, as a society and as human beings, unless we address our efforts to redressing the deep, deep wounds that we inflict on the poor, the outcast, those who somehow do not fit within our caste system—be they black or dispossessed in any way. If there is one thing that has come out of our work with the very young, it is the extent to which "being out," not having a chance as an adult, or as a parent, very quickly reflects itself in loss of hope in the child. As early as the second or third year a child begins to reflect this loss of hope.

When any group is robbed of its legitimate aspiration, it will aspire desperately and by means that outrage the broader society, though they are efforts to sustain or regain dignity. Inequity cannot be altered by education alone, another lesson we have learned in the past decade. The impact of poverty is usually transmitted through the school as well. It cannot be counteracted by words unless there are also jobs and opportunities available to express society's confidence in what is possible after school.

There must be ways in which we can think honestly of reformulation of the institutions into which our schools fit, as one integral part. Surely it requires that we redirect our resources, re-order our priorities, redefine our national effort, and come to terms with the fact that we have a deep and brutal racism in us—in all of us. We must learn how to cope with that. The young know it; they despise our failure to talk about it and our other difficulties. History may well side with them.

In the end, we must finally appreciate that education is not a neutral subject, nor is it an isolated subject. It is a deeply political issue in which we guarantee a future for someone and, frequently, in guaranteeing a future for someone, we deal somebody else out. If I had my choice now, in terms of a curriculum project for the seventies, it would be to find a means whereby we could bring society back to its sense of values and priorities in life. *I believe I would be quite satisfied to declare, if not a moratorium, then something of a de-emphasis on matters that have to do with the structure of history, the structure of physics, the nature of mathematical consistency, and deal with it rather in the context of the problems that face us.* We might better concern ourselves with how those problems can be solved, not just by practical action, but by putting knowledge, wherever we find it and in whatever form we find it, to work in these massive tasks. *We might put vocation and intention back into the process of education, much more firmly than we had it there before.*

A decade later, we realize that *The Process of Education* was the beginning of a revolution, and one cannot yet know how far it will go. Reform of curriculum is not enough. Reform of the school is probably not enough. The issue is one of man's capacity for creating a culture, society, and technology that not only feed him but keep him caring and belonging.

RELEVANCE AND THE CURRICULUM

LAWRENCE E. METCALF
MAURICE P. HUNT

Metcalf and Hunt have contributed a perceptive book on teaching the social studies through emphasis upon "the closed areas." Some of its major themes are sharply delineated here.

The authors propose that a curriculum, if it is to be relevant today, must assist young people in an examination of their own basic assumptions about society and its improvement. They call for study by young people of youth's rejection of adult culture, and they advocate the development by young people of relevant utopias and preferred worlds.

Maurice P. Hunt is professor of educational foundations at Fresno State College in California. Lawrence E. Metcalf is professor of secondary education and social studies at the University of Illinios, Urbana. Together, Hunt and Metcalf wrote Teaching High School Social Studies (*New York: Harper and Row,* 1968).

Our assignment in this article is to indicate what we mean by a relevant curriculum. We shall define curriculum not as "all the experiences a child or youth has in school" but more traditionally as "the formal course-work taken by students." We believe that formal coursework acquires relevance whenever it impinges upon what students believe, and whenever it has the effect of producing a pattern of belief that is well grounded and internally consistent.

Ours is a period of history in which youth on a mass and international scale reject the culture of the old. This rejection is not universal to all youth; some are more actively opposed to established traditions; many are in tacit support of changes initiated by the bolder and more aggressive young. To a large extent the rebellion of the young began with college students, has now been adopted by large numbers of high school students, and is beginning to filter down into junior high school. Young people are beginning to develop their own culture, and appear at times to learn more from one another than from teachers or parents. Some adults feel so turned off and rejected that they doubt that they can ever say anything that youth would accept as relevant.

Youth's rejection of adult culture—"the whole, rotten, stinking mess of it"—has become a significant social movement. This movement has assumed international proportions—practically every modern, industrial-

Reprinted by permission from *Phi Delta Kappan*, March 1970, pp. 358–361.

ized nation has felt its impact. Any school that has not made this social movement a subject of serious study on the part of its youthful clientele is about as irrelevant as it can get.

Rejection of adult culture is proclaimed overtly, not merely by verbal attack, but also by deliberate adoption of grooming habits or display of those artifacts which have been established or promoted as symbols of sophisticated rebellion. New hair styles, manners of dress, a new language (which relies heavily on traditional Anglo-Saxon monosyllables), a new music, an open sexual promiscuity, and the use of drugs or pot—all reflect a wholesale rejection of tradition and orthodoxy.

Many of the new values and customs are carefully chosen as goads to older persons. "What would my parents or grandparents least like to have me think and see me do?" When this question has been answered, often only after some tests of adult reaction, the young then adopt whatever they think will best demonstrate that they are *not* part of the main culture stream of earlier generations. In the case of males, it may require only long hair and a string of beads to make the point. For females, attendance at a love-in or rock festival attired in a mini-miniskirt may suffice. The movement has its uniforms, rituals, and badges of membership. Older people sometimes put on the uniform in order to demonstrate that they are not entirely out of sympathy with the ideas and ideals of youth. Others, who are not without sympathy, refuse the beard and beads simply because they detest all uniforms, whether worn by pigs, fascists, or revolutionaries.

But the rebelliousness of youth does not confine itself to the symbolisms of dress, language, and coiffure. Rejection of religion as traditionally practiced has become commonplace. New faiths are emergent, as among the hippies, and have more in common with Zen than anything orthodox to Christianity. Paul Goodman sees the young as primarily religious. If so, theirs is the kind of faith that mirrors John Dewey's distinction between religion and the religious.[1]

Equally significant is the anti-war and pro-love stance of our young rebels. When generalized to embrace a way of life, it runs contrary to most American traditions. We now see mass protests on a grand scale. Riots, marches, sit-ins, love-ins, and mass assemblies surpass anything in our history. When a war moratorium brings hundreds of thousands of persons into public arenas, it can truly be called a "happening." Adults are puzzled by it all, and somewhat frightened.

A CONCEPT OF RELEVANT CURRICULUM

Young people are particularly critical of established educational practice. A common charge is that education lacks relevance. Often this criticism harks back to some of the traditions of old progressives in education. Sometimes, the charge means that education has not allied

[1] See John Dewey, A *Common Faith* (New Haven: Yale University Press, 1934).

itself with the goals of revolutionaries, or that it has allied itself with business, labor, and the military.

What can education do these days that would be relevant? *We suggest that the schools incorporate in their curriculum a study of an important social movement, rejection by youth, and that this study emphasize examining, testing, and appraising the major beliefs caught up in this movement.* To pander to the instincts or impulses of rebellion would have little or no educational effect. The over-30 adult who simply "eggs on" his activist students does his clientele no service. A black studies program that fosters black nationalism or separatism would be equally obnoxious. If this is what youths mean by relevance, their wishes can not be served.

Students find it all too easy to spot contradictions in the beliefs of their elders, and to explain all such discrepancies as instances of hypocrisy. They are a good deal less proficient in spotting their own inconsistencies, and they are quite convinced of their own sincerity. We need the kind of educational relevance that would help and require young people to examine their most basic assumptions about the kind of world that exists, and how they propose to change the world from what it is into something preferable. Students who rebel not only against the establishment but also against logical analysis may not at first perceive the relevance of this kind of education.

In order to achieve this kind of relevance, teachers will have to familiarize themselves with the thought patterns of students—their attitudes, values, beliefs, and interests. This can be done. It helps just to listen carefully to what young people are saying. Sometimes teachers who listen do not bore deeply enough into the meaning of what has been heard. They learn much about the surface thought of students but little, if anything, about what students "really think."

If we look closely at what students today believe, four issues or propositions in social analysis and processes of social change seem to prevail within the movement. Taken together, these four issues suggest a rejection of the liberal-reformist tradition. Liberalism is anathema to our youthful rebels. Liberalism is a failure, they say. Liberals talk much and do little. Many of the young leaders resemble the romantics who supported totalitarian movements in pre-war Germany and Italy. A seldom observed and reported fact is that the candidacy of George Wallace in 1968 received more support from people under than over 30 years of age. A realignment in American politics that would place radicals and conservatives in alliance against liberalism is not without prospect.

A major issue that divides radicals from liberals is to be found in attitudes toward The System. Liberals tend to assume that the system can best be changed and improved by working within it. They may agree with radicals that much in the system requires fundamental and sweeping change, but they also believe that the system is basically sound in that it permits and values change when rationally determined and implemented. In contrast, the radical would work against the system from the outside. He wants no part of the system, which he views as rotten throughout.

Liberals who suggest that schools assist students to examine the system in order to determine whether it is as rotten as some claim it to be are regarded as advocates of a delaying action. Radicals tend to view analysis of this kind as a form of social paralysis. It is not clearly established how many of today's young can properly be classified as radicals. An increasing number do believe that social change must begin with a total rejection of the existing system. Drastic change is preferred to any attempt to patch the existing system.

A second assumption that divides young people from the mainstream of American liberalism is over the relationship of means to ends. Liberals tend toward the assumption that the achievement of democratic ends requires the use of democratic means. Every means is an end, and every end a means to some further end. The quality of any end we achieve cannot be separated from the quality of the means used to achieve it. In contrast, many of the young assume that our kind of society can be transformed into a more democratic system only as people dare to employ undemocratic methods. They see no inconsistency in advocacy of free speech and denial of such freedom to their opposition. Some liberals agree with radicals on the need for drastic changes in the system, but they are unwilling to achieve such change except through processes of reason and persuasion.

A third assumption expresses on the part of the young a preference for intuitive and involved thinking as opposed to rational and detached thought. Many of the hippies, for example, have voiced a distaste for the logic and rationality of middle-class Americans. In contrast, liberals have criticized middle-class Americans for not being rational enough.

A part of the issue here is over the nature of rationality. Liberals do not agree that rational thought is necessarily detached or without involvement. Thought springs from the ground of social perplexity and concern. Objectivity is not the same as neutrality. Objectivity is a means by which to express concern and achieve conclusions. It is not to be used as a method by which to avoid conclusions or commitments. In the hands of some liberals, however, it has appeared to be a method by which to avoid rather than make value judgments. When they perceive objectivity as avoidance, concerned youth will look elsewhere for their philosophy. An intuition or existential leap may be their solution to any confusion that inhabits their minds. The popularity of the drug experience as a source of awareness and insight is consistent with this preference for intuitive methods of problem solving. The growing interest in parapsychology, extrasensory perception, spiritualism, and various versions of the occult manifests the same tendency to retreat from the use of reason in the study of social affairs.

A fourth assumption, issue, or proposition is over the nature, worth, and necessity of violence. The liberal eschews violence except when an organized minority thwarts the will of the majority, if that will seems to be the outcome of free discussion and reflective study of alternatives. The young, on the other hand, often regard reason and discussion as forms of compromise. It is quite defensible to take the law into one's hands if the law is unjust. One does not obey an unjust law until one is able to presuade others of its injustice and thus get it changed. Evasion of the law or open refusal to obey the law is an acceptable form of social protest, if personal conscience so dictates.

Basic to this issue is the question of whether or not drastic system change can be achieved without use of violence. Advocates of violence have not always distinguished between impressionistic and instrumental violence.[2] Impressionistic violence is the kind of hot response that results from deep-seated frustration over existing social conditions. Instrumental violence is more disciplined in nature, and is followed deliberately and coolly as a method of social protest with social change as its objective.

The above four assumptions are basic in varying degree to the life outlook of young people who are in rebellion against established traditions. None of them is entirely new. Each has been tried and tested in a variety of social circumstances. Relevant history would reveal where such assumptions lead when acted upon under certain conditions. Yet none of these assumptions is today subjected to open, careful, and fair appraisal by a majority of schools or teachers. A relevant curriculum would take these assumptions seriously enough to make their study a major purpose of general education. Such study would help young people to understand their important personal problems but would also open up for serious study the large social problems of our time.

UTOPIAS, RELEVANT AND IRRELEVANT[3]

A curriculum that would assist young people in an examination of their basic assumptions about society and its improvement must deal with values and social policies. Yet attention to values and social policies is now almost totally foreign to public schools.

Young people today will be in the prime of life by the year 2000. They can begin to think now about what they want as a society by that time. Four questions are basic to a curriculum that would start now to build toward future-planning: 1) What kind of society now exists, and

[2] Charles Hamilton is to be credited with this distinction, as developed in a speech at Wingspread in 1968.
[3] We are indebted to Saul Mendlovitz of the World Law Fund, who is also professor of international law, Rutgers University, for development of the concept of relevant utopias.

what are the dominant trends within it? 2) What kind of society is likely to emerge in the near future, let us say by the year 2000, if present trends continue? 3) What kind of society is preferable, given one's values? 4) If the likely and prognosticated society is different from the society that one prefers, what can the individual, alone or as a member of groups, do toward eliminating the discrepancy between prognostication and preference, between expectation and desire?

These questions are relevant to anyone, but they are particularly relevant to those young people who think in utopias and who agree with Buckminster Fuller that we now have to choose between utopia and oblivion.

We define utopia as any description of a society radically different from the existing one. Some utopias, as described, are relevant. Others are irrelevant. A relevant utopia is a model of a reformed world which not only spells out in specific and precise behavioral detail the contents of that new world but, in addition, provides a behavioral description of the transition to be made from the present system to the utopian one. Irrelevant utopias omit all solutions to the problem of transition. They may be precisely defined in behavioral terms, as in Butler's Erewhon, but provide no suggestions as to how one gets from where he is to where he wants to be.

Most utopias stated or implied by today's youth are irrelevant. Youth are fairly clear as to what they oppose. They desire a drastically different kind of social system, but they are not clear in any detailed sense as to what they desire as a system, or how that undefined system might be brought into being. To be relevant, youth with encouragement from the schools will have to engage in the kind of hard thinking that results in construction of social models. Hard thinking and model building are not always prized by youth who rely upon intuition and hunches for solutions to problems. Intuition is good enough for stating irrelevant utopias. It will not work, however, for those who value precisely stated concepts and tested solutions to the problem of social transition.

The search for relevant utopias should have great appeal to those youth who feel or believe that a drastic change in the social system is required for solution of today's problems. Its appeal lies in the fact that the search for relevance requires one to take seriously, and not merely romantically, the problem of how best to achieve drastic system change. Since drastic system change has occurred in the past, some study of a certain kind of history—not the kind usually taught in the schools— should be relevant to this search.

RELEVANT UTOPIAS, PREFERRED WORLDS

We have defined as a relevant utopia any social vision or dream that has been expressed as a social model with due regard for problems of precise definition and successful transition. From studies of existing society numerous relevant utopias have been stated. In the area of international systems alone no less than nine models have been identified by Falk and Mendlovitz.[4] Each model may be used descriptively, predictively, and prescriptively. That is, each may be seen as a report of what already exists, as a prediction of what will soon exist, or as a prescription of what ought to exist in the near future. (Obviously, a model used only for descriptive purposes does not function as any kind of utopia, relevant or irrelevant. A person who sees the present international system in certain terms can encounter in another person a different description. Both persons may agree or disagree as to what they conceive utopia to be.) Much of the literature fails to make a clear distinction between descriptive and other uses of a model. The methodology of relevant utopias requires that such distinctions be consciously made. This methodology also requires us to take seriously any utopia that qualifies as relevant. But to take it seriously does not force us to prefer it.

One chooses his preferred world from the set of relevant utopias available to him. It is in the region of preferred worlds that individuality as prized by young radicals has a chance to express itself. A person who chooses his preferred world from a set of available relevant utopias must decide what risks he is prepared to take; and obviously, persons differ greatly as to what risks they perceive and what risks they are willing to take.

An illustration from international relations and systems may serve to clarify this point. Grenville Clark and Louis Sohn have developed a relevant utopia that takes the form of limited world government. Their model consists of detailed amendments to the UN Charter which would give to the United Nations sufficient authority to prevent war, but without authority to intervene in the domestic affairs of nation states. Another model, developed by Robert Hutchins and his colleagues at the University of Chicago, envisages a much more sweeping kind of world authority. The relationship within their model between the world authority and the nation states resembles that which holds within the American federal system between the national government and the several states.

If one's choice is limited to these two models, which one should become one's preferred world? One can imagine a person who would say to himself: "The federal model is superior to the modified UN model for purposes of war prevention because it can get at the causes of war by intervening in the domestic affairs of nation states. But the likelihood that any such world authority will come into being by the year 2000 is very dim. Yet some kind of world government is necessary if we are to have any chance of avoiding large-scale nuclear war. There-

---

[4] Richard Falk and Saul Mendlovitz, eds., *A Strategy of World Order* (New York: World Law Fund, 1966).

fore, I choose Clark-Sohn as my preferred world." Someone else might argue as follows: "Without an effective world government, nuclear disaster is bound to occur. Clark-Sohn, although feasible by the year 2000, could not possibly work. Hutchins, though very difficult to achieve, is my preferred world. To work for anything less would be a waste of time. I'll risk everything on reaching for the impossible. Perhaps, my preference can even have some influence on the possibilities in the case."

Students have every right to differ with one another and with their teachers in their preferred worlds. They may also disagree as to whether a given utopia has been stated relevantly, as we have defined relevance. They may even disagree as to whether a particular utopia would be either effective, if adopted, or achievable if pursued with zeal and rationality. They may also disagree as to whether utopian solutions are as necessary as some social critics claim. But these various differences are not always qualitatively the same. Whether a given model would work, or whether a given model is achievable in the near future, are factual questions; such questions can be answered only by ascertaining as rationally as possible what the probable facts are. But a difference in opinion over preferred worlds is not always a factual difference. It may be a difference involving values, preferred risks, life styles, and even personal temperament. One may use logic and evidence in choosing his preferred world, but logical men in possession of all the facts may not always agree on the world they prefer.

PERSONAL DILEMMAS, SOCIAL CONCERNS

A relevant curriculum is sometimes defined as one addressed to the personal problems of youth. This is not good enough. *It is more relevant to engage young people in a study of the problems of the larger culture in which many of their personal problems have their origin. The culture of most significance to the young consists of those aspects that are problematic—that is, the large conflicts and confusions which translate into the conflicts and confusions of individuals.*

To take one example, young people who are opposed to the war in Vietnam are reluctant to take a position against all war because the larger culture from which most of their learning continues to come expresses the same reluctance. In fact, many of the young insist upon the right to be conscientiously opposed to the war in Vietnam without a requirement that out of conscience they oppose all war. When asked the four questions basic to the methodology of relevant utopias as applied to the Vietnamese (what is Vietnam like today, what will it be like in the near future if present trends are extrapolated, what would you like it to be, and what can you do about any discrepancy between extrapolation and values?), they are prone to reply that the fate of the Vietnamese is of no concern to them and that America should mind its own business. Their vaunted idealism is thus victimized by the widespread cultural preference for some form of isolationism. Although they don't like Nixon, they find it difficult to oppose his attempts to turn over the war to the Vietnamese. The methodology of relevant utopias would ask them to consider carefully whether or not Nixon's policies and their own view of those policies are at all adequate as steps transitional to a drastic change in the existing system of international relations. Unless they make an assessment of this kind, their opinions on a number of related personal and social matters are bound to reflect a great deal of confusion. They could end up as confused as the parents and grandparents whose views they reject.

Finally, what has been said about the use of relevant utopias in social analysis and prescription also applies to personal development and self-analysis. The significant questions are: What kind of person am I now? What will I become if present habits and trends persist? What kind of person would I like to become? What can be done now about tendencies and preferences that conflict? This approach to the problem of identity is more promising than some of the programs offered these days in the name of black studies, black history, and black pride. Historical and cultural studies have maximal relevance when they help us to predict the future or to make transition.

ENLIVENING THE COMMUNITY SCHOOL CURRICULUM

EDWARD G. OLSEN

Edward G. Olsen, a long-time proponent of the community school and of problem oriented education, makes a vigorous case for dealing with "the life-and-death issues of war, nationalism, racism, sexism, poverty, environmental pollution, urban decay, consumer exploitation, and the like" through dealing with "fundamental life concerns and problems of living today and tomorrow." Though he is writing about the community school in the article reproduced here, his advocacy of a curriculum centered about human concerns applies to all schools.

Edward G. Olsen is a leader in the community school movement. His books include School and Community Programs *(New York: Prentice-Hall, 1949),* School and Community *(New York: Prentice-Hall, 1947, revised 1954, 1965) and* The School and Community Reader *(New York: McMillan, 1963). Formerly he was Director of School and Community Relations for the Washington State Office of Public Instruction. On his retirement, he was awarded the rank of Professor Emeritus by California State University, Hayward—the second such award in the history of the institution.*

Throughout this nation there is a growing crisis of public confidence, a general feeling among people of all ages and backgrounds that things are fast getting out of hand. Cities rotting ... environment poisoned ... consumers exploited ... seemingly endless, irrational war ... and a widening disbelief in anything that government at any level says or promises to do.

Affluent Americans are locked into suburbs of physical comfort and emotional insecurity; poor Americans are locked inside urban and rural ghettos of material privation and spiritual destruction. The older, solid foundations of general belief in order, reason, and progress and the confidence that must sustain a civilized society are eroding. We can almost feel the growth of a kind of social insanity that leads to national ruin. And by all the signals of today we must expect that during the seventies millions of American youth—college, high school, even junior high school students—will be alienated from the mainstream values and life patterns of traditional American society. Perhaps they should be alienated. Despite its many virtues, much of our society is sick, obsessed with moneymaking, material things, status

Reprinted by permission from *Phi Delta Kappan*, November 1972, pp. 176–178.

275

symbols, cults of sex and violence, rampant nationalism, burning racism.

Poverty and prejudice . . . crime and unemployment . . . overpopulation and racial discrimination . . . environmental pollution and consumer exploitation . . . you name it! They all dramatize in tragic terms the central human imperative of the seventies: Learn to live humanely together as one family of man in a pluralist world. U Thant, when secretary-general of the United Nations, warned that:

. . . the members of the United Nations have perhaps 10 years left in which to subordinate their ancient quarrels and launch a global partnership to curb the arms race, to improve the human environment, to defuse the population explosion, and to supply the required momentum to developmental efforts.

If such a global partnership is not forged within the next decade, then I very much fear that the problems I have mentioned will have reached such staggering proportions that they will be beyond our capacity to control.

Human community—a profound and effective sense of *common-unity*—is the essence of any enduring free society. Without that fundamental public sense of shared basic values, of widespread community aspiration, no democratic framework is likely to survive for even another generation. If we are to continue as a free and culturally pluralist people we must immediately find ways to build up the psychological basis for genuine community development—in family groups, in neighborhoods, in urban areas, in geographic regions, in the nation, and in the larger world of human beings on this planet.

Myriads of youthful Americans feel a deep hunger for genuine *community* to replace the constrictive, frustrating, and dehumanizing life patterns still dominant. Many people not so young share that longing also. Whatever their limitations of strategy for social advance, "future shock" and "consciousness III" are facts of modern life to be reckoned with, to be understood and built upon.

Listen to one cry of today's youth against what many view as a morbidly sick society: "Look at you, blowing up whole countries for the sake of some crazy ideologies that you don't live up to anyway. . . . Look at you, needing a couple of stiff drinks before you have the balls to talk with another human being. Look at you, making it with your neighbor's wife on the sly just to try and prove that you're really alive. Look at you, hooked on your cafeteria of pills, making up dirty names for anybody who isn't in your bag, and screwing up the land and the water and the air for profit, and calling this nowhere scene the Great Society! And you're gonna tell us how to live?"

Is that picture overdrawn, a bitter caricature distorted beyond validity? Or is there essential truth in its thrust?

However extreme the rhetoric and behavior of young people may be, their challenge to educators must not be ignored, evaded, or put down. For there is real hope in the new generation. And these young people are enrolled in our schools right now. Black and white, brown, yellow, and red, they have become deeply sensitive to the decadence of adult society and highly critical of its hypocrisy. Many of them are dedicated in varying degrees to the bold task of transforming our world into something far better. They are understandably impatient, and sometimes they are hostile and violent, because Establishment oldsters are so blind to that great need, so slow to move on with the task. More than that, they demand that their school education be relevant to their own lives today. If the 1960s was the decade of the Black Revolt, then the 1970s will almost surely become that of the Youth Revolt. And in dealing with militant youths as with militant blacks, the alternatives are the same: confrontation or involvement. Put them down, or bring them in.

What are youth's driving concerns today? Most young people answer as individuals: fun, money, sex, drugs, people, work, identity. But many others answer for society: war, racism, poverty, pollution, materialism, authority, hypocrisy. Many of the latter, disillusioned with adult values and behaviors, are the truly alienated. Thousands know what they are *against*, but few indeed can say what they are *for* in specific and practical terms. They only know that these are the life concerns that turn them on!

And what does the conventional high school curriculum offer to these perplexed, rebellious, and usually idealistic youth? It offers them mainly the traditional "subjects" of study, academically packaged: art, biology, chemistry, and so on, all the way to zoology. Almost nowhere are the life-and-death issues of war, nationalism, racism, sexism, poverty, environmental pollution, urban decay, consumer exploitation, and the like central in the curriculum or even included as areas for sustained individual study. Is it any wonder that classroom motivation becomes increasingly difficult, often impossible? For it is the traditional academic requirements that turn students off—except, of course, the grade-obsessed child of grade-demanding parents. Is it any wonder that socially sensitive and caring youth are among those who turn toward drugs and other cop-outs, or to the rhetoric and even the terror tactics of the violent revolutionists?

One central conclusion is inescapable: The traditional secondary school curriculum—even when enlivened by courses or units in driver training, drug abuse, sex education, race relations, and consumer protection—substantially fails to meet the vital needs of youth today. Conventional high schools are archaic, obsolescent. Their human orientation is backward, not forward. Their curricula are essentially static, not dynamic. Their administrators are often hapless bureaucrats, not educational statesmen. Their teachers are frequently weary manipulators of dreary subject matter, not enthusiastic organizers of life-significant learning experiences. And their students are captives within a social system described by San Francisco's former superintendent of schools, Thomas A. Shaheen, as almost a prison:

Our schools are organized on a semiprison approach, on crime and punishment, and cops and robbers techniques. We have lack of trust—sign-in and sign-out slips, detention systems, wardens and jailers, fear of escape, regimentation, limited opportunities for choice, barricaded or locked toilet rooms, cell-like classrooms. Why are we surprised that some youngsters rebel? Is it not surprising that more of them do not?

What might happen if alert secondary schools dared to experiment with a genuinely life-concern-centered curriculum? This would not mean adding to the traditional program a course or two or a series of units or a few student community activities related to ecology or ethnic prejudice or sex or drugs or anything else thus tacked on. It would mean eliminating from the required core of the curriculum all the traditional academic subjects and substituting for them organized learning about the fundamental life concerns and problems of living today and tomorrow.

What are these "fundamental life concerns and problems of living"? They are the major activity areas in which people spend their lives— and always have, in all cultures, in all eras. Many lists of such areas have been compiled. Years ago the state education departments of Virginia and Mississippi suggested this human-concerns approach as a curriculum organization principle. The precise delineation of the life-activity areas chosen is much less important than the use of this concept itself in curriculum redesign. Consider the following as one such list:

Securing food and shelter
Protecting life and health
Exchanging ideas
Adjusting to other people
Sharing in citizenship
Controlling the environment
Educating the young
Enriching family living
Appreciating the past
Meeting religious needs
Engaging in recreation
Enjoying beauty
Asserting personal identity

Then confront squarely these probing queries: Suppose the required curriculum of the schools consisted essentially of imaginative explorations into the ways through which people in different communities and cultures seek to deal with their major life concerns and to solve related problems, personal and social, individual and group? Of how people in the same communities and cultures did so at different periods of history? Of what they did to solve their problems within the context of their value systems? Of the alternatives for a better future which they now recognize? Of the means they are using to achieve that better future?

Let me illustrate: people all through history, everywhere, have had to secure food if they were to survive. In primitive times and places they hunted animals for food; later they developed agriculture. With specialized labor came barter, then coinage, then further specialization. Today food is produced on an increasingly mechanized basis. Thus the specific ways of getting food vary from culture to culture, but the fundamental human life concern of securing food remains the same. So it is with each of the other generic life-activity areas noted.

A further step: Persisting problems arise whenever the goal-seeking activities prove inadequate, defective, exploited, or otherwise less than desirably effective. Thus the basic life concern to protect life and health includes in all communities, cultures, and times the problems of disease. If one is a member of a primitive tribe in the Stone Age, or today in some parts of the world, and becomes ill, he may summon a medicine man to shake gourds and mutter incantations, and so hope to drive away the evil spirits presumed to be causing his sickness. An urban American, by contrast, will consult a physician for possible antibiotic medication. In short, the *procedures* for attacking problems differ according to place and time, but the basic *life concerns* are always the same.

Suppose that the required curriculum of the modern high school were structured directly around systematic study of these life-centered human concerns. Would that help young people and adults develop a wider sense of identification with other human beings who differ in ethnicity, living place, cultural patterns, or historic eras? Would it help our whole society surmount the ethnocentrism of nation, race, class, and religion which now threatens us all? Would it help to bridge the generation gap as young people in school and adults in community together tackle pressing problems of living? Could such studies and experiences relate school learning directly with actual living, and thereby make education more relevant, realistic, and meaningful to more students? Might it even help them develop the emotional commitment as well as the comprehension and the skills to build that imperative sense of humane common-unity without which the future is grim indeed?

Neoprogressive educators may contend that relevance is a matter of individual definition, that it concerns the connections between a person's uniquely individual concerns and varied aspects of the total culture. Preferences for Chaucer or crayfish dissection or ping-pong or Aztec art are obviously areas of purely personal relevance. But the massive issues such as environmental pollution, international warfare, racial hatred, overpopulation, and poverty are relevant to every individual, whatever his specifically personal interests may be. In this sense they are common to all students.

It may be objected that such a life-concern curriculum cannot be acceptable because it will not prepare students for college entrance: They will lack the 16 academic-subject Carnegie units which most colleges still demand for entrance.

The answer to that obstacle was given nearly 40 years ago when the old Progressive Education Association conducted the famous "Eight-Year Study." The Progressives had mostly abandoned the conventional curriculum in favor of serial units and learning projects organized about student interests. So they too faced the problem of college entrance requirements. The PEA persuaded some 250 colleges to admit recommended graduates of 30 selected progressive secondary schools, even though those students lacked the 16 Carnegie units. The findings of their careful follow-up were impressive:

Graduates of the progressive schools were not handicapped in their college work.

Departures from prescribed patterns of academic subjects did not lessen students' readiness for the responsibilities of college study.

Students from schools which had made the most drastic curricular revisions achieved in college distinctly higher standing than did students of equal ability with whom they were compared.

Today we need another "Eight-Year Study," this time to evaluate results of a genuine community education high school program whose required curriculum is centered in the enduring concerns, processes, and problems of living: *present* living (to discover needs and resources), *past* living (for perspective and insight), and *future* living (for planning improvement). This undoubtedly could be done, for colleges and universities these days are themselves in curricular flux. Many of them have found through evaluation of the Upward Bound programs that academic success in college is not necessarily dependent upon traditional subjects "passed" in high school. (The old belief dies hard, but it is going!)

"But wait," some may say. "Even if colleges were persuaded to admit recommended graduates of 'life-centered' curricular programs, how would these kids ever have learned their English, history, or math if the high school offered them no courses in English, history, or math?"

In answer, let's keep foremost in mind these major considerations:

—The 30 schools in the Eight-Year Study prepared their students for effective college work without the usual prepackaged formal studies in these and other academic subject areas. Community schools today could do the same.

—The proposed life-concerns curriculum is to be the generally required program of studies, the common core of systematic learning expected of all. Around this required core can be included academic and special subjects. All such conventional subjects, however, should be electives for those who want to take them, not barriers against those who do not.

—Over half of American secondary school graduates now go on to college. Probably that percentage will increase markedly during the 1970s. Most of the students who do not immediately go to college and who later desire academic discipline studies can pursue them through adult education programs, in or out of community and 4-year colleges. Then their greater maturity level and increased personal motivation will make such studies far more meaningful.

The American Association of School Administrators put it well: "The American public schools today are charged with an unprecedented task: not to perpetuate a culture but to transform it." Yet the conventional high school curriculum is still structured essentially for the convenience in *teaching the past,* not for effective *learning about the present problems and future possibilities.*

Unless learning is joined directly with living, much of it is a futile deception, a meaningless academic game. That is why the 2x4x6x9 school must go—the school which assumes that education should be confined to the two covers of the textbook, the four walls of the sheltered classroom, the six hours of the usual school day, and the nine months of the traditional school year.

In its place must come the truly functional community school— the kind of school which knows that all life educates, organizes the core of its curriculum directly around the basic life concerns of human beings today, helps everybody of all ages to become more deeply aware of the vast gulf between our democratic declarations and our discriminatory dealings, confronts students frankly and creatively with the burning issues of our time, and which thereby challenges youth and adults together to build a truly humane world-wide society with dignity and decency for all.

RACISM
AND
ETHNIC
EDUCATION

IMPERATIVES IN ETHNIC MINORITY EDUCATION

JAMES A. BANKS

Although James A. Banks agrees with the Kerner report that our nation is currently moving toward two societies, one black, one white, he believes that the school has the "potential to promote and lead constructive social change." His perceptive analysis of the requirements for affirmative change centers on the need for educators to deal creatively with racial problems which promise to destroy or dehumanize the American man.

Banks is presently professor of education at the University of Washington. He is the co-editor of Teaching Strategies for the Social Studies: Inquiry, Valuing and Decision-Making (*Reading, Mass.: Addison-Wesley, 1973*), Black Self-Concept: Implications for Education and Social Science (*New York: McGraw-Hill, 1972*) and Teaching Social Studies to Culturally Different Children (*Reading, Mass.: Addison-Wesley, 1971*). He was guest editor of the issue of Kappan *magazine in which his article appeared.*

Reprinted by permission from *Phi Delta Kappan*, January 1972, pp. 266–269.

As we approach the threshold of the twenty-first century, our nation is witnessing technological progress which has been unparalleled in human history, yet is plagued with social problems of such magnitude that they pose a serious threat to the ideals of American democracy and to man's very survival. Environmental pollution, poverty, war, deteriorating cities, and ethnic conflict are the intractable social problems which Americans must resolve if we are to survive and create a just, humane society. Our society is becoming increasingly polarized and dehumanized, largely because of institutional racism and ethnic hostility. The elimination of conflicts between the races must be our top priority for the seventies.

One of the founding principles of this nation was that oppressed peoples from other lands would find in America tolerance and acceptance, if not a utopia for the full development of their potential. People who were denied religious, economic, and political freedom flocked to the New World in search of a better life. Perhaps more than any nation in human history, the United States has succeeded in culturally assimilating its immigrants and providing them with the opportunity to attain the "good life." The elimination of differences among peoples of diverse nationalities was the essence of the "melting pot" concept.

While the United States has successfully assimilated ethnic groups which shared a set of values and behavior patterns of European origin, it has blatantly denied its black, brown, red, and yellow citizens the opportunity to share fully in the American Dream because they possess physical and cultural characteristics which are non-European. Ethnic minority groups have been the victims of institutional racism in America primarily because of their unique physical traits and the myths which emerged extolling the intrinsic virtues of European civilization and describing non-European peoples as ruthless savages. European and white ancestry have been the primary requisites for full realization of the American Dream. For most colored peoples in the United States, the dream has been deferred. The shattered dream and the denial of equal opportunities to ethnic minority groups have been the sources of acute ethnic conflict within America; it has now reached crisis proportions. The flames that burned in Watts, the blood that ran in Detroit, and now the Attica massacre are alarming manifestations of our inability to resolve conflicts between the majority and ethnic minority groups in America.

No sensitive and perceptive student of American society can deny the seriousness of our current racial problems. In recent years they have intensified as blacks and other powerless ethnic groups have taken aggressive actions to liberate themselves from oppression. Reactions of the white community to the new ethnic militancy have been intense and persisting. A "law and order" cult has emerged to eradicate ethnic revolts. To many white Americans, the plea for law and order is a call for an end to protests by ethnic groups and alienated youths. The fact that many law and order advocates demanded that Lt. Calley go free after a military jury convicted him for killing numbers of civilian colored peoples in Asia indicates that many "middle" Americans do not consistently value law, order, or human life. The law and order movement is directed primarily toward the poor, the colored, and the powerless. One example is the "no-knock" law in Washington, D.C. Although promises to bring law and order to the street often ensure victory in public elections, the most costly and destructive crimes in America are committed by powerful syndicates, corrupted government officials, and industries that pollute our environment, not by the ghetto looter and the petty thief. Also, few constructive actions have been taken by local and national leaders to eliminate the hopelessness, alienation, and poverty which often cause the ghetto dweller to violate laws in order to survive. As our nation becomes increasingly polarized, we are rapidly becoming two separate and unequal societies.[1]

Because the public school is an integral part of our social system, it has been a partner in the denial of equal opportunities to America's ethnic minorities; it has served mainly to perpetuate the status quo and to reinforce social class and racial stratification. Sensitive and perceptive writers such as Kozol and Kohl, and researchers like Pettigrew and Coleman, have extensively documented the ways in which the public schools make the ethnic child feel "invisible," while at the same time teaching the American Dream. Such contradictory behavior on the part of educators makes the ethnic minority child, as Baldwin has insightfully stated, run "the risk of becoming schizophrenic."[2]

Despite the school's reluctance to initiate social change, despite its tendency to reinforce and perpetuate the status quo, whenever our nation faces a crisis we call upon the school to help resolve it. Obviously, this is not because schools have historically responded creatively and imaginatively to social problems. It is because many Americans retain an unshaken faith in the school's *potential* for improving society. I share that faith. The school does have potential to promote and lead constructive social change. In fact, it may be the only institution within our society which can spearhead the changes essential to prevent racial wars and chaos in America. I would now like to propose a number of changes which must take place in the school if it is going to exercise a leadership role in eliminating ethnic hostility and conflict in America.

Because the teacher is the most important variable in the child's

[1] *Report of the National Advisory Commission on Civil Disorders* (New York: Bantam Books, 1968), p. 1.
[2] James Baldwin, "A Talk to Teachers," *Saturday Review*, December 21, 1963, p. 42.

learning environment, classroom teachers must develop more positive attitudes toward ethnic minorities and their cultures and must develop higher academic expectations for ethnic youths. Teacher attitudes and expectations have a profound impact on students' perceptions, academic behavior, self-concepts, and beliefs. Many teachers do not accept and respect the diverse cultures of ethnic youths, hence ethnic students often find the school's culture alien. The "cultural clash" in the classroom is by now a cliché. Studies by scholars such as Becker, Gottlieb, and Clark indicate that teachers typically have negative attitudes and low academic expectations for their black, brown, red, and poor pupils. Other research suggests that teachers, next to parents, are the most "significant others" in children's lives, and that teachers play an important role in the formation of children's racial attitudes and beliefs. A study by Davidson and Lang indicates that the assessment a child makes of himself is significantly related to the evaluation that "significant" people, such as teachers, make of him.[3]

It is necessary for *all* teachers to view ethnic groups and their cultures more positively, whether they teach in suburbia or in the inner city. The problems in the ghetto are deeply implicated in the larger society. Our future presidents, senators, mayors, policemen, and absentee landlords are taught in suburban classrooms. Unless teachers can succeed in helping these future leaders to develop more humane attitudes toward ethnic minorities, the ghetto will continue to thrive and destroy human lives.

The research on changing teacher attitudes is both sparse and inconclusive. It suggests that changing the racial attitudes of adults is a herculean task. However, the *urgency* of our racial problems demands that we act on the basis of current research. To maximize the chances for successful attitude intervention programs, experiences must be designed specifically for that purpose. Programs with general or global objectives are not likely to be successful. Courses which consist primarily or exclusively of lecture presentations have little impact. Diverse experiences, such as seminars, visitations, community involvement, committee work, guest speakers, movies, multimedia materials, and workshops, combined with factual lectures, are more effective than any single approach. Community involvement and contact (with the appropriate norms in the social setting) are the most productive techniques. Psychotherapy and T-grouping, if led by competent persons, are also promising strategies.[4]

[3] Helen H. Davidson and Gerhard Lang, "Children's Perceptions of Their Teachers' Feelings Toward Them Related to Self-Perception, School Achievement, and Behavior," *Journal of Experimental Education*, 1960, pp. 107–18; reprinted in James A. Banks and William W. Joyce (eds.), *Teaching Social Studies to Culturally Different Children* (Reading, Mass.: Addison-Wesley, 1971), pp. 113–27.
[4] For a review of this research, see James A. Banks, "Racial Prejudice and the Black Self-Concept," in James A. Banks and Jean Dresden Grambs (eds.), *Black Self-Con-*

Teachers must help ethnic minority students to augment their self-concepts, to feel more positively toward their own cultures, to develop a sense of political efficacy, and to master strategies which will enable them to liberate themselves from physical and psychological oppression. There is a movement among ethnic minority groups to reject their old identities, shaped largely by white society, and to create new ones, shaped by themselves. The calls for black, red, brown, and yellow power are rallying cries of these movements. However, despite the positive changes which have resulted from these identity quests, most ethnic minority youths still live in dehumanizing ghettos which tell them that black, brown, and red are ugly and shameful. They have many hostile teachers and administrators who reinforce the negative lessons which they learn from their immediate environment. Ethnic youths cannot believe that they are beautiful people as long as they have social contacts within the school and the larger society which contradict that belief. While current research is inconclusive and contradictory, the *bulk* of it indicates that recent attempts at self-determination *have not* significantly changed the self-concepts and self-evaluations of most ethnic minority children and youths.[5]

Despite the need for ethnic studies by *all* youths, ethnic content alone will not help minority youths to feel more positively about themselves and their cultures, nor will it help them develop a sense of control over their destinies. A school atmosphere must be created which values and accepts cultural differences, and ethnic youths must be taught how they have been victimized by institutional racism. They must become involved in social action projects which will teach them how to influence and change social and political institutions. One of the major goals of ethnic studies should be to help ethnic minority students become effective and rational political activists. We must provide opportunities for them to participate in social action projects so that they can become adept in influencing public policy which affects their lives. We now educate students for political apathy. They are taught that every citizen gets equal protection under the law, that racism only exists in the South, and that if they vote regularly and obey laws our benign political leaders will make sure that they will get their slice of the American Dream pie. The powerlessness and widespread political alienation among blacks, Chicanos, Indians, Puerto Ricans, and other poor peoples are deceptively evaded in such mythical lessons about our political system. We must teach ethnic youths how to obtain and exercise political power in order for them to liberate

---

cept: Implications for Education and Social Science (New York: McGraw-Hill, 1972), pp. 5–35.
[5] For a research summary and review, see Marcel L. Goldschmid (ed.), *Black Americans and White Racism: Theory and Research* (New York: Holt, Rinehart, and Winston, 1970).

themselves from physical and psychological captivity. Their liberation might be the salvation of our confused and divided society.

There is also an urgent need for ethnic studies to help white students expand their conception of humanity. Many whites seem to believe that they are the only *humans* on earth. To the extent that a people excluded other humans from their conception of humanity, they themselves are dehumanized. Racism has dehumanized many whites and caused them to exclude ethnic minority groups from their definition of humanity. The differential reactions by the majority of whites to the killings of blacks and whites in recent years indicate how whites often consider blacks and other ethnic groups less than human. During the racial rebellions that broke out in our cities in the early 1900's, the 1940's, and the late 1960's, hundreds of blacks were killed by police because they were protesting against injustices and grinding poverty. Many of these victims were innocent bystanders. In 1969, two black students were shot by police on the campus of a black college in South Carolina. The majority of white Americans remained conspicuously silent during these tragedies; a few even applauded. The tragedy at Kent State evoked strong reactions and protest by many white Americans, but no similarly strong reactions followed the tragedy at Jackson State. Reactions of the majority of white Americans to the My Lai massacre and the Attica incident were not as intense as the reaction to the Kent State tragedy.

Each of these dehumanizing events—the killings of ghetto blacks, the incidents at Kent State and Jackson State, the My Lai massacre, and the Attica tragedy—should have caused *all* Americans to become saddened, anguished, and outraged. The American dilemma which these incidents illuminated is that Americans are capable of reacting to the killing of human beings differently because of differences in their skin color and social class. While people may start treating others in dehumanizing ways because of their skin color or social class, the dehumanizing process, once started, continues unabated. Unless aggressive efforts are made to humanize white students, future incidents such as Kent State may leave the majority of Americans emotionally untouched. The issue of helping students become more humanized ultimately transcends race and social class. However, helping students see ethnic minorities as fellow humans is imperative if we are to eliminate our racial problems.

Ethnic content can serve as an excellent vehicle to help white students expand their conceptions of humanity and to better understand their own cultures. Since cultures are man-made, there are many ways of being human. The white middle-class life-style is one way; the Spanish Harlem culture is another. By studying this important generalization, students will develop an appreciation for man's great capacity to create a diversity of life-styles and to adapt to a variety of social and physical environments. Most groups tend to think that their culture is superior to all others. Chauvinist ethnocentrism is especially acute among dominant groups in American society. By studying other ways of being and living, students will see how bound they are by their own values, perceptions, and prejudices. The cultures of our powerless ethnic groups, and the devastating experiences of America's oppressed black, brown, red, and yellow peoples, are shocking testimony to the criminal effects of racism on its victims. Ethnic content can serve as an excellent lens to help white America see itself clearly, and hopefully to become more humanized.

We must construct new conceptions of human intelligence and devise instructional programs based on these novel ideas to improve the education of ethnic minority groups. Brookover and Erickson have summarized the conceptions of human intelligence on which most current educational programs are based: "1) that ability to learn is relatively fixed and unchangeable and 2) that it is predetermined by heredity. . . . These beliefs assume that ability is unaffected by external social forces. Another common assumption is that fixed ability of individuals can be measured with reasonable accuracy by intelligence tests."[6] These pervasive and outmoded assumptions have led to unfortunate practices in our schools. Ethnic minority youths are often placed in low academic tracks, classified as mentally retarded, and exposed to an unstimulating educational environment because they perform poorly on I.Q. and other tests which were standardized on a white middle-class population. These practices result in the self-fulfilling prophecy: Teachers assume that these pupils cannot learn, and they do not learn because teachers do not create the kinds of experiences which will enable them to master essential understandings and skills.

The traditional conceptions of human intelligence have been recently defended and popularized by Arthur S. Jensen. Jensen's research is based on unhelpful and faulty assumptions (he maintains, for example, that intelligence is what I.Q. tests measure). His argument is only a hypothesis, and should never have been presented to the general public in a popular magazine such as *Life* (since it is only a hypothesis) in these racially troubled times. I believe that *the hypothesis is immoral, misleading, and irrelevant*. Since we have no reliable and valid ways to determine innate potential, a moral assumption is that *all* students have the ability to master the skills and understandings which educators deem necessary for them to function adequately in our highly technological society; we should search for means to facilitate their acquisition of these skills and understandings and not spend valuable time trying to discover which ethnic group is born with "more" of "something"

---

[6] Wilbur B. Brookover and Edsel L. Erickson, *Society, Schools, and Learning* (Boston: Allyn and Bacon, 1969), p. 3.

that we have not yet clearly defined. As Robert E. L. Faris, the perceptive sociologist, has stated, "We essentially create our own level of human intelligence."[7]

Teachers must obtain a more liberal education, greater familiarity with ethnic cultures, and a more acute awareness of the *racist* assumptions on which much social research is based if they are to become effective change agents in minority education. Social science reflects the norms, values, and goals of the ruling and powerful groups in society; it validates those belief systems which are functional for people in power and dysfunctional for oppressed and powerless groups. Research which is antithetical to the interests of ruling and powerful groups is generally ignored by the scientific community and the society which supports it.[8] Numerous myths about ethnic minorities have been created by white "scholarly" historians and social scientists. Many teachers perpetuate the historical and social science myths which they learned in school and that are pervasive in textbooks because they are unaware of the racist assumptions on which social science research is often based. Much information in textbooks is designed to support the status quo and to keep powerless ethnic groups at the lower rungs of the social ladder.

Teachers often tell students that Columbus discovered America, yet the Indians were here centuries before Columbus. The Columbus myth in one sense denies the Indian child his past and thus his identity. Many teachers believe that Lincoln was the great emancipator of black people; yet he supported a move to deport blacks to Africa and issued the Emancipation Proclamation, in his own words, "as a military necessity" to weaken the Confederacy. Primary grade teachers often try to convince the ghetto child that the policeman is his friend. Many ethnic minority students know from their experiences that some policemen are their enemies. Only when teachers get a truly liberal education about the nature of science and American society will they be able to correct such myths and distortions and make the school experience more realistic and meaningful for *all* students. Both pre- and in-service training is necessary to help teachers to gain a realistic perspective of American society.

The severity of our current racial problems has rarely been exceeded in human history. The decaying cities, anti-busing movements, escalating poverty, increasing racial polarization, and the recent Attica tragedy are alarming manifestations of the ethnic hostility which is widespread throughout America. Our very existence may ultimately depend upon our creative abilities to solve our urgent racial problems. During the

[7] Robert E. L. Faris, "Reflections on the Ability Dimension in Human Society," *American Sociological Review*, December, 1961, pp. 835–42.
[8] For a perceptive discussion of this point, see Barbara A. Sizemore, "Social Science and Education for a Black Identity," in Banks and Grambs, *op. cit.*, pp. 141–70.

decade which recently closed, much discussion and analysis related to ethnic minority problems occurred, yet few constructive steps were taken to eliminate the basic causes of our racial crisis. Educators must take decisive steps to help create a culturally pluralistic society in which peoples of different colors can live in harmony. Immediate action is imperative if we are to prevent racial wars and chaos and the complete dehumanization of the American man.

RACISM IN AMERICAN EDUCATION

ROBERT L. GREEN

Robert L. Green traces the elements in our educational system which contribute to racism in American education. He identifies several areas in which changes would help mitigate racism, including establishment of units to combat racism and the development of multiracial schools early in the child's career.

Mr. Green is the editor of Racial Crisis in American Education *(Chicago: Follet, 1969). When he wrote this article he was professor of educational psychology and director of the Center for Urban Affairs at Michigan State University. In 1973 he also served as acting dean of Michigan State's College of Urban Development.*

For many years, whites in Northern communities and the liberal white press have been basking in self-righteousness, condemning Southern whites for "mistreating black Americans." Yet as they raised their voices in protest over the attitudes of Southern whites toward school desegregation, they refused to look at the conditions in their own communities—segregated housing, discrimination in employment, and, most importantly, segregated inferior schools for blacks. Before whites had time to reflect on racial injustice "Northern style," they were suddenly faced with urban unrest, school boycotts, and cries for integration, separatism, and community control.

Even today the North is not responding to the legitimate concerns of its black citizens. In 1971 the major confrontations over school desegregation in the U.S. occurred in a Michigan community, not in the

Reprinted by permission from *Phi Delta Kappan*, January 1972, pp. 274–276.

Deep South. Several buses were blown up the day before they were to be used to cross-bus black and white pupils in Pontiac, Michigan. The only major violent incident in 1971 that led to the arrest of Ku Klux Klan leaders was also in Pontiac. Clearly, Southern whites do not have a monopoly on racism and educational inequities.

Throughout its history, the American educational system in all regions has perpetrated the subordination of racial minorities and the poor. It has failed to provide all children with relevant education of high quality. The schools have reflected, reinforced, and sometimes promoted the same discrepant treatment of children on the basis of race and social class that exists in the larger society. As the National Advisory Commission on Civil Disorders (Kerner Commission) reported, "The schools have failed to provide the educational experience which could help overcome the effects of discrimination and deprivation."[1]

White middle-class school administrators and government officials are responsible for the inequities in public education. They have deliberately established school boundaries along racial and class lines. In Detroit, Michigan, U.S. District Judge Stephen J. Roth recently ruled that the city's schools are illegally segregated and that government action was responsible for the residential segregation in the city. Judge Roth also said that the school board, attempting to relieve overcrowding, had admitted that black students were bused past or away from nearby white schools with available classroom space to black schools that were overcrowded. In Benton Harbor, Michigan, evidence was presented in a suit against the school district which showed that black youngsters were being bused from black neighborhoods to white schools, isolated in all-black classrooms for the day, and then returned to the black neighborhoods in the afternoon.

DAMAGE CAUSED BY RACIAL ISOLATION

Racial isolation in the schools is damaging to black children because they are denied the resources that are often available to white pupils. It is also detrimental to white children because they develop a false sense of superiority. "Whites who attend racially isolated schools develop unrealistic self-concepts, hate, fear, suspicions, and other attitudes that alienate them from minorities," Preston Wilcox has written.[2] Although American public education has encouraged patriotism, it has neglected to develop respect for humanity and people of diverse backgrounds. White children learn at a very early age at home, and are

[1] *Report of the National Advisory Commission on Civil Disorders* (New York: E. P. Dutton and Co., 1968), p. 425.
[2] Preston Wilcox, "Education for Black Humanism: A Way of Approaching It," in N. Wright, Jr. (ed.), *What Black Educators Are Saying* (New York: Hawthorn Books, Inc., 1970), p. 7.

often reinforced by teachers and textbooks, not to respect people of color; whites have been socialized to feel superior to blacks and browns. As Wilcox noted, "The myth of white supremacy remains a myth perpetrated to foster the privileges of white skin."[3]

The public schools are not providing minority and poor children with the knowledge and skills they will need to earn a decent living and to participate in the social and political life of the community. More ethnic minority students than white students drop out of school and "many of those who do graduate are not equipped to enter the normal job market, and have great difficulty securing employment," the Kerner Commission reported.[4] School administrators, teachers, parents, and students all tend to regard urban schools as inferior.

LESS QUALIFIED TEACHERS

The quality of teachers and administrators in inner-city schools is a major factor which often makes the school experience for the ethnic minority child unsuccessful. Most teachers in urban schools have inferior credentials and often have fewer years of teaching experience. It was documented in the Benton Harbor, Michigan, case that teachers with inferior credentials were assigned to black schools and that teachers were also assigned by race. When faced with desegregation suits, school districts often place their best qualified black teachers in predominantly white schools. Robert Havighurst reported in 1967 that 36% of the teachers in the Chicago public schools with large minority enrollments were full-time substitutes. No other Chicago schools averaged more than 14% in this category. Eighty-two percent of all substitutes in the system were assigned to minority schools. The median years of teaching experience in those schools was four years, while in other Chicago schools it was no less than nine years and usually more.[5]

A 1963 study of the Chicago public schools showed that only 63.2% of all teachers in the 10 schools ranking lowest in socioeconomic status were fully certified.[6] Seven of the 10 schools had black enrollments exceeding 90%. Of the 10 highest ranking schools, eight were almost totally white, and of the teachers in the highest ranking schools, 90.3% were fully certified.

A major problem in inner-city schools results from the large number of permanent substitutes and individuals teaching out of their fields of specialization. To be effective, a teacher must have a strong command

[3] Ibid., p. 12.
[4] Report of the National Advisory Commission, pp. 425–26.
[5] Robert I. Havighurst, Education in Metropolitan Areas (Boston: Allyn and Bacon, 1967).
[6] Report of the National Advisory Commission, p. 428.

of his discipline. In 1968, Chicago public school officials announced that for the first time in many years they had a waiting list of teachers for their inner-city schools. The reason was that draft deferments were promised to college students who taught in low-income schools. The prospective teachers said that they would not have accepted the positions if the war in Vietnam were over; only a small percent of them planned to remain in teaching.

LESS THAN ADEQUATE FACILITIES

Inner-city schools are overcrowded and tend to be the oldest and most ill-equipped schools in the nation. In 1967, 30 of the occupied school buildings in Detroit had been dedicated during President Grant's administration. The Coleman Report stated that "Negro pupils have fewer of some of the facilities that seem most related to achievement." Curricula and materials used in urban schools are often not relevant to the experiences of the students; they are intended to serve a middle-class population.

Although some progress has been made and there are notable exceptions, most white middle-class teachers have little understanding or appreciation of minority cultures and do not instill an appreciation of different cultures in minority students. Immigrants to this country in the mid-nineteenth century faced a similar problem. Many teachers and principals viewed immigrant parents as "ignorant, prejudiced, and highly excitable people." Children of immigrants were taught to be ashamed of their parents. Although these immigrants were minorities, they were eventually able to fit into the American "mainstream." They were able to develop what the majority considered appropriate behavior. In American life, being part of the mainstream means dressing, looking, and thinking like the ideal middle-class white American. The interesting aspect of this concept of becoming a part of the American heritage is that it means feeling guilty about being Jewish, Polish, Chicano, or black.

The real barrier to the concept of equal educational opportunity and the development of democratic attitudes is related to the set of values instilled in young children. The mainstream is a myth; otherwise it would include all people. Instead, the dominant culture forces upon minority and majority children subjects that are not at all relevant to their lives. Students are often bored with sixteenth-century approaches to European literature and history. This is one reason why many children of all races drop out of school. Teachers often convince the ethnic minority child that his culture and life-style do not merit study in school. When working with ethnic children educators often violate the sound educational principle that the school experience should reflect the life-styles and interests of their pupils.

TRACKING

Minority youngsters are often placed in tracks on the basis of their performance on intelligence tests, and tracking is often a manifestation of racism. In Benton Harbor, Michigan, for example, black students were given reading tests; those doing poorly were assigned to "lower academic" tracks, no matter how proficient they were in other subjects. Court testimony showed that teachers of youngsters in lower tracks viewed them as nonachievers, and expected little from them academically. When students are provided inferior educational training in the early grades and are not positively reinforced and helped to develop adequate self-concepts, they cannot be expected to perform well on standardized aptitude tests. Beyond this, the validity of many tests used to predict the academic success of ethnic minority students has been seriously questioned by black psychologists and educators. They argue that test constructors usually exclude ethnic students when establishing group norms. Consequently, standardized test results often reinforce the negative self-images of minority youths and are frequently used to deny them equal educational opportunities.

ALTERNATIVES TO RACISM IN EDUCATION

All of the factors discussed above indicate that racism exists in the public schools. Six areas in which changes could help to mitigate racism in education are: 1) the development of multiracial schools early in the child's career, 2) improving teacher training, 3) establishing units on antiracist behavior, 4) retraining teacher trainers, 5) leadership, and 6) ongoing in-service training.

One method to achieve multiracial schools is two-way busing. Practiced in the South for many years as a means of assuring segregated schools, busing was then advocated by blacks in the North to enable black students to attend better equipped schools in white communities. But "integration" did not work as harmoniously as had been anticipated. Black children were bused miles away to white schools, while white students were not bused. Some perceived this one-way busing as punishment for blacks pursuing integration. As the Citizens Committee on Equal Educational Opportunities in Richmond, California, said, "The only real way to solve segregation problems is by two-way busing."[7]

It is not clear why parents are so opposed to busing to achieve desegregation. Many white children are bused daily to private schools with parental approval. Neither do most people object to busing a child who has a physical handicap to a school where he can get a good education. The purpose of busing should be to improve the quality of education. The arguments that center around busing today

[7] James E. Allen, Jr., "Integration Is Better Education," *Integrated Education*, September–October, 1969, p. 30.

are highly racially motivated. Other issues are merely attempts to evade the main problem.

Segregated schools foster a sense of superiority in whites and also hate, fear, and suspicion of minorities. Minorities, in turn, develop a sense of inferiority along with feelings of hostility, resentment, and resignation. Consequently, neither group is able to function properly in a multiracial setting. It is a vicious circle, but the circle must be broken. Multiracial settings contribute to improving minority self-perception; improvement of the minority youngster's self-image can lead to greater academic achievement.

Another way to achieve multiracial schools is by developing magnet schools or high-caliber schools attractive to all, with interdistrict busing. This provides for alteration of school districts and the creation of wider metropolitan school boundary lines.

Educational leaders must also apply pressure to metropolitan governments to end racism in housing. President Nixon's recent negative stand on expanded housing opportunities was a blow to those striving for multiracial communities; the federal government has not assumed an active role in creating racial harmony in America.

IMPROVED TEACHER TRAINING

Teacher training institutions must develop programs that reflect and promote ethnic diversity. How do we do this? We must begin to desegregate teaching staffs systematically at every level in teacher training programs within colleges of education in large universities. The largest colleges of education throughout the U.S. have essentially all-white staffs. We cannot realistically expect to help students develop nonracist attitudes when teaching staffs are selected from a population that has been trained to be biased. A complete sequence of curriculum development and in-service training should be planned and initiated, and minority members must be included in this planning and used in teaching roles.

The first two years of teacher training might parallel the VISTA or Peace Corps experience. Students should spend less time in the classroom and more time in field projects with racial minorities and the poor. Internships with such individuals as Cesar Chavez and the Reverend Jesse Jackson, with groups like the black poor in Green County, Alabama, and with institutions such as the Martin Luther King, Jr., Memorial Center and the Institute of the Black World should be structured for students early in their training programs. Two years of academic course work in the classroom could well be enough. Students should spend more time learning about people from diverse backgrounds and becoming more humanistic by actually participating in work projects with urban and rural residents from all walks of life and from diverse racial backgrounds.

UNITS TO COMBAT RACISM

There should be lesson plans and units in the public schools that teach children how to develop nonracist attitudes. Units on democracy, living with people who are different, and units teaching respect for the life-style of the poor would help children to develop more positive racial feelings.

TRAINING AND LEADERSHIP

Ongoing in-service training for all teachers should be established, focused on eradicating biased attitudes toward the poor and racial minorities. Individuals who have demonstrated that they are very sensitive to the plight of the poor and racial minorities should be selected to head these workshops.

The National Education Association and local education groups must speak out against injustice. Educators cannot purport to be neutral when minorities are discriminated against in housing, employment, and education. Poor people have always been suspicious of teachers and administrators, not only because they have failed to educate their children but because organized educational bodies have seldom spoken out against racial injustice. Teachers' unions, unfortunately, often parallel other unions such as the electrical workers' union and the carpenters' union, in that they struggle mainly for higher salaries rather than for human or civil rights. They can no longer remain neutral on race-related issues. They cannot remain neutral when quality education is at stake. They cannot remain neutral when the rights of minorities are threatened.

Replying to the attorney for the Detroit Board of Education who stated that the school board could not be held responsible for the acts of other governmental bodies, Judge Stephen Roth countered that ". . . the actions or the failures to act by responsible school authorities . . . were linked to actions of . . . other governmental units."[8] Therefore, if the educational system is to serve all of the nation's children, it must change its direction and pace. Unless it changes its posture toward ethnic minorities and the poor, our schools will continue to be the sources of conflict and turmoil in the community.

[8] William Grant, "Suit Unraveled Long History of Race Segregation in City," *Detroit Free Press*, October 11, 1971, p. 4B.

CHANGING THE CURRICULUM

PRIORITIES IN CHANGE EFFORTS

FRED T. WILHELMS

Fred T. Wilhelms, a versatile educator, issues a clear call for programs which go directly to the human person and to the great social agenda of today. In his words, "It may seem odd to advocate an 'innovation' which consists simply of deciding on purposes first and then finding subject matter and experiences to achieve those purposes. But an 'innovation' it would be—the most important innovation I can think of."

Wilhelms has been a professor, a school administrator, and staff member of organizations dealing with problem areas in education. He was executive secretary of the Association for Supervision and Curriculum Development in Washington, D.C. and, later, senior secretary of this curriculum leadership organization.

I believe that there are two needs so pressing that they place absolutely overriding demands on us to produce curriculum that does what it is meant to do. One is for programs de-

Reprinted by permission from *Phi Delta Kappan*, March 1970, pp. 368–371.

liberately designed to offer maximum effective help to each young person in his personal becoming. The other is for programs designed to go straight to the great social agenda of the here and now.

Around these two peaks lie wide ranges of other important needs. We must produce real mastery of knowledge and skills in a great diversity of areas: in reading, for instance, in mathematics, and in all that complex that makes up our scientific technology and the vocational life of people in it. These needs are real and basic and important. We dare not ignore them or slight them because the competencies they represent are vital both to the persons in our society and to the society itself.

Yet I believe the two overriding demands I have named tower above all the others, simply because they go directly to what is crucial to life in our culture—and the survival of the culture itself.

I know of no objective way to declare one or the other of these two the more important, both being essential. Certainly our society is in a state of emergency. Along with its wonderful productivity, our technology has generated side effects that suddenly converge upon us with bewildering speed: pollution, contamination of the earth and sea and air, urban rot, the depletion of key resources, and simultaneously the prospect of annihilation and of more people than the world can hold —to mention but a few. Alongside these, perhaps out of different parentage, rushes the blessed but troublous urgency for social justice and equity, with all its hostilities of race and class.

Every one of these problems is massive. Every one of them demands resolution in an incredibly short time—or else. Even if they could be taken one at a time, no one of them would yield a quick, simple solution. Taken together—as they must be taken—they constitute the most formidable agenda ever to face any society. Obviously they demand a nation of aggressive, effective, and dedicated problem-solvers. Obviously our schools are not producing enough of them. Our social studies drone on. Our so-called civic education is mostly a sterile analysis of structure, almost without effect. The whole thing is out of touch with reality. Until painfully recently, even the attempts at improvement were dominated by goals of mere academic virtuosity. That is changing now; but the inertia of the system is awesome. Only a massive effort, bringing to bear resources of mind-stretching diversity, has any chance of generating programs that can bring each youth face-to-face with his realities and teach him to help. We cannot depend forever on the political socialization of the street corner.

Yet, subjectively, I believe there is a still higher order of need in our culture. The salient problems of our day lie *within the individual person* —*within us*. Historians will see it more clearly one day; it is hard to see clearly while we stand inside the whirlwind. Old religions, old systems of values and morals and mores are crumbling. Life changes at a fantastic pace, and the old stabilizers are weakening. Very probably we stand at one of the great swing-points in human history. And no matter how courageously or even buoyantly we hold to the faith that what will emerge will be better, the present is a time of trouble.

Our youth are especially (only especially, not exclusively) hard hit. One cannot lump them all together. They react in many different ways, make their search in many different corners. Some reject virtually the whole tradition—perhaps in sullen withdrawal, perhaps angrily or even violently. Some have a sweetness about them that has rarely been equalled. Many stay within the system and throw themselves into great idealistic ventures, putting into action the finest of the old tradition and maybe something more. And the great "silent majority"? What mature adult really believes that even they are the same as he was at their age?

Underneath all the turbulence, surfacing often in forms that may seem bizarre to us, and sometimes in forms that may genuinely be subversive, destructive, and dangerous—beneath all this, it seems to me, lies a bedrock quest for "something better," for a higher social ethic, and a finer relation of man to man. The vision is inchoate; the goals are seen dimly, if at all. The search for "leads" goes everywhere—into old, quietist oriental religions, into existentialist philosophies, into human-relations experimentation, and even into consciousness-expanding drugs. The search is daring and courageous, but it is also, to be blunt about it, inept, sensation-ridden, and fumbling.

And how much have we done to help, we gray-heads in whom so much wisdom resides? How much chance have we provided a learner in our school to dig down into the immanent questions of values, of the significance of life, of the possibilities inherent in his humanity? How much help do we ever offer him to see the great options he has as to how to spend himself? What is there in our program that helps him to hammer out his own personal set of values, make his own commitments, and decide what to *be*?

I believe our next great task is to work out programs that will go *directly to the human person*—disregarding subject-matter rubrics at first, searching for subject matter and experience, from whatever source, that will help the person realize himself—starting bare-handed with nothing but the determination to help human becoming to its ultimate.

That will be the toughest, most sophisticated job ever undertaken by our profession. But we know enough now about human potential and its actualization to make the try. Anyway, as the kids say, "that's where it's at." The job of a school is to assault the deepest problems of its time. And I believe I have named them.

All this may be an unconscionably long prelude to an article that is supposed to be about innovation. But it is not a put-down of those brisk new developments one thinks of first when the word "innovation" is used. We shall need them—and more—if we are to master the challenges sketched above.

Obviously, if we are to have programs that "go directly to the human person," we have got to develop something beyond individualization—*personalization*—and yet keep it in a milieu of intimate human contact. Team teaching will be near-essential. Flexible scheduling that leaves much of each student's time free (and, hopefully, unpoliced) will help greatly. Assuming a considerable dependence on literature, art, and music, we shall need a wide array of materials that facilitate use by individuals or by two or three at a time—including books, but also including stereo record players with headphones, desk-size projection outfits, and so on, to the more complex devices. We need to be able to use motion pictures for even one student at a time. And we need individualized space for *doing* activities. The shapes of buildings and rooms will change radically, and all the new media for message-transmittal will be in great demand.

Yet it will be taking nothing from great adaptations such as these—which are commonly read as synonymous with "innovation"—to say that there must be other innovations of a far higher order. In teaching, for example. Consider for a moment the innovations in teaching that will be essential if we are to use literature optimally as an aid to human becoming.

The standard didactic mode upon which we chiefly rely in "teaching literature" is sufficient to do just what that phrase implies: to help students "know" a certain number of classics, to master lists of authors and their works, to survey literary movements, etc. But all this—important as it may be in an academic way—has very little to do with a young person's *use* of a poem or a novel as something to form himself upon. In all truth the standard didactic treatment gets in the way of such truly intrinsic learning.

It is hard even to visualize, let alone to practice, the sort of teaching that will let a youngster soak in literature that has direct meaning for him. I can scarcely imagine the tranquility, the warm, supportive environment, the uncrowded leisureliness it will take if individuals or small groups are to be free simply to look at themselves with clear eyes, talk through their deepest concerns, and forge out values to which they can commit themselves. I suspect that the highest forms of teaching will look to the unsophisticated observer like non-teaching. The sensitivity of feedback interpretation and progressive guidance will make the crude assign-quiz-test routine we now call teaching look as ridiculous as it is.

Probably the change in teaching need not be as radical in all areas as it must be in the deeply personal humanistic fields, but the change throughout must likely be in the same direction. What this will demand of pre-service and in-service teacher learning staggers the imagination. In 10 years we have not been able to generate even the relatively simple teaching changes envisioned by the pioneers in science and mathematics. By and large, the visionary new ventures have suffered a massive regression to the mean as most teachers have translated the dreams of discovery learning into the comfortable routines of good old "standard didactics."

One hesitates to call a spade a spade in discussing the practice of teaching, because we have a fellow feeling for teachers, and we secretly know that they are not all that much to blame, being caught in a tradition and a system they didn't invent. But the cold truth is that, by any system of scoring with even the slightest element of the visionary in it, the typical teacher, if he were a golfer, would rarely break a hundred. The result is a dreary wasteland of mediocrity. And it is worse than that: From the viewpoint of the learner it is repression and all too often sheer oppression. There is really little use doing much of anything else in education unless we devise a system of education for teachers that sets them on a different track and then—more fundamentally important—helps teachers toward a *way of life* consonant with what they are expected to deliver.

We are just "playing house" as long as we expect a high school teacher, for example, to think and feel deeply about individual learners, to innovate fundamentally in his use of subject matter—to reach for the stars—as long as he has to teach five classes a day, meeting a new group every hour on the hour, with maybe 15 or 20 minutes to prepare each lesson. He is ground down by the system; he goes home bone-tired —all the wearier because he knows in his heart that much of his work has been futile.

There has been a great deal of talk and some action—valuable enough in its way—about relieving teachers of clerical, milk-money duties. It is time we got up the nerve to talk about the sheer, massive volume of teaching-at-classes. Try saying sometime to an educational audience that teachers have to be able to live in the life-style of an intellectual, even of a scholar—and watch the blank looks. It is, to say it softly, not a part of our dream. How many educational leaders even believe that every secondary teacher needs a private office, with the appurtenances of systematic pursuit of study, and with room to confer privately with one or a few students? It is, to me, literally shocking, what we reveal we think about teachers. Maybe the most profitable innovation of them all would be to get serious about the total way of life that superior teaching has to be based on.

Just how to get at the necessary changes remains mostly to be worked out. But let us, at the least, face up to a grim truth: Unless somehow we provide teachers a breakaway from the stultifying school life we now force upon them, most of them will remain virtually inaccessible to new ideas and new insights. The savants in the schools of education may go on elaborating their intricate "scenarios" for educational revolution; the scholars in the background may penetrate deeper and deeper into the mysteries of human potential and the ways of learners; but the typical teacher will go on, practically untouched by it all, placidly administering the old routines of standard didactic method.

It is a tempting target for contempt. Teachers ought to be "professional," we tell ourselves; they ought to be alert to new knowledge, new insights, new content, and new materials. But who among us could or would do all that if we carried the load they carry and lived in the environment that people like us have made for them? If we want anything significant in further improvements in our schools—anything more fundamental than the sharpening of existing competencies—we had better make ourselves "tribunes for the teachers" and fight for a way of life that will free them for a quest a lot of them want to make.

And then there is the curriculum. Obviously it is too chopped up. John Donne might almost have had it in mind when he moaned,

> 'Tis all in peeces, all cohaerence gone;
> All just supply, and all relation.

In the past decade we have had splendid developmental work on many of the "peeces." The next great innovative surge had better be toward unification.

My own perception is that to begin by trying to balance and integrate the whole curriculum at one time is to court defeat; the job is just too big. On the other hand, confining ourselves to the individual course only accentuates fragmentation. I propose that we start serious work with each of what I see as the three great streams in the common curriculum:

> Science-Math
> The Social Studies
> The Humanities

I suggest that in each of these broad areas we ("we" meaning variously a single school, a school system, a state, a professional association, etc.) form a comprehensive "area committee."

In terms of personnel, such an area committee should include broad representation of parents, the public at large, and students as well as professionals of all appropriate types. About half of the professionals should deliberately be drawn from *outside* the disciplines directly affected; e.g., the humanities area committee should include science persons, physical educators, vocational education staff members, etc.

In terms of purpose, each area committee should be charged primarily to inquire into the *kind of program* needed; e.g., what should an entire social studies program be designed to *do?* Only very slowly should such a committee move into specific organizational plans and content areas. It should never dictate details of particular courses— that is a job for specialists.

Such a committee, because of its heavy loading of nonspecialists, can work wonders to move the emphasis in curriculum-forming back to where it belongs—to the *purposes to be achieved,* with subject matter selection in an ancillary role. The fundamental mistake we make over and over is to start with subject matter.

In fact, the fundamental mistake lies even deeper. To put it in terms of systems analysis, *we have confused input with output.* So we keep acting as if "putting across" informational content (input) is our job, and as if the students' knowing it is the output. Most of the time nothing could be further from the truth. For example, a history teacher may labor mightily to put across chronological details of presidential administrations (input); if she is honest she knows that nearly all of those details will quickly be forgotten. If, then, there is no other output than the students' knowing those details, there is nothing left—and the teacher is essentially goal-less in her teaching.

That confusion of output with input—and that consequent goal-lessness—are extremely deepseated in American education. It may seem odd to advocate an "innovation" which consists simply of deciding on purposes first and then finding subject matter and experiences to achieve those purposes. But an "innovation" it would be—the most important innovation I can think of.

And if we go at it that way we shall reap one other benefit. To unify curriculum across wide areas is very difficult if we start with subject matter, for the disciplines are discordant among themselves. To integrate around fundamental purposes is relatively easy. If we go to the fundamentals, organization will fall into place rather naturally.

THE MULTIPLE FORCES AFFECTING CURRICULUM CHANGE

RONALD C. DOLL

A curriculum worker, professor, and adminis-trator who specializes in the process of curricu-lum change, Ronald C. Doll writes about and participates in curriculum development. Here he examines the current roles of four forces: power, the dollar, growth in knowledge, and human needs and concerns.

Doll is professor of education at Richmond College of the City University of New York. He is the author of Curriculum Improvement: De-cision-Making and Process *(Boston: Allyn and Bacon, 1964), the co-editor of* Children Under Pressure *(Columbus, Ohio: Charles E. Merrill, 1966), and the co-author of* The Elementary School Curriculum *(Rockleigh, N.J.: Allyn and Bacon, 1973).*

William Van Til, in his foreword to the 1953 yearbook of the Association for Supervision and Curriculum Development, told of William H. Burton's attempts during the Forties "to rouse the concern of the educational profession over new developments in forces affecting education."[1] During the subsequent decade, edu-cators were jarred from their lethargy when practices in elementary and secondary education were virulently attacked or urgently criticized. Educator concern about "outside" forces reached a peak after October, 1957, when the Soviet Union launched its first Sputnik. Within the decade of the Sixties, both beneficent and hostile influences have con-tinued to play upon American school systems.

Groups and individuals of varied rheums and viewpoints have, then, for generations affected American schools. Today those of us in cur-riculum work recognize that some agents of forces, and thus some forces themselves, affect the curriculum intimately and consistently. These special and permanent forces, with their temporary agents, tend to cause curriculum change, though sometimes they hold it back. Be-cause the curriculum is where people are, the special, permanent forces bringing about and otherwise affecting curriculum change are clearly human. Each force, in its quality of humanness, holds potential for good and potential for evil. Each lies deep in human motivation.

Four forces affecting curriculum change have become especially prominent: 1) the drive for power; 2) the appeal of the dollar; 3) growth in knowledge, with corresponding efforts at evaluating acquisi-

[1] William Van Til (ed.), *Forces Affecting American Education*, 1953 Yearbook, Association for Supervision and Curriculum Development. Washington, D.C.: The Association, 1953, p. ix.

Reprinted by permission from *Phi Delta Kappan*, March 1970, pp. 382–384.

tion of knowledge; and 4) the needs and concerns of people in schools, within surrounding social and cultural milieux.[2]

THE DRIVE FOR POWER

Consider people's drive for power over the curriculum. During the Forties, for instance, this drive revealed itself in the urge of a man or a group to speak loudly, to alert other citizens to an alleged danger, to become nationally prominent, or, as we say today, "to shake up the troops." Sometimes the drive had a helpful end; often it seemed only a quest for power for power's sake. During eras of attack on the curriculum, school people tend to think of man's natural drive for power as being malicious and threatening. During quieter, saner moments, they think of the drive for power as a force which could possibly result in improvement.

Within recent years we have seen several major attempts at shifting loci of power over the curriculum. Among them are the following:

1. A push by scholars in the subject fields, often at the expense of professional educators and especially curriculum leaders, to give elementary and secondary school pupils choice content from their fields and, whether incidentally or not, to enhance their own status as curriculum workers.
2. Prods from the far left to promote particular brands of political education, with countering prods from the far right against alleged dangers like sex education and sensitivity training.
3. Militancy by teachers' organizations, which have learned that when one begins to talk about teacher welfare, he must soon discuss organization of schools and children's curricula, both of which matters have previously been in the preserve of boards of education and their administrative staffs.
4. The increasing strength of highly localized community groups, especially in the big cities, at the expense of centralized control of schools.
5. The militant behavior of youth, beginning in the colleges and moving to the secondary schools.
6. The new thrust of quasi-governmental regional or national agencies, like the Education Commission of the States, which have developed prestige and sometimes real power.
7. Forays toward control of the curriculum by the United States Office of Education and other federal agencies, at the expense of state departments of education and local school districts.
8. Campaigns for a black curriculum and, to a minor degree, a red

[2] Students in the course 76.701, Supervision and the Improvement of Instruction, winter semester, 1969–1970, at Richmond College have helped in defining these forces.

curriculum, a Puerto Rican curriculum, a Mexican-American curriculum, and so on.

While systems and formal arrangements for decision making about the curriculum have not materially changed during the 1960's, the persons who have initiated and sanctioned curriculum ideas have often come from groups other than teachers, administrators, and school board members. Power has shifted, in part, to scholars in the subject fields, conductors of summer in-service institutes, people who complain most loudly, those who have special programs to promote, the inner councils of teachers' unions and associations, self-appointed community leaders, paraprofessionals and other climbers on career ladders, designers and reviewers of project proposals, bureaucrats at state and federal levels of government, and specialists at sitting-in, impeding, and taking over meetings for decision making. These individuals and groups have sought power in obvious, open ways. Other quieter participants in a new drive for power, like owners of wealth and persons high in the power structures of communities, have also been at work.

Inasmuch as every action is likely to trigger a corresponding reaction, vocal demands for power have made current wielders of power "run scared." After making some initial resistance, the currently powerful have often said in effect, "Oh, all right, let *them* try to improve things. They'll soon find out how complex the whole problem is!" A consequence of this viewpoint has been a bending of the decision-making system so that decisions which are less-than-legal and sometimes— though not always—poorer than before have eventuated. In exercising their new-found power to make curriculum decisions, inexperienced participants have inevitably gained a certain amount of valuable experience.

THE APPEAL OF THE DOLLAR

A second fundamental force which has affected curriculum change in the United States is the strong appeal which money has for curriculum makers in a materialistic society. Always in need of funds to do what they have wanted to do for children, curriculum personnel have found a bonanza in grants-in-aid, which have frequently proved to be mixed blessings. Whereas under a time-honored arrangement school boards and administrators waited for all their funds to be sent them by tax collectors, state finance officers, and (sometimes) federal agencies, school officials have become seekers of special grants to augment school district income.

State governments, along with accrediting agencies, still have something to say about ways in which funds are to be used for supporting and expanding the curriculum. But state regulations concerning the curriculum have always been fewer than classroom teachers or laymen have realized. For example, the states have often limited subject requirements in elementary schools to reading, writing, arithmetic, and health, while subject requirements in secondary schools may consist only of English, American history, and health. In the language of school administrators, state aid has been almost exclusively "general" and therefore usable largely at the discretion of personnel in local districts.

On the other hand, financial aid supplied during recent years by the federal government has frequently been earmarked, designated, or "categorical." Both acts of the Congress concerning education and guidelines prepared by private foundations have so predetermined the scope, direction, and precise nature of curriculum reform supported by the federal government and independent grantors that these agencies have been said by some school officials to stifle creativeness and skill development among local planners, as well as to cause excessive dependence on persons who are geographically remote and have little understanding of pupil needs in local districts.[3]

While grants have emphasized, for example, particularized cognitive development and special attention to poverty areas, producers of educational materials have sought financial profit through new educational ideas and the increase in child population. The appeal of the dollar for these producers has brought a flood of instructional materials which are conditioning, increasingly, what children learn. Thus one may say that both the curriculum hobbies of grantors and the sales promotion schemes of businessmen are now having unprecedented impact on curriculum decision making. Priorities in the curriculum have been realigned as control has continued to follow the dollar.

GROWTH IN KNOWLEDGE

A third force persistently affecting curriculum change is growth in knowledge, which formerly occurred slowly and quite steadily but now shows marked, erratic bursts of speed. The teacher is no longer able to "cover the book." Instead, many books now cover the teacher. The eight-to-12-year doubling of knowledge in the natural sciences which Robert Oppenheimer noted has not been duplicated in other subject fields. Nevertheless, knowledge abounds embarrassingly in all fields, so that Herbert Spencer's question, "What knowledge is of most worth?" becomes more and more pertinent. Against a backdrop of educational objectives, curriculum planners are forced to seek new answers to Spencer's question.

Apparently the well-advertised reforms in subject matter content, sponsored by national curriculum projects, have not affected the

[3] See, for instance, Galen Saylor, "The Federal Colossus in Education—Threat or Promise?" *Educational Leadership*, October 1965, pp. 7–14.

achievement of pupils in American schools as much as sponsors had hoped they would. But the public seems to be convinced that after "softness" in the schools had been revealed during the Fifties, a subsequent period of "hardness" brought reassuring improvement in the curriculum. Interestingly, though the schools were blamed in 1957 for our failure to keep with the Russians' space program, few persons have seriously credited teachers with helping to put men on the moon.

Though the scholars in subject fields have failed to affect the curriculum as thoroughly as they have wished, in part because they have not faced the hard, human problems in curriculum change, they have shown new interest in ideas which have been talked about for a long time: experimentation, discovery, acquisition of meaning, inquiry, development of major concepts, and intellectual excitement. Our experience with organizing human knowledge for teaching now suggests the need to team academic scholars with curriculum specialists, behavioral scientists, and specialists in research and evaluation.

With increased growth of knowledge have come definite attitudes toward the effects of its growth. While one of these attitudes has been concern with how to sort out elements of knowledge and place them within the curriculum, another attitude has been fear that even the former elements are not being learned. Hence a flurry of effort at evaluation and assessment. Enter, for instance, national assessment, research and development centers, and new contracts for firms which develop and sell tests.

Proponents of national assessment have declared its purpose to be evaluation of educational performance as a means of gauging strengths and weaknesses in schooling and of assisting research. It could, under the wrong conditions, become a direct determiner of the curriculum in the same way that Regents Examinations have been one of the determiners of the high school curriculum in New York State. Dangers in the current anxiety about evaluation may well include confusion of means and ends in the curriculum, pressures which pupils and teachers feel in preparing for major examinations, and a tendency to sacrifice all-round development of children to a new set of remote goals. Though the elementary and secondary schools obviously did not cause the current burgeoning of knowledge, they are seriously caught up in its effects.

THE NEEDS OF PEOPLE IN SCHOOL

A fourth major force affecting curriculum change is the needs and concerns of pupils, teachers, administrators, parents, and other persons who work together to provide the best education for children. To dedicated educators, this is the most satisfying, meaningful force with which they deal. Always the real needs and concerns of people have part of their foundation in societal, subcultural, and community milieux. Therefore, parents and other community members should be expected to contribute to in-school education and to education beyond the confines of the school. The experiences children have in schools must be related increasingly to the life space of youngsters throughout the day.

Findings in human development and learning and in the impact of social and cultural influences on learners have been accumulating throughout the twentieth century. Very recently, we have come to realize more poignantly what various forms of disadvantage do to children. An economic order assisted by a new technology requires that pupils be introduced to new sets of skills. Experiments in urban education call for us to face live social problems. Furthermore, the current crisis in values makes us seek better ways of educating in the affective domain. Attempts at shaping human behavior through reinforcement are being made by one school of psychologists, though these attempts are being opposed by other psychologists and educators. More encouraging views of human potential are being expressed; clearer understandings of cognitive development are seen as having important applications in curriculum making. Curriculum workers are striving to develop pupil experiences which use children's learning styles, stimulate learners intellectually, offer them new opportunities for success, encourage their reasoning and critical thinking, help them understand other persons, help them clarify their values, and increase their ability to cope with their world in other ways. All in all, we live in an exciting era for attending to the needs and concerns of people in schools, within changing social and cultural contexts.

A major concern of teachers and administrators is for pre-service and in-service development of teaching skills which will help teachers do their best in classrooms. Studies of the teaching act which have resulted in more than two dozen ways of analyzing teaching give promise of indicating new emphases in teacher education and educational supervision.

THE INTERRELATIONSHIP OF FORCES

Curriculum leaders find that the four prominent forces which have been discussed above sometimes become merged and blurred because human motivation is almost never single or pure. Actions which are taken by professionally minded teachers for the good of children may be aided, for instance, by teaching devices manufactured by profit seekers and by ideas developed by power-hungry community groups. Is it possible that when a society begins to age and to become more complex, the impact of single forces on the curriculum of its schools become less clear-cut and distinctive by combining at times into a major, fused force? If so, discussions of "outside forces" versus "inside" or institutional ones become unreal, and efforts to identify separate forces according to any criteria become more difficult.

INSTRUCTIONAL
OBSOLESCENCE:
HOW NOT
TO KEEP
UP WITH
THE JONESES!

J. MERRELL HANSEN

J. Merrell Hansen, a member of the staff of the Department of Curriculum and Instruction at the University of Kentucky, believes that much of what passes for innovation needs tough-minded reappraisal. He suggests that all changes are not synonymous with improvement. He calls for more consideration of objectives and more experiences within the curriculum. He asks for evaluation in terms of objectives. Writing for secondary school principals, he urges a new breed of administrators.

Curriculum innovation and instructional improvement are popular terms in educational circles. Success frequently is measured by the extensiveness of the coverage rather than by the improvement of teaching or the facilitation of learning.

In an era of change for the sake of change and innovation without rationality, the educator needs a new perspective on curriculum improvement. This perspective need not reflect pessimism or intimidation; it need not be directed by impulsive showmanship or bandwagon "me-too-ism." Indeed, public hesitancy to support public education, administrative reluctance to innovate, and high pressure demands have contributed to the re-examination of what is called curriculum improvement.

HISTORICAL PERSPECTIVE NEEDED

Historical perspectives provide some insights into the change process in education. Instructional programs are directly influenced by external pressures and demands. Sputnik and the NDEA reflected a fundamental interest in national needs, public priorities, and academic emphases. During the 1960's, the disciplines and the structures of knowledge gained popularity as new fields of study entered the classroom. By the

Reprinted by permission from the *National Association of Secondary School Principals Bulletin*, February 1973, pp. 27–33.

late 1960's, reflecting youth and public concerns for human values, humanization and sensitizing educational programs became more evident.

From these changes, both in national priorities and individual needs, the schools emerged as conflicting bases for change. A mediocre product, a persuasive salesman, and an anxious school district seemed to be the elements of change.

However good the intentions of the innovators, much of their past activity now reflects no significant difference. Despite the excitement about the subjects chosen by the NDEA—foreign language, science, mathematics, and guidance—little visible evidence remains of its impact. The claims for compensatory education have also been diminished with conflicting research. Currently, the enthusiasm for performance contracting has waned substantially. Rush programs, whether to placate the public or calm governmental fears, seem inadequate in generating programs with improved educational qualities.

EFFICIENCY, AN ERRANT DETERMINANT

Much of that disguised as "innovation" has philosophical and psychological foundations of sand. The assumptions are elaborate and ornate, but inconclusive. Instead of identifying the means of improving the instructional program and hence the betterment of the learning process, concentrated efforts are expended upon hardware, gadgetry, and organizational manipulation. Prescribed programs, whether in the form of behavioral objectives, programed instruction, or computer programs, failed to individualize the students' needs, interests, or learning. Rather, these popular programs reflected efficiency in operation, standardization in procedures, and contrived experiences. Seldom was change directed to the activities of the teacher or the processes of the learner.

Instructional improvement under the misnomer of efficiency and expediency has not satisfied the variables of learning. Evidence that a child has performed at a certain level of proficiency indicates neither his desire to maintain that skill or his internalization of its worth. Successful and valued experiences frequently are done with the least expenditure of time and money, are most subjective, and are personally valued by the individual. Efficiency has been an errant determinant of much of that done to change the instructional program. Calculating coolness and methodical procedures may replace any humane interaction, but it may also retard the development of human curiosity and creativity.

Partially responsible for this tendency is an administration that is held accountable by a power system that is critical of unmeasured performance. Principals and superintendents are often hounded by community and public expectations. The public demands quality education with a minimum of cost. The district office and local school board want to avoid difficulties and controversies.

Under the pressure to be all things to all people, administrators have abandoned their primary responsibility—the improvement of the instructional process and the innovation of curricular experiences. Managerial functions, such as ordering books, meeting community leaders, completing volumes of office forms, conducting faculty meetings, providing for students' social events, and ensuring adequate facilities and conveniences, have become primary functions of an administrator.

A new generation of administrators, dedicated to facilitating teachers' effectiveness and promoting students' learning, is needed. Conversations with current and prospective administrators provide evidence that this new generation is not finding itself in the profession. Indeed, many are admitting that concerns over instruction and curriculum should be the responsibilities of others. Programs that are implemented seldom reflect needs and purposes of the school. The array of programs, accepted, poorly implemented, and then discarded for newer fads, is something directly responsible to the educational leader of the school system.

The enterprising administrator, free from inhibitions and intimidations, would launch his school in a program of change. The instructional staff could be sensitized to the developmental stages and learning processes of the child. New programs would be implemented when the staff is qualified and receptive, when the programs serve the objectives and goals of the community and the students, and when the facilitation of the program provides experiences adapted to the school's philosophical position. In-service will sharpen the abilities of the teachers.

OVERHAUL IS NECESSARY

Materials will complement rather than dictate the type of practices that occur in the school. Facilities will be altered to serve the needs of the teacher and his students, rather than the conveniences of the janitorial staff or the extrinsic value of apparent neatness in the building. The leader of this innovation will not be just a manager or business executive, but a curriculum designer and an instructional facilitator. Such an overhaul is not only desired but necessary if the public schools are to remain the social and viable institution that they ought to be.

In addition to instructional leadership changes, another perspective might be gained from an analysis of historical traditions that have molded and directed the public schools. Objectives in education have been responsive to society's needs. Yet, educators are still discussing the Seven Cardinal Principles with eager intent.

New definitions must be applied in describing the objectives of the schools. By identifying objectives reflecting today's problems, providing experiences relating to those objectives, sequencing these experiences into a meaningful relationship, and evaluating in terms of those objectives, the educator uses rationality instead of impetuous judgment.

Schools that attempt to be the sole agents for moral education neglect the other institutions, including the family and the church. Indeed the schools cannot accomplish all purposes and functions. The schools already have multiple tasks and sufficient responsibilities. Therefore, the program should expend its efforts in fulfilling these tasks rather than seeking to appropriate other and less educational designated objectives.

DON'T BE IMPULSIVE

Sacrosanct, but archaic practices persist despite all logic and understanding. Rationality and inspection provide tools for evaluating the worth of these practices. However, iconoclasts are not needed; destroying sacred cows may be a pleasant pastime for the nihilist but not for the instructional innovator. Many current practices reflect the highest degree of value and rationality and in haste, these might be discarded by impulsive decision makers. The romantic critics and the pessimistic doomsday prophets have been too vocal and too influential in the public schools.

Now, the teacher and innovational leader need to review their practices and decide what is worthwhile and what should be rejected. Under such examination, libraries hopefully will become centers of exciting learning, rather than quiet domains of books, periodicals, and dust. Four-walled classrooms could serve as convenient meeting centers, rather than confining limitations.

Scheduling may reflect periods of learning instead of "efficiency-bound" determinants. If a student needs four hours to accomplish a learning task, the school ought to provide that time. The sacred 50-minute period, the six-period day, the five-day week, and the nine-month year ought to be suspect. Learning occurs beyond the guarded period of time that the student sits passively in a classroom.

Indeed, the McLuhan generation is learning from numerous sources, many totally involuntary and uncontrollable. Interference with a student's mode of learning only encourages him to drop out academically or tune-out psychologically.

TRADITIONAL PRACTICES REMAIN

The source of curriculum decisions is another quixotic windmill to be assaulted. By defining curriculum in terms of experiences and events, changing the curriculum involves changing the experiences in school. Yet curricular changes have been exceptionally resilient.

History remains primarily a regurgitation of trivial facts. Mathematics includes endless and contrived theorems and axioms for undefinable reasons. English includes the teaching of traditional grammar as if some mystical improvement will occur despite the research indicating otherwise. Foreign language remains distant, inconsequential, and peripheral to the value of understanding other cultures, languages, humanistic creations, or other meaningful goals.

Many of these practices remain as shadows from the past because of the conservatism of the profession and the "other directedness" of curriculum decision making. Other groups and other interests are highly significant in determining the experiences to be had in the classroom. The teachers and students appear manipulated rather than manipulating. One anthology in literature, a chronological approach to history, sequential and abstract mathematics, and programed science experiences all reflect the decisions made by others than the students or the teachers.

Much of that adopted as instructional innovation and curriculum improvement is timed with "planned-obsolescence." The textbook will automatically self-destruct after "x-number" of years. Machines will cease functioning after so much use. New concepts will date the current concepts. Last year's investment is outmoded with this year's new gadgets.

External influences upon the curriculum should be acknowledged. Teachers who teach students to pass college board examinations or national merit programs are admitting that their classroom experiences are being legislated by others. National curriculum projects, with scholars, financial assistance, and publicity, become desired programs. The community, having experienced an educational process, condones current practices but fears any change. To allow change, citizens might suggest that their education was somehow inferior. They remember, expect, and demand experiences similar to those they had. Such myopia neglects the differences that have occurred between the generations.

CHANGE NOT SYNONYMOUS WITH IMPROVEMENT

In what terms may instructional improvement be defined? Change is not synonymous with improvement and the endurance of a practice is not justification either. An experience need not be included because it is prescribed by a textbook company, a state legislature, a community norm, a reluctant administrator, or an unimaginative teacher.

An experience is justified in terms of the vitality and utility incorporated by the teacher and the perceptiveness of the student in evaluating the worth of the experience. As a facilitator, the teacher attempts to vitalize the material so that its value is perceived by the student. Unless this occurs, the teacher continues to spoon-feed the student who continues to endure the "mutilation of spontaneity, of joy in learning, of pleasure in creating, of sense of self."[1]

When the teacher encourages intellectual and emotional experiences in the child, the instructional program is improved. In the past, improvement was measured by amount of change, by new facilities and equipment, and complying with the varieties of curriculum decision makers. The result has been "team teaching" that became "turn teaching"; programed materials reflecting the same concepts and ideas as before; and packages in new wrappings but with the same old content. The result was change—but no change.

CONCLUSION

All innovation, all the materials and paraphernalia, and all the acclaimed successes are inappropriate unless the teacher behaves more effectively and the student relates to the experiences more meaningfully. Otherwise, the charade is a small drama, with roles and scripts, ending when the class ends. Many children survive despite the barren time spent in school. The hurdles, barriers, and intimidations are endured by these children. But woefully, there are many bearing scars of emotional disappointment and intellectual abuse.

The applause for the successful is greatly diminished by the social cripples discarded along the way. To such an end, the public schools must either accept the blame or instigate real instructional improvement. The choice is an imperative and an opportunity. Too much may be left to chance unless the schools visualize their objectives, institute experiences that make the curriculum a life experience, and evaluate in terms of their objectives. Success is not determined by additional renovations of buildings, inappropriate technology and paraphernalia, and complex rigamarole. Instructional improvement or obsolescence—instructional enhancement or bandwagon impulsiveness—these decisions need to be made by the sincere educator.

[1] Silberman, Charles F., *Crisis in the Classroom* (New York: Random House, 1970), p. 10.

PART FOUR

CURRICULUM
FOR
THE
FUTURE

*A new development has emerged in contem-
porary curriculum-making. Professional
educators, including curriculum workers, are
joining scholars in other disciplines in speculating on the alternative futures which lie
ahead for Americans.*

*Today's futurists often encounter skepti-
cism among colleagues who remind them of
the failures of previous efforts by intellectuals
to predict the future. The skeptics point to
the long history of utopian thought, from
Plato to the optimistic nineteenth century
writer Edward Bellamy, and to the new
phenomenon of negative prophecies characteristic of the twentieth century, such as the
fantasies of H. G. Wells and the despairing
visions of George Orwell and Aldous Huxley.
(The latter forecasts are more accurately
described as Infernos than as Utopias.)*

*The editor has observed in his introduction
to* Education, A Beginning, *that the 1970s,*

best described by borrowing Dickens' phrase "the best of times and the worst of times," have seen the arrival of neither Utopia nor Inferno. Instead, the residents of the United States experience a peculiar blend of both realms. Since neither the Utopian dream nor the Infernal nightmare has yet materialized, some skeptics maintain that speculation on the future is akin to astrology and that the work of scholars who deal with futurism is about as reliable as farmers' almanacs.

Yet speculating on the future is different from prophesying Utopia or Inferno. For one thing, today's futurists have better tools with which to shape their speculations than their predecessors had. More important, the most perceptive of today's futurists speculate on alternative futures rather than setting forth a single static prediction. Contemporary futurism recognizes the existence of "system breaks," which is Kenneth E. Boulding's perceptive phrase for the discontinuities, turning points, and surprises which occur in modern society. Consequently, today's futurism is much more than extrapolation from current trends or the whimsical projection of some tendency which has impressed a particular writer.

A frequent criticism of futurism is that it is escapist. Futurists are charged with dodging present problems by keeping their heads in the clouds of the future. Actually, the opposite is true. Studying alternative futures is a way of clarifying the alternative courses and possible value options available in the present. In other words, the study of alternative futures is a highly effective method of forcing human beings to confront their present problems and to consider the results of their present choices.

Futurism has a long history in Europe. More recently it has been taken up by American intellectuals. One of the best explorations of alternative futures was conducted by the American Academy of Arts and Sciences for the Summer 1967 issue of Daedalus. The issue was devoted to a report by the Academy's Commission on the Year 2000, which offered outstanding scholars the opportunity to present papers on various aspects of the future and to interact with each other on ideas concerning the future. The issue was then published in book form. The prestige of the American Academy of Arts and Sciences gave the futurist movement substantial momentum. The Year 2000, by Herman Kahn and Anthony J. Wiener, provided futurists an extremely helpful factual basis for speculation concerning the future. Unfortunately, these publications give practically no attention to education and, consequently, implications were not drawn for the curriculum.

This defect was soon remedied by educators themselves. In the late 1960s, a project titled Designing Education for the Future and sponsored by eight western states (Arizona, Colorado, Idaho, Montana, Nevada, New Mexico, Utah, Wyoming) cooperatively published a series of books. Scholars and educators in a variety of disciplines and

specializations collaborated on books about education and the future.
Among the better volumes are those on prospective changes in society,
the educational implications of such changes, and on teacher education
to meet emerging needs. Prospective Changes in Society by 1980 *is*
composed largely of articles by scientists and humanists dealing with
their own fields of specialization. Implications for Education of Prospective Changes in Society *consists of speculation by educators on*
possible educational directions; it is a lively and provocative volume
which takes into account the extrapolated trends and system breaks
described in the earlier volume. Only rarely does a contributor interpret
his role as a futurist to be that of supplying support for an educational
innovation with which he is already associated. Preparing Educators to
Meet Emerging Needs *deals forthrightly with teacher education for the*
future.

Meanwhile, nineteen contributors were at work on their reactions to
a chapter in Kimball Wiles' The Changing Curriculum of the American
High School *in which Wiles had speculated on the curriculum of 1985.*
The 1970 symposium, a memorial volume for Wiles, is titled The High
School of the Future *and deals perceptively with possible futures for*
American secondary education. Another useful book is The Unprepared
Society: Planning for a Precarious Future *by Donald N. Michael, an*
expansion of a John Dewey Society lecture. Michael clearly believes
that difficulties are in store for the "unprepared society," unwilling to
plan ahead.

As Harold G. Shane points out in The Potential of Educational
Futures, *in the 1970s futures research was being carried on by large*
corporate complexes such as Rand Corporation and the Singer Corpora-
tion, by consultation groups such as the Institute for the Future, by
educational policy research centers at Stanford and Syracuse Universi-
ties, by schools such as the University of Massachusetts and Alice
Lloyd College and the University of Minnesota, by groups such as
Hudson Institute and the Academy for Educational Development.
Reports of current research are often carried in The Futurist, *a maga-*
zine published by the World Future Society.

In addition to the books mentioned above, many excellent specula-
tions on alternative futures have appeared in article or pamphlet form.
Such material is often less accessible to curriculum students than are
books. So the fourth and final part of this anthology is largely made up of
selected articles and pamphlets on possible futures. The
rest of this introduction will comment on interrelationships among the
ideas espoused by those willing to speculate on possible alternative
futures.

As a prologue, the editor contributes a pamphlet he has written on
teacher education in the year 2000. From your vantage point in the mid
1970s please enjoy agreeing and disagreeing with the editor's 1968 projec-

tion! *The selection includes comments on speculating on the future, a description of alternative futures before American society, and a discussion of the consequent alternatives available to American education as a whole. Only then does the pamphlet consider possible directions for teacher education in the year 2000. The editor foresees conflict between technologists, who may be charged with stressing things and ignoring people, and the social emphasizers, who may be charged with stressing people and ignoring things.*

Undoubtedly the best known contemporary futurist is Alvin Toffler. His book, Future Shock, *has been enormously successful and influential. The phrase "future shock"—defined as the disorientation brought about by the premature arrival of the future—has become part of the American language. Though his implications are sometimes frightening, Toffler is essentially optimistic in his orientation as to education. He hopes that his Councils of the Future will help overcome educational obsolescence and help education cope with the future. We have reproduced here in part an interview with Toffler; however, his analysis as a whole deserves your careful reading.*

The impact which Toffler and other futurists are having on contemporary education is demonstrated in the article from Nation's Schools. *Some American schools are introducing studies of the future into the curriculum. Though varied and creative, the approaches are only in their beginning stages. Current approaches which you might wish to consider for incorporation in your own teaching include games, science fiction, the use of the Delphi technique, the writing of scenarios, and the extrapolation of trends, all described in this magazine staff report.*

In "Youth Revolt: The Future Is Now," anthropologist Margaret Mead suggests that it is later than we think and that the future is actually upon us. In synthesizing ideas from her book, Culture and Commitment, *she urges that we must relocate the future in the present as elders work with the young on the questions which only the young can think to ask. Since Mead regards the future as unknown and unknowable, she would probably regard with skepticism any suggestion that life in the year 2000 will partially depend upon action by today's adults and any implication that today's educators can influence the kinds of human beings we wish to produce. We are, both young and old, strangers in an unknown land, says Mead, and we can only attempt to insure communication between elders and children and seek answers to children's questions.*

Carl R. Rogers, in his speculation on alternative routes we may take in interpersonal relationships as we move toward the year 2000, interrelates two forces: the ability of democratic societies to deal with human survival problems, and the spread of such intensive group experiences as sensitivity training, encounter groups, and T-groups.

Rogers, a proponent of such experiences, sees great promise for society and education if the trend toward openness, love, and reality in relationships prevails. Not only will the schools be environments for learning, but industry will also be increasingly humanized and religion will be related to a sense of true community.

Those who speculate upon the future must also come to grips with the role of technology. The place of machines, especially the computer, is particularly important in any consideration of future curriculums. Harold E. Mitzel supplies a helpful overview of the development of technology in his "The Impending Instruction Revolution." He examines the development of individualized instruction, including five concepts of individualization which have emerged. He predicts that adaptive education, involving the tailoring of subject matter presentations to fit each learner, will be a next step. Such adaptive programs should be accompanied by teaching for student mastery. With the revolution growing out of computer-assisted instruction should come new concepts in student appraisal and adaptation to the increasing heterogeneity among students. Mitzel looks forward with confidence to his version of a genuine instructional revolution.

Though futurists are committed to the idea of alternative futures characterized by differing scenarios, they are still tempted to speculate on those trends which seem most fundamental to them. For instance, despite their interest in developing a variety of scenarios, Kahn and Wiener, in The Year 2000, set forth what they described as the "Basic, Long-term Multifold Trend." Similarly Michael Marien, an able student of the future, writing in The Futurist, sets forth an outline of such a basic trend in education. As Marien sees it, the trend of the future in education is from closed teaching systems to open learning systems. The reader may wish to check the reported trend against the projections and advocacies of other authors in this volume. He will find that, in general, their desires are consistent with Marien's expectations.

Unlike some writers, Warren G. Smith reaches his conclusions on the future of education from a base within an innovating school system. Smith is the director of Nova High School in Fort Lauderdale, Florida. Smith would probably not quarrel with the basic trend reported by Marien; indeed many of the characteristics of open learning systems have been adopted by Nova High School. However, Smith would probably include in the trend certain interdisciplinary studies, for he believes that "present disciplines must be dropped and a new set of categories should be established." The interdisciplinary fields related to the future which Smith would stress are technology, ecology, and esthetic concepts through the humanities.

In closing this anthology, we readily turn to Harold G. Shane for summary. Included here are two digests by this prolific futurist. The first reports on a survey of educators in which Shane and his collaborator, Owen N. Nelson, describe what a cross section of educators believe that the schools of the future will become. The second summary by Shane is a commentary on future oriented curriculums. His curriculum views are excerpted from his larger essay on issues related to the future of American education.

The futurists are varied in their ideas and provocative in their approaches. They are not escapists; instead, they force us to recognize that what we do or leave undone today affects tomorrow.

PROLOGUE: THE YEAR 2000: TEACHER EDUCATION

WILLIAM VAN TIL

Part Four begins with an editorial prologue. The Year 2000: Teacher Education serves both as an overview of alternative futures for the curriculum of teacher education and as an introduction to Part Four. Speculation on future programs of teacher education necessarily involves preliminary consideration of problems encountered in studying the future and of possible patterns that may emerge in society and the schools. The Year 2000: Teacher Education originated as my presidential address to the National Society of College Teachers of Education in 1968. More than half a decade later, much of my early venture into futurism seems to me to stand up well enough despite time's remorseless marching on.

ON SPECULATING ON THE FUTURE

Some may say, "But the year 2000 is far away!" Is it, really? The year 2000 is as far in the future as the year 1936 is in the past. From 1968, the year 2000 is thirty-two years away; so is the year 1936.

Historians will point out parallels between 1936 after the initiation of Franklin D. Roosevelt's New Deal program and 1968 after the initiation of Lyndon B. Johnson's Great Society program.[1] But they will also point out some major "system breaks," to use Kenneth E. Boulding's phrase,[2] meaning sudden changes in the characteristics of systems. Such discontinuities, sometimes termed "turning points" or "surprises,"

---

[1] Historians report that 1936 was the year of Roosevelt's second election during the era of the New Deal. The backbone of the Great Depression was being broken and such acts of social legislation as the establishment of the Social Security system and the Tennessee Valley Authority were already established historical facts. In Europe, Adolph Hitler, in power for three years, marched into the Rhineland and, in America, a struggle between isolationists and internationalists accelerated.

Historians will probably report that 1968 was the year of Lyndon B. Johnson's "completely irrevocable" decision not to seek or accept the nomination of his party after his term of office had expired. A war against poverty had been declared, with the outcome in doubt, and such acts of social legislation as Medicare and extended categorical federal aid to education were already established historical facts. In Asia, a war in Vietnam engaged American forces and drained our resources while the confrontation between whites and blacks in American cities escalated.

[2] Kenneth E. Boulding, "Expecting the Unexpected: The Uncertain Future of Knowledge and Technology," *Prospective Changes in Society by 1980*, ed. Edgar L. Morphet and Charles O. Ryan (Denver: Designing Education for the Future, July, 1966), p. 203.

From William Van Til, *The Year 2000: Teacher Education* (Terre Haute: Indiana State University, 1968), pp. 9–35. Copyright © 1968 by William Van Til. Reprinted by permission.

develop because of powerful social forces, unpredictable or only partially predictable in advance.

The Role of System Breaks   For the 1936–68 period, major system breaks included such events as World War II, 1939–1945; the first atomic bomb dropped on Japan, 1945; the outer space pioneering dating from the Soviet Union's Sputnik, 1957; and the United States participation in Asiatic land wars during the 1950's and 1960's.[3]

If we look for parallels and continuities between 1936 and 1968, we can find them. If we look for system breaks and discontinuities between 1936 and 1968 we can also find them.

What is the shape of things to come in the year 2000, thirty-two years away? Can we envision at all the tomorrow of 2000 from the viewpoint of 1968? Or will major system breaks with respect to war or technology or biology or international development so change the current scene that a contemporary Rip Van Winkle falling asleep in 1968 would, like Rip, wake to a totally unimaginable and incomprehensible environment in the year 2000?[4]

WORLD WAR OR FAMINE AS SYSTEM BREAKS   So, before venturing any extrapolations of data and trends, we will formulate and invoke Rip Van Winkle's law, "All bets are off if such major system breaks as world war or world famine occur." In a time when the grinning horror of a nuclear war marked by incalculable devastation or a population growth culminating in famine must be regarded as a nightmare possibility, Rip Van Winkle's law must more than ever be respected.

TECHNOLOGICAL DEVELOPMENTS AS SYSTEM BREAKS   But what about the role of technological developments in making the year 2000 unimaginable and incomprehensible from the viewpoint of 1968? How about the possibility of the wizardry and marvels of gimmicks and gadgets in a time of accelerating technology transforming the recog-

---

[3] While prophets of 1936 might have predicted (and indeed did) the Second World War, no one could have predicted even from the vantage point of 1936 the exact alignments (the German-Russian non-aggression pact came in 1939) and certainly not the military development, extent, weaponry, or outcomes of the war. Few were the insiders in nuclear devastation. The science fiction writers had a monopoly on speculation on outer space conquest in 1936. Few students of the international scene in 1936 could have envisioned American men fighting in local wars on the Asian mainland following a victory in a major World War.

[4] Rip, you may remember, fell asleep in the Catskill mountains "while the country was yet a province of Great Britain" and returned twenty years later to his village to hear his fellow residents talking about "rights of citizens—elections—members of congress—liberty—Bunker's Hill—heroes of seventy-six—and words which were a perfect Babylonish jargon to the bewildered Van Winkle" and to hear "that there had been a revolutionary war—that the country had thrown off the yoke of old England—and that, instead of being a subject of his Majesty George the Third, he was now a free citizen of the United States." *Selected Writings of Washington Irving*, ed. Saxe Cummins (New York: Modern Library, 1945), pp. 14, 18.

nizability of the year 2000? Sociologist Daniel Bell, writing early in the *Daedalus* explorations, ventured a sober and unromantic assessment: "The simple point is that a complex society is not changed by a flick of the wrist. Considered from a viewpoint of gadgetry, the United States in the year 2000 will be more *like* the United States in the year 1967 than *different*. The basic framework of day-to-day life has been shaped in the last fifty years by the ways the automobile, the airplane, the telephone, and the television have brought people together and increased the networks and interactions among them. It is highly unlikely that in the next thirty-three years (if one takes the 2000 literally, not symbolically) the impending changes in technology will radically alter this framework."[5]

Sociologist Bell's judgment may be influenced by what another *Daedalus* contributor would term his nonscience background. In a *Daedalus* discussion, Ithiel Pool pointed out, "When I looked at the Rand Delphi predictions, I was struck by the difference between the predictions made by the science panel and those made by other panels. The nonscience panels essentially predicted that whatever was recently happening was going to continue, only a little more so."[6]

Today some scholars are speculating on system breaks which may grow out of technological developments. One possible system break relates to the encompassing social implications of the growth of computer technology. Economist Kenneth E. Boulding speculates, "The crucial problem here is whether the development of electronics, automation, cybernation, and the whole complex of control systems does not introduce as it were a new gear into the evolutionary process, the implications of which are as yet only barely apparent. The computer is an extension of the human mind in the way that a tool or even an automobile is an extension of the human body. The automobile left practically no human institution unchanged as a result of the increase in human mobility which it permitted. The impact of the computer is likely to be just as great, and indeed of the whole world electronic network which represents, as McLuhan has pointed out, an extension of the human nervous system and what is perhaps even more important, a linkage of our different nervous systems. It seems probable that all existing political and economic institutions will suffer some modifications as a result of this new technology; in what directions, however, it is hard to predict."[7]

William T. Knox of the Office of Science and Technology, Executive Office of the President, predicts flatly and positively, "*The impact on*

[5] Daniel Bell, "The Year 2000—The Trajectory of an Idea," *Daedalus* XCVI (Summer 1967), 641–42.
[6] "Baselines for the Future," *Daedalus* XCVI, 659.
[7] Boulding, *Prospective . . . 1980*, p. 209.

U.S. society of this (computer systems) development will exceed the impact of the automobile."[8,9]

BIOLOGICAL DEVELOPMENTS AS SYSTEM BREAKS   Another possible "system break" grows out of developments in biology. Some observers believe that we are leaving a century in which physics was queen of the sciences and entering a new era. Robert Wood, an urbanist, says, "I think one shrewd point of departure would be to recognize that the physical sciences have had their day for a while, that there is an innovative turn to the life sciences, and that most of our problems will come from the new advances in genetics, pharmacology, artificial organs, and medicine."[10] Ernst Mayr, a biologist, comments in the *Daedalus* discussions that one of his colleagues regards our times as "the beginning of the century of biology."[11]

The biological transformation of man via genetics, DNA developments, chemicals, and drugs is on the threshold.[12]

INTERNATIONAL DEVELOPMENTS AS SYSTEM BREAKS   Still another foreseeable system break relates to the international scene. In the broadest terms, the problem is the extent to which the world will be nationally or globally oriented during the next thirty-two years.[13] In the narrower

8 William T. Knox, "The New Look in Information Systems," *Prospective . . . 1980*, p. 223.
9 "If the middle third of the twentieth century is known as the nuclear era, and if past times have been known as the age of steam, iron, power, or the automobile, then the next thirty-three years may well be known as the age of electronics, computers, automation, cybernation, data processing, or some related idea." Herman Kahn and Anthony J. Wiener, *The Year 2000: A Framework for Speculation on the Next Thirty-three Years* (New York: Macmillan Co., 1967), p. 86.
10 "Baselines for the Future," *Daedalus* XCVI, 663.
11 *Ibid.*
12 The century of biology is both welcomed and deplored. Richard L. Shetler, as the President of General Learning Corporation, comments on "another era in which there may be some massive break-throughs by 1980—the field of molecular biology, of imposing changes in and around the living cell, thus possibly changing the character and quality of life itself. All the overtones of 1984, of Orwell and Huxley, are there, of course. But there are other and more hopeful overtones, too—of conquering disease and ignorance, and of opening boundless new horizons to human experience. I hope we have the good sense and humanity to use such a tool wisely and not monstrously, if we are able to use it at all. But I have enough faith in our instincts to hope that we do not shrink from the adventure of using it." "Major Problems of Society in 1980," *Prospective . . . 1980*, p. 268.
On the other hand, Joseph Wood Krutch viewed man's possible use of biological developments with alarm. In his article, "What the Year 2000 Won't Be Like," humanist Krutch carried on his long-term feud with the determinists in which an earlier battle was his assault in *The Measure of Man* on B. F. Skinner's *Walden Two.* " 'Would you like to control the sex of your offspring? Would you like your son to be six feet tall? Seven feet? . . . We know of no intrinsic limitations to the lifespan. How long would you like to live?'
"How would *you* like to be able to determine this or that? To me, it seems that a more pertinent question would be: 'How would you like *someone else* to answer these questions for you?' And it most certainly would be *someone else!*" *Saturday Review*, January 20, 1968, p. 43.
13 "Will the world separate out into two cultures, both within countries and between countries, in which a certain proportion of the people adapt through education to the

sense, the question is the extent to which the United States will follow the course of enhancing the immediate twentieth-century consumption of its citizenry as contrasted to the course of supporting the development of human and material resources abroad among underdeveloped peoples because of some combination of humanitarian and long-range survival considerations. If one extrapolated some current trends, the result would be ambivalent. Simultaneously, the United States is the long-range and altruistic nation of the Marshall Plan, the Agency for International Development, and the Peace Corps. It is also an immediate-consumption-oriented nation which reduces appropriations for foreign aid and which responds inadequately as the economic gap between the developed and underdeveloped lands grows wider and wider while the rich get richer and the poor get children. A world famine in the era of the population explosion might be the precipitator of a system break toward the global view. A system break might also be brought about by aggressive threats by coalitions of nations, newly industrialized and reaching for power.

THE EXPECTED AND THE UNEXPECTED Thus, anyone who attempts to envisage the shape of things to come in 2000 for the sake of considering alternative futures in his own field of inquiry (in this case teacher education), and possibly helping to shape directions in his field of inquiry, must face a paradox. The paradox is that he must report as though assuming that there will occur no major system breaks or surprises. Yet, at the same time, his historical sense tells him that system breaks or surprises (and not necessarily those mentioned above) are likely to occur and may be unpredictable.[14] In such a dilemma,

---

world of modern technology and hence enjoy its fruits, while another proportion fail to adapt and perhaps become not only relatively worse off but even absolutely so, in the sense that what they have had in the past of traditional culture collapses under the impact of technical superculture and leaves them disorganized, delinquent, anemic, and poor?" Boulding, *Prospective* . . . 1980, pp. 209–10.

[14] Those who attempt to envisage the shapes of things to come must even take into account the possibility that they are now living through an actual system break as they speculate and write. For instance, we may now be living through a period of literal social revolution which may be moving toward a culmination in open warfare between whites and blacks and toward new patterns of social arrangements imposed by the victors, rather than simply living through a period of swift social change in relationships between Negroes and whites within established precedents. We may be living through a period of triumph of anarchy as world-wide youth revolt spreads, as alienation characterizes masses of mankind, as more and more of the young and old withdraw from the Establishment, rather than simply a period of youth dissent marked by temporary withdrawals which the established society can absorb.

Even between the first draft and the final editing of this pamphlet, President Johnson terminated the bombing of Hanoi and asked for negotiations in the war in Vietnam; simultaneously, President Johnson announced his decision to neither seek nor accept the nomination for presidency; Martin Luther King was assassinated and violence and destruction ensued in 125 communities; a general strike swept France; student protests with attendant violence developed at Columbia University; Robert F. Kennedy was assassinated at the close of the Democratic Primary in California; the problem of violence in America dominated political discussion. Swift and astounding social change? Definitely. An indication of major system breaks? Quite possibly.

some would educate simply for surprises and forego all speculations, recognizing the wisdom of the early suggestion of Heraclitus that there is no permanent reality except the reality of change. Perhaps the only thing of which the prophet can be sure is that his predictions are bound to be wrong, in large or in small part, if not totally. He must recognize, with Boyd H. Bode, that the gods give no guarantees.

Yet, despite the inevitability of surprises in the pattern of change, men must try to see where they seem to be going. They must attempt to see what now seem to be reasonable possibilities, so that they can have some possible participation in influencing the future, in tempering trends with their values, in considering realistic alternatives, in short, in planning ahead. Educators who are committed to the improvement of the educational process and product must necessarily attempt to plan for educational change and participate in its direction and control as best they can. Abraham Lincoln said it well, "If we could first know where we are and whither we are tending, we could better judge what to do and how to do it." Not to attempt to look ahead is to be unintelligent. To look ahead without recognizing that surprises must be also anticipated is also to be unintelligent.

Consequently, the writer will attempt in this paper to follow the advice of Fred Charles Iklé, a *Daedalus* contributor; to infer from past observations to future ones, to use predictions which seem logically true, to depend on common sense, and to be aware of one's own inclinations to Utopianism.[15] Yet he will also recognize the role of the unexpected, as advised by Boulding.[16] He will regard such social changes as local or regional wars, extensive computer technology, extensive biological developments, and expanding international participation as likely to affect American life. But he will not regard these as system breaks. He will reserve that term for nuclear World War, the computer influential as the automobile, biological transformations, and sharply increased gap-reducing globalism; he will regard such sweeping developments as authentic system breaks, turning points, surprises.

So let us plunge into a description of the probable United States in the year 2000 (assuming current trends and substantial social changes, yet excluding system breaks) as the U.S. is envisaged by the scholar-prophets who are willing to speculate on possibilities or alternatives. Later, we will identify factors in this projection of the year 2000 which may influence education in 2000. Finally, we will attempt to describe the possible resultant nature of teacher education and the value choices

---

[15] "As said above, for the first step in 'guiding predictions' we have to infer from past observations to future ones, using theories and empirical laws from all branches of science as much as we can. Second, we should not overlook the usefulness of logically true predictions. Third, we also have to rely on common sense . . . . Fourth, the greater the role of this tacit reasoning, the more we must beware of the distorting effect of our emotions." "Can Social Predictions Be Evaluated?" *Daedalus* XCVI, 751.
[16] Boulding, *Prospective . . . 1980*, pp. 199–213.

as to alternative futures which may be before teacher education in the year 2000.

AMERICAN SOCIETY IN THE YEAR 2000

Some Projections The prophets assume that in the year 2000 the United States will still exist both as a nation and as a major world power. The states of the Union (by then possibly fifty-two in number, including the states of Puerto Rico and the Virgin Islands) will be more heavily populated than the United States of 1968.

POPULATION PROJECTIONS The Bureau of Census machine in Washington, D.C., which tolls off the population, recorded 200 million Americans on November 20, 1967. In a recent projection by the Bureau of Census, the total population for the United States is calculated as 241 million in 1980.[17] Philip M. Hauser and Martin Taitel of the University of Chicago write, "The population of the United States . . . is being projected to exceed 300 million by the turn of the century."[18] They add, "The projections utilize conservative assumptions about the future. The critical one is the birth rate. If it should not decline during the sixties, and then remain at a lower level, the total population of the United States may well be over 250 million by 1980 and close to 350 million by the end of the century."[19,20] [In the year 1973, experts recalculated probable population in 2000 as below 300 million—Ed. note.]

URBANISM AND METROPOLITANISM Both the anticipated Americans of 2000 and the Americans already born will live in urban territory. "By 1980, between 75 and 80 percent of our population may live in urban territory, which would place almost as many persons in urban territory in 1980 as there are in the entire United States today."[21,22]

As for the year 2000, Harvey S. Perloff says, "At present about 140 million Americans, out of a total of 200 million, are classed as urban

17 Philip M. Hauser and Martin Taitel, "Population Trends—Prologue to Educational Problems," *Prospective . . . 1980*, p. 25.
18 *Ibid.*, p. 24.
19 *Ibid.*, p. 54.
20 Sensibly, they hedge their bet because of the great imponderable, fertility. No population analyst can ever forget the great miscalculation of the 1930's, based on the society of the Great Depression, when the experts predicted 165 million as the peak population of the United States to be reached about the year 2000. Hauser and Taitel say, "Experience is lacking with regard to reproductive behavior in an era of easy and effective birth-control, relative affluence and nuclear power as a factor in world politics." *Ibid.*, p. 25. [Ed. note: As you read on, recognize that "reproductive behavior" in the 1970s again betrayed the experts.]
21 *Ibid.*, p. 41.
22 William L. C. Wheaton, Professor of City Planning and Director, Institute of Urban and Regional Development, University of California, Berkeley, says, "In short, during the next fifteen years, we must build about as many cities as were created in the first 200 years of this nation's existence. The population of the United States is moving to cities, and primarily to metropolitan areas." "Urban and Metropolitan Development," *Prospective . . . 1980*, p. 139.

dwellers. By 2000 at least 280 million, out of a total population of about 340 million, are expected to be living in urban areas."[23]

Not only will the future America be urban, it will also be metropolitan. Americans will reside largely in what the Bureau of the Census now terms Standard Metropolitan Statistical Areas.[24,25]

By 2000, some predict the agglomeration of many metropolitan areas into three megalopolises. Herman Kahn, formerly of Rand Corporation and now Director of Hudson Institute, and his colleague Anthony J. Wiener, report, "We have labeled these—only half-frivolously— "Boswash," "Chipitts," and "Sansan." Boswash identifies the megalopolis that will extend from Washington to Boston and contain almost one quarter of the American population (something under 80 million people). Chipitts, concentrated around the Great Lakes, may stretch from Chicago to Pittsburgh and north to Canada—thereby including Detroit, Toledo, Cleveland, Akron, Buffalo, and Rochester. This megalopolis seems likely to contain more than one eighth of the U.S. population (perhaps 40 million people or more). Sansan, a Pacific megalopolis that will presumably stretch from Santa Barbara (or even San Francisco) to San Diego, should contain more than one sixteenth of the population (perhaps 20 million people or more)."[26]

THE GROSS NATIONAL PRODUCT   The residents of the United States in the year 2000 are expected to have a substantially higher Gross National Product and GNP per capita.[27] Kahn and Wiener say, "The surprise-free United States economic scenario calls for a $1 trillion economy in 1975, $1.5 trillion in 1985, and about $3 trillion in year 2000. . . . The assumptions used in the projections for the 'Standard Society' yield a GNP for year 2000 (in terms of 1965 dollars) of $2.2 to $3.6 trillion; based upon a 1965 GNP of 681 billion, this range implies average annual rates of growth of GNP of 3.4 percent and 4.9 percent, respectively. Considering a year 2000 population of 318 million, per capita GNP would be slightly more than double the 1965 amount

[23] "Modernizing Urban Development," Daedalus XCVI, 789.
[24] Hauser and Taitel, Prospective . . . 1980, p. 30.
[25] Standard Metropolitan Statistical Area (SMSA) is defined by Hauser and Taitel as "one or more central cities of 50,000 or more persons, the balance of the county or countries containing such a city or cities, and such contiguous counties as, by certain criteria, are 'essentially metropolitan in character and are socially and economically integrated with the central city.' " Ibid., p. 30.
   Even for 1980, the predictions are for 70 percent of our population living in metropolitan areas. "By 1980, of some 170 million people in metropolitan areas, about 100 million are projected to be in suburbs, about 70 million in central cities." Ibid., p. 37.
[26] "The Next Thirty-Three Years: A Framework for Speculation," Daedalus XCVI, 718–19.
[27] Joseph L. Fisher, President of Resources for the Future, says, "A two-thirds increase in GNP in the next fifteen years seems altogether reasonable; indeed if the rather higher rate of increase in the last several years continues, the 1980 GNP will be near the high estimate shown in the table rather than the medium." (His high estimate for 1980 in his table is 1,250 billions; medium estimate 1060 billions in 1960 dollars), "Natural Resource Trends and Their Implications," Prospective . . . 1980, p. 9.

under the assumption of the low rate of productivity increase, and, under the high rate of increase, would be about 3.5 times the 1965 figure."[28]

TECHNOLOGICAL DEVELOPMENTS   In a United States which is more heavily populated, more densely urbanized, and wealthier, some recent social trends may be expected at least to continue and probably to accelerate. For instance, scientific knowledge and technological development are expected to expand further. As an illustration, nuclear power plants should be producing much of our power in 2000. The computer should be a remarkable influential force by the year 2000.[29],[30]

THE NATIONAL SOCIETY AND CREATIVE FEDERALISM   The nation may be expected to become increasingly "a national society," as Daniel Bell phrases it, characterized by more use of instrumentalities such as government, mass media, and modern transportation.[31] Yet this "national society" may not necessarily see governmental power concentrated in a highly centralized national government.[32] Some foresee a "creative federalism." Organizations may be expected to flourish, according to Grant McConnell, Professor of Political Science, University of Chicago, who quotes Tocqueville and judges that "it seems reasonably safe to predict that in the next few decades private and non-government associations will be important factors in our common social and political life."[33]

THE ROLES OF WORK AND LEISURE   In the economic realm, the trend

---

[28] *The Year 2000 . . .*, pp. 167–68.
[29] "It is necessary to be skeptical of any sweeping but often meaningless or nonrigorous statements such as 'a computer is limited by the designer—it cannot create anything he does not put in,' or that 'a computer cannot be truly creative or original.' By the year 2000, computers are likely to match, simulate, or surpass some of man's most 'human-like' intellectual abilities, including perhaps some of his aesthetic and creative capacities, in addition to having some new kinds of capabilities that human beings do not have." *Ibid.*, p. 89.
[30] There are some observers like Joseph Wood Krutch who says, "And although the man in the street still thinks of a brighter future only in terms of more, rather than less technology, there are at least a few who are beginning to ask if we are not becoming more dependent and vulnerable rather than more and more dependent and safe."
"If You Don't Mind my Saying So . . ." *American Scholar* XXXII (Spring, 1966), 183–184.
[31] Bell, *Daedalus* XCVI, 643.
[32] Daniel J. Elazar, Political Scientist, Temple University, foresees for 1980 that
  (1) All governments will continue to grow.
  (2) Sharing will be equally important in the future and will even seem to increase. ("One of the characteristics of the Great Society Programs has been the increased emphasis on federal aid to anybody.")
  (3) The states will have to act constantly and with greater vigor to maintain their traditional position as the keystones in the American governmental arch.
  (4) Localities will have to struggle for policy—as distinct from administrative—control of the new programs.
"The American Partnership: The Next Half Generation," *Prospective . . . 1980*, pp. 111–15.
[33] "Non-Government Organizations in America," *Prospective . . . 1980*, pp. 123–24.

in the American democracy which was also early reported by the French observer Alexis de Tocqueville, is anticipated to continue—what the few have today, the many will demand tomorrow.[34] So, despite probable continuing inequalities, goods and services will probably be diffused throughout the general population.

With the problem of production largely solved through the persistence of the historical American combination of facilities, geographic location, substantial resources base, and an innovating technology, the question of the work distribution among the population may become critical. Current trends indicate that the population may be increasingly characterized by what some term the masses and an elite or, if you prefer, the common man and a leadership group. Many Americans may work about a thirty to thirty-two hour week.[35] The sabbatical, once the exclusive fringe benefit of professors, may be extended to labor, along with long vacations and opportunities for early retirement.[36] Other workers may do only nominal or occasional work, resting content with their relatively low level of societal provision for maintenance.[37] But a vital group of Americans should be needed to man the specialized key positions which they hold by virtue of varied types of intellectual mastery. These key men may be expected to overwork themselves because of a variety of drives, including prestige, status, differential income, and desire for accomplishment.

THE KNOWLEDGE EXPLOSION   The knowledge explosion may be anticipated to continue its convulsive leaps. But since time is not expansible and since human beings are limited in the amount they can retain, more and more emphasis will probably be placed on storage and retrieval facilities and on computers to reduce the intellectual version of manual labor. The mastery of knowledge sources may well become an imperative educational goal for the individual who aspires to leadership and social regard.[38]

34 Bell, *Daedalus* XCVI, 643.
35 Kahn and Wiener, *The Year 2000* ..., p. 175.
36 "However, hours of work now average about 38½ per week, and by 1980 we anticipate something like a 36-hour work week. In addition, it may become common to have a sabbatical for labor; that is, a period in which a worker, after several years of work, may need retraining or additional training, travel, or to pursue some other activity of his choice." Gerhard Colm, "Prospective Economic Developments," *Prospective* . . . 1980, p. 92.
37 "Let us assume, then, with expanded gross national product, greatly increased per capita income, the work week drastically reduced, retirement earlier (but active life-span longer), and vacations longer, that leisure time and recreation and the values surrounding these acquire a new emphasis. Some substantial percentage of the population is not working at all. There has been a great movement toward the welfare state, especially in the areas of medical care, housing, and subsidies for what previously would have been thought of as poor sectors of the population." Kahn and Wiener, *The Year 2000* ..., p. 194.
38 Many such individuals will temporarily be placed in a relatively new occupation, that of graduate student, since, as Professor Joseph W. Gabarino tells us, "For a num-

GOALS AND DIRECTIONS   More questionable as to predictability are a nation's norms. Yet likely, if present trends are extrapolated, is a further shift in American orientation away from Max Weber's "Protestant ethic" of hard work, thrift, and spare living and toward leisure-oriented, free-spending and hedonistic living.[39]

It seems likely that the democratic way of life will continue to be the official ideology of the country and that the basic documents of democracy will probably continue to be venerated by the citizens and reinterpreted by the philosophers. Of the Jeffersonian trilogy, "life, liberty, and the pursuit of happiness," it seems quite possible that the latter may come into its own as never before. "Life" having been cushioned economically, and protected and extended medically, may increasingly be taken for granted.[40] "Liberty" should still be a heated focus of struggle, particularly on the part of the sensitive who reject massive invasions of privacy by governmental fact banks and law enforcement agencies and who resist impersonal controls by extended bureaucracies. But "the pursuit of happiness" may well be the aspect of the official democratic ideology which will engage the energies of most Americans and which will perturb the reflective.

While hobbies proliferate, travel expands, and educational opportunities enlarge, the present trend of spectatoritis may also grow via sports, movies, concerts, wide screen TV, etc. Discussion may be rife among intellectuals as to how man and woman should best pursue happiness in a society of multiple options.

Utopia will not have arrived by 2000. Americans of the year 2000 may well have their particular social problems, even as Americans of 1968 now have theirs—Vietnam war, Negro-white relations, the persisting slums and ghettos, the urban jungle, alienated youth, etc. Some of the social problems we now face in 1968 were readily predictable by the forecasters; the contributors to the *Daedalus* discussions comment frequently on the prescience and wisdom of *Recent Social Trends*, a publication of the Hoover era, in foreseeing 1968 dilemmas.[41]

THE PERSISTENCE OF PROBLEMS   Problems that lend themselves to technological solutions seem easier for Americans to cope with than

---

ber of reasons, including the competition for good students and the early age of marriage in recent years, a growing proportion of our university students have been converted into a special type of 'employee'." "The Industrial Relations System," *Prospective . . . 1980*, p. 159.

[39] There Is a Basic, Long-Term, Multifold Trend Toward . . . Increasingly Sensate (empirical, this-worldly, secular, humanistic, pragmatic, utilitarian, contractual, epicurean, or hedonistic) cultures." Kahn and Wiener, *Daedalus* XCVI, 706.

[40] Indeed, debate may center on how long the old should be kept alive in the century of biology in which transplants of organs are taken for granted.

[41] In retrospect, was it not also apparent that, with respect to Negro-white relations, our nation must sometime inherit the wind during the 20th century as a heritage of years of slavery and segregation for Negroes, while whites mouthed what Myrdal termed the American Creed?

problems which have largely social answers.[42] So one might anticipate that some problems now looming large for the last third of the twentieth century may well yield to the ingenuity of technology by the year of 2000. Illustrations that leap to mind are air and water pollution, with the attendant problem of waste disposal. But possibly more difficult for the year 2000 may be the struggle against social problems which eventually come home to roost. Such problems could include organized crime, environment, housing, governmental structures, and operation of voluntary associations.[43]

CRIME   By organized crime, we mean the planned lawlessness of criminal syndicates rather than "crime in the streets," today's euphemism for Negro rioting and violence. Today's struggles against the Cosa Nostra are clearly ineffectual, though the Mafia-type operations of today may appear child's play compared with the procedures of future organizations making maximum use of technology, brain power, and apparent respectability. Tomorrow's struggle against criminal syndicates which may operate systematically and precisely, will, in all probability, take place in a land rendered more vulnerable to organized crime by population density accompanied by individual invisibility, by a structure of living both more independent and more fragile, and by a climate of values in which striving for present gratifications is taken for granted.

ENVIRONMENT   Similarly, the year 2000 may be an era when Americans struggle for a better quality of the natural environment. As Joseph L. Fisher, President of Resources for the Future, suggests, "Conservation now and for the future will be at least as much involved in preserving the quality of the natural environment as it will be in maintaining a capacity to produce quantities of goods. As technology and management assure raw materials for the future, our attention will switch to the qualitative aspects of abating water and air pollution, preventing pesticide damage, and improving the design and use of both the rural and urban landscape."[44]

HOUSING   In relationship to the natural environment, housing may prove a continuous problem. Possibly, after many blighted areas in central cities are rebuilt with high-rise apartments, or cleared for urban recreation, the suburban rings may have become obsolescent and be

[42] Bell writes in his introduction to *The Year* 2000, "The Connecticut Yankee at King Arthur's Court was able to introduce quickly all kinds of wonderful inventions from the nineteenth century, but he foundered when he sought to change the religion and the monarchy—a lesson in the comparative recalcitrance of technology and belief systems in social change." P. xxiii.

[43] Should we expect that by the year 2000, America will have resolved its major Negro-white problems through a major social drive on this obvious difficulty? How long, O Lord, how long? Or is the more realistic possibility to anticipate half-measures and the consequent persistence of the Negro-white confrontation into the twenty-first century?

[44] *Prospective* ... 1980, p. 14.

candidates for reconstruction.[45] Or areas of metropolises may have become " 'slurbs'—a partially urbanized area in which the countryside has been effectively destroyed."[46,47]

GOVERNMENTAL STRUCTURE Perhaps it will have taken the development of the megalopolises of Boswash, Chipitts, and Sansan predicted by Kahn and Wiener to drive home the absurdity and obsolescence of our governmental structures in metropolitan areas. We refer to the multiple local governments which proliferate in the suburbs which ring the metropolises in a nation of 56,508 local governments, not counting school districts.[48] Already the political scientists are agreed on the unreality of our local governmental structures. Authors predict, "With the continuation of extensive urbanization and metropolitanization during the next few decades *will come increased recognition that our 20th-century technological, economic and demographic units have governmental structures of 18th and 19th-century origin and design.*"[49, 50] Perhaps the culmination of the drive for Negro rights will provide the crucial element in achieving consolidation in metropolitan areas and the breaking down of city-suburban isolation, rather than the continuance of the current 1968 pattern of central cities which are increasingly Negro and suburbs which are almost all white.[51] But possibly Black Power will result in black separatism, rather than racial integration, while white power preserves white separatism in a nation even more sharply divided.

ASSOCIATIONS The role of voluntary associations and internal and external controls in such associations may be among the crucial problems of the year 2000. Grant McConnell points out that studies of private associations show that "they generally lack the constitutional restraints which we have learned to regard as essential in our public

[45] Hauser and Taitel, *Prospective* . . . 1980, p. 37.
[46] Wheaton, *Prospective* . . . 1980, p. 145.
[47] William L. C. Wheaton points out that already "Our newer metropolitan areas are also beginning to suffer from obsolescence in neighborhood shopping centers. While they still contain tawdry and obsolete string shopping centers, vestiges of the streetcar era, they also contain small shopping centers which were quite modern in the 1930s, but have been rendered obsolete by the more advanced designs and merchandising skills of the 1950s and 60s." *Ibid.*, p. 148.
[48] Hauser and Taitel, *Prospective* . . . 1980, p. 42.
[49] *Ibid.*
[50] Wheaton, writing about aspects of urban and metropolitan government in which growth and change are necessary, says, "First among these is surely the establishment of metropolitan area governments or policies. Some of our older metropolitan areas have as many as a thousand local governments, the accumulation of a hundred years of political history and of slow growth both in urban population and in urban services. Under these circumstances of multiple governments, no effective local government is possible." *Prospective* . . . 1980, p. 143
[51] Hauser and Taitel comment that today for the 24 Standard Metropolitan Statistical Areas which contain the 24 larger cities, the central city Negro population numbers 83% of all Negroes in those Standard Metropolitan Statistical Areas. Hauser and Taitel, *Prospective* . . . 1980, p. 45.

institutions of government."[52] He says that "their governing institutions and modes of operation often do not adequately reflect the diversity of interest and will among their members; it is also that sometimes they do not serve the principle of liberty well. We can expect this to be a continuing problem in our common life."[53, 54]

SUMMARY ON SOCIETY   To this point we have reviewed four major "system breaks" or "surprises" which are, paradoxically, foreseeable and have forewarned of their possible havoc to extrapolation prophecies—the catastrophe of the occurrence of war or famine, the computer having become as influential as the automobile, the biological transformation of man, and the development of highly accelerated international support by the developed nations with substantial gap reduction between have and have-nots. We also have reviewed the data predictions of the scholar-prophets, hedged against "surprises"—expanded population, increased urban territory and metropolitan areas, higher Gross National Product and GNP per capita. We have reviewed trends predicted by the scholar-prophets—expansion of scientific knowledge and technological development, the national society marked by creative federalism and voluntary associations, diffusion of goods and services, less working time required of the common man and much expected of an intellectual leadership group, new communication tools to cope with the knowledge explosion, and a leisure-oriented pursuit of happiness. We have predicted the persistence of social problems, such as crime, environment, obsolescence in housing, governmental structures, and roles of associations and members.

AMERICAN EDUCATION IN THE YEAR 2000

Breaks and Trends   In the light of the above, what might education in the year 2000 be like? The question brings us again to the problem of "system breaks." In the event of major war, education becomes a zeal-for-our-side operation, a war support apparatus; in atomic catastrophe, what is left becomes a giant subsistence housing barracks. In the event of overwhelming impact of computer technology, the school becomes a clean factory in which workers quietly use machines. In the event of biological transformation, schools have a different population to educate. In the event of global emphasis, schools become oriented to vicarious and actual travel abroad and an American appropriation for education widely shared with the underdeveloped world. But if

[52] McConnell, *Prospective . . . 1980*, p. 128.
[53] *Ibid.*, p. 129.
[54] McConnell also points out that "inside a small association, an individual can find community and a sense of relation with his fellow man and need not feel alone or helpless. . . . In this setting he is not alienated. Thus, he and his fellows are unlikely to engage in activities that might disrupt society and they can be brought into line when necessary." *Ibid.*, p. 126.

In terms of other social trends discussed earlier, this sounds like an important prescription for the year 2000.

such system breaks do not occur, the following are likely developments in American education. (Whether these developments are desirable or undesirable is a completely different question on which the reader is invited to judge.)

THE EDUCATIONAL POPULATION As to the population to be educated, elementary education should be quite manageable. By 1968 we have already achieved, in effect, elementary education for all of the children of all of the people. In the years to 2000, the numerical task for elementary schools will be only to absorb the population increase.[55]

For secondary education, by 1968 we had reduced the dropout rate with respect to high school graduation to less than one in three persons. We did this by almost doubling high school enrollment between 1950 and 1965 as secondary school enrollment rose from 6.7 million to 13 million. To absorb most of the youth population increase plus to hold many of the one-third who now drop out, "the high schools still have a few more years of rather rapid enrollment increases (about 13 percent between 1965 and 1970) before relief arrives in the form of smaller enrollment increases," as Hauser and Taitel point out.[56] Then to 2000 the increase will represent simply population increases plus completion of secondary education for those who formerly dropped out.

The greatest increase in enrollment percentages between 1968 and 2000 is expected to come on the college and university levels. Past increments include 61 percent in the decade of the 50's and 60 percent in the first half of the 1960's. A 61 percent increase is expected from 1965 to 1980.[57, 58] The period from 1980 to 2000 should be marked by still more growth in college and university attendance, though the volume is not easily predictable. In addition, adult education may expand markedly.[59] [As of 1973, these projections seem too high—Ed. note.]

As to urbanization and metropolitanism, the typical student of year

[55] "During the sixties and seventies, the pressure on the grade schools will sharply decrease. Between 1965 and 1980, enrollment may increase by over 4 million or by only 12 percent. This is approximately an average of 1 percent per annum, an easily managed rate. The major problems, therefore, will not be those of rapidly achieving net increases in total quantities of facilities and personnel. Rather, emphasis will be upon the relocation, improvement and replacement of physical facilities, upon the improvement of personnel and upon the innovation and development of materials and techniques." Hauser and Taitel, *Prospective . . . 1980*, p. 52.
[56] *Ibid.*
[57] *Ibid.*, p. 53.
[58] According to Gerhard Colm, Chief Economist, National Planning Association, as to sheer numbers, the enrollment on the college level, from 1960 to 1980, will rise by more than 7 million human beings while enrollment on the elementary school level, from 1960 to 1980, will rise by just about the same number, more than 7 million. *Prospective . . . 1980*, p. 83.
[59] "Because men will live longer, the life cycle will become more and more of a problem as people do not pursue simply one career, but go through different career cycles . . . The problem of indecisiveness about what to educate for will increase. . . ." Bell, *Daedalus* XCVI, 667.

2000 will be among the millions living in urban areas.[60] The very large majority will be living in metropolitan areas described by Hauser and Taitel.[61] Almost half may live in the Boswash, Chipitts and Sansan described by Kahn and Wiener.[62] So schools will be very largely located in urban settings, except for some universities consciously located by their founders on open land and temporarily away from the enveloping grasp of urbanism.[63]

SUPPORT FOR EDUCATION   The American student of the year 2000 will be living in a nation which, barring "surprises," can afford to support education out of its GNP.[64] For education will go on in a nation in which Kahn and Wiener suggest as their "Standard Society" projection, a low per capita GNP in 1965 dollars of $6,850 and a high per capita GNP of $11,550.[65]

Even more important, the student generation should be living in an era in the year 2000 in which education will probably be respected for its economic power. Even today, in 1968, leading economists stress the value of education in the economic development of the nation[66] while advertisers exhort potential dropouts to stay in school through familiarizing them with the relation between income and increased years of schooling.[67]

By 2000, this continuing trend of respect for education may result in advanced education being taken for granted as the indispensable key to membership in an intellectual elite at the social controls. Indeed, as Michael Young predicts in Rise of The Meritocracy, 1870–2034, elitism based on education may be becoming so advanced as to provoke dissent from the masses by 2000.

The likelihood of the continuance of the explosion of knowledge

---

[60] Perloff, Daedalus XCVI, 789.

[61] Hauser and Taitel, Prospective . . . 1980, pp. 29–42.

[62] Kahn and Wiener, Daedalus XCVI, 718–19.

[63] "Institutionalized escapism may be imperative if the social order of the future continues to be subject to pathologies such as those so visible currently. The society of the future may be forced to introduce mechanisms for utilizing living time in nonfriction-producing settings." Luvern L. Cunningham, "Leadership and Control of Education," Implications for Education of Prospective Changes in Society, ed. Edgar L. Morphet and Charles O. Ryan (Denver: Designing Education for the Future, January, 1967), p. 186.

[64] Whether it will adequately support education is another question. By 2000 education will still have its problems but they should not be financial support problems—yet there will probably be financial crises throughout the later decades of the twentieth century which will be related to obsolete tax systems.

[65] The Year 2000 . . . , p. 168.

[66] As Kenneth E. Boulding says, "A great many studies have indicated that in terms of sheer rate of return on investment, investment in education brings a higher rate of return than that of any competitive industry." Prospective . . . 1980, p. 212.

[67] Nor is anyone particularly startled when Thomas A. Vanderslice of General Electric points out that "When a company, particularly a scientifically oriented company, contemplates moving into a community, quite often the decisive factor is not taxes, not the labor supply, and not the nearness to market. What really makes the difference is the quality of the school system. . . ." Saturday Review, January 13, 1968, p. 48.

trend should result in expanded use of computers and retrieval facilities at all educational levels, since man's cognitive apparatus is definitely finite rather than illimitably expansible, barring biological system breaks. How to accumulate relevant data will be regarded as far more significant than an outmoded stuffing of the memory.[68, 69]

CURRICULUM DEVELOPMENT In a national society characterized by creative federalism, curriculum making may be more and more the province of federations of professionals who develop concepts and create materials to implement their concepts. The parochialism of projects in the fifties and sixties which involved few others than specialists in a discipline may have been outgrown. It may be taken for granted in the development of projects and learning materials that specialists in the foundations—social, philosophical, and psychological —specialists in varied media, and curriculum specialists will be heavily utilized, in addition to liberal arts scholars in the disciplines. Rather than a single curriculum design for a field, such as PSSC physics, multiple designs may have been created, many by regional research and development laboratories which were first initiated in the 1960's.[70]

EDUCATIONAL ASSOCIATIONS AND EDUCATOR'S ROLES In the world of the year 2000, educational associations may be larger because of the increase of educators numerically and the necessity for the salary advancement, welfare provisions, and professional information which associations provide. Quite possibly, one major organization may bargain collectively and negotiate professionally for teachers.[71] Character-

[68] "Computers will also presumably be used as teaching aids, with one computer giving simultaneous individual instruction to hundreds of students, each at his own console and topic, at any level from elementary to graduate school." Kahn and Wiener, *The Year 2000 . . .*, p. 90.

[69] As Shetler says, "Just imagine the staggering possibilities of having all the world's great libraries, the accumulated knowledge of mankind, at your fingertips, of being able to select from them the information that is desired, and at the same time having a machine that can analyze, sift, integrate and calculate for us. There are machines that can, in a moment's time, go through successive calculations that would require hundreds of years in the slow motion calculating ability of our minds." *Prospective . . . 1980*, pp. 266–67.

[70] "I regard it as urgent that by 1980 the most resourceful administrative units such as cities, subdivisions of states, entire states, or clusters of states become aggressively engaged in curriculum development so that all schools will have a diversity of high-quality programs to choose from and we will not have drifted into nationwide curricular uniformity by default." Henry M. Brickell, "Local Organization and Administration of Education," *Implications . . .*, p. 231.

[71] My crystal ball tempts me to predict that the most remarkable and remarked-upon development as to educational organization will be the creation of the National Education Federation of Teachers, a coalition of the former National Education Association and the former American Federation of Teachers. NEFT, as it will inevitably be abbreviated, will grow out of a steady evolution of the National Education Association toward welfare concerns and the American Federation of Teachers toward professional concerns. After years of internecine warfare, rank and file movements in both organizations will result in amalgamation, despite the opposition of the managerial hierarchies and the swollen bureaucracies of the two organizations. Thus says the crystal ball— which possibly is cracked.

istic also may be both proliferation of organizations to match new job titles in an increasingly specialized educational profession[72] and co-ordination through super-organizations or holding companies to relate the work of specialized groups to a larger focus.

By the year 2000, the roles of most teachers will have been heavily influenced by the existence of supporting personnel, the available technology, and the extension of specialization. Secretarial staff, teacher aides, instructors and assistant teachers may be the personal supporting staff of the coordinating teacher in the discharge of his responsibilities. A pool of technicians, evaluators, and researchers, available to the teacher, may also be drawn upon.[73] The coordinating teacher increasingly may be the master of the mix, as O. K. Moore has phrased it, drawing upon readily accessible libraries or banks of books, films, television programs, sound tapes, computer consoles, etc., and utilizing trips, individual guidance, independent study, guests, etc., for instructional purposes with the aid of his staff. Perhaps a third of the coordinating teacher's six-hour working day may be spent supervising student learning of content in the existent disciplines and interdisciplines. Another third may be spent with various staff members in coordinating and planning future learning experiences. The final third may represent his specialization in education; consequently, some teachers would be engaged in individual therapy; others in conducting analysis groups for discussion with students; others in preparing television presentations and tapes; others in association with specialists programming computers; others in developing evaluation techniques and tests, etc. These specializations would reflect the personalities and preferences of individual teachers, as well as their academic backgrounds.

Overall management of the individual school may be shared by an administration specialist and a curriculum specialist. Coordination of schools and other community enterprises, often physically clustered in an educational park, will be the responsibility of the superintendent,

---

[72] "The present role of teacher will gradually evolve into a cluster of roles encompassing such discrete functions as team leader, formulator of detailed objectives, instructional sequence planner, script writer, presenter of information, evaluator of pupil responses, and designer of supplementary pupil experiences. The new administrative and supervisory specialties will include position titles such as Specialist in Outside Developments, Supervisor of Professional Training, Director of Equipment Acquisition and Maintenance, Chief of Materials Production, Program Assessor, Coordinator of Temporary Personal Assignments, Professional Librarian, and Travel Officer. We can anticipate that an Assistant Superintendent for Development and Training will cap off the pyramid of such positions in the central office of the school system." Brickell, *Implications . . .* , p. 227.

[73] "We can expect, even by 1980, an enormous expansion in sub-professional or paraprofessional full-time and part-time workers. Some will be attached to teachers as general aides, while others will serve as instructional machine operators, playground supervisors, information room clerks, data assistants, equipment maintenance technicians, travel aides, and so on." *Ibid.*, p. 227.

largely a political force in school and community, and his complex supporting staff. Some of the supporting staff may be worried about teachers who seem unable to utilize varied resources with ingenuity and who spend most of their teaching time standing before the class and talking at them.[74]

THE PURSUIT OF KNOWLEDGE AND LEISURE For the students of the year 2000, both the pursuit of knowledge and the pursuit of leisure will be important. Their lives outside of schools will, as now, be divided variously between study and recreation but the settings will be different. More prosperous homes may be able to afford, in the year 2000, a home learning and information center. Such a center might include "video communication for both telephone and television (possibly including retrieval of taped material from libraries or other sources) and rapid transmission and reception of facsimiles (possibly including news, library materials, commercial announcements, instantaneous mail delivery, other printouts)."[75,76] The home center might mainly be used by young people but also by adults, much as a collection of books, or a telephone, or an encyclopedia in the home is used today by youth and also by parents.

We may see an absorption of recreational facilities into recreational parks, a process somewhat similar to the absorption of recreational facilities onto college campuses through student unions, gymnasiums, natatoriums, etc. Instead of returning to the neighborhood for recreation after school, the youth of 2000 may turn to centers for sports, arts, gossip, etc., which are embraced in the master plan for the youth environment. His excursions into the countryside may be made in part via the school camp, while his younger brother and sister may visit the farm maintained by the school system for educational purposes.[77]

SUMMARY ON EDUCATION As to education in general in the year 2000, to this point we have commented on the possible influence of societal "system breaks" on education, on the probable especial increase in the college and university populations, on relations of education to increased urbanism, metropolitanism and per capita GNP, and on increasing emphasis on the importance of education. We have

[74] "Very probably (I regret to assume) if one opens the door to a typical 1980 classroom and walks inside, the teacher will be standing up front talking." *Ibid.*, p. 216.
[75] Kahn and Wiener, *Daedalus* XCVI, 714.
[76] "The sum of all these uses suggests that the computer utility industry will become as fundamental as the power industry, and that the computer can be viewed as the most basic tool of the last third of the twentieth century. Individual computers (or at least consoles or other remote input devices) will become essential equipment for home, school, business, and profession, and the ability to use a computer skillfully and flexibly may become more widespread than the ability to play bridge or drive a car (and presumably much easier)." Kahn and Wiener, *The Year* 2000 ... , p. 91.
[77] "It is much better to think in terms of the positive use of the countryside: for example, maintaining farms city children can visit for both recreational and educational purposes, or leasing open land for use by various groups in camping and in other related recreational activities." Perloff, *Daedalus* XCVI, p. 793.

speculated on increased use of educational technology (especially computers), on future coordinated use of education personnel in projects, on development of associations, on changing teacher roles and on resources for students for learning and leisure.

TEACHER EDUCATION IN THE YEAR 2000

We now turn to teacher education in the year 2000.[78] What might be some possible developments reflecting the social scene and related to the total education enterprise of the year 2000? What are some alternative future value choices?

Possible System Breaks in Education   Again, as in our consideration of the social setting of the year 2000, a question immediately arises. How about major "system breaks" or "surprises"? The answer is much the same as that for education as a whole. But what of the possibility of minor system breaks in that smaller system called teacher education?

Teacher education may undergo its version of system breaks or surprises by 2000. Forces leading in the direction of system breaks include persistent sharp criticism of the efficacy of teacher education by students, teachers, and scholars; slow adaptation of teacher education to such fast-moving social forces as technology; general conservatism in teacher education; and admission of weaknesses by teacher educators themselves. Forces leading away from system breaks include the considerable autonomy of key social institutions in teacher education such as schools of education, teachers' colleges, and state departments of education; the success of resistance to past "outside" proposals for change; and the lack of realistic alternatives to the present system.

If a system break appears in teacher education between 1968 and 2000, what form might it take? Among the possibilities are sharply reducing professional education preparation, and turning what remains of the teacher education effort over to the liberal arts scholars. Yet the need for some body of professional education content and the unwillingness of the liberal arts scholars to take over, as distinct from criticizing, have militated against broad acceptance of this type of system break.

Another possibility is teacher education taken over by teachers through their unions and organizations. Teachers then would be inducted into the profession through fellow teachers in on-the-job relationships. Yet, teachers are so involved in salary and welfare campaigns and in adaptations to new curricula and technology that presently they show no eagerness to assume the burden of preparing their successors.

Possibilities sometimes proposed include take-over of education by

[78] At this point, footnotes and supporting data will be abandoned to dramatize that what follows is a beginning on speculation through material for dialogue, an attempt to open rather than close possibilities.

state departments of education. It seems likely that state department take-overs would result in either other versions of schools of education, though under differing auspices and perhaps located in state capitals, or apprenticeship systems of training, conducted by teachers stressing practice and supervised by college professors moved into state departments.

Another possible system break is teacher education in 2000 planned and conducted through an industry-government complex composed of the private corporations which will have developed technologies and a U.S. Office of Education operating as does a European or Asian Ministry of Education. Militating against this development are the Constitution of the United States, the historic American distribution of power among local, state, and national levels, and the prophecy of creative federalism.

The Continuing Program   If such system breaks do not occur within teacher education, we will assume that teacher education will probably continue primarily under the aegis of colleges and universities in increasingly urban settings. It will probably include as program-influencing forces liberal arts college specialists in disciplines or interdisciplines and specialists in professional education, whether organized in departments, schools or colleges. The programs implemented by these college and university staff members may be influenced, but in changing ways, by such institutions as federal government, state departments of education, unions, and certification bodies. An additional influencing force may be the future teachers themselves, for the voices of students will probably be heard in the land. Both implementing and influencing agents will be heavily affected by the social setting of the year 2000 which we have sketched above and by the education taking place in this social setting.

MACHINES AND MEN IN TEACHER EDUCATION   Expanded population, expanded enrollments, and expanded teaching personnel combined with developing technology, the continuing knowledge explosion, and new social problems may result in a teacher education which, by the year 2000, differentiates between what can be learned through machines and what can be learned through the personal presence of liberal arts professors and teacher educators. Books will still be read in 2000 but, additionally, students individually and in groups will utilize film and television collections, computer-aided instruction, simulation, models, and various information and concept-oriented laboratories. The personal presence of teacher and liberal arts educators, no longer regularly required for lectures, may take the form of individual and group planning conferences, discussion leadership, research planning, field work leadership, and occasional major lectures on new insights not yet recorded by technology.

The first four years of higher education may stress general liberal education and specialization in a discipline or interdiscipline. These college years may be set in locales comparable to present day universities, though characterized by many more laboratories reflecting technological developments. But students may often be away from the campus, both for immersion in the field studies which may by then characterize instruction in the social sciences and humanities and for retreat to camp settings in the diminished countryside for absorption and contemplation of insights from field work and campus study carried on in urban and metropolitan areas.

A minimum of two intensive years beyond the general liberal education years may be devoted to study and practice of professional education as the minimum preparation for teaching. While centers of professional education, emphasizing laboratories for use of technology and for research, will probably persist on university campuses, a substantial proportion of the teacher education program may take place within public school settings. As educational parks develop in old and new cities, teacher education centers, university-related, may increasingly be included among the park facilities. Professional teacher educators may work within systems both as partners in the total educational enterprise and as teachers of teachers, pre-service and in-service. Those ghetto and other slum schools which persist may present a more formidable space problem for such programs, but rental of empty store fronts and other obsolescent space will probably provide headquarters for teacher educators and teachers-to-be at the scene of the action.

SEQUENCES OF PROFESSIONAL EDUCATION   In such public school settings, students in training may experience evolutionary sequences beginning with observation, going on to participation, including student teaching and culminating in internship. Each student, from his entrance into the two-year program, may have one continuing advisor throughout the entire program. Characteristics of the advisor may well include recent teaching experience on the level on which he now supervises beginning teaching, knowledge of professional education and subject content, and demonstrated skill in fostering self-actualizing personalities.

Observation may take place in a variety of settings; participation may be consciously planned to include both upper and lower income situations, largely urban and metropolitan, occasionally rural. Taking the cue from the development of field work in the social sciences, specialists in the foundation areas and the theory and practice areas may be concerned with both substantive content and field experiences in school and community. Instruction in the foundations areas and in theory and practice may be timed to coincide with observation and participation experiences. Some scholars in the foundation areas and in theory and practice may be engaged in research and study to be embodied in books and technology; other scholars may have as their role the interrelating of issues and ideas with the school and community experience being encountered by the future teacher.

All student teaching may be televised for frequent individual replay and study by the individual and also by the advisor and the individual, and for large and small group discussion by specialists in teacher education and teachers in training. For instance, the specialist in reading would include in his armory of materials television depiction of successful reading procedures as well as programs presenting problems posed for discussion.

Internship may be the transitional phase between preparation and independent teaching. As the focus of the final months of the program, internship may be accompanied by culminating seminars in which representatives of foundations, theory and practice, and the continuing counselor may participate, sometimes in the school and sometimes in the university research and laboratory settings.

More functional use of summer vacation periods by future teachers is a likely social development by 2000. The three summer vacations related to the two-year teacher education concentration may be divided among subsidized travel experiences abroad resembling more the Experiment in International Living than the traditional packaged Grand Tour, paid employment involving working with youth in summer school and community projects, and apprenticeship in research and development with educators who are carrying on studies or developing learning materials for the various technologies.

If a system break toward globalism, a highly accelerated American participation in foreign nations, should develop, the second year of the teaching preparation period for many young Americans may take place in under-developed countries, with, possibly, Puerto Rico and the Virgin Islands as staging areas and take-off points. Teaching, like diplomacy, may involve rotation in international assignments with occasional sabbatical-type returns to the United States for vacation, observation of American developments, and sharing of experiences.

ADVANCED STUDY OF EDUCATION Bi-annual extended vacation periods, subsidized leaves of absence, and taken-for-granted sabbatical years for all teachers may often be given over by teachers to retooling and doctoral work. The return would often be from the public school scene of the action to the university or regional laboratories and centers of discussions. Some sabbatical experience may result in career shifts, from, for instance, coordinator teaching roles to material development, computer programming, evaluation development, supervision, or curriculum development, accompanied by the attainment of the doctoral degree in a credentials society which requires this demonstration of specialization for a major career shift. Such periods may also provide opportunities for the expanding number of paraprofessionals, assistant teachers, retreads from other occupations including housewifery, to be educated to become coordinating teachers.

But we should not forget that in a leisure-oriented society in which teachers are well organized in the interest of salary and welfare, many teachers may not aspire beyond their original posts and the ascending salary steps won by their negotiators. Vacations and sabbaticals may be used by many for leisure and renewal. Consequently, if teachers are to keep up with fast-developing educational technology and practice, in-service education as a part of the basic teacher working day would be essential. Here teacher education based in school systems, local and metropolitan, or operating from regional centers, would play a crucial role.

Thus teacher educators of the year 2000 may be involved in conducting two-year pre-service training programs in school and university settings; helping paraprofessionals to professional status via institutes, workshops, etc.; educating specialists at the doctoral level in university settings; and participating as partners with school systems in in-service education of the permanent teaching staff.

Possible Splits in Teacher Education   One may predict with fair safety that in the year 2000 there will still be splits among educators over teacher education. It is probable that the liberal arts-professional education schism may persist. Yet it may be less virulent than during the 1950's when open warfare prevailed. Perhaps we may have reached, by the year 2000, a type of 38th parallel in the struggle, with a stalemate resulting in four collegiate years allotted to liberal arts and subject specialization and two years allotted to professional education.

It is also probable that philosophers will not have become completely reconciled. We may still be hearing, under whatever titles, the cases for essentialism, reconstruction, progressivism, realism, idealism, etc. But the discussion may be increasingly ecumenical and oriented to dialogue rather than acrimonious.

THE TECHNOLOGISTS AND THE SOCIAL EMPHASIZERS Possibly such historic splits may be muted by a new split which may now be on the horizon—the split between the scientific research wing of teacher educators, here termed the technologists, and the humanistic philosophical wing of teacher educators, here termed the social emphasizers. The two wings are likely to perceive education differently and to stress differing values.

The technologists may stress the compression and synthesis of exploding knowledge into a variety of technologies for learning. The social emphasizers may stress examination of the human dilemmas of mankind through the posing and testing of alternatives.

The technologists may foster research, based largely on physical science models, which can be translated into quantitative terms and embodied in storage and retrieval technology. The social emphasizers may foster research, based largely on social science models, which can be synthesized and made available to decision-making bodies ranging from the electorate to institutionalized in-groups.

The technologists may point to past educational breakthroughs in technical competencies based on scientific research and development, and involving innovation, evaluation, feedback, and diffusion. They may see man's technological quests as mankind's best bet. The social emphasizers may point to past gains in control over social difficulties through use of problem-solving in the educational process and to catastrophes which continue to threaten human survival. They may urge that the world can afford technological failure while social failure would be fatal.

The technologists may look forward to increased experimentation into affecting human potential through controlled conditioning, drugs and chemicals, and influences on intellectual acuteness. The social emphasizers may view with distinct reserve the extension of experimentation on modifying human potential, citing the dignity of human personality, unsuccessful genetic experimentation toward a new breed, and reminding the public of the horrors of the Hitler regime.

The technologists may be preoccupied with closely defined, value-free laboratory studies of education-related techniques intended to foster production and efficiency. The social emphasizers may be preoccupied with the quality of life, work, and leisure, the possible ways for man to pursue happiness, and attendant value-oriented consideration of alternatives through schools.

The technologists may argue for acceptance of a split between elite and masses by pointing out the accelerating concentration of knowledge for decision-making in elites and uncertainty about decisions on the part of the common man under the severely restricted condition of information in the communication system, upon which the masses depend. The social emphasizers may claim that such acknowledgment merely defines the urgent problem to be faced by mankind: finding ways of making the knowledge of the elite accessible to the masses so that the common man may use intelligence in problem-solving and the leaders may be humanely oriented in their endeavors.

The technologists may be impressed by the order and efficiency of the new technology which is increasingly characteristic of school and society. The social emphasizers may be impressed by the planlessness and even chaos related to persistence of crime, poor land use, obsolete housing, ineffective government structures, competing interest groups, and other problems currently unpredictable.

The technologists may be pleased by the logic and clarity of the content developed in many subjects by projects which continually update knowledge. The social emphasizers may be troubled by the turbulence within man and disorder in society.

The technologists may develop and support teacher-proof materials. The social emphasizers may develop and support creativity in teaching and autonomous self-actualizing teachers.

The technologists may be charged with stressing things and ignoring people. The social emphasizers may be charged with stressing people and ignoring things.

Occasional versatile teacher educators may have the educational background and personality structure to harmoniously reconcile both the technologist and the social emphasis viewpoints. But the majority may lean to one or the other persuasion and may combat their opponents academically. They may even be heard speaking disparagingly of them at parties at which both old and new forms of libations and stimulants are served.

There is only one way in which to close the venture into the year 2000 represented by this paper. It is to predict, with appropriate uncertainty, that before the year 2000 is reached, one or more major and minor system breaks, whether anticipated or not even dimly envisaged, will take place. These developments will have a profound influence on the future of mankind, including the activity termed teacher education. One insignificant pigmy outcome of such developments will be that the venture into the future represented by this paper on tomorrow's teacher education will largely be of historical interest to whoever might come upon it in the year 2000.

ALTERNATIVE FUTURES

A
CONVERSATION
WITH
ALVIN
TOFFLER

JAMES J. MORISSEAU

In "A Conversation with Alvin Toffler," James
J. Morisseau, a freelance writer who has worked
with the prominent futurist on common projects, elicits Toffler's ideas on education and the
future. Toffler is the author of Future Shock
(New York: Random House, 1970), which has
been a best seller during the 1970s. In this interview, Toffler comments on the problem of adaptation of the individual child to future shock.
He calls for more attention to the future in
teaching. The interview provides for the reader a
useful introduction to Toffler's thought, which
might well be followed by reading Future Shock.
At the New School for Social Research,
Toffler taught the "sociology of the future"—
one of the first such courses in the world. He is a
past editor of Fortune Magazine and has written
numerous articles and the prize-winning volume
The Schoolhouse In The City (New York:
Praeger, 1968).

Reprinted from The National Elementary Principal, January 1973, pp. 8–15. Copyright 1973, National Association of Elementary School Principals. All rights reserved.

Alvin Toffler is a journalist, an author, and, above all, a futurist. Unlike some of his fellow forecasters of the future, he sees the world of tomorrow not simply as an oversized, overblown extension of the present, but as a world that will be dramatically, even radically different. He sees a world characterized by rapid and accelerating change, not only in our technology but in our values, in our sexual attitudes, in our relationships with family, friends, organizations, and in the way we structure government, politics, business . . . and education. And he questions whether the human being is prepared to experience—and survive—the traumatic changes that lie ahead.

"I think," he says, "that we are in the process of a tremendous human revolution that will dwarf the industrial revolution and all the political revolutions, from the Russian to the French to the American, and make them look small by comparison."

The new revolution, he feels, will produce—indeed already is rapidly generating—a new, "superindustrial" society, one that will be "fast paced, highly diverse, nonuniform, filled with intergroup variety and conflict, nonbureaucratically organized."

This vision of the future, he adds, is "180 degrees the opposite of the vision of the future as presented in *Brave New World*, *1984*, and much of science fiction, all of which, despite their brilliance, picture a uniform future and a homogenized, regimented form of society."

The future as seen by Huxley, Orwell, and others is not impossible as Toffler sees it. But he believes that "there are powerful pressures leading toward diversity, variety, and heterogeneity rather than uniformity. Indeed, some of the real dangers may eventually come from a society so fragmented that its members no longer can communicate."

Alvin Toffler's ideas, set forth in *Future Shock*, already have had a powerful, worldwide impact. The impact can be measured by the fact that *Future Shock* has been published in fifteen countries, already has sold more than four million copies, and in 1972 was honored as the best foreign book published in France.

Future Shock includes a chapter on education that should be must reading for anyone involved in the public schools or interested in their future. Meanwhile, the editors of *The National Elementary Principal* asked me to interview Toffler and to obtain a more detailed view of the implications of the future shock syndrome for the schools and for public education.

MORISSEAU: *Educators will be concerned at the outset with a crucial question: Can the individual and, in particular, the individual child, adapt to the rapid, traumatic changes you envision?*

TOFFLER: In order to understand the adaptive abilities and limitations of the individual you must first ask: "What does this revolutionary upheaval do to the individual?" It does a number of things that ought to be of extreme concern, especially to educators. One is that it creates a world of temporary relationships. The individual no longer can suround himself with objects, people, organizations, and other environmental components that are permanent. Take friends, for example. When I was a child, a best friend was one who lasted all of one's childhood and indeed right on through adolescence. . . .

MORISSEAU: *And sometimes through adulthood.* . . .

TOFFLER: And sometimes throughout life. But that's rarely the case in our society. More and more you can visit schools, even elementary schools, in this country and ask the children: "How many of you have lost a best friend in the last year because that best friend moved away?" The hands go up in very large numbers. That fact begins to condition the child to believe that temporariness is the essential characteristic of human relationships.

The same thing is true of relationship with things—the toys the child plays with, the building he lives in or sees every day, the classroom he works in. More and more we find ourselves moving toward throwaway toys, throwaway classrooms, and portable playgrounds. We begin to create a temporary physical environment as well as a temporary social environment around the child.

We do the same thing with respect to the informational environment. We used to teach that there were certain eternal verities, not only moral verities but factual, empirical verities. Now, we know that the latest verity is likely to be found untrue next week. Information becomes a perishable product; the individual's image of the world is forced to undergo continual revision.

Even the individual's relationship with his own images becomes temporary. Instead of having a permanent relationship between himself and his or her image of the reality the relationship becomes telescoped, temporary, impermanent.

MORISSEAU: *But is the human animal psychologically capable of handling such impermanence? Are we talking about a massive explosion in mental illness?*

TOFFLER: I'm not sure that I would use those terms, but I would put it this way: When you accelerate the rate of change and create a milieu based primarily on temporary relationships, you increase the rate at which the individual is called on to make adaptive decisions. You're asking individuals to make more coping decisions in shorter intervals of time.

But you ask whether people can handle this. If all we do is ask the individual to decide faster, I suppose he could handle it. But we are also changing the nature of the decisions, making them more complex. When you introduce change into a social order, you introduce new things—surprises, unpredictable situations, new circumstances, bizarre or unusual conditions, crises, and opportunities. This means that the individual is less and less able to deal with reality through pre-programed decisions, through habitual responses, and through routines. He is forced into more creative decision making, which relies on inventing a response rather than repeating one. The faster the rate of change, the more nonroutine the responses.

I believe all this creates a fundamental cultural conflict that has very painful effects for the individual. But I also believe the individuals have a much greater potential for adapting to change than most of us realize. I think we can vastly enhance the individual's ability to cope, particularly if we pay attention to these questions in our dealings with children.

MORISSEAU: *Doesn't the phenomenon you described earlier—children losing their friends at an early age—help in that process?*

TOFFLER: That's part of it. They are being conditioned to change. On the other hand, there are certain very expensive costs involved. If you live in a world of temporary friends, there usually appears to be a decline in emotional involvement, in committedness, and in warmth. We're moving from a society that is based essentially on hot emotional relationships to one that is based on cool emotional relationships punctuated by explosions of heat and violence.

MORISSEAU: *There's a potential for trauma?*

TOFFLER: There's a potential for trauma, and I'd like to argue that the human potential is not, as most liberal educators like to believe, infinite. I know it's a controversial position, but I believe that we are biologically limited, that the rate at which we can accept information and make decisions is bound by certain biological limitations. Short of some biological mutation (or tremendously dangerous experimentation with genetic engineering), we must operate with the biological equipment we have. That imposes certain limits. I do not think we're near those limits; I think that if we were smart about education, we could do wonders. But I think it is a mistake to simply assume, in blind faith, that human beings are going to be able to adapt smoothly to this revolutionary upheaval without some kind of difficulty, pain, and, in some cases, traumatic upheaval within the individual.

MORISSEAU: *You said that, if we were smart about education, we could develop a lot of untapped potential in the human animal. What do you mean by being smart about education?*

TOFFLER: I think, first, we must recognize that we're dealing with a revolutionary situation. That means that the changes in education must be directed to the *goals* of education, not just to its methods and techniques.

But how does one design goals for an educational system, particularly when you are talking about a system that involves some fifty million human beings in the United States alone? How do you begin to think rationally about goals or objectives for education unless you first think sensibly about the future?

Now, it's easy to know what the future is going to look like if you live in a static society, because you know that the future is going to look like the past and like the present. But in a society of high speed change, such as ours, you can no longer make the assumption that the future is going to resemble the present. The question then becomes, "Can we in any way anticipate the outlines of that new world, and, from our assumptions about the future, can we work back to some sort of rational curriculum?"

MORISSEAU: *And, in your view, we can?*

TOFFLER: We can, if we recognize that it is extremely difficult to *know* anything about the future, to make any precise, hard, fast, accurate statements about the future—and impossible if we are looking for scientific certainty. On the other hand, it must be recognized that, even today, we base our curriculum on assumptions about the future. The fact, for example, that we teach children to read is based on our assumption that reading is going to be a required skill. The only difference between what I am proposing and what is currently done is that we be explicit about the dilemma of the future and thoughtful about it, rather than making implicit, unexamined assumptions.

MORISSEAU: *Explicit about it?*

TOFFLER: I mean that right now we make assumptions about the world without ever stopping to think about them. We make the linear assumption that the world is going to be the same basically, but in large outline. To me, that's a highly simple-minded form of forecasting, a dangerous one for a world caught up in profound upheaval. It leads to a curriculum that conditions children, that sets them up to be candidates for future shock. It means that when big changes do come, children are going to be bowled over by them.

Let me give you an example. Some time ago, I asked a high school class to write down seven events that were going to happen in the future. These students, being very sophisticated, came up with a phenomenal list—advanced computers in 1977, a Soviet-Red China rapprochement by 1993, food supplies from the oceans, manned stations on the planets. But, on examination, virtually all of the forecasts had to do with "the world out there" and not with the future of the individual.

I then asked them to predict seven things they thought would happen to them, personally, in the future. For the most part, their responses indicated an unchanged way of life. There was an absolute gulf between their perception of rapid change in the environment and their lack of understanding that the changes would have an effect on their personal lives. It was as though they were describing themselves living in yesterday and the world living in tomorrow.

MORISSEAU: *Does that represent a commentary on education?*

TOFFLER: It suggests to me that the educational system—and in that I would be forced to include the mass media and all of the influences that bear on the education of young people—has done a very poor job of integrating a knowledge or picture of the future and of preparing young people in any way for the jolt or jolts that face them. Basically, what today's system does is to say to youngsters that the world of the future is going to be more of the same, only bigger and more bureaucratized.

But if I am correct, the future is not going to be more of the same. We need another set of assumptions about what it is going to be like. I believe that, if we are in fact moving toward more and more temporary relationships, there will be increasing pressure on young people to know how to relate to other human beings in that kind of world. It seems to me that one of the tasks education must concern itself with is the task of relationships. If we are moving into a world of increasing variety and heterogeneity, that by definition means a world of greater individual choice.

MORISSEAU: *But is that the sort of thing that can be taught?*

TOFFLER: Yes, I think it is possible to design experiences within the framework of education that at least give people a taste of what they might later experience. As an example, let me return to the point that we are moving toward a world of more fluid relationships—not only with things, with people, and with information, but with organizations. Individuals no longer work with the same company all their lives, or belong to the same church, the same PTA, or the same political organization.

We are moving away from the bureaucratic form of organization, based on permanence, toward a structure honeycombed with temporary organizations, ad hoc committees, task forces, problem-solving teams, or the Nader style protest movement that disappears and then springs up someplace else. The implication is that, in the course of a lifetime, an individual will have to deal with many different kinds and sizes of organizations, many different styles of organizational behavior, and many different levels of complexity.

But how do we teach children about organization? We put them in a class of twenty-five or thirty with a single teacher. Then, year after year, we move them through an organization that resembles the first organization we ever had anything to do with. At the end of the line, out comes a teenager, almost an adult, who has experience with being, in effect, a subordinate in a group dominated by a single person. But he has no experience with other organizational designs.

MORISSEAU: *But what you're describing is no longer universal.*

TOFFLER: I know that. I'm describing the typical, industrial style school system. I'm well aware that it's beginning to break down, that there is a lot of experimentation, and that's a good adaptation of the system. But I'm willing to bet that most children still go through the standard organizational training.

If you believe that you're moving into a world of temporary and complex organizations, you want to design into the educational process experiences that give children a taste or smell of different kinds of organizational life.

Similarly, if you're going to be dealing with high diversity in the society—a plethora of different consumer products, conflicting subcultural values, a kaleidoscopic value system—then it becomes a world of very difficult choices. This suggests that the schools must give students some experience not only with organizational styles but with the definition and clarification of their own value systems. To me, one of the crucial things the schools must focus on is the issue of values, but not in the traditional sense of inculcating a set of fixed, permanent values. Rather, the schools need to deal with the question of better values, to accept the value of value clarification.

Schools should create conditions in which students are encouraged to ask, debate, and discuss; to explore such topics as sex, politics, religion and drugs; to discuss the morality of different kinds of work. I certainly don't think we should aim toward uniformity in the values of our children; we would fail if we tried. The nature of the new society itself demands variety, creativity, and individuality. We should be careful not to try to impose a homogenized, uniform value system, but that does not mean ducking the issue of values.

MORISSEAU: *You've said that the schools should pay more attention to interpersonal relationships, expose students to organizational variety, and deal more effectively with the issue of values. What other changes would you propose?*

TOFFLER: I would add two more suggestions. One is more attention to what happens outside the classroom. I believe much of what now happens in the classroom ought to be moved out into the community. We have experiments with this under way around the country, and I think they are on the whole very healthy.

Unlike previous societies, we live in a world that, through the interminable prolongation of adolescence, robs children and young people of the sense of being needed. In our well-intentioned hurry to spare children the misery of child labor, we have taken away the sense of being needed and replaced it with a lot of rhetoric about love and a lot of rhetoric that says, "You are going to be the leaders of the future."

In reality, the message to the child from most families and most schools is: "You are not needed." This is the most debilitating, crippling, painful message any human being can receive. We need to create a system that does not look on students as parasites—as they are frequently regarded by conservatives—or as investments—as they are viewed by liberals and the majority of educators. I prefer to look on students as neither parasities nor investments but as resources for the community.

MORISSEAU: *What sort of resources?*

TOFFLER: We have enormous problems in every community that are not being met by government or by the private sector. Whenever we ask why a problem—air pollution, noise, traffic congestion, or crime —is not being resolved, we are usually told we don't have the budget or the resources to solve it. And yet there are more than fifty million young people in our society, representing an enormous pool of imaginative, energetic, enthusiastic, but as yet relatively unskilled resources for helping us deal with some of these problems. I would like to move much of education into the community, with teams of young people working with community adults, as well as with faculty, on the whole range of neighborhood problems that are presently neglected due to "lack of resources."

And I would extend this idea to the elementary schools by selecting small tasks. We did this in a rudimentary way when we gave a handful of children Sam Browne belts and sent them out to direct traffic on school crosswalks. That was a very small start, but if we were imaginative about it, we could develop enormously enriching activities for elementary school children.

MORISSEAU: *What about education itself? Why not use students as teachers?*

TOFFLER: Absolutely—each one, teach one. Ironically, this is done both in Red China and in the U.S. military academies. It seems to me that the schools have missed a fantastic opportunity here.

MORISSEAU: *Yes, and I think it comes to grips with another problem. In the low income communities of this country, there is no visible career ladder, no organized way for the deprived to take the first steps toward a paraprofessional or professional career. Why not, then, let youngsters at age six start on their way toward a teaching career?*

TOFFLER: That makes so much sense. Simultaneously, it seems to me that the schools—and here I must be critical of the NEA and the teacher unions—through an overemphasis on professionalism, have been backward in taking advantage of community resources, adults who know things that children ought to know.

It seems to me that we could create a system of mentorships for any number of occupations—accounting, carpentry, or photography, to name a few—and recruit a list of community people in these occupations who are willing to sit down periodically with one child and demonstrate and discuss what they do. The value of this lies in the fact that inevitably they are not only going to talk about the occupation, but also about the world. It would serve as a great improvement in intergenerational communication, a "generational bridge," instead of the breakdown in communication we are now experiencing.

MORISSEAU: *From your vantage point, is the schoolhouse as we now know it going to survive? Is it going to be effective in housing the new education?*

TOFFLER: Most schools are built, physically, in a way that parallels the way they are organized. Both their physical shape and their organizational structure are essentially modeled after the factory. They are built for mass production in education. I believe the superindustrial revolution is going to change most of our assumptions about the way society ought to be organized. It is going to force a reevaluation of the notion that mass production equals economy. This is already having an impact on education; we are already beginning to move toward more individualization of instruction. We're experimenting with efforts, such as the voucher system, to break the lockstep of big city school systems. We are having struggles over community control, which is part of the battle to overthrow standardization.

I think all of this is eventually going to be reflected in new conceptions of architectural designs for schools. If we are not running groups of students through a mechanical process but, instead, paying attention to individual needs and individual schedules and teaching different things to different people, we obviously need a different kind of physical structure. Moreover, if we recognize that a great deal of learning can go on outside the classroom, perhaps we will realize that we need less in the way of physical structure—fewer seats and fewer "classrooms," if indeed that is what we will call them.

Now, I wouldn't go so far as to say that we will no longer have lectures or seminars, or that we will have no more need for classrooms. But the idea that the classroom is the heartland of education, that it is where education takes place, is absurd, and it's going to fall by the wayside. The day of the massive, factory style school is at its end. But it is hard to say what exactly will replace it.

We are not moving from one uniform system to another uniform system, but from a uniform system to a heterogeneous system. Therefore, there is no single answer to what the school of the future ought to look like. Maybe it ought to look like a local office, a local store, a world's fair, an automated factory, or a sports arena. There are different purposes to be served, and therefore different environments required for learning to take place.

MORISSEAU: *We have a prototype in Philadelphia, the Parkway*

School, where an insurance company, governmental offices, the courts, the museums, and the scientific institutions all serve as the "school-house."

TOFFLER: I would add one dimension to that. The idea of moving the school into the community and its existing institutions is an enormous forward step. It's probably administratively and architecturally inconvenient, but it is educationally highly sensible. The only cavil I have is that, while it is a very good way for students to learn about their present environment, it is still focused on the present society. I would like to see an emphasis on possible futures built into such a program.

MORISSEAU: *But doesn't that relate to the curriculum rather than the physical environment?*

TOFFLER: Yes, it certainly ought to be in the curriculum. But a student working in a government office and learning about governmental procedure, for example, ought to be exposed to a discussion of governmental operations of the future. And that discussion might include questions about the architectural requirements of future governmental operations. While it is difficult for us to actually create the physical environment of the future, we can imagine it and we can simulate some of it. We can represent it in physical form, through scale models and drawings. Indeed, through the use of sophisticated audiovisuals, we can even simulate the feeling of what it might be like to be in such a place.

At any rate, I think the schoolhouse is the last place in the world in which education is likely to be focused in the future.

FUTURISTICS:
CRYSTAL
BALL
FOR
CURRICULUM

(NATION'S SCHOOLS)

Nation's Schools is a magazine which is read by many administrators of public schools. That developments in futurism are reported on in Nation's Schools is indicative of the impact currently being made by study of the future. This article by the editorial staff of Nation's Schools reviews some approaches to futurism in American elementary and secondary schools.

Sixth-graders at the Fox School in Belmont, Calif., spend the day writing science fiction stories about purple monsters on Mars and the colonization of the moon. Their assignment: Describe your life in the 23rd Century.

In Melbourne, Fla., juniors and seniors come to class to find themselves "doubling up" with their classmates since half the desks in the room are roped off. The kids don't know it yet, but they're playing a "future theater game" about the effects of overpopulation.

Elementary school children in Amherst, Mass., design their future bodies—adding wings and extra legs—in a class called "genetic engineering." In Minneapolis, youngsters are building geodesic domes as part of a grand-scale plan for the "City of the Future."

What's all this about? In a word, futuristics—the study of the future. Until recently that activity was left pretty much to fortunetellers and science fiction writers. But no more. Now standing beside English and physics, futuristics has been accorded curricular status on many college campuses and "futures courses" are beginning to filter down to elementary and secondary classrooms as well.

Along with them comes a whole new set of tools for teachers, thanks to "think tanks" like the RAND Corporation and the Hudson Institute, and futurist thinkers like designer R. Buckminster Fuller and author Alvin Toffler. The tools—Delphi studies, scenarios, simulations, trend analyses—are unfamiliar to most educators now, but it seems likely that they won't be much longer if the current interest in futures courses continues to expand.

According to one expert, American elementary and secondary schools may be at approximately the same point reached by colleges and universities in 1968. At that time, a handful of teachers on various campuses were offering courses that focused on futuristic interests. The idea took hold fairly quickly in the colleges, and today more than a hundred postsecondary institutions, including Dartmouth, Stanford and the University of Massachusetts, now offer futures courses.

What does the typical course look like? There doesn't seem to be one at either the college or precollege level. One reason is that futures educators tend to stress the ecumenical nature of their field. Like history, they claim, futuristics can be applied to any part of the curriculum, indeed, to any area under the sun. Most frequently, however, the courses broach traditional subjects in a future-oriented manner, a manner which talks about the future of a given area—say politics in the year 2,000—and how students in the present can help shape the style and course of politics in that not-too-distant time. More than any other single aim, futuristics attempts to get youngsters to develop *a way of thinking* which will help them look beyond today and *anticipate* what they may be faced with tomorrow.

THINKING ABOUT THE UNTHINKABLE

If the idea sounds far-out, it really isn't anymore. Since the days of Sputnik, scholars and scientists have been developing a style of thinking which would facilitate looking into tomorrow. An entire literature has grown up encompassing close to a thousand books and essays which deal with the theme of predicting the future. The authors include some highly respected schoolmen: David Riesman, Erik H. Erikson, Daniel Bell, Robert Heilbroner.

In the non-academic world there has been considerable activity as well. The federal government, for one, has backed futuristic "think tanks" like the RAND Corporation of Santa Monica, Calif., and the Hudson Institute in New York State for several years. These firms both focus on forecasting in attempting to assess some highly crucial questions for Washington: What is the likelihood of nuclear war? Can man survive nuclear fallout? What would life be like in a post World War III society?

The popular media hasn't neglected the subject either. Consider the success of Toffler's *Future Shock* or the popularity of Ray Bradbury and Robert Heinlein's science fiction. Or the movies, *2,001: A Space Odyssey, The Andromeda Strain,* or *Dr. Strangelove.*

As futures expert Billy Rojas points out in a recent article,[1] all of this activity is only an effect, not the cause, of a deepening interest in academic futuristics. Most compelling cause is the perception of many people that tomorrow's individual will have to develop increased amounts of "cope-ability"—to deal with change even more hectic than the change we know today. The faster the rate of change, the more attention must be paid to discerning the pattern of future events. What kinds of jobs will be needed five, ten, twenty years from now? What

[1] Rojas, Billy. "The Meaning of Futuristics," *World Order*, Fall, 1970 (published by the National Spiritual Order of the Bahais of the U.S., 2011 Yale Station, New Haven, Conn. 06520).

Delphi

Numbers indicate percent of date estimations

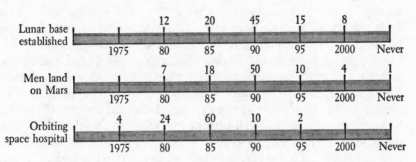

Distribution of responses from a panel of experts is believed to give a more reliable guide to future events than trust in any single source. Shown above are Delphi questions.

Trend Extrapolation

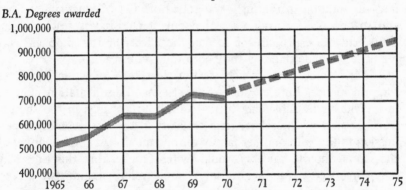

Extrapolating the mean of fluctuations of past data is the method used by many forecasters. Some teachers use the same technique in their futuristics classes.

kinds of family relationships will we live with? What kinds of technology will shape our lives? What kinds of political and social institutions will we create?

Of course no one knows the answers to these questions. Unlike Nostradamus or any latter-day prognosticators, futurists don't claim any special foreknowledge. What they do claim, along with English novelist John Galsworthy, is that "if you don't think about the future, you can't have one"—at least not one over which you feel any measure of control. Futurist educators ask: "Do we want students to be able to face the future intelligently, with 'cope-ability' and some feeling of purpose and control?" If the answer is yes, then schools have to deal with the future now.

FUTURISTICS IN THE CLASSROOM

How are elementary and secondary schools handling futuristics? One approach, which some educators have dubbed the "Toffler style," was designed for a "21st Century course" at Melbourne High School in Melbourne, Florida. The author of *Future Shock* served as chief consultant for the course, developed simulation games, and pulled together a variety of materials, including magazine articles, science fiction stories, nonfiction books and contemporary novels, and films for the class to study. [The *Nation's Schools* article included a course outline and bibliography—Ed. note] In all parts of the course, the teacher attempted to use scientific thinking to extrapolate trends or draw analogies with the past to predict the future. A good deal of time was spent playing "future theater games" to illustrate the idea of possible futures.

In the population game designed by Toffler, youngsters came to class on Monday to find one row of desks roped off, supposedly for repair work. The students were forced to double up. On Tuesday another row—in addition to the first—was roped off. On Wednesday, another and so on until by Friday a real population crisis was reached. Students had the experience of feeling the effects of this problem as a requisite for understanding the books they were reading.

Another Toffler game, which was not played at Melbourne, illustrates the principle of "Future Shock"—the stress and disorientation induced in individuals by subjecting them to too much change in too short a time. At start of the school term students in the class would get permission to live with another family for one month. At the beginning of the second month, students would switch families, but this time stay only three weeks. Another turnover would follow, lasting two weeks. Each stay would be proportionally reduced in length so that at the end of the term each student would spend three, then two, then one day with a different family. Students would not only read about "Future Shock" they'd feel it and hopefully find a way to deal with it which they could then discuss with their classmates. Admittedly, the "games" don't sound like much fun, but both are intended to motivate serious thinking and study.

Another approach involves not an entire course, but brief units built around a future theme. One effort along these lines was a project at the Mark Meadows Elementary School in Amherst, Mass., designed by teacher Patricia Bourke. First through sixth-graders were introduced to the concept of genetic engineering—the idea that at some time we may be able to redesign parts of our bodies to suit individual needs and preferences. Aim of the project was to get students to grasp the relationship between a study of the achievements and potentialities of biological science and their lives.

SCIENCE FICTION STUDIES

Science fiction is being used by a number of elementary and secondary teachers to look at future societal and technological alternatives. A sample effort is a weekly class for sixth-graders at the Fox School in Belmont, Calif. Teacher Judi Driessel and her class discussed seven different types of science fiction, including works dealing with science and technology, future inventions, and the social sciences (1984 by George Orwell). One guest lecturer was a science fiction instructor at Stanford University. Along with the reading, the class was given certain problems to talk about. For example: What would you do right now if you walked out of school and saw a giant blob of protoplasm? Or, if man no longer contracted cancer, what might be the social consequences? Final assignment for the class: "Pretend you found yourself in the 23rd century. Write a letter to your parents explaining how you arrived there and what your life is like now."

In other approaches, teachers try to involve pupils in creating futuristic models and environments. In Minneapolis and Berkeley, Calif., schools, youngsters spent a term trying to design a "city of the future" during which they got the chance to work with geodesic domes and other modern architectural forms. In some classes, students work with a variety of activity-oriented learning experiences—cooking their own macrobiotic lunches for example. On "Media Day" in a Minneapolis high school, students explored the future of communications. Youngsters were asked to communicate with each other by using only portable TV units, Polaroid cameras, and tape recorders.

These are only a few of the current experiments in futuristics.[2] To pull together the work teachers all over the country are doing in this area and to provide a resource and training center for elementary and secondary educators, the program for the Study of the Future in Education was set up at the University of Massachusetts in July 1969. At present the program offers both undergraduate and postgraduate level courses to help teachers "futurize" classroom work.

According to program director Chris Dede, the broad aim of the teacher training is to offer instructors a "content-free process" for getting a group of students to think about: the future potentialities of a given subject; what future they would like to see emerge; and how they can affect its emergence.

Implicit in this process—and a point which teachers are asked to press with students—is the idea that it is within the power of people

[2] For more information about curriculum experiments in futuristics, schoolmen should take a look at the Spring, 1971 issue of TREND magazine published by the Cooperative School Service at the University of Massachusetts. Copies can be purchased for $1.50 or $1.00 when two or more are ordered. Available from: Nathaniel S. French, Managing Editor, School of Education, University of Massachusetts, Amherst, Mass. 01002.

who are alive at this moment to *choose* the kind of future they want. How? By doing what modern government and industry have been trying to do for many years: to plan for the future and to base these plans on realistic appraisals of tomorrow's world.

Teachers are introduced to the following techniques, used by professional futurists, which they can modify according to their own preferences for classroom use.

DELPHI TECHNIQUE

Developed by the RAND Corporation, the Delphi has been used by government and industry for a number of activities, including forecasting, long-range planning, and decision-making. Basically, the Delphi is a questionnaire. When futurists use it, each question asks when (what year) the respondent thinks a particular event will take place, if he thinks it will take place at all. Delphi rests on the assumption that a panel of experts, say a group of top aerospace engineers, can reach an accurate consensus on the time range within which a given event (*e.g.* the exploration of Mars) will occur in the future. Results from the first questionnaires are tabulated and sent back to the experts so that during the second polling or the third their answers will tend to converge. Futurists then design a set of alternative futures on the basis of the probable date. Naturally the time range the experts arrive at is only as accurate as their ability to predict the future, but the distribution of responses from a panel is believed to give a more reliable guide to events than trust in one source.

The technique is a simple one to modify for the classroom with any content the teacher deems appropriate. In fact, Dede claims, one of the reasons why the Delphi has been widely touted is not because it's so good, but because it's so simple to use. At the University of Massachusetts where the teachers learn futurist techniques by using them just as their students will, questionnaires are distributed in class, the mean and median of the first poll results are computed and then passed back to the class. The second and third rounds include asking people who are at the end points of the continuum their reasons for their answers. This generates a lot of discussion almost immediately, Dede points out, because there are, of course, no *right* answers. One answer may seem better than another because it sounds more reasonable.

"Whatever its shortcomings as a forecasting tool," says Dede, "the Delphi is a good introductory technique because it gets people talking about the future and sharing their perceptions."

Teachers have gone on to use the Delphi in classroom settings that range from a "World Problems" course for high school seniors to elementary science and social studies classes in which very young children were given a list of provocative questions (How old will you be when people get all their food from the ocean? When the U.S. has a Secretary of Peace?) and asked to compare answers with others.

FUTURE "HISTORIES"

The "scenario" is the device most often used by professional futurists to design alternative futures and teachers in the U. Mass. program use it in exactly the same way. A scenario is a narrative that combines the future with a history leading up to it. The writer begins by describing the future state of *x* (say, urban education in 1990). He then tries to construct a probable history of the evolution of the current state of big city schools to his future state.

If the history he writes sounds rational and probable, the future state he has constructed is also probable. Generally, professional futurists construct a whole series of scenarios in which they try to exhaust all of the likely futures for *x*, taking into account all the factors in the present they possibly can. Scenario writing is the most famous of the techniques developed by Herman Kahn, the key figure at the Hudson Institute, to enable futures researchers to predict, with some degree of sophistication, alternative futures and ways to deal with them.

In the classroom, scenarios can provide a good stimulus for students to unshackle their imaginations and project their own visions of the future on paper. At this point, teachers can help them to make the distinction between desirable futures and probable futures, and, hopefully, get them to think about what must be done to make the desirable future emerge. U. Mass. instructors feel that the exercise involved in scenario writing—concentration on developing and organizing a sequence of events, each shaped by the one preceding it—can be helpful in giving students a feeling of control over their own personal futures as well. A number of teachers are trying out the technique in history and social studies, and at least one teacher has reported some success in using the scenario as a chance to motivate disadvantaged youngsters —by getting them to consider alternative possibilities in their own lives.

TREND ANALYSIS

This technique asks students to identify trends in a given area, then project them into the future. By extrapolating several trends, relying on their own knowledge and appropriate data, students can also construct probable futures. Then the class can turn to comparing again the desirable future with the one they've arrived at on the graph. From this point they work back to the scenario approach to talk about what needs to be done in the present to shift probable futures to desirable futures.

A host of other techniques, including computer and gaming simulations, are in the works now at the U. Mass. and other centers of activity. The goal, says Dede, is to make these approaches easily accessible to teachers who could then use them without needing any special training or expertise.

To help educators right now who want to learn about futuristics, the program has developed a number of resources of value to the classroom teacher. These include a comprehensive Future Studies Bibliography, a Future Studies Directory listing many futures organizations and professional futurists. The program has also developed a Future Studies Newsletter which would inform readers about promising innovations in the field, new literature and the like.

Thus far, there are no commercial future curriculum units on the market, but the proliferation of books, films and magazine articles on the subject, plus available simulation games, can provide an imaginative teacher with resources enough.

Clearly, the study of the future need not be an esoteric goal that only the initiates can pursue. Instead, it can be used by schoolmen both inside and outside the classroom to reorient education towards a future perspective—a future they can help to mold. Futurists prod educators to consider that, in our rapidly changing society, such a reorientation may well be a necessity for survival.

YOUTH REVOLT: THE FUTURE IS NOW

MARGARET MEAD

The indefatigable Margaret Mead is a distinguished anthropologist and an effective mediator between young and old. This selection is an overview of her recent book, Culture and Commitment: A Study of the Generation Gap. *Unlike the futurists, Mead believes that the emerging prefigurative future is unknown and unknowable, and thus stresses questing for answers to questions only the young can raise in a future which is already upon us. In Mead's view, there are no guides for the new immigrants in time.*

Margaret Mead is the author of many books in anthropology. She has served as curator of ethnology for the American Museum of Natural History and has been chairman of the social sciences division of Fordham University and a professor of anthropology at both Columbia and Fordham Universities. Recently she published a volume of autobiography, Blackberry Winter.

Our present crisis has been variously attributed to the overwhelming rapidity of change, the collapse of the family, the decay of capitalism, the triumph of a soulless technology, and, in wholesale repudiation, to the final breakdown of the Establishment. Behind these attributions there is a more basic conflict between those for whom the present represents no more than an intensification of our existing cofigurative culture, in which peers are more than ever replacing parents as the significant models of behavior, and those who contend that we are in fact entertaining a totally new phase of cultural evolution.

Most commentators, in spite of their differences in viewpoint, still see the future essentially as an extension of the past. Edward Teller can still speak of the outcome of a nuclear war as a state of destruction relatively no more drastic than the ravages wrought by Genghis Khan, and historians can point out that time and again civilization has survived the crumbling of empires. Similarly, many authorities treat as no more than an extreme form of adolescent rebellion the repudiation of present and past by the dissident youth of every persuasion in every kind of society in the world.

Theorists who emphasize the parallels between past and present in their interpretations of the generation gap ignore the irreversibility of

Reprinted from *Saturday Review*, Jan. 10, 1970, pages 23–25, 113. "Youth Revolt: The Future Is Now" copyright © 1970 by Margaret Mead from the book *Culture and Commitment*. Reprinted by permission of Doubleday & Company, Inc.

the changes that have taken place since the beginning of the Industrial Revolution. This is especially striking in their handling of modern technological development, which they treat as comparable in its effects to the changes that occurred as one civilization in the past took over from another such techniques as agriculture, script, navigation, or the organization of labor and law.

One urgent priority, I believe, is to examine the nature of change in the modern world, including its speed and dimensions, so that we can better understand the distinctions that must be made between change in the past and that which is now ongoing. To do so, I make distinctions among three different kinds of culture: *post-figurative*, in which children learn primarily from their forebears; *cofigurative*, in which both children and adults learn from their peers; and *prefigurative*, in which adults learn also from their children.

Although it is possible to discuss both post-figurative and cofigurative cultures in terms of slow or rapid change without specifying the nature of the process and to compare past and present situations when the focus is kept on generation relationships and on the type of modeling through which a culture is transmitted, it is only when one specifies the nature of the process that the contrast between past and present change becomes clear.

The primary evidence that our present situation is unique, without any parallel in the past, is that the generation gap is world-wide. The particular events taking place in England, Pakistan, the United States, New Guinea, or elsewhere are not enough to explain the unrest that is stirring modern youth everywhere. Recent technological change or the handicaps imposed by its absence, revolution or the suppression of revolutionary activities, the crumbling of faith in ancient creeds or the attraction of new creeds—all these serve only as partial explanations of the particular forms taken by youth revolt in different countries.

Concentration on particularities can only hinder the search for an explanatory principle. Instead, it is necessary to strip the occurrences in each country of their superficial, national, and immediately temporal aspects. The desire for a liberated form of communism in Czechoslovakia, the search for "racial" equality in the United States, the desire to liberate Japan from American military influence—these are particularistic forms. Youthful activism is common to them all. The key question is this: What are the new conditions that have brought about the revolt of youth around the world?

The first of these is the emergence of a world community. For the first time human beings throughout the world, in their information about and responses to one another, have become a community that is united by shared knowledge and danger. As far as we know, no such single, interacting community has existed within archaeological time. The largest clusters of interacting human groups have always been fragments of a still larger unknown whole, and the idea that all men are, in the same sense, human beings always has been either unreal or a mystical belief.

The events of the past twenty-five years changed this drastically. Exploration has been complete enough to convince us that there are no humanoid types on the planet except our own species. World-wide air travel and globe-encircling TV satellites have turned us into one community, in which events taking place on one side of the earth become immediately and simultaneously available to peoples everywhere else. No artist or political censor has time to intervene and edit as a leader is shot or a flag is planted on the moon. The world is a community, though it still lacks the forms of organization and the sanctions by which a political community can be governed.

Men who are the carriers of vastly different cultural traditions are entering the present at the same point in time. It is as if, all around the world, men were converging on identical immigration posts, each with its identifying sign: YOU ARE NOW ABOUT TO ENTER THE POST-WORLD-WAR-II WORLD AT GATE 1 (GATE 23, etc.). Whoever they are and wherever their particular points of entry may be, all men are equally immigrants into the new era. They are like the immigrants who came as pioneers to a new land, lacking all knowledge of what demands new conditions of life would make upon them. Those who came later could take their peer groups as models. But among the first comers, the young adults had as models only their own tentative adaptations and innovations.

Today, everyone born and bred before World War II is such an immigrant in time as his forebears were in space—a pioneer struggling to grapple with the unfamiliar conditions of life in a new era. Like all immigrants and pioneers, these immigrants in time are the bearers of older cultures, but today they represent all the cultures of the world. And all of them, whether they are sophisticated French intellectuals or members of a remote New Guinea tribe, land-bound peasants in Haiti or nuclear physicists, have certain characteristics in common.

Whoever they are, these immigrants grew up under skies across which no satellite had ever flashed. Their perception of the past was an edited version of what had happened. Their perception of the immediate present was limited to what they could take in through their own eyes and ears and to the edited versions of other men's sensory experience and memories. Their conception of the future was essentially one in which change was incorporated into a deeper changelessness. The industrialist or military planner, envisaging what a computer, not yet constructed, might make possible, treated it as another addition to the repertoire of inventions that have enhanced man's skills. It expanded what men could do, but did not change the future.

When the first atom bomb was exploded at the end of World

War II, only a few individuals realized that all humanity was entering a new age. And to this day the majority of those over twenty-five have failed to grasp emotionally, however well they may grasp intellectually, the difference between any war in which, no matter how terrible the casualties, mankind will survive, and one in which there will be no survivors. They continue to think that a war, fought with more lethal weapons, would just be a worse war. Our thinking still binds us to the past—to the world as it existed in our childhood and youth.

We still hold the seats of power and command the resources and the skills necessary to keep order and organize the kinds of societies we know about. We control the educational systems, the apprenticeship systems, the career ladders up which the young must climb. Nevertheless, we have passed the point of no return. We are committed to life in an unfamiliar setting; we are making do with what we know.

The young generation, however—the articulate young rebels all around the world who are lashing out against the controls to which they are subjected—are like the first generation born into a new country. They are at home in this time. Satellites are familiar in their skies. They have never known a time when war did not threaten annihilation. When they are given the facts, they can understand immediately that continued pollution of the air and water and soil will soon make the planet uninhabitable and that it will be impossible to feed an indefinitely expanding world population. As members of one species in an underdeveloped world community they recognize that invidious distinctions based on race and caste are anachronisms. They insist on the vital necessity of some form of world order.

No longer bound by the simplified linear sequences dictated by the printed word, they live in a world in which events are presented to them in all their complex immediacy. In their eyes the killing of an enemy is not qualitatively different from the murder of a neighbor. They cannot reconcile our efforts to save our own children by every known means with our readiness to destroy the children of others with napalm. They know that the people of one nation alone cannot save their own children; each holds the responsibility for all others' children.

Although I have said they *know* these things, perhaps I should say that this is how they *feel*. Like the first generation born in a new country, they listen only half-comprehendingly to their parents' talk about the past. For as the children of pioneers had no access to the landscapes whose memories could still move their parents to tears, the young today cannot share their parents' responses to events that deeply moved them in the past. But this is not all that separates the young from their elders. Watching, they can see that their elders are groping, that they are managing clumsily and often unsuccessfully the tasks imposed on them by the new conditions. The young do not know what must be done, but they feel that there must be a better way and that they must find it.

Today, nowhere in the world are there elders who know what the children know, no matter how remote and simple the societies are in which the children live. In the past there were always some elders who knew more than any children in terms of their experience of having grown up within a cultural system. Today there are none. It is not only that parents are no longer guides, but that there are no guides, whether one seeks them in one's own country or abroad. There are no elders who know what those who have been reared within the last twenty years know about the world into which they were born.

True, in many parts of the world the parental generation still lives by a post-figurative set of values. From parents in such cultures children may learn that there have been unquestioned absolutes, and this learning may carry over into later experience as an expectation that absolute values can and should be re-established.

There are still parents who answer such child's questions as why he must go to bed, or eat his vegetables, or learn to read with simple assertions: Because it is *right* to do so, because *God* says so, or because *I* say so. These parents are preparing the way for the re-establishment of post-figurative elements in the culture. But these elements will be far more rigid and intractable than in the past because they must be defended in a world in which conflicting points of view, rather than orthodoxies, are prevalent.

Most parents, however, are too uncertain to assert old dogmatisms. They do not know how to teach these children who are so different from what they themselves once were, and most children are unable to learn from parents and elders they will never resemble. In the past, in the United States, children of immigrant parents pleaded with them not to speak their foreign language in public and not to wear their outlandish foreign clothes. They knew the burning shame of being, at the same time, unable to repudiate their parents and unable to accept simply and naturally their way of speaking and doing things. But in time they learned to find new teachers as guides, to model their behavior on that of more adapted age mates, and to slip in, unnoticed, among a group whose parents were more bearable.

Today, the dissident young discover very rapidly that this solution is no longer possible. The breach between themselves and their parents also exists between their friends and their friends' parents and between their friends and their teachers.

These young dissidents realize the critical need for immediate world action on problems that affect the whole world. What they want is, in some way, to begin all over again. They are ready to make way for something new by a kind of social bulldozing—like the bulldozing in which every tree and feature of the landscape is destroyed to make way for a new community. Awareness of the reality of the crisis (which is, in fact, perceived most accurately not by the young, but by their discerning and prophetic elders) and the sense the young have that their elders do not understand the modern world, because they do not understand their children, has produced a kind of rebellion in which planned reformation of the present system is almost inconceivable.

Nevertheless, those who have no power also have no routes to power except through those against whom they are rebelling. In the end, it was men who gave the vote to women; and it will be the House of Lords that votes to abolish the House of Lords—as also, in the final analysis, nations will act to limit national sovereignty. Effective, rapid evolutionary change, in which no one is guillotined or forced into exile, depends on the co-operation of a large number of those in power with the dispossessed who are seeking power.

These, in brief, are the conditions of our time. These are the two generations—pioneers in a new era and their children—who have as yet to find a way of communicating about the world in which both live, though their perceptions of it are so different. No one knows what the next steps should be. Recognizing that this is so is, I submit, the beginning of an answer.

I believe we are on the verge of developing a new kind of culture, one that is as much a departure in style from cofigurative cultures as the institutionalization of cofiguration in orderly—and disorderly—change was a departure from the post-figurative style. I call this new style "prefigurative," because in this new culture it will be the unborn child, already conceived but still in the womb—not the parent and grandparent—that represents what is to come. This is a child whose sex and appearance and capabilities are unknown, but who will need imaginative, innovative, and dedicated adult care far beyond any we give today.

No one can know in advance what the child will become—how swift his limbs will be, what will delight his eye, whether his tempo will be fast or slow. No one can know how his mind will work—whether he will learn best from sight or sound or touch or movement. But knowing what we do not know and cannot predict, we can construct an environment in which a child, still unknown, can be safe and can grow and discover himself and the world.

Love and trust, based on dependency and answering care, made it possible for the individual who had been reared in one culture to move into another, transforming, without destroying, his earlier learning. It is seldom the first generation of voluntary immigrants and pioneers who cannot meet the demands of a new environment. Their previous learning carries them through. But unless they embody what is new post-figuratively, they cannot pass on to their children what they had acquired through their own early training—the ability to learn from others the things their parents could not teach them.

Parents, in a world where there are no more knowledgeable others to whom they can commit the children they themselves cannot teach, feel uncertain and helpless. Still believing that there should be answers, parents ask how they can tell their children what is right. So some try to solve the problem by advising their children, very vaguely, that they will have to figure it out for themselves. And some parents ask what the others are doing. But this resource of a cofigurative culture is becoming meaningless to parents who feel that the "others"—their children's age mates—are moving in ways that are unsafe for their own children to emulate, and who find that they do not understand what their children figure out for themselves.

It is the adults who still believe that there is a safe and socially approved road to a kind of life they have not experienced who react with the greatest anger and bitterness to the discovery that what they had hoped for no longer exists for their children. These are the parents, the trustees, the legislators, the columnists and commentators who denounce most vocally what is happening in schools and colleges and universities in which they had placed their hopes for their children.

Today, as we gain a better understanding of the circular processes through which culture is developed and transmitted, we recognize that man's most human characteristic is not his ability to learn, which he shares with many other species, but his ability to teach and store what others have developed and taught him. In the past men relied on the least elaborate part of the circular system—the dependent learning by children—for continuity of transmission and for the embodiment of the new. Now, with our greater understanding of the process, we must cultivate the most flexible and complex part of the system: the behavior of adults. We must, in fact, teach ourselves how to alter adult behavior; we must create new models for adults who can teach their children not what to learn, but how to learn, and not what they should be committed to, but the value of commitment.

In doing this we must recognize explicitly that the paths by which we came into the present can never be traversed again. The past is the road by which we have arrived where we are. Older forms of culture have provided us with the knowledge, techniques, and tools necessary for our contemporary civilization.

The freeing of men's imagination from the past depends on the development of a new kind of communication with those who are most deeply involved with the future—the young who were born in the new world. In the past, in cofigurational cultures, the elders were gradually cut off from limiting the future of their children. Now the development of prefigurational cultures will depend on the existence of a continuing dialogue in which the young, free to act on their own initiative, can lead their elders in the direction of the unknown. Then the older generation will have access to the new experiential knowledge, without which no meaningful plans can be made. It is only with the direct participation of the young, who have that knowledge, that we can build a viable future.

Instead of directing their rebellion toward the retrieval of a grand-parental utopian dream, as the Maoists seem to be doing with the young activists in China, we must learn together with the young how to take the next steps. Out of their new knowledge—new to the world and new to us—must come the questions to those who are already equipped by education and experience to search for answers. The children, the young, must ask these questions that we would never think to ask, but enough trust must be re-established so that the elders will be permitted to work with them on the answers.

I feel that we can change into a prefigurative culture, consciously, delightedly, and industriously, rearing unknown children for an unknown world. But to do it we must relocate the future.

Here we can take a cue from the young who seem to want instant utopias. They say the future is now. This seems unreasonable and impetuous, and in some of the demands they make it is unrealizable in concrete detail; but here again, I think, they give us the way to reshape our thinking. We must place the future, like the unborn child in the womb of a woman, within a community of men, women, and children, among us, already here, already to be nourished and succored and protected, already in need of things for which, if they are not prepared before it is born, it will be too late. So, as the young say, the future is now.

INTERPERSONAL RELATIONSHIPS: U.S.A. 2000

CARL R. ROGERS

Carl R. Rogers is a distinguished psychologist and a pioneer in the development of open interpersonal relationships. In this article, based on his contribution to a symposium entitled "USA 2000," sponsored by the Esalen Institute, Rogers hopefully stresses the promise inherent in intensive group experiences for the realization of future interpersonal relationships. He presents a "new picture of man—this flowing, changing, open, expressive, creative person."

Rogers, a former president of the American Psychological Association and a guiding force in client-centered therapy, psychotherapy, and study of personality, is now a member of the Center for Studies of the Person in La Jolla, California.

I want to make it very clear at the outset that I am not making predictions about the year 2000. I am going to sketch possibilities, alternative routes which we may travel.

One important reason for refusing to make predictions is that for the first time in history man is not only taking his future seriously, but he also has adequate technology and power to shape and form that culture. He is endeavoring to *choose* his future rather than simply living out some inevitable trend. And we do not know what he will choose. So we do not know what man's relation to man will be in this country thirty-two years from now. But we can see certain possibilities.

MAN'S GREATEST PROBLEM

Before I try to sketch some of those possibilities, I should like to point to the greatest problem which man faces in the years to come. It is not the hydrogen bomb, fearful as that may be. It is not the population explosion, though the consequences of that are awful to contemplate. It is instead a problem which is rarely mentioned or discussed. It is the question of how much change the human being can accept, absorb, and assimilate, and the rate at which he can take it. Can he keep up with the ever increasing rate of technological change, or is there some point at which the human organism goes to pieces? Can he leave the static ways and static guidelines which have dominated all of his history and adopt the process ways, the continual changingness which must be his if he is to survive?

There is much to make us pessimistic about this. If we consider

the incredible difficulties in bringing about change in our great bureaucracies of government, education, and religion, we become hopeless.
When we see how frequently the people take action which is clearly
against their long-range welfare—such as the resolute refusal to face
up to the problem of the urban ghettos—we become discouraged.

But I see two elements on the other side of the balance. The first
is the ability of the Western democratic cultures to respond appropriately—at the very last cliff-hanging moment—to those trends which
challenge their survival.

The second element I have observed in individuals in therapy, in
intensive encounter groups, and in organizations. It is the magnetic
attraction of the experience of change, growth, fulfillment. Even
though growth may involve intense pain and suffering, once the individual or group has tasted the excitement of this changingness, persons
are drawn to it as to a magnet. Once a degree of actualization has
been savored, the individual or the group is willing to take the
frightening risk of launching out into a world of process, with a few
fixed landmarks, where the direction is guided from within. So, in this
field of interpersonal relations, though there is much reason for despair,
I believe that if our citizens experience something of the pain and risk
of a growth toward personal enrichment they will grasp for more.

With this context of uncertainty about our ability or willingness to
assimilate change, let us look at some specific areas of interpersonal
relationships.

URBAN CROWDING AND ITS POSSIBLE EFFECTS

The world population will more than double in the next thirty-two
years, a ghastly trend which will affect us in unknown ways. The population of the United States, which was comfortably remembered in my
grammar school days in 1915 as 100 million, fifty-two years later
reached 200 million, twenty-two years from now is predicted to reach
300 million, and in the year 2000 will be between 320 and 340 million,
though hopefully it will be starting to stabilize itself at about that time.
The great bulk of these millions will reside in a great megalopolis, of
which there will probably be three. One trend which we may follow
is to crowd more and more closely together, as we are now crowded
in our ghettos. I understand that Philip Hauser, the noted demog-
rapher, has stated that if all of us were crowded together as closely
as the residents of Harlem, all of the people in the entire United States
could be contained in the five boroughs of New York City. The future
may resemble this, if we choose to push in more and more closely
together.

Such crowding has consequences. Even in rats, as Calhoun[1] has so

[1] J. B. Calhoun, "Population Density and Social Pathology," *Scientific American*, 206,
2 (1962), 139–50.

vividly shown, overcrowding results in poor mothering, poor nest building, bizarre sexual behavior, cannibalism, and complete alienation, with some rats behaving like zombies, paying no attention to others, coming out of their solitary burrows only for food. The resemblance to human behavior in crowded rooming house areas, the complete lack of involvement which permits people to watch a long-drawn-out murder without so much as calling the police, the poor family relationships—this could be a trend which will be carried even further by the year 2000.

On the other hand, we could learn to decentralize our great urban areas, to make them manageable, to provide not only for more efficiency but for warmer and more human interpersonal relationships. We could use more space, build smaller cities with great park and garden areas, devise plans for neighborhood building which would promote humanization, not dehumanization. What will the choice be?

CLOSENESS AND INTIMACY IN THE YEAR 2000

In my estimation, one of the most rapidly growing social phenomena in the United States is the spread of the intensive group experience— sensitivity training, basic encounter groups, T groups (the labels are unimportant). The growth of this phenomenon is rendered more striking when one realizes that it is a "grass roots" movement. There is not a university nor a foundation nor a government agency which has given it any significant approval or support until the last five or six years. Yet it has permeated industry, is coming into education, and is reaching families, professionals in the helping fields, and many other individuals. Why? I believe it is because people—ordinary people— have discovered that it alleviates their loneliness and permits them to grow, to risk, to change. It brings persons into real relationships with persons.

In our affluent society the individual's survival needs are satisfied. For the first time, he is freed to become aware of his isolation, aware of his alienation, aware of the fact that he is, during most of his life, a role interacting with other roles, a mask meeting other masks. And for the first time he is aware that this is not a *necessary* tragedy of life, that he does not have to live out his days in this fashion. So he is seeking, with great determination and inventiveness, ways of modifying this existential loneliness. The intensive group experience, perhaps the most significant social invention of this century, is an important one of these ways.

What will grow out of the current use of basic encounter groups, marathons, "labs," and the like? I have no idea what *forms* will proliferate out of these roots during the coming decades, but I believe men will discover new bases of intimacy that will be highly fulfilling. I

believe there will be possibilities for the *rapid* development of closeness between and among persons, a closeness which is not artificial, but
is real and deep, and which will be well suited to our increasing mobility of living. Temporary relationships will be able to achieve the
richness and meaning which heretofore have been associated only
with lifelong attachments.

There will be more awareness of what is going on within the person,
an openness to all of one's experience—the sensory input of sound and
taste and hearing and sight and smell, the richness of kaleidoscopically
changing ideas and concepts, the wealth of feelings—positive, negative,
and ambivalent, intense and moderate—toward oneself and toward
others.

There will be the development of a whole new style of communication in which the person can, in effect, say, "I'm telling you the way
it *is*, in me—my ideas, my desires, my feelings, my hopes, my angers,
my fears, my despairs," and where the response will be equally open.
We shall be experimenting with ways in which a whole person can
communicate himself to another whole person. We shall discover that
security resides not in hiding oneself but in being more fully known, and
consequently in coming to know the other more fully. Aloneness will
be something one chooses out of a desire for privacy, not an isolation
into which one is forced.

In all of this I believe we shall be experimenting with a new ideal
of what man may become, a model very *sharply* different from the
historical view of man as a creature playing various appropriate roles.
We seem to be aiming for a new *reality* in relationships, a new openness in communication, a love for one another which grows not out of
a romantic blindness but out of the profound respect which is nearly
always engendered by reality in relationships.

I recognize that many individuals in our culture are frightened in
the depths of their being by this new picture of man—this flowing,
changing, open, expressive, creative person. They may be able to stop
the trend or even to reverse it. It is conceivable that we shall go in for
the manufactured "image" as on television, or may insist more strongly
than ever that teachers are *teachers*, parents are *parents*, bosses are
manipulators—that we may rigidify every role and stereotype in new
and more armorplated ways. We may insist with new force that the
only significant aspect of man is his rational and intellectual being and
that nothing else matters. We may assert that he is a machine and no
more. Yet I do not believe this will happen. The magnetism of the
new man, toward which we are groping, is too great. Much of what I
say in the remainder of this paper is based on the conviction that
we are, for better or for worse, in labor pains and growth pains, turning
toward this new view of man as becoming and being—a continuing,
growing *process*. . . .

LEARNING IN INTERPERSONAL RELATIONSHIPS

What of education in the year 2000, especially as it involves interpersonal relationships? It is possible that education will continue much as it is—concerned only with words, symbols, rational concepts based on the authoritative role of the teacher, further dehumanized by teaching machines, computerized knowledge, and increased use of tests and examinations. This is possible, because educators are showing greater resistance to change than any other institutional group. Yet I regard it as unlikely, because a revolution in education is long overdue, and the unrest of students is only one sign of this. So I am going to speculate on some of the other possibilities.

It seems likely that schools will be greatly deemphasized in favor of a much broader, thoughtfully devised *environment for learning*, where the experiences of the student will be challenging, rewarding, affirmative, and pleasurable.

The teacher or professor will have largely disappeared. His place will be taken by a facilitator of learning, chosen for his facilitative attitudes as much as for his knowledge. He will be skilled in stimulating individual and group initiative in learning, skilled in facilitating discussions-in-depth of the *meaning* to the student of what is being learned, skilled in fostering creativity, skilled in providing the resources for learning. Among these resources will be much in the way of programmed learning, to be used as the student finds these learnings appropriate; much in the way of audiovisual aids such as filmed lectures and demonstrations by experts in each field; much in the way of computerized knowledge on which the student can draw. But these "hardware" possibilities are not my main concern.

We shall, I believe, see the facilitator focusing his major attention on the prime period for learning—from infancy to age six or eight. Among the most important learnings will be the personal and interpersonal. Every child will develop confidence in his own ability to learn, since he will be rewarded for learning at his own pace. Each child will learn that he is a person of worth, because he has unique and worthwhile capacities. He will learn how to be himself in a group —to listen, but also to speak, to learn about himself, but also to confront and give feedback to others. He will learn to be an individual, not a faceless conformist. He will learn, through simulations and computerized games, to meet many of the life problems he will face. He will find it permissible to engage in fantasy and daydreams, to think creative thoughts, to capture these in words or paints or constructions. He will find that learning, even difficult learning, is fun, both as an individual activity and in cooperation with others. His discipline will be self-discipline.

His learning will not be confined to the ancient intellectual concepts and specializations. It will not be a *preparation* for living. It will be, in itself, an *experience* in living. Feelings of inadequacy, hatred, a desire for power, feelings of love and awe and respect, feelings of fear and dread, unhappiness with parents or with other children—all these will be an open part of his curriculum, as worthy of exploration as history or mathematics. In fact this openness to feelings will enable him to learn content material more readily. His will be an education in becoming a whole human being, and the learnings will involve him deeply, openly, exploringly, in an awareness of his relationship to the world of others, as well as in an awareness of the world of abstract knowledge.

Because learning has been exciting, because he has participated heavily and responsibly in choosing the directions of his learning, because he has discovered the world to be a fantastically changing place, he will wish to continue his learning into adult life. Thus communities will set up centers that are rich environments for learning, and the student will *never be graduated*. He will always be a part of a "commencement."

In view of my past prejudices I find it somewhat difficult but necessary to say that of all of the institutions of present-day American life, industry is perhaps best prepared to meet year 2000. I am not speaking of its technical ability. I am speaking of the vision it is acquiring in regard to the importance of persons, of interpersonal relationships, and of open communication. That vision, to be sure, is often unrealized but it does exist.

Let me speculate briefly on the interpersonal aspect of industrial functioning. It is becoming increasingly clear to the leaders of any complex modern industry that the old hierarchical system of boss and employees is obsolete. If a factory is turning out one simple product, such a system may still work. But if it is in the business of producing vehicles for space or elaborate electronic devices, it is definitely inadequate. What takes its place? The only road to true efficiency seems to be that of persons communicating freely with persons—from below to above, from peer to peer, from above to below, from a member of one division to a member of another division. It is only through this elaborate, individually initiated network of open human communication that the essential information and know-how can pervade the organization. No one individual can possibly "direct" such complexity.

Thus if I were to hazard a guess in regard to industry in the year 2000 it would be something different from the predictions about increasing technical skill, increasing automation, increasing management by computers, and the like. All of those predictions will doubtless come true but the interpersonal aspect is less often discussed. I see many industries, by the year 2000, giving as much attention to the quality of interpersonal relationships and the quality of communication as they currently do to the technological aspects of their business.

They will come to value persons as persons, and to recognize that only out of the *communicated* knowledge of all members of the organization can innovation and progress come. They will be forced to recognize that only as they are promoting the growth and fulfillment of the individuals on the payroll will they be promoting the growth and development of the organization.

What I have said will apply, I believe, not only to persons in management but to persons classed as "labor." The distinction grows less with every technological advance. It also applies, obviously, to the increasingly direct and personal communication between persons in management and persons in the labor force, if an industry is to become and remain healthily productive.

Historically, much of man's life has revolved around his relationship to his God or gods and around his relationship to others who share his religious views. What will be the situation three decades from now?

It is definitely conceivable that out of a deep fear of the rapidly changing world he is creating, man may seek refuge in a sure dogma, a simplistic answer to life's complexities, a religion which will serve him as security blanket. This seems unlikely, but I can imagine the circumstances under which it might occur.

The more likely possibility—or so it appears to me—is that by the year 2000, *institutionalized* religion, already on the wane as a significant factor in everyday life, will have faded to a point where it is of only slight importance in the community. Theology may still exist as a scholastic exercise, but in reality the God of authoritative answers will be not only dead but buried.

This does not mean at all that the concerns that have been the basis of religion will have vanished. The mysterious process of life, the mystery of the universe and how it came to be, the tragedy of man's alienation from himself and from others, the puzzle of the meaning of individual life—these mysteries will all be very much present. There may, indeed, be a *greater appreciation* of mystery as our knowledge increases (just as theoretical physicists now marvel at the true *mystery* of what they have discovered).

But religion, to the extent that the term is used, will consist of tentatively held hypotheses that are lived out and corrected in the interpersonal world. Groups, probably much smaller than present-day congregations, will wrestle with the ethical and moral and philosophical questions that are posed by the rapidly changing world. The individual will forge, with the support of the group, the stance he will take in the universe—a stance that he cannot regard as final because more data will continually be coming in.

In the open questioning and honest struggle to face reality which exist in such a group, it is likely that a sense of true community will

develop—a community based not on a common creed nor an un-
changing ritual but on the personal ties of individuals who have become deeply related to one another as they attempt to comprehend
and to face, as living men, the mysteries of existence. The religion of
the future will be man's existential choice of his way of living in an
unknown tomorow, a choice made more bearable because formed in
a community of individuals who are like-minded, but like-minded only
in their searching.

In line with the thread which runs through all of my remarks,
it may well be that out of these many searching groups there may
emerge a more unitary view which might bind us together. Man as a
creature with ability to remember the past and foresee the future, a
creature with the capacity for choosing among alternatives, a creature
whose deepest urges are for harmonious and loving relationships with
his fellows, a creature with the capacity to understand the reasons
for his destructive behaviors, man as a person who has at least limited
powers to form himself and to shape his future in the way he desires—
this might be a crude sketch of the unifying view which could give
us hope in a universe we cannot understand. . . .

THE IMPENDING INSTRUCTION REVOLUTION

HAROLD E. MITZEL

*Stanley Elam, editor of Kappan, the liveliest
of today's educational journals, calls this article
"one of the best summaries we have seen of the
early stages of a revolution which, Mr. Mitzel
believes, will be completed by the turn of the
century." Mitzel describes different concepts of
individualized instruction and calls for adaptive
instruction, "the tailoring of subject matter
presentation to fit the special requirements and
capabilities of each learner."*

*Harold E. Mitzel is professor of educational
psychology at Pennsylvania State University. His
article is a version of a paper he presented to the
American Society for Engineering Education; it
appeared in both* Engineering Education *and*
Kappan.

First, let me explain my choice of the above
title. It is fashionable in these days of rhetorical excess to describe
change as revolutionary in scope. The mass media remind us daily that

Reprinted by permission from *Phi Delta Kappan*, April 1970, pp. 434–439, and from
Engineering Education, March 1970, pp. 749–754.

revolutions are occurring right under our noses. We hear of (and see) the Social Revolution, the Sexual Revolution, the Technology Revolution, the Student Revolt, the Faculty Revolt, and so on. Apparently any complete or sudden change in the conduct of human affairs, with or without a violent confrontation or an exchange of power, may properly be called a revolution.

It is my thesis that the last three decades of the twentieth century will witness a drastic change in the business of providing instruction in schools and colleges. Change by the year 2000 will be so thorough-going that historians will have no difficulty in agreeing that it was a revolution. You will note the omission of words like "teaching" and "learning" in describing the coming revolution. Teaching connotes for most of us an inherently person-mediated activity and the vision of the "stand-up" lecturer comes most immediately to mind. One of the concomitants of the impending change is a major modification of the role of teacher. It is likely that future terms for teacher may be "instructional agent" or "lesson designer" or "instructional programmer." As for learning, we take the position that the word is not a way of describing an *activity* of the student, but rather a way of characterizing change in the student's behavior in some desired direction between two definite time markers. Pask[1] has pointed out that teaching is "exercising control of the instructional environment by arranging scope, sequence, materials, evaluation, and content for students." In other words, instruction is the general term for the process and learning is the product.

My objective is to challenge you with the shape of the instruction revolution, to point out how you as a teacher or administrator can cooperate and cope with it, and to suggest some of the social changes which are currently fueling this revolution.

INDIVIDUALIZED INSTRUCTION

At the secondary school level, American educators, beginning with Preston W. Search[2] in the late nineteenth century, have been interested in the goal of individualization. Between 1900 and 1930, disciples of Frederick Burk (see Brubacher[3] and Parkhurst[4]) devised and implemented several laboratory-type plans for self-instruction in the lower schools. These were self-pacing plans for the learner and demanded a great deal of versatility on the part of the teacher. Additional impetus for the theoretical interest of educators in individualization

[1] G. Pask, "Computer-Assisted Learning and Teaching," paper presented at Seminar on Computer-Based Learning, Leeds University, September 9–12, 1969.
[2] P. W. Search, "Individual Teaching: The Pueblo Plan," *Education Review*, February, 1894, pp. 154–70.
[3] J. S. Brubacher, *A History of the Problems of Education*, 2nd ed. (New York: McGraw-Hill, 1966).
[4] H. H. Parkhurst, *Education on the Dalton Plan* (New York: E. P. Dutton & Co., 1922).

stemmed from the mental testing movement, beginning with the seminal work of Binet[5] about 60 years ago. Early intelligence tests clearly showed differences in speed of task completion among pupils, and these differences were easily confirmed by a teacher's own observations of mental agility. At the practical level, a great deal of individualization took place in rural America's one-room schools. Fifteen to 25 children spread unevenly through ages 6 to 14 necessarily committed the teacher to large doses of individual pupil direction, recitation, and evaluation. With population increases and school consolidations, most village and rural schools began to look like rigidly graded city schools. Teachers found themselves responsible for larger and larger groups of children of approximately the same age and about the same physical size. It is little wonder that some of the zest, enthusiasm and obviousness of need for individualized teaching was lost. When teachers complained about too-large classes, the lack of time to spend with individual pupils, the wide diversity in pupil ability levels, many not-so-smart administrators introduced "tracking" or "streaming" strategies. Separating children into homogeneous classes according to measured mental ability within age groups has been shown conclusively to fail to increase the achievement level of groups as a whole.[6] Homogeneous ability grouping has, on the other hand, seriously exacerbated social problems connected with race and economic levels by "ghettoizing" classrooms within the schools, even though the schools served racially and economically mixed neighborhoods.

Whereas the common schools have *some* history of experimentation with individualized instruction methods, higher education, led by the large state universities, has pushed the development of mass communication methods in instruction. The large-group lecture and the adaptation of closed-circuit television are examples of higher education's trend away from individualized instruction. Of course, the outstanding accomplishments of American university graduate schools could never have been achieved without the cost-savings introduced by mass communications techniques in their undergraduate colleges.

Interest in individualized instruction had a surge about 15 years ago when Harvard's B. F. Skinner[7,8] advocated an education technology built around the use of rather crude teaching machines. It soon became apparent that there was no particular magic in the machines, since they contained only short linear series of questions and answers to

[5] A. Binet and T. Simon, *The Development of Intelligence in Children*, trans. Elizabeth S. Kite (Vineland, N.J.: The Training School, 1916).
[6] J. I. Goodlad in *Encyclopedia of Educational Research*, 3rd ed., (ed. C. Harris) (New York: Macmillan, 1960).
[7] B. F. Skinner, "The Science of Learning and the Art of Teaching," *Harvard Educational Review*, Spring 1954, pp. 86–97.
[8] B. F. Skinner, "Teaching Machines," *Science*, 128, 1958, pp. 969–77.

word problems called "frames." These programs were quickly put into book form and the programmed text was born. Although it enjoyed initial success with some highly motivated learners, the programmed text has not caught on in either the lower schools or in higher education as a major instructional device. Industry and the military forces seem to have made the best use of programmed texts, perhaps because of a high degree of motivation on the part of many learners in those situations.

Most recently, an educational technique for the lower schools has been developed out of the work of the Learning Research and Development Center at the University of Pittsburgh. The method, called "individually prescribed instruction" or IPI, is described by Lindvall and Bolvin,[9] by Glaser,[10] and by Cooley and Glaser.[11] Behind the method lies the careful development of a technology based on precise specification and delineation of educational objectives in behavioral terms. Pupils work individually on a precisely scaled set of materials with frequent interspersed diagnostic quizzes.

It must be clear, even after this sketchy review of the history of individualized instruction, that the concept has been pursued in a desultory fashion. I have heard hour-long conversations on individualization by educators who have only the vaguest notion of what is encompassed by the concept. Let me review five *different* concepts of individualization and acknowledge that I am indebted to Tyler[12] for some of these distinctions.

First, most educators agree that instruction is "individual" when the learner is allowed to proceed through content materials *at a self-determined pace that is comfortable for him.* This concept of self-paced instruction is incorporated into all programmed texts and is perhaps easiest to achieve with reading material and hardest to achieve in a setting that presents content by means of lectures, films and television. Oettinger,[13] in his witty but infuriating little book, *Run, Computer, Run,* refers to this self-pacing concept of individualization as "rate tailoring."

[9] C. M. Lindvall and J. O. Bolvin, "Programed Instruction in the Schools: An Application of Programing Principles in Individually Prescribed Instruction," in *Programed Instruction,* ed. P. C. Lange, The Sixty-Sixth Yearbook of the National Society for the Study of Education, Part II (Chicago: The University of Chicago Press, 1967), pp. 217–54.
[10] R. Glaser, *The Education of Individuals* (Pittsburgh: Learning Research and Development Center, University of Pittsburgh, 1966).
[11] W. W. Cooley and R. Glaser, "An Information Management System for Individually Prescribed Instruction," Working Paper No. 44, Learning Research and Development Center, University of Pittsburgh, mimeographed, 1968.
[12] R. W. Tyler, "New Directions in Individualizing Instruction," in *The Abington Conference '67 on New Directions in Individualizing Instruction* (Abington, Pa.: The Conference, 1967).
[13] A. G. Oettinger and S. Marks, *Run, Computer, Run* (Cambridge, Mass.: Harvard University Press, 1969).

A second concept of individualized instruction is that the learner should be able *to work at times convenient to him*. The hard realities of academic bookkeeping with the associated paraphernalia of credits, marks, and time-serving schedules make this concept difficult to implement in colleges or in the common schools.

That a learner should *begin instruction in a given subject at a point appropriate to his past achievement* is a third way of looking at individualization. This concept makes the assumption that progress in learning is linear and that the main task is to date the learner's present position on a universal continuum. Once properly located, he can continue to the goal. These notions seem to have their optimum validity for well-ordered content like mathematics or foreign languages. In fact, the advanced placement program, which provides college credit for tested subject matter achievement during secondary school, is a gross attempt to get at this kind of individualization.

A fourth concept of individualization is the idea that *learners are inhibited by a small number of easily identifiable skills or knowledges*. The assumption is that the absence of these skills is diagnosable and that remedial efforts through special instructional units can eliminate the difficulty. Colleges and universities seeking to enroll a higher proportion of their students from among the culturally disadvantaged and the economically deprived will be forced to bring this concept to bear if they wish to maintain current academic standards.

A fifth concept is that individualization can be achieved by *furnishing the learner with a wealth of instructional media from which to choose*. Lectures, audio tapes, films, books, etc., all with the same intellectual content, could theoretically be made available to the learner. The underlying notion is that the learner will instinctively choose the communication medium or combination of media that enable him to do his best work. The research evidence to support this viewpoint and practice is not at all strong.[14] Perhaps even more persuasive than the lack of evidence is the vanity of instructors who cannot understand why a student would choose a film or an audio tape in preference to the instructor's own lively, stimulating, and informative lectures.[15]

I have reviewed five concepts of individualization which have some credence in education, but by far the most prevalent interpretation is the one of self-pacing, or rate tailoring. These notions lead us directly

[14] S. N. Postlethwait, "Planning for Better Learning," in *Search of Leaders*, ed. G. K. Smith (Washington, D.C.: American Association for Higher Education, NEA, 1967), pp. 110–13.
[15] D. T. Tosti and J. T. Ball, *A Behavioral Approach to Instructional Design and Media Selection*, BSD Paper Number 1, Observations in Behavioral Technology (Albuquerque, N.M.: The Behavior Systems Division, Westinghouse Learning Corporation, 1969).

to the idea of adaptive education in responsive environments, which I want to discuss shortly. But first, one more distinction. "Individual instruction," where one studies in isolation from other learners, should probably be distinguished from "individualized instruction," where the scope, sequence, and time of instruction are tailored in one or more of the five ways I have just described. "Individualized instruction" can still be in a group setting and, in fact, was commonly practiced in rural one-room schools, as mentioned earlier. On the other hand, "individual instruction" can be singularly rigid, monotonous, and un-responsive to the needs of the learner. You could, for instance, take pro-gammed text material which is designed for individualized instruction and put it into an educational television format. Each frame could be shown to a large group of students for a short time, allowing the students to pick a correct option and then going on to another frame. This procedure would be individual instruction with a vengeance. But it forces a kind of lockstep on students of varying abilities and inter-ests that is the antithesis of "individualized instruction."

ADAPTIVE EDUCATION

I predict that the impending instruction revolution will shortly bypass the simple idea of individualizing instruction and move ahead to the more sophisticated notion of providing *adaptive education* for school and college learners. By adaptive education we mean the tailoring of subject matter presentations to fit the special requirements and capa-bilities of each learner. The idea is that no learner should stop short of his ultimate achievement in an area of content because of idiosyncratic hang-ups in his particular study strategies.

We have seen how the concept of individualized instruction has been pretty well arrested at the level of encouraging the learner to vary and control his task completion time. Many additional, more psy-chologically oriented variables will have to be brought into play to achieve the goals of adaptive education, as well as the adoption of individualizing techniques. We know a great deal about individual differences among people in regard to their sensory inputs, their reac-tion times, their interests, their values and preferences, and their or-ganizational strategies in "mapping" the cognitive world. What we do not know very much about is the extent to which, or how, these easily tested, individual difference variables affect the acquisition and reten-tion of new knowledge. Psychological learning theory has been pre-occupied with the study of variables in extremely simple stimulus-re-sponse situations, and investigations of meaningful learning phenomena have clearly dealt with human subjects as if they were all cut from the same bolt. The exception to this observation is, of course, the variable of measured mental ability, which has been shown to be related to

achievement in conventionally presented instruction and has been carefully controlled in many learning experiments involving human subjects.

Essential to the idea of adaptive education is the means of utilizing
new knowledge about individual differences among learners to bring a
highly tailored instructional product to the student. As long as we are
dealing with static or canned linear presentations such as those contained in books, films, video tapes, and some lectures, there seems to be
little incentive to try to discover what modifications in instructional
materials would optimize learning for each student. To plug this important gap in the drive toward vastly improved learning, the modern
digital computer seems to have great promise. About a decade ago,
Rath, Anderson, and Brainerd[16] suggested the application of the computer to teaching tasks and actually programmed some associative
learning material. In the intervening decade, a number of major universities, medical schools, industries, and military establishments have
been exploring the use of the computer in instruction. Five years ago
we instituted a computer-assisted instruction laboratory at Penn State
and have been trying to perfect new instructional techniques within the
constraints of available hardware and computer operating systems.[17, 18,
19, 20] There are, according to my estimate, some 35 to 40 active computer-assisted instruction (CAI) installations operating in the world
today, and fewer than 100 completed, semester-length courses or their
equivalent. Almost none of these courses have been constructed according to the ideals I mentioned for adaptive education. Indeed, many
of them look like crude, made-over versions of programmed textbooks,
but this does not disturb me when I recall that the earliest automobiles
were designed to look like carriages without the horses. The fact is that
the modern computer's information storage capacity and decision logic
have given us a glimpse of what a dynamic, individualized instruction
procedure could be, and some insight into how this tool might be
brought to bear to achieve an adaptive quality education for every

[16] G. J. Rath, N. S. Anderson, and R. C. Brainerd, "The IBM Research Center
Teaching Machine Project," in Automatic Teaching: The State of the Art, ed. E. H.
Galanter (New York: Wiley, 1959), pp. 117–30.
[17] H. E. Mitzel, The Development and Presentation of Four College Courses by Com-
puter Teleprocessing. Final Report, Computer-Assisted Instruction Laboratory, The
Pennsylvania State University, June 30, 1967. Contract No. OE-4-16-010, New
Project No. 5-1194, U.S. Office of Education.
[18] H. E. Mitzel, B. R. Brown, and R. Igo, The Development and Evaluation of a
Teleprocessed Computer-Assisted Instruction Course in the Recognition of Malarial
Parasites. Final Report No. R-17, Computer-Assisted Instruction Laboratory, The
Pennsylvania State University, June 30, 1968. Contract No. N00014-67-A-0385-0003,
Office of Naval Research.
[19] H. E. Mitzel, Experimentation with Computer-Assisted Instruction in Technical
Education. Semi-annual progress report, R-18, Computer-Assisted Instruction Labora-
tory, The Pennsylvania State University, December 31, 1968.
[20] "Inquiry," Research Report published by Office of the Vice President for Research,
The Pennsylvania State University.

student. We do not claim that the achievement of this goal is just around the corner or that every school and college can implement it by the turn of the century. We do believe that progress toward a program of adaptive education will be the big difference between our best schools and our mediocre ones at the end of the next three decades.

What individual difference variables look most promising for adapting instruction to the individual student via CAI? At Penn State we are testing the idea that a person learns best if he is rewarded for correctness with his most preferred type of reinforcement.[21] Thus some students will, we believe, learn more rapidly if they receive encouragement in the form of adult approval. Others will perform better if they receive actual tokens for excellence at significant places in the program, the tokens being exchangeable for candy, cokes, or other wanted objects. Still others respond to competitive situations in which they are given evidence of the superiority or inferiority of their performance compared to that of their peers. It is a fairly simple matter to determine a learner's reward preference in advance of instruction and to provide him with a computer-based program in which the information feedback is tailored to his psychological preference.

Perhaps the most dynamic and relevant variable on which to base an adaptive program of instruction is the learner's immediate past history of responses. By programming the computer to count and evaluate the correctness of the 10 most recent responses, it is possible to determine what comes next for each learner according to a prearranged schedule. For example, four or fewer correct out of the most recent 10 might dictate branching into shorter teaching steps with heavy prompting and large amounts of practice material. A score of five to seven might indicate the need for just a little more practice material, and eight or more correct out of the 10 most recent problems would suggest movement onto a fast "track" with long strides through the computer-presented content. The dynamic part of this adaptive mechanism is that the computer constantly updates its performance information about each learner by dropping off the learner's response to the tenth problem back as it adds on new performance information from a just-completed problem.

There are two rather distinct strategies for presenting subject matter to learners. One is *deductive*, in which a rule, principle, or generalization is presented, followed by examples. The other strategy is *inductive* and seeks, by means of a careful choice of illustrative examples, to lead the learner into formulating principles and generalizations on his own initiative. In the lower schools, inductive method is called "guided discovery"and has been found useful by many teachers. Our belief at

21 C. A. Cartwright and G. P. Cartwright, *Reward Preference Profiles of Elementary School Children*, mimeographed, Computer-Assisted Instruction Laboratory, The Pennsylvania State University, 1969. Paper presented at the meeting of the American Educational Research Association, Los Angeles, February, 1969.

the Penn State CAI Laboratory is that these two presentation strategies have their corollaries in an individual differences variable and that, for some students, learning will be facilitated by the deductive approach; others will learn more rapidly and with better retention if an inductive mode is adopted. A strong program of adaptive education would take these and other identifiable learner variables into account in the instructional process.

EVALUATION AND STUDENT APPRAISAL

One of the important concomitants of the instruction revolution will be a drastic revision in the approach to learner evaluation and grading practices by faculty. Even the moderate students on campus are saying that letter grades are anachronistic. On many campuses, including our own, students have petitioned for, and won, the right to receive "satisfactory" and "unsatisfactory" evaluations of their work in certain non-major courses. Other students have attacked all grades as a manifestation of a coercive, competitive, materialistic society. Without admitting to being a tool of a sick society, we should change this part of the business of higher education as rapidly as possible.

It seems to me that most formal instruction has been predicted on the notion that a course is offered between two relatively fixed points in time. In addition, the tools of instruction, such as lectures, textbooks, references, and computer services, are all relatively fixed and are the same for all learners. To be sure, the students do vary the amount of time they spend with these tools. Even there, the college catalogue tells the students that they should all study three hours outside of class for every hour in class. At the close of the period of instruction or end of the course, usually the end of the term, we give the students an achievement test that is constructed in a way that will maximize the *differences* among their scores. To get this seemingly important differentiation between our students in achievement, we have to ask extremely difficult questions. Sometimes we even go so far as to ask questions about footnotes in the text. In fact, we often have to ask questions on topics or objectives that we have made no attempt to teach. Our rationalization for this tactic is that we want the students to be able to *transfer* their knowledge. After obtaining the achievement examination results, we consult the trusty "normal curve" and assign A's, B's, C's, D's, and F's according to our interpretation of the grading mores of the institution. With time and materials fixed, we are essentially capitalizing upon the same human abilities that are measured by intelligence tests. Thus it is not surprising that intelligence and teacher-assigned grades tend to be highly correlated.

We could, as collegiate educators, do society and ourselves a big favor by making a fundamental shift in our approach to teaching and examining. (Incidentally, we might generate some relevance "points" with our students.) First, we should say (and mean) that our job is helping each of our students to achieve *mastery* over some operationally defined portion of subject matter.[22] Furthermore, failure by any student putting forth an effort is a failure on our part as teachers, or a breakdown of the selection system. Now, to do this job we will have to get rid of a lot of the present practices and irrelevancies of higher education. There is no point in maintaining an *adversary* system in the classroom, with the students against the instructor and each of the students against each other. Society may think that it wants us to mark our students on a competitive scale, but how much more sensible it would be if we could say, on the basis of accumulated examination evidence, that John Jones has achieved 85 percent of the objectives in Engineering 101, rather than say that he got a "B." If our job is to help the student master the subject matter or come close—say, achieve 90 percent or greater of the objectives—then we are going to have to adapt our instruction to him. As a starter, we could individualize by letting the student pace his own instruction. We know, for example, from preliminary work with class-sized groups in computer-assisted instruction, that the slowest student will take from three to five times as long as the fastest student in a rich environment of individualized teaching material. During a recent computer-mediated in-service teacher education course presented by Penn State in Dryden, Virginia, to 129 elementary school teachers, the average completion time was 21 clock hours. The fastest student finished in 12 hours and the slowest took 58 hours.[23]

Student evaluations should also be based on the concept that an achievable mastery criterion exists for each course. We should no longer engage in the sophistry of classical psychometrics, in which we prepare a test or examination deliberately designed to make half the students get half the items wrong. It is true that such a test optimally discriminates among the learners, which we justify by claiming need for competitive marking information. If, however, 50 percent of the students get 50 percent of the items wrong, then either we are asking the wrong questions or there is something seriously wrong with our non-adaptive instructional program.

Under optimum circumstances, we might get an enlightened view of the faculty's need to adopt mastery-type student evaluation procedures and we might get professors to talk less, but we would still be faced with the psychological problem of instructor dominance or instructor power. The power over students which the "giving" of grades confers on professors would not be yielded easily by many in college teaching today. As Pogo says, "We have met the enemy and he is us."

[22] B. Bloom, "Learning for Mastery," *UCLA Evaluation Comment*, 1968.
[23] K. H. Hall, *et al.*, *Inservice Mathematics Education for Elementary School Teachers via Computer-Assisted Instruction*. Interim Report, No. R–19, Computer-Assisted Instruction Laboratory, The Pennsylvania State University, June 1, 1969.

If we, as faculty and administrators in higher education, embraced the notion of teaching for student mastery by means of individually adaptive programs, then these are some of the concomitants:

1. Instructors would have to state their course objectives in behavioral terms.
2. Achievement tests keyed to course objectives would have to be constructed and used as both diagnostic placement and end-of-course determiners.
3. The bachelor's degree might take from two to eight years instead of the traditional four, because of the wide variability in mastery achievement.
4. Instead of telling three times a week, instructors might have to spend their time listening to students individually and in small groups where progress toward subject mastery required careful monitoring.
5. Instead of being primarily concerned with a discipline or with a specialization, those who profess for undergraduates would have to make the student and his knowledge their first concern.
6. Evaluation for promotion and salary increments for college teachers would be based on measured amounts of growth exhibited by their students and on numbers of students who achieved a specific mastery criterion.

If professors and deans ignore the reasoned demands for reforms of undergraduate instruction which come from the students, the government, and a concerned citizenry, then the revolution will be ugly and wrenching. The so-called "free universities," with their obvious shortcomings, are already harbingers of the chaos into which traditional higher education could slip if there is no responsiveness on the part of a majority of academicians to the need for change.

In the current wave of student unrest, many of the best articulated issues are local in nature, like the quality of food in the cafeteria or the relaxation of dormitory visiting rules for members of the opposite sex. Underneath these surface issues, however, lies the *one big issue*, which the students themselves haven't spelled out clearly. This is the issue of the relevance of contemporary collegiate instruction for students' lives. It seems to me students are saying, albeit not very clearly, that they want some wise adult to care about them, to pay attention to them, to listen and to guide them. We sit on our status quos and ignore their cry for help at our peril.

INCREASING HETEROGENEITY

Part of the fuel breeding the revolution in instruction is the increasing heterogeneity in mental ability and scholastic preparation among college students. The combined power of the teaching faculty, regional accrediting agencies, and shortage of spaces for students has, until recently, enabled many public universities to become increasingly selective. In fact, prestige among higher education institutions has been closely correlated with the height of the norms for entrance test scores. Even the great state universities, which began under the land-grant aegis as people's colleges, have a kind of "elitist" aura about them. Rising aspirations of minority groups, particularly blacks, have pointed up the fact that the poor, the disadvantaged, and the dark-skinned of our society do not share equally in whatever benefits a post-secondary college experience confers. A recent study and report by John Egerton for the National Association of State Universities and Land-Grant Colleges[24] was based on 80 public universities which enroll almost one-third of the nation's college students. He found that less than two percent of the graduate and undergraduate students were Negro in these institutions and that less than one percent of the faculty were black. Yet approximately 11 percent of the total U.S. population is black. It seems irrefutable that, with society's new awareness of the inequality in higher education, university entrance standards will have to be lowered for sizeable groups of blacks who have been poorly educated in the nation's secondary schools. Accounts of City University of New York's open admissions plan for fall, 1970, provide ample proof of the beginning of this trend, and Healy's[25] recent article firms up the humanitarian and social theory for the change in this great university. The lowering of entrance requirements will inevitably increase the heterogeneity of scholastic skills which makes the conventional teaching job so difficult.

Another source for increasing individual differences among college undergraduates is their stiffening resistance to required courses. Students clearly want more freedom of choice in devising their education programs. They want to determine what subjects are relevant to their lives and are increasingly impatient with elaborate prerequisites and multi-course sequences. Although the activists are not likely to win a complete victory on this score, the pressure which they generate will serve to breach the walls and gates around courses that have carefully been built by faculty over the years in order to make the conventional job of teaching somewhat more manageable. In addition to the student rejection of required courses, there is a corresponding need for the teaching of interdisciplinary subjects. Students see, perhaps more clearly than the faculty, that solution of the nation's problems such as urban decay, congestion, air and water pollution, and war and peace are not going to be solved by the unitary application of knowledge from traditional disciplines. For purposes of this discussion, the drive toward

24 B. Nelson, "State Universities: Report Terms Desegregation 'Largely Token,'" *Science,* June 6, 1969, pp. 1155–56.
25 T. S. Healy, "Will Everyman Destroy the University?" *Saturday Review,* December 20, 1969, pp. 54–56+.

more interdisciplinary courses of study can only increase the heterogeneity among students which the faculty has labored to minimize.

CONCLUSION

I have argued that we are now living with the early stages of a revolution in instruction which will be more or less complete by the turn of the century. The major changes will be primarily characterized by individualization of instruction leading to sophisticated systems of adaptive education. Two concomitants of the revolution which seriously concern college faculty and administrators are the need for new fundamental concepts of student appraisal and adaptation to increasing heterogeneity among the students in our charge.

THE BASIC LONG-TERM MULTIFOLD TREND IN EDUCATION

MICHAEL MARIEN

Michael Marien was Research Fellow, Educational Policy Research Center, Syracuse University Research Corporation, in Syracuse, New York. He is project director for Information for Policy Design, a World Institute project. Marien is one of the futurists who has given evidence of his deep interest in applying futures research to education. To Marien, the fundamental future trend in education is from closed teaching systems to open learning systems, as his chart graphically demonstrates.

One of the most widely-known and respected volumes in contemporary futures literature is *The Year 2000* by Herman Kahn and Anthony J. Wiener. The central concept within this volume is the "Basic, Long-term Multifold Trend," which, somewhat condensed, involves:

Increasingly sensate cultures (empirical, secular, humanistic, hedonistic).

Bourgeois, meritocratic elites; literacy and education.

Institutionalization of change and increasing tempo of change.

Reprinted by permission from *The Futurist*, December 1970, pp. 220–223, published by the World Future Society, P.O. Box 30369, Bethesda Branch, Washington, D.C. 20014.

Population growth, urbanization, and megalopolitanization.

Worldwide industrialization and modernization.

The Basic, Long-Term Multifold Trend (BLTMT) provides a general sense of societal direction, and dips into somewhat greater complexity with 8 "Canonical Variations" in 3 major categories, each a major alternative to the "Standard World."

The major orientation of *The Year* 2000, however, concerns international relations, and little or nothing is said about knowledge, communication, education, and internal conflict. Although international conflict is surely a critical concern, it is perhaps equally important to consider the nature of education and learning, which will be a central concern of a complex, dynamic, super-industrial, and knowledge-based society. Indeed, the future configuration of "who learns what and how" may well determine the manner in which international problems are responded to, and could mean the difference between a viable planetary society or global cataclysm.

The chart presented with this article is an initial attempt to outline a BLTMT for education. Conceived as a trend from closed teaching systems to open learning systems, the BLTMT for education is a distillation of empirical trends, forecasts, and prescriptive future states at all levels of education, and offers an overview of the transformation of present day schools into learning environments that will better suit men's needs. The chart is an attempt to start people thinking about how the present homogeneous institutions, whose main goal is inculcating the values of our industrial, linear society might become heterogeneous, open learning systems that will encourage lifelong learning in a post-industrial society.

There are many reasons for this long-range shift, among which the following are suggested:

The growing quantity and complexity of knowledge and ignorance.

The growing demands for a skilled labor force and a sophisticated citizenry, increasingly raising the minimum level of functional literacy.

Social and technological change, increasingly requiring lifelong learning and unlearning.

Leisure, affluence, and increasing access to social position through educational attainment—all increasing the demand for educational services.

Mounting evidence that all people have a far greater capacity to learn than has been admitted.

Obsolescent institutions requiring personnel retraining.

There is a widespread sense of ferment and change, all in the direction of open learning systems, but it is difficult to determine the degree

From Yesterday to Tomorrow:
The Basic Long-Term Multifold Trend in Education

Closed teaching systems	*Open learning systems*
ALTERNATE TITLES	
Teacher and/or institution centered	Student and/or child centered
Tight system; Rational mechanics; Cause-effect paradigm	Loose system
Control-centered	Learning-centered; Inquiry approach; Developmental; Discovery education
SOCIETAL CONTEXT	
Agricultural; Industrial	Postindustrial; Knowledge-based, Service society
Autocratic; Plutocratic; Gerontocratic	Democratic; Meritocratic; Self-renewing
Static and simple	Dynamic and complex
BELIEFS ABOUT LEARNING	
Teaching results in learning	Good teaching aids learning, bad teaching inhibits it
Learning requires discipline, work, drill, memorization, pain control	Learning is enjoyable, follows from pursuit of interests
Teacher as source of knowledge, student as passive absorber	Learning from many sources, including peers; student as active participant
Capability confined to a few; the genius, the gifted	Extensive latent potential in all
ADMINISTRATION	
Input oriented	Input-Service-Benefit oriented, PPBS
Hierarchical leadership	Pluralistic, participatory
CURRICULUM	
Narrow, fixed, retrospective	Broad, changing present and future-oriented
Classics, Principles, Truth, facts, deduction, Maxims	Methods, principles, induction, creativity, intuition, randomness
Determined by teacher and/or extra-classroom authority	Determined by teacher and/or student
Programmatic, sequential; Lesson plans strictly followed	Interchangeable programettes, Modular learning; Lesson plan as guide to options
Group study prescribed for all students	Independent study designed to fit individual needs and interests
Western culture as superior to primitives, heathens, Noble Savages, and the underdeveloped; Us-Them: emphasis on differences	Humanistic, pan-cultural; Us: emphasis on similarities

Closed teaching systems	Open learning systems
STUDENT-TEACHER RELATIONS	
Students are a collectivity	Compensatory education for exceptional children, the physically and linguistically handicapped, the underprivileged
Teacher as Authority, student as follower; control as instrumental technique	Professional as Learning Facilitator or Senior Learners; student as junior colleague
Feeling Withheld; I-It	Feelings exposed and respected, student evaluation of teachers; I-Thou
Single Teacher	Multi-adult exposure, team teaching, guests, differentiated staffing
STUDENT CONDUCT	
Compulsory attendance: no choice of institution	Optional participation: alternatives offered
Physical punishment for "Misbehavior"	Counseling for personal difficulties
No student recourse for injustice	Ombudsman, legal measures
Dropping out is fault of student; shaming for ignorance	Many possible sources of failure: environmental, institutional and individual
Established rules and routines	Democratic development of rules and routines as necessary
FEEDBACK	
Formal, mechanistic, "Right" answers	Multi-faceted, formal and informal, open-ended
Strong reliance on quantitative measures	Use of quantitative measures as necessary
REWARDS	
Grades, fixed proportion of failures, class rankings, honors, medals, degrees	Pass-fail, non-grading
Recognition through competition in a few areas of excellence	Deemphasis of competition, promotion of diversity and many areas of excellence; a taste of success for all
Learning has vocational and social utility	Rewards of learning are inherent
GOALS	
Socialization, training, moral education, passing on civilization, knowing; education of intellect only	Development of whole individual, investigation of cultural heritage, questioning
Getting an Education, being educated, terminal education	Learning how to learn, lifelong learning, education as a beginning

Closed teaching systems	Open learning systems
EXTRA-CLASSROOM ENVIRONMENT	
Restrictive, "In Loco Parentis"	Permissive, largely peer controlled
Physical and intellectual separation from world	Interlinkage of school and life, "School Without Walls"
SPACE	
"Grid" architecture, stationary furniture	Omnidirectional space and flexible furnishings, choice of environments
Arbitrarily assigned seats	Student freedom to choose seats
Teaching in classrooms	Learning in classrooms, learning resource center, home, dormitory, community, world
Specially designated learning institutions, outside learning ignored	Recognition and encouragement of formal and informal learning opportunities throughout society, equivalent credit for outside learning
TIME	
Collective pace	Individual pace
Ordered structure of class hours and course credits	Flexible scheduling
Uninterrupted schooling, followed by uninterrupted work	Learning and work interspersed throughout lifetime; learning a living

Reprinted by permission from *The Futurist*, pp. 222–223
December 1970, published by the World Future Society, P.O. Box 30369, Bethesda Branch, Washington, D.C. 20014.

of change and where it has occurred. Uncertainty is compounded by glowing proclamations of what has happened—in the midst of bitter attacks on "the monolithic system"—or of what has not happened. Do the reforms, innovations, and experiments reflect a visible minority of schools and colleges, or are they but the tip of an iceberg of change? Are the changes widespread and permanent, or are they superficial and temporary? Finally, are the actual changes keeping pace with or outpacing the growing desires and need for change?

THREE SCENARIOS FOR THE FUTURE OF EDUCATION

The major question for the future is the rate of transition and the extent to which open learning systems become a reality for all. (A parallel shift, also of uncertain dimensions, might be noted in the goals and activities of prisons and mental hospitals, from a "custodial" orientation to a "treatment" orientation.) However, no matter which outcome obtains—non-adaptation, differential adaptation, or full adaptation—an aggravation of some present social problems appears likely.

1. *Non-Adaptation and Conflict* The first scenario to consider is that open learning systems will not be widespread, and that the changes taking place are superficial, isolated, and short-lived. Although there is no evidence that open learning systems are more expensive than traditional systems, a period of severe financial famine at all levels of education (likely at least in the short-run) may inhibit the thoroughgoing changes that are required. Change is not necessarily expensive, especially considering social cost savings. But it may be 20 years before public decision-makers begin to think intelligently about social costs.

The general consequence of non-adaptation would be an additional impetus to create alternatives outside the regular educating system that would compete with and possibly replace existing forms of education. At the grade school level one can already see the rise of privately operated "Discovery Centers," outside learning contractors, and free schools. At the high school and college level, student-run free schools and experimental colleges are being developed as alternatives. At the same time, frustration and conflict can be expected to rise in the schools and colleges, as students increasingly develop the view that education should promote learning skills, rather than hand out obsolescing "facts" and shallow platitudes.

2. *Differential Adaptation and Equality of Opportunity* Although there is a general trend toward a national system of education, there is still considerable variation among states and within states, as well as a lack of coordination between levels of education. Consequently, although the national system may be moving toward some condition called "open learning systems," differential adaptation can be expected both in the horizontal dimension (between and within states) and in the vertical dimension (between levels).

Trend data is not only lacking on a national aggregate basis, but also within states and metropolitan areas. In the absence of such data, the location of change can only be surmised. At lower levels, one might expect to find open learning systems in affluent and suburban school districts in the Northeast and the West reflecting the cosmopolitan upper-middle class constituencies that are disposed to change and learning. Conversely, closed system traits are most apt to be found in bureaucracy-ridden inner cities, isolated rural areas, the small towns of "Middle America," and the South—although islands of experimentation (especially in big city ghettoes) may prove exceptions to this rule.

At higher levels, open system conditions which largely characterize the small, high quality liberal arts college, may increasingly be found in the large national universities that attract the brightest and most vocal students. Conversely, closed system conditions will continue at fundamentalist Bible colleges and obscure state colleges.

If access to open learning systems is considered to be desirable, a possible result of differential adaptation in the horizontal dimension may be an increasing inequality of opportunity if, as suggested, the best schools are getting better at a faster rate than the poorest schools.

Differential adaptation between levels may also lead to serious problems. Students who have been acclimated to closed teaching systems in high school may not take advantage of open learning systems opportunities on the college level. Conversely, students acclimated to open learning systems at an early age may lose the impetus toward self-directed learning or display considerable hostility if closed teaching systems are encountered at later ages. Many of the benefits of the Head Start program, for example, have been lost when students have encountered the traditional closed systems practices of elementary schools. Similarly, students who have tasted independence in high school would certainly expect nothing less in college.

3. *Full Adaptation and Generational Inversion* It can hardly be expected that all educating institutions at all levels will ultimately offer open learning system conditions. Nevertheless, the overall transformation may be so widespread as to suggest an outcome of "full" adaptation, whereby all students are provided opportunities to maximize the development of their abilities.

Such an idealized state nevertheless suggests a profound consequence, for each age cohort would have a better chance of developing human potential than the preceding, older age cohorts. Students presently in a new open system have more opportunities to learn than those who have graduated from a closed system; and students at elementary levels who have known only open system conditions will be further advanced at the high school level than the present high school students who may be encountering open learning systems for the first time. With each age cohort increasing its capabilities relative to the one preceding it, generational inversion may become increasingly evident.

Although the young have much to learn, especially in the broad area of experience that we call "wisdom," one can already see the early signs of generational inversion in what is euphemistically called the "generation gap." For, in many respects, the young are better fitted to this world and the world of tomorrow than their elders. Political education campaigns launched on university campuses are an early form of the young teaching the old in what Margaret Mead has called "Prefigurative Culture."

WAYS TO HASTEN THE FUTURE

Although the variations in the BLTMT in education have been presented singly, societal complexity is such that the most probable future will contain a complex mixture of all three situations. In turn, this suggests the necessary paths of action for those who are sympathetic to open learning systems and wish to hasten the future while guarding against undesirable consequences.

1. *Better Understanding of Open Systems* To avoid stagnation, conflict, and threats of supersession, attempts must be made to define open learning systems fully and to make clear their superiority both in learning and in social benefits. One of the functions of the synoptic chart is to facilitate an appreciation of the many facets that are involved in a fully open system. Too many open system innovations, launched singly, are made ineffective by largely closed systems. Educators may feel giddily innovative and therefore complacent in the absence of any model that indicates how far they have to go.

2. *More Knowledge of Inequality* To avoid greater inequality, a far more sophisticated educational data system is required to monitor what is happening and where. Ultimately, we may require a thoroughgoing Census of Education and Learning, similar to the quinquennial Census of Manufactures that has provided information for the industrial society that we are leaving behind.

Inequality of learning opportunity is not only to be found in schools. Affluent families, living in information-rich homes and communities, also provide for many extra-school learning opportunities such as summer camps, trips abroad, tutors, and music lessons. It is to be expected that the affluent parents will be the first to take advantage of video cassettes to promote the learning of their children, similar to the provision of encyclopedias at home—which presently serves as a further means to one-up the disadvantaged. Indeed, one of the problems of our future society may be to simply keep the present level of inequality from worsening, let alone attempt to narrow the gap.

3. *More Adult Education* Efforts at adult education will require far more attention in the future, such that, in accord with the open learning system model, school and work are interspersed throughout everyone's lifetime. There may well be a growing gap between what is known by the young and what is known by the old, and, similar to the widening gap of opportunity, considerable efforts may be required to simply maintain the present balance. Among many traditional notions that will be painfully discarded is the obsolete view that "education is for the young." To survive in our new society, we will all have to learn, unlearn, and learn.

To move from "yesterday to tomorrow" the key factor in promoting open learning systems may well be the disposition toward learning that is held by adults: teachers, educational authorities, and—perhaps most importantly—parents. To change the schools and colleges, then, would first require a change in the American public. In other words, to restate an obvious but often overlooked point, educating institutions reflect their constituents and their surrounding communities, and cannot be expected to rise very far above their surrounding intellectual milieu.

A LOOK INTO THE FUTURE

WARREN G. SMITH

Warren G. Smith is the director of Nova High School, Fort Lauderdale, Florida. Thus Mr. Smith approaches the future from the standpoint of one identified with a highly future oriented high school. In its short history, Nova has established a national reputation for creative experimentation in education.

One of the recent popular pastimes of educators is to write papers and make speeches predicting the education in our world of the future. These papers range from treatises on individualized instruction by use of technology to a complete student demand curriculum, dependent upon the sophistication of the presenter. I would like to join the group but perhaps with a fresh approach that will give me an advantage over my peers. I wiped from my mind all of the customs, mores, taboos, traditions and contexts of present-day education and, with this clean mind, looked into the future.

To set the theme for this mind-cleaning process, I borrowed an idea from a colleague, Mr. John Arena, that was used by a discussion group in a graduate class. The group imagined that the human race, by design or by accident, had succeeded in eliminating nearly all of its members from the face of the earth, a not-too-fantastic idea based on the exerted efforts toward this end going on all around us every day. A small group of humans, perhaps a million or fewer, has escaped this terrible destruction. They are concentrated in one geographical area and they know that they are the last remaining humans on earth. The educators among them are challenged by the group to design a system of education for the children of the survivors that will prepare them to face the future with an educational background that will, for all time, prevent a recurrence of the disaster that struck the rest of the world.

The situation described is so horrible and awesome that if you can fantasize yourself into this group, you might have a fair opportunity of designing the type of education necessary under those conditions. Regardless of the cause of the destruction of human life in the situation described above, whether atomic war, man-made biological pestilence, or worldwide pollution, any form of educational model or design must first attempt to combat such an occurrence. In this article I am not going to try to decide for you an educational system to meet the needs of this group of survivors. Rather, I am going to attempt to relate present-day conditions and predicted future conditions to present-day education.

It is only natural that the first thought when one attempts to change education is of content, which is probably the farthest from a realistic approach. Each content area has supporters who vehemently defend its importance to the whole child. The explosion of knowledge, which is now spiraling all around us, is adding to the content at such an increased rate that we could never hope to expose the student to all of the possibilities. The common cry is that there just isn't time to teach everything necessary to prepare our students to face the world of the future, but what we really are saying is that there isn't time to acquaint him with all of the content of the past as well as to insert into our present-day school system the content of the present and to make room for the content of the future.

If time is an important factor, then more time would be the obvious answer, but I don't believe that we will be given more time. I don't believe that we will have a longer school day for each individual student. Six hours of bombardment, plus expected home study, would task almost any human. Under present methods there must be some limit to the amount of exposure that a student can take in a given day. Therefore, I discount the possibility of a longer learning day. I am not prepared for a longer school week. All of business and industry seem to be turning towards a shorter work week with increased recreation or leisure time. Our students, who are also members of our society, are equally interested in recreational and leisure time. For us to expose them to a six or six-and-one-half-day school week in order to accomplish our predetermined task of acquainting them with all of the "necessary" content would be self-defeating.

Much is being said presently about extending the school year. We must not confuse this with the four-quarter school year, a device to make use of buildings, equipment and teachers on a year-'round basis, which does not, in reality, provide more school days per year for the individual student. Very few school systems in the world have extended the school year for students, because it also increases the cost of education, and the American taxpayer seems to be on the verge of rebelling against increased taxes for education or for any other purpose.

I think we must discount the increasing of time as an answer to our educational problems. We can also discount a great increase in expenditure for education which would provide for more teachers and more equipment and more materials, which could substantially help in the learning of content material. I think we must face reality and accept the fact that we will have our children about the same length of time that we now have them, with the same amount of staff, with the same amount of material, and perhaps a slight improvement in equipment. Therefore, all of our thoughts should be on increasing efficiency of time that students *are* with us.

There are several ways that this efficiency can be increased. One, a painful one, is to remove from the curriculum those things that are obsolete now or are close to obsolescence. Each time an item of content is removed from the curriculum, certain groups of people who depend on that content for their livelihood defend it. Obsolete items must be eliminated from the required content. Perhaps there is a better way to approach the problem.

An easier method of increasing efficiency is to eliminate repetition. A careful analysis of content being taught in the various departments of the present-day schools would reveal a great deal of repetition. Some items, such as measurement or wave action, etc., are taught in several different areas at different times. There isn't even consistency in the manner in which these concepts are presented. Not only is this wasteful, but it is very confusing to the student.

A more drastic way to improve efficiency—and perhaps the only way to succeed—would be to make a very careful and complete analysis of the real needs of the students in his future and balance them against the needs as expressed by the professionals. To go back to our group of survivors, if we could borrow some of the insight that such a group would attain, we might be able to identify student needs for existence in the future in a very relevant manner without falling back into the trap of traditionalism or convention in education.

These student needs should meet certain criteria which might be defined in terms of relevance, motivation, interest, identity with peers and teachers, and success, and the only educational or school needs that should be considered are efficiency, accountability and techniques.

As the student needs are identified, they should be categorized and grouped in order to meet the efficiency requirement and accountability of the schools. The first impulse of educators is to try to drop the identified student needs into the present department of disciplines that are in the schools today. It quickly becomes apparent that some of them cross over discipline or departmental lines, and, therefore, there is a certain amount of effort toward interrelating disciplines to achieve efficiency and relevance. I believe a much more drastic step must be taken. All identity with present disciplines must be dropped and a new set of categories should be established. As long as educators can identify themselves with a specific discipline, I believe they will be unable to interrelate truly with others, and the only possible way to achieve true relevance and efficiency is to eliminate the present and create a new set. For my purposes, I have done so.

The dramatic technological advance is providing our world with conveniences and necessities to meet nearly every physical need. To cite a few, I might mention the space program, medical science, the communications media, transportation, and food production. This force (technology) is doing its job with a gusto never before witnessed. This very gain, however, is not without loss. Because of technological gain, we are despoiling our environment. Our rivers and lakes are the dumping ground for industrial wastes. Our land is scarred, robbed of its minerals and then left. The very air we breathe is saturated with the waste from industrial combustion—in blast furnaces, electrical generating plants, automobile exhausts, etc. We cannot kill the goose, so we must devise a system of education to prepare our future citizens to cope with this dilemma.

The progress made by technology is evident. We must now learn to reap its benefits without paying the penalties. Each individual must become competent in all manners of preventing the polluting of our environment and the people who inhabit it. Conservation of resources, physical and human, must be made an important part of the student's world. Every concept related to preservation and rejuvenation of our environment and its inhabitants should be grouped into a discipline so that each child is exposed to them just as he is exposed to the other basic skills. The ecology of our world is everyone's responsibility, and only by emphasizing it in this manner throughout the public school years will we ever achieve perpetual security. Ecological thinking must be a natural and involuntary response.

If we advance only technology and ecology, we will have a healthy and comfortable place to live, but one more ingredient must be added to make life have meaning and beauty—the humanities. This group of aesthetic concepts seems to be a natural division to add to technology and ecology, thus making up a trilogy of disciplines for the school of the future.

Nova has taken the first steps to reach this ambitious, long-range goal. With conservation of pupil and teacher time as a pressing need, the staff has begun to interrelate some of the disciplines. LAPs are being written in mathematics and science to treat common concepts so that a relevance is established. Many technical science activities are becoming a part of English LAPs. Art and music are integrated into science, literature, home economics and social studies.

A reorganization of teaching teams across discipline lines for planning and curriculum development will move the plan another step forward. Study groups will identify commonalities in the courses of study and will negotiate changes that will tend to eliminate redundancy. Several other subtle attempts will be made to advance the school toward their goal.

Even though it is painful, innovation is necessary. Ideas must become experiments and then, if feasible, pilot programs. Each such program must be researched for its ultimate value to the education of our youth. These steps can best be done in a school complex that is staffed and equipped for the process and in an environment where both success and failure are accepted as valuable.

WHAT WILL THE SCHOOLS BECOME?

HAROLD G. SHANE

OWEN N. NELSON

Harold G. Shane is one of the most knowledgeable and widely read educators studying the future and the curriculum. Here with his collaborator, Owen N. Nelson, assistant professor of education at Wisconsin State University, he presents the results of a survey of educators on what the schools will become. The respondents were school administrators (72), subject matter specialists (42), curriculum professors (37), doctoral students (87), public school teachers (95). Shane is University Professor of Education at Indiana University, where he was formerly Dean of the School of Education. In 1973–74, he served as president of the Association for Supervision and Curriculum Development.

Man has always had a keen interest in his future. In the present climate of speculation, how does the U.S. educator perceive our changing schools in the interval between 1975 and 2000? *What* does he believe may happen, *when* is it likely, and

Reprinted by permission from *Phi Delta Kappan,* June 1971, pp. 596–598.

does he *like* what he anticipates? What changes seem likely to come about easily, and where will the schools resist change most vigorously?

In an effort to obtain thoughtful conjectures about developments just over the horizon, the authors invited 570 persons to react to 41 possible educational futures, all of them discussed in more than 400 books and articles dealing with alternatives for the next 30 years. Of the respondents, 58% answered 205 queries which dealt with 1) curriculum and instruction, 2) new organizational patterns and pupil policies, 3) economic and political influences, 4) teacher preparation and status, 5) the school's relationships to society, and 6) biological intervention and mediation tactics such as the use of drugs to increase children's teachability.

The responses reveal the status and direction of educators' thinking. They merit added consideration because of the "self-fulfilling prophecy" phenomenon, which suggests that the beliefs of our sample, if widely held, could perceptibly influence future developments in education. A few of the questions in all six areas have been selected for discussion here.

CURRICULUM AND INSTRUCTION

Multimedia Almost all of the educators (93%) anticipate that a mix of learning resources will replace the traditional monopoly that the textbook has enjoyed as a mainstay of instruction. Virtually everyone (96%) agrees that a multimedia approach is desirable, that such approaches would be fairly easy to bring about, and that they will become prevalent between 1975 and 1985.

Student Tutors The use of student tutors (for example, 11-year-olds working with six-year-olds in reading) will be commonplace if not a standard procedure by the early 1980's, in the opinion of almost three-quarters of the survey participants. Four out of five feel the idea is excellent, and two-thirds think it would be easy to start such programs.

A New English Alphabet The predictions and enthusiasm of a few linguists notwithstanding, most respondents are pessimistic about the prospects for a phonetic alphabet of approximately 45 letters, which more nearly coincides with the number of phonemes (significant speech sound units) in English. While three out of four concede the virtue of such a change, over half think it is unlikely to be adopted and assign a low priority to the task.

Increased Time for the Expressive Arts. Teachers of drama, art, and music will be cheered to know that over half of their fellow educators participating in the survey are convinced that work in the expressive arts will double its present time allotment in the curriculum within 10 to 15 years. Seventy-five percent also believe the 100% increase is desirable.

Controversial Issues An overwhelming 91% of the educators feel that, before 1980, instruction in the social studies will come to grips with controversial topics (activist movements, discrimination, and so on), and over 90% think that it is high time to give top priority to the forthright study of these social issues. Opinion is split as to how much public resistance there might be to controversial content and issues on which the schools took a stand.

With reference to sex education, and despite the fact that 60% feel it would be difficult, 89% of the educators believe that comprehensive study of human sexuality in all its aspects should begin in the primary years. Four-fifths urge that the introduction of sex education programs receive high priority.

ORGANIZATION AND PUPIL POLICIES

A 12-Month-Year and Personalized Programs The organization of U.S. education and many of its long-familiar policies are due to change sharply and rapidly if the views of professors, teachers, and administrators are accurate. No later than the mid-Eighties, 84% believe, our schools will be open for 12 months and students' programs will be so personalized that the individual can leave school for three months each year, choosing both the time and the length of vacations. Educators concede, however, that the public will be reluctant to accept such flexibility. Noncompetitive "personalized progress records" are endorsed, but a strong minority (38%) foresee that grades will be used to report pupil achievement for another 10 to 15 years.

Early Childhood Education Respondents were optimistic when asked whether school services would extend downward to enroll three-year-olds and to provide health services for babies no later than at age 2. Three-quarters of the replies favor such early childhood programs. Some 73% further urge that high priority be assigned to early childhood education and estimate that programs for the youngest will be a universal reality by around 1985. A large majority of the sample is convinced that the British infant schools will influence practice, and they believe this is a good thing.

Revision of Compulsory Attendance Laws Opinions of the survey population are almost evenly divided on whether compulsory attendance laws will be relaxed, although 63% favor the idea if exit from and reentry into school can be made more socially acceptable, personal, and flexible. Attendance policies will be hard to change, 60% said, although most feel that they ought to be eased to permit students to leave school sooner to enter the world of work.

FUNDING AND FINANCIAL POLICIES

Government Agencies The respondents forecast (62%) and endorsed (88%) rapid consolidation of federal education programs. Strong and united professional action is required to accomplish this goal, and 82 out of 100 urge a high priority for coordinated action by school officials. Even so, 10% of the respondents conjecture that it will be the year 2000 before cooperation among governmental agencies replaces duplication and competition. One extreme cynic cast a write-in vote for 2500 A.D. as the probable year of consolidation for overlapping agencies.

Differentiated Staffing Despite heated opinions on differentiated staffing, 74% of the educators favor differentiation with teacher-pupil *ratios*, but with paraprofessionals and educational technology utilized to decrease teacher-pupil *contact hours*. This is viewed as a means of increasing productivity, efficiency, and wages. Another large group, 66%, indicates that differentiated staffing probably will be accepted, though not without a struggle. If the respondents' hunches prove accurate, a substantial degree of differentiation will be attained within the decade.

Performance Contracting The average respondent is opposed to the idea of corporation management of school systems, but feels there is an even chance it will be more widely adopted. Estimates on when business may engage in increased school management responsibilities vary somewhat, but four out of five educators feel it could occur quickly. Ten percent believe that the purchase of instruction from corporations will be far more widespread as soon as four years from now.

Vouchers for Tuition Payments Little enthusiasm is indicated for a voucher system. Seventy-one percent of the sample feel that such a plan will not get off the ground, and 67% condemn the idea. If vouchers ever are distributed, fewer than 15% see them coming into general use before 1985.

Salary and Teacher Performance The antipathy toward merit rating which teachers have expressed for many years apparently has transferred to salary schedules based on teaching performance. Nearly 54% feel that performance-based wages and increments are not likely in the future. However, two-thirds of the replies acknowledged the desirability of basing salaries on competence.[1]

[1] This does not necessarily accurately reflect classroom teachers' attitudes. Only 95 of the 333 respondents were employed as teachers.

TEACHER PREPARATION AND STATUS

Teacher Education and Certification   Major changes in the preparation and licensing of teachers are widely accepted by those polled. For example, 92% feel that teacher education will be drastically modified to prepare pre-service students to work in teams or partnerships, to individualize instruction, to make use of educational technology, and to encourage greater pupil participation in the process of education. Routine use of sensitivity training in teacher education is foreseen by 64% of the respondents. Virtually all respondents (98%) favor major changes. There is also a pronounced feeling (82%) that alternatives to state-controlled teacher licensing are desirable, that they will be instituted (73%), and that they will be widely accepted by 1980 or 1985.

A strong current of opinion suggests that ways of obtaining teaching certificates should be liberalized (67% said "yes") and that few if any of the new avenues should involve merely adding courses in professional education. Major changes are presumably to be inaugurated in the immediate future and, for the most part, completed in 10 to 15 years.

The Self-Contained Classroom   "One teacher-one group" instruction is on the way out, according to 69% of the respondents predicting the shape of the future. Another larger group (75%) apparently say "good riddance" to this venerable institution.

In place of the self-contained classroom, 67% of the educators see (and 79% cheerfully accept) some form of "flexible teaching partnerships." Presumably, such partnerships would be an extension of the team concept, but would involve greater "horizontal" and "vertical" deployment of a differentiated staff; that is, a given teacher would work "vertically" with more children of different ages and "horizontally" in more varied capacities.

THE SCHOOL AND SOCIETY

Societal Services   The school is viewed as an agency responsive to social change by most of the participants. Judging by majority opinions of social engineering, we can anticipate 1) psychiatric treatment without cost to students (76% said "yes," 87% "desirable");[2] 2) massive adult education and vocational retraining programs (92% said "yes," 95% "desirable"); and 3) school programs designed to help adults adjust to increased leisure and longer periods of retirement (85% said "yes," 94% "desirable").

Mandatory Foster Homes   Respondents were asked whether they thought that children, before age three, might be placed in foster

[2] Most (76%) of the educators expect public schools to assume routine responsibility for identifying and treating incipient mental and psychological disorders or problems beginning in early childhood; 89% favor the idea.

homes or kibbutz-type boarding schools to protect them from a damaging home environment. Opinions are about evenly divided on whether this is a good or bad policy, but the likelihood of such a development in the U.S. is rejected by over 70%.

INTERVENTION AND MEDIATION

One of the more controversial items among the 41 in the educational futures instrument is whether or not, in the years ahead, schools should and will use chemical compounds to improve the mood, memory, power of concentration, and possibly the general intelligence of the learner. Most of the respondents feel that what is measured as intelligence can be increased substantially. Ninety percent of the survey participants consider it appropriate to try to increase the IQ through such mediation tactics as enriched environment in early childhood, and 82% also express confidence that measurable intelligence will be increased by or before 1990.

However, the use of drugs to increase "teachability" was labeled as both unlikely (57% say it will not occur on a widespread scale) and a bad practice to boot. Fifty-six percent rejected the idea of using stimulants, tranquilizers, or antidepressants.

"Intervention" in early childhood The presumed importance of education under school auspices in the learner's early years is supported by survey respondents. Over 70% feel that "preventive and corrective intervention" before age six might, within the next 25 years, make the annual per-pupil expenditures for the early-childhood group even higher than per-student costs at the university level.

CONCLUSION

Our small sample—directly or by implication—expresses great confidence in the influence of and financial support for education between 1975 and 2000. The respondents expect and desire substantial educational changes; their dissatisfaction with the status quo comes through clearly. If the 333 respondents who struggled patiently through the survey instrument represent U.S. educators as a whole, then the coming decade should attain levels of humaneness and educational zest and venturesomeness reminiscent of the 1930's, the heyday of the progressive education movement.

LOOKING
TO THE
FUTURE:
REASSESSMENT
OF
EDUCATIONAL
ISSUES
OF THE
1970s

HAROLD G. SHANE

Harold G. Shane is also a versatile writer on various educational issues. Author of dozens of books and articles, his recent major works include publications on improving language arts instruction and on linguistics for the classroom teacher. Yet he found time to cooperate with Kappan in analyzing a study of issues in education identified by the Phi Delta Kappa membership. The excerpt which follows is from an encompassing, future oriented review of current issues in education. Included here are some of Shane's introductory comments and his section on curriculum.

FORCES RECASTING VINTAGE EDUCATIONAL ISSUES

The Crisis of Transition The unprecedented development that has most severely shaken society and the school is the crisis of transition.[1] Scientifically and psychologically, most men and women in 1910 were closer to ancient Rome of 73 B.C. than they were to the America of 1973 A.D. Sixty or 70 years ago horses were a main source of power, and medical knowledge was more akin to Claudius Galen's than to Christiaan Barnard's. Cooking and preserving food were laborious tasks generally left to women, a substantial meal including pie could be had for 12 cents, opium to ease the pangs of "female problems" was sold over the counter and through the Sears, Roebuck catalog, and children of 8 and 10 worked 12-hour days in the coal mines. Furthermore, these youngsters were expected to be seen rather than heard at the evening meal that brought the family together from a variety of tasks, many of which are unknown to the present generation.

At the risk of digression, note that much of the importance of the great transition that was to follow between 1920 and the present resided in a whole series of inventions such as the refrigerator, which, in freeing women from the drudgery of the kitchen, set the stage for an upheaval in the way the family of 1910 lived. Today approximately 40% of mothers of young children in the U.S. work full-time *outside* the home. As William H. Kilpatrick foresaw with remarkable prescience in 1926, children now learn neither extensively nor exclusively from their parents—both of whom are away for many hours in a mysterious place

[1] I am indebted to John Platt for this term. See "What We Must Do," *Science*, November 28, 1969, pp. 1, 115–21.

Reprinted by permission from *Phi Delta Kappan*, January 1973, special section on Issues, pp. 326–328, 332–333.

"out there."[2] Although our developmental data are incomplete, this lack of contact may well account for a host of ills in the child and in the adolescent he becomes: disorientation, identity crises, lack of understanding of how goods are produced, a love-deficit that leads to faulty intrafamily relationships, and comparable problems with major implications for both school and society.

By the early 1920s portentous changes were under way, and in the 50 years that have intervened, more changes have taken place than occurred in the previous 50,000 years. Even now that we have begun to take them almost for granted, the developments seem fantastic: atomic power, jet travel, instantaneous communication via satellite, artificial life, genetic manipulation, oral contraception, repeated moon landings, unmanned flights to planets other than ours, the science of data processing, and universal TV. Although it is probably impossible to place them in precise rank order of importance with respect to their impact on the lives of the young or with respect to their potential impact on schooling, high on the list would be widespread TV, developments in communication, jet travel, and new, diversified energy sources.

Having started these five decades threatened by an uncompromising natural environment that had limited what man could do for a thousand generations, man abruptly turned the tables. He himself became a menace to nature—and an even greater threat to himself. In this process the life-style of millions of Americans changed from the taut austerity of life aboard a Viking longboat to the opulence of Cleopatra's barge—plus modern plumbing! *Dreams* of the twenties and thirties became the *hopes* of the forties and fifties, and then the *expectations* of the sixties. Now, in the 1970s, yesterday's wistful fancies have become *demands:* demands for both human rights and for material things that were not coveted 50 years ago because—like TV and electrical air conditioning—they hadn't been invented or, as in the case of foreign travel and gourmet dishes, they were the rare prerogatives of the very rich.

The Crisis of Crises   A few years ago, somewhere in the middle sixties, the crisis of transition—for those who longed for stability—took a turn for the worse. Crisis began to pile on crisis and, like a knight worn out because he was called upon to defend his realm from attack at all times, for a while it seemed that the U.S., too, might become too weak to fend off its problems.

There was discontent, protest, and confrontation on the campus, violence and disaster in the ghetto. An undeclared war that no one wanted destroyed a president's credibility and left us with years of slaughter that seemed impossible to end. Most forms of authority, no

[2] William H. Kilpatrick, *Education for a Changing Civilization* (New York: Macmillan, 1926).

matter how legally constituted, were questioned with vehemence, with rancor, and occasionally with physical force. Many of the moral maps that the church had long provided did not seem to fit the terrain we were crossing; crime and personal violence climbed to a level of medieval intensity. As for the young, some sought "authenticity" in drugs or tried to "find themselves" through experiments with sex, in new life-styles, through imaginative and sometimes weird personal grooming and nongrooming, or in combinations of all four.

Perhaps no more than 15% of the population participated directly in either confrontations or in new life-styles, but virtually everyone felt their impact. Inevitably, most Americans were motivated to reassess their views toward the "Grave New World" that, in varying degrees, either threatened or alarmed or inspired and encouraged them. And ineluctably the schools became involved in the self-examination in which the American segment of humankind was deeply and irreversibly engaged.

'So much to do.' As he lay on his deathbed in 1902, one of the more powerful Englishmen of the Victorian era, Cecil John Rhodes, said, "So little done, so much to do." In a wholly different context, Rhodes's last words provide a fitting bumper-sticker slogan for today. Human-kind has very much to do and very little time in which to do it—even if only a few of the alarming auguries of catastrophe prove to be true.

The growing literature of disaster gives a note of documented urgency to social and economic decisions that probably must be made between 1973 and 1985. Most students of the biosphere's problems appear to agree that we have about a dozen years in which to adopt policies that will keep our naive use of technology from becoming a disease that could leave our planet with its beauty gone and only its helplessness remaining.[3]

The "crisis of crises" problems inventoried above, plus such world-wide problems as famine, dwindling resources, impure water and foul air, and the overuse of chemical fertilizers and insecticides give us "so much to do." The projections of social or physical scientists such as Jay W. Forrester and Goesta Ehrensvaerd also urge upon us the need to recognize that time could run out on us—*conceivably in the next generation*. Plainly, as they reexamine great educational issues of the day, U.S. educators also must concern themselves with the problem-issues of their society *and with their implications for changes in what is now taught and for the processes that children and youth now experience in our schools and through related educational agencies, the mass media in particular.*

The ways in which our long-standing issues such as "What should

---

[3] Books dealing with problems lying before us have appeared in large numbers since 1970. Some of the better and more readable are listed in the bibliography. See Barry Commoner's *The Closing Circle*, Barbara Ward and Rene Dubos, *Only One Earth*, and the Club of Rome Report, *The Limits of Growth*.

the curriculum include?" need to be answered seem almost self-evident.
We cannot, for instance, continue to teach that ever-expanding growth
is "good." Our space probes—among other things—have taught us that
our badly maintained globe is not only the sole piece of decent property
in the vicinity; it also is a closed system. The refuse from our technology must be recycled; we must move into an era of controlled
growth. *Growth* is necessary lest innovation languish and man's struggle
for a portion of a finite quantity of goods become intensified until it
is unbearable. *Social control* is essential lest we destroy more of what
Barry Commoner has called our "biological capital." Much of the U.S.
technology which created crucial problems because we used it too care-
lessly must be reordered to bring it into a more harmonious relationship
with the biosphere. Education should be accountable for putting this
point across to the next generation as quickly as possible.

On a crowded, limited earth we also need to temper nationalism
with internationalism, to use the neutrality of the young as a foundation for a new race structure which at long last will finally begin to
shed today's veneer of prejudice, and courageously to tackle the sur-
passingly dangerous problem of class strife.

This brings us up against the have and have-not problem, the really
threatening danger behind the tragic mask of the class problem. Specifically, the challenge is to sensitize the young and help them learn
ways of coping with the dilemmas of a new quest for *equity* among the
world peoples—equity as distinct from egalitarianism.

Equality, as Boulding points out, denies the principle that one
should receive in rough proportion to his expenditure of talent and
effort.[4] Equalitarianism thus gives the "deserving" less than they deserve and the "undeserving" more. Our generation has an *obligation*
to attack this dilemma with our young in the arena that education
provides and to begin to understand the subtleties of *real* equity.

Perhaps we can move toward an era in the third millennium in which
"growth"—that is, building what we can simply because our technology permits us to build it—can be redirected in human channels and
supplemented by a new concept of maturity through which

. . . human energies can be devoted to qualitative growth—knowledge,
spirit, art, and love. One might even romantically regard the twenty-first
century as symbolizing the achievement of this maturity.[5]

To put it bluntly, however, if we are ever to move toward this
millennium we shall have to begin to help children and youth find
satisfaction in sources other than creature comforts and consumer
goods. Likewise, we will need to study with care the apparent world-
wide need for zero population growth and seek to create a major new

[4] Kenneth E. Boulding, "The Stationary State," *Resources*, September, 1972, p. 3.
[5] Ibid., p. 3.

concept of productivity aimed at human needs, including the *re-transformation* of our technological community so as to reverse certain counter-ecological trends that have developed since World War II.

And at the risk of hearing cries of heresy, it seems essential that we reverse some of our long-ingrained ideas and vigorously emphasize that "success" does not necessarily reside in the nineteenth-century dictum that the able child should rise above his father's station in life. With social conditions and social attitudes changing (and with chemists, engineers, psychologists, lawyers, teachers, anthropologists, et al. unemployed or underemployed), there appears to be new and great merit in school climates—and in mass media— which would encourage some cobblers' sons to remain cobblers' sons, lest we end up unshod a few years hence.

Whatever our decisions and actions may be between 1973 and 1985, the crisis of transition, the exponential increase in crises, and the deadlines imposed by a deteriorating and prematurely aging planet demand that educators seek new and courageous answers to questions that have been asked for many generations. . . .

WHAT SHOULD THE CURRICULUM INCLUDE AND HOW SHALL IT BE ORGANIZED?

What Shall the Curriculum Include? Once we have established the nature of societal and individual needs, goals, and purposes, we can, with some confidence, examine the curriculum to determine to what extent it encourages us to meet them. However, when attempting to respond to the question of content to be included in the curriculum, certain ground rules need to be established. For one thing, we need to be in some agreement as to what *curriculum* means. In the following paragraphs its meaning is limited to learnings that are encouraged through *schooling*. We need to make this distinction between schooling and the learner's total *education*, because the latter is influenced by many things—mass media, the home, the street, the self-instructional materials, what one learns on the job and what he learns from his peer group.

Within the parameters of the educational community, the matter of what shall be in the curriculum leaves educators with the melancholy burden of three difficult preliminary decisions. First, shall we settle for more equal education or shall we explore what constitutes an *equitable* one—the latter implying preferential opportunities based upon human need rather than on egalitarian policies. I choose to argue for equity in the belief that it will eventually lead us toward equality.

Second, what shall we judge to be essential learnings which children and youth should confront sometime during their schooling once certain basic skills, such as reading, have been acquired? I am rash enough to suggest some "essentials" below. And, finally, some kind of agreement is needed with respect to what constitute the best teaching methods. What kind of mix do we want to compound from among didactic, heuristic, and humanistic prescriptions? As one whimsical elderly teacher put it, "Do I *tell* 'em, do I have them try to *discover* the answers, or do I just *love* 'em and stop worrying about whether they think the world is a globe or a cube?" Here, I would suggest that all three approaches have merit or each would not have so many proponents! The task of the teacher is to develop a talent for knowing what mix works best for *whom*, *when* it works, and in *what* circumstances.

Having recognized and skirted these three contemporary problems— philosophical, substantive, and methodological—let us speculate about content: about whether we should concentrate on the roots or on the branches of learning, and what the roots and branches *are*.

Proposals for Curriculum Content   At the moment let us forget the three R's, since there seem to be few advocates of basic illiteracy, and assume that the schools will, without much squabbling, continue to promote reading and ciphering. Let us ask instead, What are the "Big Questions" as to content for 1973–85? While the schools traditionally have provided a basis rather than an arena for social change, accumulating data suggest that at least a few crucial topics need to be phased into the curriculum beginning no later than during the primary school years. Specifically, there are *future*-oriented skills input, and attitudes that need to become a part of the personal resources that young citizens bring to bear on the problems that confront us all. To serve this end:

1. Schooling needs to focus on the dangers that ruthless exploitation of resources, pollution, warfare, and waste are creating for mankind.
2. The curriculum needs to become more specific in recognizing that the rate of population increase is a real and present threat *now*, not in the third millennium.
3. Young learners should begin to ponder the point that maintaining the U.S. standard of living as of 1972 requires processing about 65% of the world's annual output of raw materials for the 6% of the world's population residing in our 50 states.
4. Deliberate study should be made of mass media—especially inevitable misrepresentation because TV can't actually show us the world "the way it is." We also need to help the young to understand the propaganda power and image-building impact of press and screen[6];

[6] Anthony Tovatt and Ted DeVries, quoting an American Academy of Pediatrics speaker, say, "By age 14, a child has seen 18,000 human beings killed on television." (See Tovatt and DeVries, "This World of English," *English Journal*, November, 1972, p. 1,248.)

the passive, mind-numbing aspects of being forever a spectator of, rather than a participant in, the beat of life.

5. As noted earlier, a great effort should be made through school experiences to build the personal inner strength, discipline, and self-control that enable a human being to live effectively in a climate of mutual trust and respect with his fellows.

6. Much more thought should be given to developing with and for the young learner a future-focused role image, a projected self-concept of what he can become 10, 20, and 30 years hence and which promises the merited respect, dignity, and a measure of security needed to motivate the learner *now*.

Many similar examples might be given, but one in particular seems an important contemporary challenge to the schools: 7) developing content that will sensitize youth to the fact that many Americans—judging by what they *do*—tacitly reject democracy, or at least ignore its egalitarian implications. Democracy generally is construed to be a means to self-improvement and a channel to personal gain, the ballot is a lever with which to gain a real or fancied advantage. Yet more often than not today's curricula reflect the folklore of democracy—information of a contrary nature that indirectly leads to disillusionment and a loss of faith in the democratic process.

Undoubtedly, one of the most difficult aspects of imparting future-oriented learnings is that children and youth tend to learn by example rather than precept, from the world as it is rather than through admonition. This means that *we* need to think and to act in a manner which reflects *our* belief in the importance of points like those listed above. If we don't we have only ourselves to blame for a deteriorating physical and psychological environment.

Innovations in Curriculum Organization for the Next Decade Only a few generalizations can be made about so broad an issue as curriculum *organization*. One can point out, however, that faulty approaches to organizing the school for learning probably have caused more justifiable griping among teachers than any other single topic—including the salaries they are paid!

One important point regarding instructional designs is that we need to make them more congruent with what has been learned regarding human development. When this is done:

1. Since children learn all of the time, curricular experiences will extend throughout the year rather than for the present September–June academic year.

2. Since each human is unique, arbitrary comparative measures of social, physical, and academic performance will be abandoned in favor of evaluating personalized growth patterns.

3. Because education is a lifelong process, schooling and its inevitable concomitant, the curriculum, will provide opportunities for mature learners in their 30s, 50s, and 70s.[7]

4. Human values will receive greater emphasis in a lifelong curriculum continuum characterized by unrestricted exit and reentry privileges as learners move back and forth between schooling and the additional educative experiences provided by the world of work.

5. The importance of subject matter steadily will be upgraded, despite recent retreats from excellence. At the same time, uniformity in what is learned will diminish—except for more uniform levels of competence in postsecondary programs such as those designed for teachers, paramedics, engineers, technicians, dentists, architects, physicians, and the like.

Novel ways of deploying faculty members also promise to be an integral part of changes in both curriculum and school organization. In view of present trends, we should see an increase in the variety of a given teacher's assignments as he or she works in more fields with students of more varied ages—including adults. The idea of *team* teaching is likely to evolve into a concept of teaching *partnerships*—a more versatile type of teacher assignment—and these will become more common in secondary and postsecondary education.[8]

Resolved: *That, while the basic issue of what our children and youth shall learn actually has been partly obscured by most curriculum reform in substantive fields such as mathematics and linguistics, which are indispensable means to improved education, the ends of education—future-oriented knowledge and survival skills needed to cope with technology, mass media, pollution, the peace deficit, inflation, and a myriad of similar problems—now be given "compensatory attention."* Further resolved: *That the curriculum be more fully anchored to the lifelong "human needs" concept of womb-to-tomb educational experience provided under the sponsorship of the schools.*

[7] The appetite for education shown by older persons already has been demonstrated at Hennepin State Junior College in suburban Minneapolis. In 1972, 400 persons from 55 to past 80 years of age were enrolled in tuition-free courses. Four-fifths of them had not gone beyond grade eight. Other programs for "senior learners" are under way both here and abroad. See *Time*, July 17, 1972, p. 48.

[8] For a chapter-length discussion of curriculum change and staff deployment, see Chapter XV, "Prospects and Prerequisites for the Improvement of Elementary Education: 1973–1985," in John I. Goodlad and Harold G. Shane (eds.), *The Elementary School in the United States*, 72d Yearbook, Part II, The National Society for the Study of Education (Chicago: University of Chicago Press, 1973).

INDEX

Kahn, Herman, 318, 321, 330, 335, 365, 394
Kant, Immanuel, 215
Kelleher, Alice, 204
Keller, Charles B., 16
Kennan, Richard Barnes, 2
Kenney, Bill, 115–16
Kerner Commission, 291, 292
Kilpatrick, William Heard, 9, 10, 11, 412
Knebel, Fletcher, 256
knowledge: growth in, and curriculum change, 304, 307–8; explosion of, in U.S. in 2000, 332; pursuit of, in 2000, 341
Knox, William T., 325–26
Kohl, Herbert, 2, 25–36, 47, 197, 284; background of, 5; and authoritarianism, 112; successes of, 121; Other Ways School, Berkeley, 130, 179
Kozol, Jonathan, 2, 37–46, 47, 161 194–201; and authoritarianism, 70, 112; and Dewey's influence, 82; and free schools, 111, 127–128, 262; and reform, 124; and "invisibility" of minority child, 284

LaBrant, Lou, 111, 202–5
language, progressive development of, 31–32
LAP, 405, 406
learner, activation of, 262–65
learning: programmed, 14; capacity for, 19; relationship to teaching, 51, 75–77; and experience, 52; centers, 128, 129; environment for, 379; and interpersonal relationships, 379–82; as life-long process, 380
Learning Research and Development Center, 385
Leicestershire Model, 114, 115, 119, 167
leisure: work and, roles in 2000 of, 331–32; use in U.S. in 2000, 333; pursuit in 2000 of, 341; and retirement programs, adult, 410
Leonard, George, 82, 168
Lerner, Max, 257
Levine, Sol, 110, 154–59

liberalism: opposed by youth, 268
liberals: as seen by young people, 268–69
life concerns, and curriculum change, 278–81
life-styles, application of education to, 264
Lindvall, C. M., 385
Lippmann, Walter, 225
literacy, dependence of industrial society on, 66
Lockley, Arnold, 178
Lucas, George, 256

man, greatest problem of future, 375–76
Marcus Garvey Institute, 179
Marien, Michael, 321, 394–402
Marin, Peter, 122, 124–25
Marsubian, P. O., 146
Martin Luther King, Jr. Memorial Center, 295
Marx, Karl, 87
mass media: quality of, 100; and ethical problems of education, 168–69; study of in future curriculum, 417–18
materials, school, proper emphasis on, 312
Mayer, Martin, 10, 17, 100
Mayr, Ernst, 326
McCarthyism, education in era of, 2
McClelland, David, 163–64
McConnell, Grant, 331, 335
McLuhan, Marshall, 325
McMurrin, Sterling, 10
Mead, Margaret, 320, 367–74, 400
means of change, attitude of youth toward, 269
media, instructional, and individualization concept, 386
megalopolis, 376
Melby, Ernest, 2
Mendlovitz, Saul, 272
mental ability, and individualization, 387–88; heterogeneity in, 392–94
mentorship system, 356–57
Merton, Thomas, 68
Metcalf, Lawrence E., 229, 266–74